THE CAMBRIDGE COMPANION TO
AMERICAN ISLAM

The Cambridge Companion to ⌐_____ ⌐ ____ _ scholarly
overview of the state of research on American Muslims and American
Islam. The book presents the reader with a comprehensive discussion of
the debates, challenges, and opportunities that American Muslims have
faced through centuries of American history. This volume also covers
the creative ways in which American Muslims have responded to the
serious challenges that they have faced and continue to face in constructing a religious praxis and complex identities that are grounded in
both a universal tradition and the particularities of their local contexts.
The book introduces the reader to some of the many facets of the lives
of American Muslims that can only be understood in their interactions
with Islam's entanglement in the American experiment.

Juliane Hammer is associate professor and Kenan Rifai Scholar in
Islamic Studies at the University of North Carolina at Chapel Hill. Her
research focuses on American Muslims, discourses on gender and sexuality, and Sufism. She is the author of *Palestinians Born in Exile* (2005)
and *American Muslim Women, Religious Authority, and Activism:
More than a Prayer* (2012). Her work has appeared in *The Muslim
World, Hawwa, Contemporary Islam*, and *Islam and Christian-Muslim
Relations*, as well as in several edited volumes. She is currently working on a research project analyzing American Muslim efforts against
domestic violence.

Omid Safi is professor of Islamic Studies at the University of North
Carolina at Chapel Hill, specializing in contemporary Islamic thought
and classical Islam. He is the author of *Politics of Knowledge in
Premodern Islam* (2006) and *Memories of Muhammad* (2010). He is also
the editor of two volumes, *Progressive Muslims: On Justice, Gender,
and Pluralism* (2003) and *Voices of Islam: Voices of Change* (2006). He
has a forthcoming book on the famed mystic Rumi and is currently
working on a monograph discussing contemporary Islamic debates
in Iran.

CAMBRIDGE COMPANIONS TO RELIGION

This is a series of companions to major topics and key figures in theology and religious studies. Each volume contains specially commissioned chapters by international scholars, which provide an accessible and stimulating introduction to the subject for new readers and nonspecialists.

THE CAMBRIDGE COMPANION TO

AMERICAN ISLAM

Edited by

Juliane Hammer
University of North Carolina at Chapel Hill

Omid Safi
University of North Carolina at Chapel Hill

CAMBRIDGE
UNIVERSITY PRESS

32 Avenue of the Americas, New York, NY 10013-2473, USA

Cambridge University Press is part of the University of Cambridge.

It furthers the University's mission by disseminating knowledge in the pursuit of
education, learning, and research at the highest international levels of excellence.

www.cambridge.org
Information on this title: www.cambridge.org/9780521175524

© Cambridge University Press 2013

This publication is in copyright. Subject to statutory exception
and to the provisions of relevant collective licensing agreements,
no reproduction of any part may take place without the written
permission of Cambridge University Press.

First published 2013

Printed in the United States of America

A catalog record for this publication is available from the British Library.

Library of Congress Cataloging in Publication data
The Cambridge companion to American Islam /
[edited by] Julianne Hammer, Omid Safi.
    p.   cm.
Includes bibliographical references and index.
ISBN 978-1-107-00241-8 (hardback) – ISBN 978-0-521-17552-4 (pbk.)
1. Islam – United States.   I. Hammer, Juliane.   II. Safi, Omid.
BP67.U6C355   2014
297.0973–dc23   2012046780

ISBN 978-1-107-00241-8 Hardback
ISBN 978-0-521-17552-4 Paperback

Cambridge University Press has no responsibility for the persistence or accuracy
of URLs for external or third-party Internet Web sites referred to in this publication,
and does not guarantee that any content on such Web sites is, or will remain,
accurate or appropriate.

ACC LIBRARY SERVICES AUSTIN, TX

Contents

Figures

Notes on Contributors

Su'ad Abdul Khabeer is assistant professor of Anthropology and African American Studies at Purdue University. Her work explores the intersection of race, religion, and popular culture through ethnography and performance art. Her publications include "Rep That Islam: The Rhyme and Reason of American Muslim Hip Hop" (*Muslim World*, 2007) and "Black Arabic: Some Notes on African American Muslims and the Arabic Language," in *Black Routes to Islam* (edited by M. Marable and H. Aidi, 2010). In addition to her academic writing, Abdul Khabeer's poetry is included in the anthology *Living Islam Out Loud: American Muslim Women Speak*. She has written for TheRoot.com, the *Washington Post*, and the Huffington Post.

Zain Abdullah is associate professor in the Religion Department at Temple University. His research focuses on topics related to religion and society, Islam and the West, and the formation of global and transnational Muslim identities. He is the author of *Black Mecca: The African Muslims of Harlem* (2010), and his articles have appeared in the *Journal of the American Academy of Religion*, *Anthropological Quarterly*, the *Journal of Islamic Law and Culture*, the *Journal of History and Culture*, *African Arts*, the *Middle East Journal*, and other periodicals. Abdullah is currently writing a book about Black Muslim conversion and the Nation of Islam in mid-twentieth-century America.

Liali Albana is a high school world history teacher and freelance writer. She holds a B.A. from Rutgers University in Political Science and Middle Eastern Studies. She is involved in a statewide social studies curriculum revision initiative through the New Jersey Arab Heritage Commission and the Rutgers University Center for Middle Eastern Studies.

Maytha Alhassen is a University of Southern California Provost Ph.D. Fellow in American Studies and Ethnicity, studying historical encounters between African Americans and Arabs, critical race studies, youth popular culture, social movements, oral histories, narratives, and storytelling. Her writings have appeared online on CNN, Huffington Post, and Counterpunch and in academic journals. In addition to her journalistic and academic writing, she has appeared on CNN and Al Jazeera English and contributed an essay to *I Speak for Myself* (2011), a book of American Muslim women's stories. Alhassen is the coeditor (with Ahmed Shihab-Eldin) of *Demanding Dignity: Young Voices from the Frontlines of the Arab Revolutions* (2012).

Sylvia Chan-Malik is assistant professor in the Departments of American Studies and Women's and Gender Studies at Rutgers University. Her research and teaching examine the intersections of race, religion, gender, and sexuality through critical frameworks of American transnationalism and comparative ethnic studies, with a focus on the history of Islam in the United States. Before joining the faculty at Rutgers, she was a UC President's Postdoctoral Fellow at the University of California at Santa Cruz and a Ford Foundation Diversity Fellow. Her articles appear in the *Annals of the American Academy of Political and Social Science*; the *Journal of Race, Ethnicity, and Religion*; *The Encyclopedia of Women and Islamic Cultures*; *The Encyclopedia of Muslim-American History*; The Immanent Frame; and edited anthologies.

R. David Coolidge is the Associate University Chaplain for the Muslim community at Brown University. Previously, he was the Muslim adviser at Dartmouth College and an adjunct lecturer in the Department of Philosophy and Religious Studies at St. Francis College. His publications relating to Islam in America have appeared in *Islamica, Islamic Horizons,* and *Illume Magazine* and on various sites online. In addition, he is a member of the Board of Directors for Ta'leef Collective.

Edward E. Curtis IV is Millennium Chair of the Liberal Arts and professor of Religious Studies at Indiana University–Purdue University Indianapolis (IUPUI). He is the author or editor of *Muslims in America: A Short History; Encyclopedia of Muslim-American History; Black Muslim Religion in the Nation of Islam, 1960–1975; Islam in Black America;* and the *Columbia Sourcebook of Muslims in the United States*. A former NEH Fellow at the National Humanities Center, Curtis has been awarded Carnegie, Fulbright, and Mellon fellowships. He serves as founding coeditor of the *Journal of Africana Religions*.

Nabil Echchaibi is assistant professor and associate director of the Center for Media, Religion and Culture at the University of Colorado at Boulder. His research focuses on religion and the role of media in shaping and reflecting modern religious subjectivities among Muslims in the Middle East and in the diaspora. His work on diasporic media, Muslim media cultures, and Islamic alternative modernity has appeared in publications such as the *Journal of Intercultural Studies, Nations and Nationalism, Journal of Arab and Muslim Media Research, Media Development,* and many book publications. He is the author of *Voicing Diasporas: Ethnic Radio in Paris and Berlin between Culture and Renewal* (2011) and the coeditor of *International Blogging: Identity, Politics and Networked Publics* (2009).

Kambiz GhaneaBassiri is associate professor of Religion and Humanities at Reed College. He is the author of numerous publications on Islam in America, including *A History of Islam in America: From the New World to the New World Order* (2010) and *Competing Visions of Islam in the United States* (1997). His research has been supported by fellowships from the Carnegie Scholars Program and the Guggenheim Foundation.

Zareena A. Grewal is assistant professor in the Departments of American Studies and Religious Studies and in the Program in Ethnicity, Race, and Migration at Yale University. She is a historical anthropologist and documentary filmmaker and has directed and produced two films for television, *By the Dawn's Early Light: Chris Jackson's Journey to Islam* (2004) and *Swahili Fighting Words* (with Mohamed Yunus Rafiq, 2009). Her book, *Islam Is a Foreign Country: American Muslim Youth and the Global Crisis of Authority* (2013), as well as articles in journals and book chapters in edited collections, explores the intersections of race, gender, class, and religion across a wide spectrum of American Muslim communities. Grewal is also the Director of the Center for the Study of American Muslims at the Institute for Social Policy and Understanding.

Juliane Hammer is associate professor and Kenan Rifai Scholar in Islamic Studies in the Department of Religious Studies at the University of North Carolina at Chapel Hill. Her research focuses on American Muslims, discourses on gender and sexuality, and Sufism. She is the author of *Palestinians Born in Exile* (2005) and *American Muslim Women, Religious Authority, and Activism: More than a Prayer* (2012). Her work has appeared in the *Muslim World*, *Hawwa*, *Contemporary Islam*, *Islam and Christian-Muslim Relations*, and the *Bulletin for the Study of Religion*, as well as in several edited volumes. She is currently working on a research project analyzing American Muslim efforts against domestic violence.

Rosemary R. Hicks is a visiting scholar at Bard College with the Bard Prison Initiative, which she joined after completing a two-year Mellon Fellowship with the Center for the Humanities at Tufts University. Hicks earned a Ph.D. in North American Religions in 2010 from Columbia University, where she was a Mellon Fellow with the Institute for Social and Economic Research and Policy and an American Association of University Women Fellow. Hicks specializes in issues of secularism, pluralism, and challenges facing religious minorities in the United States. She has published in journals including *Religion*, *Comparative Islamic Studies*, *American Quarterly*, and the *Journal of Feminist Studies in Religion*.

Sally Howell is assistant professor of History in the Center for Arab American Studies and the Department of Social Sciences at the University of Michigan-Dearborn. Her books include *Citizenship and Crisis: Arab Detroit after 9/11* (coauthored with Wayne Baker et al., 2009) and *Arab Detroit 9/11: Life in the Terror Decade* (with Amaney Jamal et al., 2011). Her essays have appeared in *Anthropological Quarterly*, *Diaspora*, *Food and Foodways*, *International Journal of Middle East Studies*, *UCLA Journal of Islamic and Near Eastern Law*, and *Visual Anthropology*.

Amaney Jamal is associate professor of Politics at Princeton University. Her research focuses on democratization and the politics of civic engagement in the Arab world. Among Muslim and Arab Americans, she has examined the pathways that structure their patterns of civic engagement in the United States. Jamal is the author of *Barriers to Democracy* (2009) and *Of Empires and Citizens* (2012), the coauthor of *Arab Detroit 9/11: Life in the Terror Decade* (with Sally Howell et al., 2011), and the coeditor of *Race and Arab Americans Before and After 9/11* (with Nadine Naber, 2008). Jamal is a principal investigator of the "Arab Barometer Project" and Senior Advisor on the Pew Research Center projects focusing on Islam in America (2006) and Global Islam (2010–12). In 2005 Jamal was named a Carnegie Scholar.

Akel Ismail Kahera is professor of Architecture and associate dean for research and graduate studies in Clemson University's College of Architecture, Arts and Humanities. Kahera is the author of more than two dozen scholarly essays on history, the theory of architecture, and urbanism, as well as the author of three books: *Deconstructing the American Mosque: Space, Gender, and Aesthetics* (2002); *Design Criteria for Mosques* (2009); and *Reading the Islamic City* (2011). He received a bachelor's degree in Architecture from the Pratt Institute in Brooklyn; a master's in Architecture from the Massachusetts Institute of Technology; and a Ph.D. in Near Eastern Studies (in the fields of architecture, law, and urbanism) from Princeton University.

Michael Muhammad Knight is the author of nine books, including a monograph on the Five Percenter movement, *The Five Percenters: Islam, Hip-Hop, and the Gods of New York* (2007); an American Muslim travelogue, *Blue-Eyed Devil* (2006); a hajj narrative, *Journey to the End of Islam* (2009); and the novel, *The Taqwacores* (2004). He obtained his master of Theological Studies degree from Harvard in 2011 and is currently a doctoral student at the University of North Carolina at Chapel Hill. His doctoral research investigates engagement of the *sunnah*, the personal example of the Prophet Muhammad, in American Islamic discourses.

Karen Leonard currently chairs the Anthropology Department at the University of California at Irvine, where she is also a professor of Anthropology. She is the author of *Locating Home: India's Hyderabadis Abroad* (2007), a multisite ethnography of the diaspora from Hyderabad to Pakistan, the United Kingdom, Australia, Canada, the United States, and the Gulf states of the Middle East (2007); and *Muslims in the United States: The State of Research* (2003). Leonard has published on the history and culture of India, especially the former Hyderabad state, and on Asian American and Muslim American history and culture.

Debra Majeed is professor of Religious Studies at Beloit College. She is the first African American female and first Muslim to be tenured in the 166-year history of Beloit College. She has published in the *Journal of Feminist Studies in Religion*, *The Encyclopedia of Women and Religion in America*, *The Encyclopedia of Women in Islamic Cultures*, and *Delving Deeper Shades of Purple: Charting Twenty Years of Womanist Approaches in Religion and Society*. She is completing a manuscript on polygyny and African American Muslims that is forthcoming from the University Press of Florida.

Kathleen M. Moore is professor of Religious Studies at the University of California at Santa Barbara, where she specializes in law and religion. Her research interests lie at the intersection of politics, religion, and law. She has authored three books and several articles on the topic of Islam and Muslims in the United States and Britain, the legal status of Muslim Americans, immigration politics, and pluralism. Titles include *Al Mughtaribun: American Law and the Transformation of Muslim Life in the United States* (1995; revised and expanded edition forthcoming), *Muslim Women in America* (coauthored with Yvonne Haddad and Jane Smith, 2006, 2011), and *The Unfamiliar Abode: Islamic Law in the United States and Britain* (2010).

Omid Safi is professor of Islamic Studies at the University of North Carolina at Chapel Hill, specializing in contemporary Islamic thought and classical Islam. He is the editor of the volume *Progressive Muslims: On Justice, Gender, and Pluralism* (2003) and of *Voices of Islam: Voices of Change* (2006). He is also the author of *Politics of Knowledge in Premodern Islam* (2006) and *Memories of Muhammad* (2010). He has a forthcoming volume from Princeton University Press on the famed mystic Rumi and is currently working on a monograph discussing contemporary Islamic debates in Iran, to be published by Harvard University Press.

Richard Brent Turner is professor of Religious Studies, African American Studies, and International Studies at the University of Iowa. He is the author of *Islam in the African-American Experience* (1997, 2003) and *Jazz Religion, the Second Line, and Black New Orleans* (2009). Other writings have appeared in the *Muslim World, Souls, Journal of Religious Thought*, and the *Black Studies Reader*.

Gisela Webb is professor of Comparative Religion and Islamic Studies at Seton Hall University. Her research and publications include studies on medieval and contemporary Islamic mysticism and spirituality, Islam and Sufis in the United States, women and gender in Islam, death and dying in Islam, and religious approaches to Alzheimer's. Her publications include the edited volume *Windows of Faith: Muslim Women Scholar-Activists in North America* (2000), *Intimations of the Great Unlearning: Interreligious Spirituality and the Demise of Consciousness Which Is Alzheimer's*, and "Third Wave Sufism in America and the Bawa Muhaiyaddeen Fellowship" in *Sufism in the West* (edited by Jamal Malik and John Hinnells, 2006).

Timur R. Yuskaev is assistant professor of Contemporary Islam and director of the Islamic Chaplaincy Program at Hartford Seminary in Hartford, Connecticut. His forthcoming book, *Speaking Qur'an: The Emergence of an American Sacred Text*, reflects his academic interests, which include anthropology of the Qur'an, Qur'anic hermeneutics, the study of Muslim modernities, American religious history, and memory studies.

Note on Transliteration

It is customary for Islamic studies scholars to explain their transliteration system, in part as proof that we are aware of the complex rules guiding our field and the languages associated with it. We have used a very simplified transliteration system for Arabic, Persian, Urdu, and Turkish words. Those familiar with these languages will easily identify the correct terms and those who are not will benefit more from the explanation in the glossary. In addition to ease of reading, we have refrained from using a more complicated system because American Muslims generally use simplified transliterations of key religious vocabulary that has been integrated into American Muslim English, including the use of English plurals for Arabic words.

Glossary

adhan. The call to prayer, for five daily prayers (see *salat*).

da'wah. Literally "invitation." Used to describe missionary activities to spread Islam.

dhikr (or *zikr*). Invocation or remembrance. The term for a particular Sufi practice involving the invocation of one of the Divine names, or the very term Allah, with the aim of attuning the consciousness of the faithful with that of Divine Presence.

Eid al-fitr. Feast of Fastbreaking. The celebration at the end of the month of Ramadan.

fatwa. A ruling or decree issued by an Islamic legal scholar.

fiqh. Human interpretation of *shari'ah* (Divine law), Islamic jurisprudence.

hadith. A saying of the Prophet Muhammad. Also used for the collected sayings of Muhammad.

hajj. Pilgrimage to Mecca, one of the five pillars of Islam.

halal. Lawful or permissible according to Islamic law.

hijab. One of the terms for the Muslim headscarf.

ijma'. Consensus of a community of scholars on a legal issue.

imam. In Sunni Islam, the leader of congregational prayer. In a Shi'i context, the title for the immediate descendants of the Prophet Muhammad. Also used as a title for mosque and community leaders in the American context.

marja' (pl. *maraji'*). The title of a leading Islamic legal scholar in Twelver Shi'ism, one to whom the followers turn for authoritative interpretations.

mawlid. Celebration in honor of the birthday of an important religious figure, including that of the Prophet Muhammad.

mazar. Tomb or mausoleum of an important religious figure.

Mi'raj. The night journey and heavenly ascension of the Prophet Muhammad.

muezzin. Caller to prayer.

nikah. Marriage ceremony.

niqab. Face "veil" or cover that some Muslim women wear.

pir. Elder religious leader figure, especially in Sufism. Same as shaykh.

qutb. Literally "pole." Term for the function of a high-ranking Sufi teacher as a vertical axis that connects this world to God.

Ramadan. The month of fasting in the Islamic calendar.

salat. The five daily prayers, one of the five pillars.

shahadah. The Muslim testimony of faith, first of the five pillars of Islam, declaring "There is no god but God, and Muhammad is God's messenger."

shari'ah. Divine law, sometimes used for Islamic Law. To be distinguished from fiqh, which is jurisprudence.

shaykh. Elder religious leader figure.

sunnah. The life acts of the Prophet Muhammad, including his sayings (see *hadith*).

tariqas. English plural of the Arabic term tariqa, which literally means "mystical path." A hierarchically structured Sufi community led by a Sufi shaykh or pir (teacher).

tawhid. Oneness of God. Article of Islamic belief in the absolute unity and oneness of the Divine.

'ulama. Religious scholars, with expertise in Qur'anic interpretation and law.

ummah. Muslim community.

zakat. Alms, charitable giving, one of the five pillars of Islam.

Introduction: American Islam, Muslim Americans, and the American Experiment

JULIANE HAMMER AND OMID SAFI

The conversation about where American Muslims fit into the larger fabric of American society far predates the election of Barack Hussein Obama to the presidency in 2008. To critically assess the anxiety over American Muslims as part of a historical chronology and continuum, we should start with the ratification of the United States Constitution.

The date was July 30, 1788. The site was North Carolina, and the occasion was the convention to ratify the proposed U.S. Constitution. The speaker on this occasion was a certain William Lancaster, who was a staunch Anti-Federalist. Lancaster spoke of what would happen not if, but when, a few centuries down the road a Muslim would be elected to the highest office in the land, the presidency of the United States of America.

> But let us remember that we form a government for millions not yet in existence. I have not the art of divination. In the course of four or five hundred years, I do not know how it will work. This is most certain, that Papists may occupy that chair, and Mahometans may take it. I see nothing against it.[1]

"Mahometan" was the common designation for Muslims back then, now considered derogatory, and was derived from the also obsolete and equally offensive "Muhammadan." In 1788 there were no Muslim Americans running for the office of the president. As far as we know, there were not even any Muslim citizens of the newly formed American republic – though there were thousands of slaves from Africa in America who came from Muslim backgrounds. As legal scholars have noted, the putative conversation about a Muslim president was a fear tactic used by Anti-Federalists

---

[1] Jonathan Elliot, ed., *The Debates in the Several State Conventions on the Adoption of the Federal Constitution, as Recommended by the General Convention at Philadelphia, in 1787*, 5 vols. (Philadelphia, 1888), 4:215; cited in Denise A. Spellberg, "Could a Muslim be President? An Eighteenth-Century Constitutional Debate," *Eighteenth-Century Studies* 39:4 (2006): 485.

to put pressure on Federalists. In other words, the conversation about where Muslims fit into the fabric of the American politic was one that was concomitant with the passage of the U.S. Constitution.

The source of controversy was Article VI of the United States Constitution:

> The Senators and Representatives before mentioned, and the Members of the several State Legislatures, and all executive and judicial Officers, both of the United States and of the several States, shall be bound by Oath or Affirmation, to support this Constitution; *but no religious Test shall ever be required as a Qualification to any Office or public Trust under the United States.* (emphasis added)

The issue of whether a Muslim could become the president of the United States moved from a theoretical debate "four or five hundred years" in the future – as the representative Lancaster had imagined in 1788 – to a very real campaign issue in Barack Obama's successful presidential run in 2008. The conversation in 2008 was about whether the presidential candidate Senator Obama, whose father was a secular Kenyan Muslim, was himself a Muslim. In spite of Obama having been a committed Christian, a regular churchgoer for decades, one who got married and had his daughters baptized in a church, a significant percentage of Americans believed – and continue to believe – that he was a Muslim. At the time of the 2008 presidential election, 13 percent of all Americans acknowledged that they suspected Obama to be Muslim;[2] other polls put the number closer to 20 percent. One study of people who voted for the Republican candidate, Senator McCain, in 2008 found that between 56 and 77 percent of those voters thought Obama was Muslim. It would be fair to assume that the overwhelming majority of those who mistakenly held this view also held this against the candidate Obama.[3] Insinuations and assumptions about Obama's "Muslimness" did not disappear during his presidency and had risen to 24 percent by 2010.[4] Even in 2012, one in three Republicans continued to believe, in spite of the available evidence, that Obama was Muslim.[5] It was ultimately the Republican Colin

---

[2]   See the Newsweek poll: http://nw-assets.s3.amazonaws.com/pdf/1004-ftop.pdf.

[3]   "Smearing the Opposition," http://news.msu.edu/media/documents/2010/08/a8099abf-c5dd-439f-95d5-64178e629848.pdf.

[4]   Jonathan Alter, "The Illustrated Man," http://www.thedailybeast.com/newsweek/2010/08/28/alter-how-obama-can-fight-the-lies.html.

[5]   Moustafa Bayoumi, "Did Islamophobia Fuel the Oak Creek Massacre?" *Nation*, August 10, 2012. http://www.thenation.com/article/169322/did-islamophobia-fuel-oak-creek-massacre#.

Powell who offered a forceful refutation of the whole debate. Speaking of Barak Obama, Powell stated:

> Well, the correct answer is, he is not a Muslim, he's a Christian. He's always been a Christian. But the really right answer is, what if he is? Is there something wrong with being a Muslim in this country? The answer's no, that's not America. Is there something wrong with some seven-year-old Muslim-American kid believing that he or she could be president? Yet, I have heard senior members of my own party drop the suggestion, "He's a Muslim and he might be associated with terrorists." This is not the way we should be doing it in America.[6]

"Is there something wrong with being a Muslim in this country?" Colin Powell asked in 2008, and that question has hovered over the American Muslim community at least since September 11, 2001, and in many ways for much longer.

The present volume offers a scholarly overview of the state of research on American Muslims and American Islam and presents the reader with a comprehensive discussion of the debates, challenges, and opportunities that American Muslims have faced through centuries of American history. This volume also covers the creative ways in which American Muslims have responded to the serious challenges that they have faced and continue to face in constructing a religious praxis and complex identities that are grounded in both a universal tradition and the particularities of their local contexts. The book then introduces the reader to the many facets of the lives of American Muslims, which in turn can be understood only in their interactions with Islam's entanglement in the American experiment.

AMERICAN ISLAM BETWEEN THE ERA OF THE FOUNDING FATHERS AND TODAY

Muslims have a long history of accommodation, engagement, resistance, and official acknowledgment in America. One of the first known acknowledgments came not in the aftermath of the horrific events of 9/11, or even as a result of the monumental 1965 immigration laws introduced under the Johnson administration, but much earlier, during the holy month of Ramadan in the year 1805. The host of the event, held

---

[6] "Meet the Press," transcript from October 19, 2008, http://www.msnbc.msn.com/id/27266223/ns/meet_the_press/t/meet-press-transcript-oct/.

on December 9, was none other than the president of the United States and the author of the Declaration of Independence, Thomas Jefferson. The Muslim guest was Sidi Soliman (Sulayman) Mellimelli, who was the envoy from the Bey of Tunis, a North African Muslim state. Dinner would have ordinarily been served at 3:30 P.M., but the president held that, to honor his guest's religious preferences, he would have dinner served "precisely at sunset."[7]

The legacy of this event was acknowledged in a more lavish ceremony held in August 2012, when President, Barack H. Obama held a White House Iftar dinner (meal to break a fast during the month of Ramadan) on August 10, 2012.[8] During his speech at the dinner, the American president pointed back to that early Ramadan dinner as proof for the centuries of the presence and inclusion of Muslim Americans as part of the fabric of American society:

> As I've noted before, Thomas Jefferson once held a sunset dinner here with an envoy from Tunisia – perhaps the first Iftar at the White House, more than 200 years ago. And some of you, as you arrived tonight, may have seen our special display, courtesy of our friends at the Library of Congress – the Koran that belonged to Thomas Jefferson. And that's a reminder, along with the generations of patriotic Muslims in America, that Islam – like so many faiths – is part of our national story.[9]

President Obama's reference to Thomas Jefferson's copy of the Qur'an is also apropos here, as it shows the intertwined roots of the American experiment and Islam. In 1765 a young Thomas Jefferson was studying law and sought to acquaint himself with a wide variety of legal traditions and natural law. He purchased for his own personal library the recently published two-volume translation of the Qur'an, called *The Koran, Commonly Called the Alkoran of Mohammed*, which had been undertaken by the British scholar George Sale.[10] It was his library that would in time form the basis of the Library of Congress.

---

[7] http://iipdigital.usembassy.gov/st/english/inbrief/2011/07/20110729153019kramo.35 08199.html#axzz24NUokUoo.

[8] http://www.whitehouse.gov/the-press-office/2012/08/10/remarks-president-iftar-dinner.

[9] http://www.whitehouse.gov/the-press-office/2012/08/10/remarks-president-iftar-dinner.

[10] Jefferson purchased the 1764 second-edition printing of the George Sale translation. For a history of Jefferson's encounter with the Qur'an, see Kevin J. Hayes, "How Thomas Jefferson Read the Qur'an," *Early American Literature* 39:2 (2004): 247–261; also see http://www.saudiaramcoworld.com/issue/201104/thomas.jefferson.s.qur.an.htm.

Jefferson's interest in Islam and "Oriental wisdom" more broadly was no passing fancy. He had begun the study of Arabic language and grammar and obtained many books on the history of Islam and Muslim civilizations. He had supported the establishment of academic programs for the study of "the Orient." Jefferson's primary interest in Islam was through the legal tradition, and in doing so he mirrored the concerns of the translator of the Qur'an, George Sale:

> If the religious and civil Institutions of foreign nations are worth our knowledge, those of Mohammed, the lawgiver of the Arabians, and founder of an empire which in less than a century spread itself over a greater part of the world than the Romans were ever masters of, must needs be so.[11]

In Jefferson's autobiography, he used language that indicated his desire to see this country not merely as a Christian country but as a home for all. His discussion of the Virginia Statute of Religious Freedom in 1786 makes this point emphatically:

> Where the preamble declares that coercion is a departure from the plan of the holy author of our religion, an amendment was proposed, by inserting the word "Jesus Christ," so that it should read, "a departure from the plan of Jesus Christ, the holy author of our religion." The insertion was rejected by a great majority, in proof that they meant to comprehend, within the mantle of its protection, the Jew and the Gentile, the Christian and Mahometan, the Hindoo, and infidel of every denomination.[12]

Jefferson's remarkable reference to religious freedom was not a one-time occurrence. In his "Notes on Religion," he had approvingly cited a passage from Locke's *Letter Concerning Toleration* that "neither Pagan nor Mahometan, nor Jew, ought to be excluded from the civil rights of the commonwealth because of his religion."[13]

Thomas Jefferson was not the only one of the Founding Fathers to engage with Islam. Without taking the Founding Fathers to be paradigms of universalist pluralism, one can situate them in a broad Enlightenment tradition that actually looked to Islam as a more "rational" religion and

---

[11] http://www.saudiaramcoworld.com/issue/201104/thomas.jefferson.s.qur.an.htm.
[12] *The Writings of Thomas Jefferson* (Washington, D.C., 1904), p. 67. The text of this statement can be accessed at the Library of Congress Web site: http://memory.loc.gov/cgi-bin/ampage?collId=mtj1&fileName=mtj1page052.db&recNum=516.
[13] Cited in Barbara McGraw, ed., *Taking Religious Pluralism Seriously: Spiritual Politics on America's Sacred Ground* (Waco, 2005), p. 11.

offered fairly positive evaluations of the tradition. This evaluation of Islam as a "rational faith" was often an implicit critique of Christianity, especially its mysticism and alleged opposition to rationality. In other words, the praise of Islam was often a veiled critique of the Christianity they found in their own era, and an implicit prioritization of rationality over revelation as a means of access to the truth. Benjamin Franklin and George Washington can be counted among those including Islam in a list of religions to be accommodated. When George Washington was asked in 1784 what kind of workers should be hired to work on Mount Vernon, he responded by stating that they should hire the best workers, regardless of their background: "If they are good workmen, they may be from Asia, Africa or Europe; they may be Mahometans, Jews, Christians of any sect, or they may be Atheists."[14] Since the 1990s, American presidents have repeatedly come back to emphasize the notion of Muslim Americans fulfilling this promise of being hardworking and contributing citizens of this society.

In identifying the spaces and places for Muslim Americans in American society, it is important to point out the extent to which some of these early possibilities are there to be excavated and resurrected in our own age.

AMERICAN MUSLIMS IN THE TWENTY-FIRST CENTURY

Much has changed between the era of the Founding Fathers and our post-9/11 era of early twenty-first-century America. Thomas Jefferson's copy of the Qur'an, which eventually became part of the holdings of the Library of Congress, gained attention when it was used in the swearing-in ceremony of Keith Ellison, the first Muslim American elected to the U.S. Congress in 2007. Right-wing bloggers and alarmists saw the choice of the Qur'an (instead of the more commonly used Bible) as yet another slippery slope that would lead to the implosion of American identity and called Ellison unpatriotic and a threat to American values. The low point in these attacks came from the Virginia congressman Virgil Goode:

> I fear that in the next century we will have many more Muslims in the United States if we do not adopt the strict immigration policies that I believe are necessary to preserve the values and beliefs traditional to the United States of America.[15]

---

[14] George Washington, *Letters and Addresses* (New York, 1908), p. 257.
[15] http://www.washingtonpost.com/wp-dyn/content/article/2006/12/20/AR2006122001318.html.

Ellison's response was both firm and polite. He offered that Goode was mistaken both on Islam and on the constitutional rights of religious minorities in America. Furthermore, Ellison reminded Goode that Ellison's own standing as a Muslim was not due to immigration, as his ancestors had been in the United States since 1742: "I'm not an immigrant ... I'm an African-American."[16]

Even more powerful words would come after the presidential election in 2008. Perhaps the most powerful declaration of support for Islam from an American political leader was the June 2009 speech of President Obama in Cairo. In this historic speech, Barack Obama began by offering:

> I have come here to seek a new beginning between the United States and Muslims around the world; one based upon mutual interest and mutual respect; and one based upon the truth that America and Islam are not exclusive, and need not be in competition. Instead, they overlap, and share common principles – principles of justice and progress; tolerance and the dignity of all human beings.[17]

He then went on to cite from the Qur'an ("Be conscious of God and speak always the truth") and offered that he too promised to follow the spiritual and moral guidance of this verse and speak truthfully. He recalled many of the historic markers between Islam and America, including Morocco (a Muslim nation) having been the first to recognize the United States of America, John Adams's comments on the Treaty of Tripoli, and the election of Keith Ellison. In quite possibly the most emphatic statement of support any American president has ever made on behalf of Islam, he stated: "And I consider it part of my responsibility as president of the United States to fight against negative stereotypes of Islam wherever they appear."[18]

While there are the positive engagements with Islam, the overall trend in the country has been much more negative. An August 2010 study by the Pew Foundation found 38 percent of all Americans admitting to having "unfavorable" opinions of Muslims.[19] This unfavorable opinion also appeared among members of the U.S. Congress, including

---

[16] http://www.nytimes.com/2006/12/21/us/21koran.html?_r=1.

[17] http://www.whitehouse.gov/the_press_office/Remarks-by-the-President-at-Cairo-University-6-04-09/.

[18] http://www.whitehouse.gov/the_press_office/Remarks-by-the-President-at-Cairo-University-6-04-09/.

[19] http://pewresearch.org/pubs/1706/poll-americans-views-of-muslims-object-to-new-york-islamic-center-islam-violence.

New York congressman Peter King, the powerful chair of the House Homeland Security Committee, who openly asked whether there are "too many mosques" in the country.[20] At the time of King's statement, there were approximately 2,000 mosques in the country, compared to over 330,000 churches.[21] Muslim organizations wondered whether any member of the U.S. Congress would have stated with equal ease that there were too many churches or synagogues. Congressman King cited Islamophobes Steven Emerson (the discredited "terrorism expert" who falsely identified Muslims as being behind the Oklahoma City bombing committed by Timothy McVeigh)[22] and the equally notorious Daniel Pipes as his sources.[23] Not surprisingly, the congressman also stated that 85 percent of American mosques were controlled by Islamic extremists, and as such the majority of American Muslims represent "an enemy living amongst us."[24]

The issue of Muslims' presence in the broader fabric of American civic life has continued to occupy American media headlines and debates in the public sphere. Events from the 2010 controversy over a Muslim community center in New York City (the Park51 controversy) to a series of attacks on mosque building projects throughout the country continued to demonstrate the ambivalent status and perception of American Muslims in American society. The cover of *Time Magazine* in August 2010, rightfully so, asked "Is America Islamophobic?"[25]

It is worth noting that Muslim American leaders and scholars have responded to these controversies not only by defending their religious tradition but also by reminding people of American values and traditions. Hamza Yusuf, one of the most influential living American Muslim leaders and a white convert to Islam, wrote a powerful essay in which he traced his own family's lineage to his great-great-grandfather, Michael O'Hanson, who arrived in America from Ireland in the 1840s. Yusuf placed Muslims in this broader American genealogy by proclaiming that "Muslims are the new Irish" and encouraged Muslims

---

[20] http://thinkprogress.org/security/2011/03/10/149817/peter-king-too-many-mosques-fact-check/.

[21] http://features.pewforum.org/muslim/controversies-over-mosque-and-islamic-centers-across-the-us.html.

[22] On Steve Emerson, see "Meet An Islamophobia Network 'Expert': Steven Emerson," http://thinkprogress.org/politics/2011/08/31/308537/steve-emerson-investigative-project/?mobile=nc.

[23] For more on Daniel Pipes, see "Fear, Inc.," http://www.americanprogress.org/wp-content/uploads/issues/2011/08/pdf/islamophobia.pdf.

[24] http://onfaith.washingtonpost.com/onfaith/panelists/john_esposito/2011/03/islamophobia_draped_in_the_american_flag.html.

[25] http://www.time.com/time/magazine/article/0,9171,2011936,00.html.

to take heart and follow the example of previous ethnic and religious minorities who successfully became a part of the American mosaic. It was surely no slip of the tongue when Yusuf identified the city that his great-, great-grandfather arrived in, Philadelphia, as "the Mecca for Irish-Americans" in the 1840s. As Keith Ellison had done before Yusuf, in referring to his own family's long lineage in America, Yusuf was also pointing out the intertwined nature of American and Muslim identities.[26]

FRAMEWORK OF THE VOLUME

Clearly, more than ever, we are in need of accurate and accessible discussions that portray the full complexity and subtlety of vibrant Muslim communities and advance the discourse beyond the often shallow and sensationalist journalistic accounts. The present volume brings together scholars in the continuously growing field of scholarship that addresses American Islam. While many of the popular discussions of American Islam deal with American Muslims as only partially "Americanized," as a "problem," or in a situation of crisis, this volume also speaks of the many opportunities that exist in Muslim communities for exploring new discourses and practices in areas such as new emerging religious authority, arts, gender, pluralism, and citizenship.

It is also important here to explain the title of this volume: *The Cambridge Companion to American Islam*. The choice of this title reflects use of a term now common in the scholarly literature, one that supports the claim that American Muslims have indeed forged their own version of Islam (one of many "Islams," alongside Iranian Islam, Turkish Islam, Egyptian Islam, etc.). This American Islam is at the same time a vision and a reality on the ground. Muslim communities, discourses, and practices have had an impact and significantly helped shape the American religious landscape at least since the 1900s. Conversely, American religion, politics, and culture have had an even more significant impact on the formulation of Muslim American practices, institutions, politics, and communities. The title "American Islam" implicitly rejects the assumption that Muslims are somehow a temporary or simply migratory phenomenon in America, as implied in terminology such as "Muslims in America" or "Islam in America."

[26] Hamza Yusuf, "Amid Mosque Dispute Muslims Can Look to Irish Catholics for Hope," *Christian Science Monitor*, September 16, 2010, http://www.csmonitor.com/Commentary/Opinion/2010/0916/Amid-mosque-dispute-Muslims-can-look-to-Irish-Catholics-for-hope.

As for the human beings who inhabit and animate this American Islam, the contributors to the volume refer to "American Muslims" and "Muslim Americans." The two terms are of course related but carry slightly different valences. The term "American Muslims" locates Muslims as part of a global community (the *ummah*) and then focuses on the American members of that global community. The term "Muslim Americans," on the other hand, begins with the genus of Americans and then locates the group marked as Muslim within that broader American umbrella. Some contributors prefer one term over the other, while others use them interchangeably, and in the variation of their usage is demonstrated both the significance of terminology ("What's in a name?") and the varied and negotiated approaches to the subjects of study and their complex identities.

It also needs to be pointed out that "American" is here used in its most limited geographic understanding as designating the borders and boundaries of the United States. This focus on Islam and Muslims in the United States is a concession to the limits of an edited volume and the expectation of comprehensiveness as well as depth and breadth of coverage. There are, of course Muslim communities in Canada, and Muslims have also had a continuous presence in the Caribbean and South America. Muslims in Canada have had some similar but also some vastly different historical experiences as part of the fabric of American society, and the editors thought it cumbersome and confusing to compel the scholars who wrote for this volume to include, compare, and differentiate between U.S. and Canadian Muslims. This is even truer for Caribbean and South American Muslims with their diverse and complex local histories. There is surely a need for subsequent studies of the whole North American and South American Muslim contexts, but including them here would not have done justice to any of the countries, regions, and communities.

The geographic focus on the United States has been paired with a set of basic premises that each contributor to the volume was charged to incorporate into her or his chapter. These premises reflect developments in the fields that contribute to the study of American Islam, while simultaneously pushing the boundaries imposed on many of those fields in the past.

The first of these premises focuses on the necessity to include gender as a category of analysis in all aspects of the study of American Muslims. As women compose roughly half of the American Muslim population (even if this was not always the case in the past), their presence, contributions, and frequent absence from documents and historical narratives needed to be problematized and discussed in the contributions to the volume. In addition to the final chapter, which focuses on American Muslim women, women appear in almost all of the chapters as historical subjects, as well as objects and subjects of debate and discourse.

Historically, the fields of study focusing on American Muslims, including sociology, history, anthropology, African American studies, Islamic studies, and religious studies, had proved to be reluctant to fully explore the long intertwined narratives of Islam and America, especially by being too respectful of the artificial divisions between immigrant and African American narratives. In part, this division has been perpetuated by scholars, mainly because African American Muslims have more frequently been studied from within the framework of African American studies and American religions, while the study of immigrant Muslim communities has often been carried out from the various fields associated with Islamic studies. To make matters worse, many of the scholars who have written on "Muslims in America" have shown little interest in the study of American religions. The contributions to this volume incorporate and intentionally emphasize the complex and multifaceted character of American Muslim communities, be it on the level of ethnicity, discourse, gender, class, or background. Recent scholarship on the role of race categories in the construction of Black and Arab Muslim identities and the interplay of race, class, and gender have contributed to our understanding of the topic and have made it possible to revisit earlier binary constructions of immigrant and African American Muslims, or sometimes immigrant and indigenous Muslims.

The claim to an American Islam as a construct, a project, and a reality should not overlook the fact that American Muslim communities are simultaneously indigenous and a product of migratory movements. Consequently, any topic in regard to the study of American Muslims needs to take into account the interplay between domestic and localized dynamics and translational ties, connections, and exchanges. Each contributor was asked to connect domestic American conditions and politics with global and transnational trends and developments as they have shaped and continue to shape American Muslim communities in their politics, practices, and discourses.

Finally, the volume does not contain a separate chapter on Shi'ism in America. Shi'a communities and Shi'ites in communities have been and continue to be part of the America Muslim fabric; however, their community dynamics cannot be understood without the larger context of Sunnis as the majority of a religious minority community and the ensuing alliances, convergences, and divergences in practice and politics.

Some of these premises proved to be more challenging to address on the basis of the available research and documentation, and the chapters reflect the continuous negotiation of these foundational assumptions. Readers will find contributors to the volume agreeing as well as disagreeing with each other in their frameworks, methodologies, and analyses. In this sense, the chapters in this volume should be seen as part of a larger conversation in which knowledge is produced precisely through exchange of ideas and debate of methods and conclusions.

STRUCTURE OF THE VOLUME

The volume begins with an overview over the history, debates, and scholarly literature in the study of American Muslims, written by Edward E. Curtis IV. This chapter provides the reader with the tools to situate and evaluate the arguments and materials provided by the other contributors to the volume.

The chapters by Richard Brent Turner (Chapter 2 on African Muslim slaves in the Americas), Sally Howell (Chapter 3 on Muslim American history from 1865 to 1965), and Zain Abdullah (Chapter 4 on the history of American Muslims from 1965 to the present) provide a chronological and thus historical treatment of the subject at hand. The authors focus on available documentation, historical timelines, and institution building, while also offering insight into the trends, debates, and discourses that inform the events described in the chapters. Michael Muhammad Knight (Chapter 5) provides a thematic as well as chronological discussion of the role of "converts and conversion" to Islam and argues for the significance of converts as markers of debates over race, authenticity, and gender.

The remaining fourteen chapters build on the aspects of continuity and change introduced in the historical chapters. Each has a thematic focus and thus allows glimpses into some of the many facets and dimensions of American Muslim lives. The authors represent a range of academic disciplines and their methodologies and sources. Amaney Jamal and Liali Albana (Chapter 6) address the difficulty of demographic analysis of American Muslims as well as their patterns of political participation. Nabil Echchaibi (Chapter 7) takes up the issue of mostly negative media representations and stereotypes but balances the effects of such anti-Muslim and Islamophobic discourses by spotlighting the many ways in which American Muslims have participated in media production and representation.

Kathleen M. Moore (Chapter 8) provides a framework for understanding the experiences of American Muslims with the American legal system. Rosemary R. Hicks (Chapter 9) focuses on the 2010 controversy over a Muslim community center in New York City as part of a broader framework for thinking about American Muslims as a religious minority community in a secular state, as participants in interfaith dialogues, and as both objects and subjects of debates over religious pluralism. Karen Leonard (Chapter 10) synthesizes and analyzes research on American Muslim institution building and provides an overview of organizations, networks, and groups of American Muslims including an appendix listing the major organizations in the United States. Gisela Webb (Chapter 11) offers insight into a particular subset of communities, those associated with Sufism (or Islamic mysticism). By discussing a particular Sufi community in significant detail, Webb offers both a qualitative and historical understanding of Sufi discourse and practices in the United States.

Kambiz GhaneaBassiri (Chapter 12) delineates approaches to Muslim religious practices and the particular role of Islamic Law in a minority community. He discusses models of engagement with religious authenticity and authority in the American context. Akel Ismail Kahera (Chapter 13) provides insight into the special dynamics of religious practice and Muslim presence in the United States. Zareena A. Grewal and R. David Coolidge (Chapter 14) present an overview of institutions as well as discourses on Islamic education in America from elementary-level schools to higher education and professional religious training. Timur R. Yuskaev (Chapter 15) connects many of the scholars, leaders, and intellectuals involved in Islamic education with their roles as public intellectuals and their contributions to global Muslim thought.

Sylvia Chan-Malik (Chapter 16) offers a glimpse into the rich history and breadth of American Muslim cultural production in genres from music to literature. Su'ad Abdul Khabeer and Maytha Alhassen (Chapter 17) link this cultural production to expressions in youth culture, including music, fashion, and Internet forums. Debra Majeed (Chapter 18) discusses American Muslim discourses and practices related to marriage, sexuality, and women's dress. Juliane Hammer, in the final chapter, situates the study of American Muslim women as part of the broader field and reflects on the roles of American Muslim women scholars in the secular academy and beyond.

In many ways this volume is simultaneously a stocktaking of what the study of American Muslims has so far offered to the academy and the public, as well as an invitation to explore further the rich histories, multiple identities, and complex realities of American Muslim lives. The list of further readings at the end of each chapter provides a starting point for such exploration. Much more can be found as American Muslims continue to write their stories and live their lives, while scholars continue to advance our understanding of the particular aspects and larger frameworks of American Muslim experiences as part of the fabric of American society.

1 The Study of American Muslims: A History

EDWARD E. CURTIS IV

Though popular images and amateur ethnographies of Muslim slaves and visitors circulated in the nineteenth-century United States, the formal study of American Muslims did not begin until the 1930s. This chapter explores the history of the field, which began as the sociological study of "Black Muslims" and a few immigrant groups and by the 1980s became a religious studies subfield sometimes called Islam-in-America studies. The field's focus in the 1980s on post-1965 Muslim immigration, however, obscured the presence of African American Muslims and mistakenly analyzed the Muslim American experience as a whole through the lens of a first-generation struggle between American modernity and Islamic tradition. As studies of African American and other Muslim groups multiplied in the 1990s and then increased dramatically after 9/11, however, the leading paradigm of the field was challenged. A new generation of scholars arose to analyze Islam as an American religious tradition and to narrate the lives of Muslims as mundane Americans.

THE SOCIOLOGY OF SECURITY THREATS, OR THE STUDY OF BLACK MUSLIMS

Anticipating a contemporary motive for the study of Muslim Americans, the first research conducted in the field was generally concerned with Muslims as a security threat. The U.S. Federal Bureau of Investigation (FBI) and a few sociologists led the way. Though it did not produce peer-reviewed scholarship, the FBI was by far the most prolific student of Muslim groups in the first half of the twentieth century. The Bureau produced thousands of pages on both the Moorish Science Temple of America (MSTA), established in the middle 1920s by Noble Drew Ali, and the Nation of Islam (NOI), established by W. D. Fard in 1930, during the first three decades of these organizations' existence. The FBI was worried about the radical potential of such groups, a concern that continued to define the FBI's relationship to any African American movement that threatened white supremacy in the United States through the 1960s.[1]

Following in Marcus Garvey's footsteps, the Moorish Science Temple of America, the Ahmadiyya movement, and the Nation of Islam urged Blacks to challenge their second-class citizenship in the United States by converting to Islam. Both the MSTA and the NOI explicitly questioned whether the American nation-state was the proper object of Black Americans' loyalty, instead encouraging African Americans to imagine their national identity as located in other sites – like the "nation" of Islam. In the 1930s, some members of these groups were attracted to Japanese national Satokata Takahashi's movement to unite all nonwhite people in the United States behind the Empire of Japan. This sympathy for Japan never amounted to a direct threat to the national security of the United States but was a symbolically important challenge to Jim Crow and white supremacy.[2]

The fact that these groups were simultaneously religious and political posed another problem for the federal government, because religious activity was protected under the U.S. Constitution. In order to remove this legal impediment to persecution, it was in the interest of the federal government to deny these groups' religious legitimacy. Both field agents and scholars in the employ of the FBI did just that, insisting that the MSTA and NOI were not religious groups but "cults." Religion was a veil, they said, that hid the subversive politics of movement members and the chicanery of movement leaders. The white press repeated this message, depicting Black Muslims as "improper" religious believers, as Sylvester Johnson has pointed out.[3] The press demeaned movement members by representing them as pitiful and poor Negroes who had been duped by religious charlatans interested only in making money or in leading Blacks toward political radicalism.

In confronting the question of whether Muslims posed a direct or indirect threat to the internal security and cultural cohesion of the United States from the 1930s to the 1950s, sociologists were among the very few scholars outside of the FBI to track the burgeoning institutional growth of

[1]   See "Moorish Science Temple of America," http://foia.fbi.gov/foiaindex/moortemp. htm, accessed November 11, 2010, and "Nation of Islam," http://foia.fbi.gov/foiaindex/nation_of_islam.htm, accessed November 11, 2010.

[2]   Ernest Allen Jr., "When Japan Was 'Champion of the Darker Races': Satokata Takahashi and the Flowering of Black Messianic Nationalism," *Black Scholar* 24 (1994): 23–46.

[3]   Sylvester A. Johnson, "Religion Proper and Proper Religion: Arthur Fauset and the Study of African American Religions," in Edward E. Curtis IV and Danielle B. Sigler, eds., *The New Black Gods: Arthur Huff Fauset and the Study of African American Religions* (Bloomington, 2009), pp. 245–284.

American Islam in the twentieth century. As popular and media images of American Muslims oscillated between images of the scary political radical and of the sad religious cultist, sociologists employed both functionalist and reductionist paradigms to understand these movements. In 1938, for example, sociologist Erdmann Beynon's misnamed article, "The Voodoo Cult among Negro Migrants in Detroit," addressed police suspicions that the Nation of Islam engaged in ritual human sacrifice. He argued that the movement was better understood as a creation of displaced, working-class African Americans attempting to attain higher social status.[4]

This thesis was later reiterated in C. Eric Lincoln's 1961 *The Black Muslims in America*, likely the first full-length academic book about Muslims of any kind in the United States. Repeating the claim of Beynon and anticipating the analysis of Martin Luther King Jr., in the 1963 "Letter from a Birmingham Jail," Lincoln argued that the Nation of Islam was first and foremost a Black nationalist group. It was a "defensive response to external forces – hostile forces that threaten their creative existence." Its single most important aspect was its social function as a response to the anger of working-class Blacks toward their white oppressors: "It matters little," wrote Lincoln, "whether the homeland of the dispersal Black Nation is said to be Asia or Africa. For the black nationalist, the black Zion is wherever whites are absent."[5] Lincoln discounted the importance of Islamic religious practice, narrative, and scriptures to the group's functions as a social protest movement. Islam worked to shroud Black anger in religious clothes, according to Lincoln.[6]

Addressing the NOI as a Black nationalist group was meant to show the need for a civil rights bill that would remove the underlying social conditions that led to such protest movements. But in downplaying the Islamic elements of the NOI, Lincoln also supported, no doubt unconsciously, the arguments of immigrant and some African American Muslim competitors who dismissed the Islamic legitimacy of the NOI. After World War II, though Elijah Muhammad and Malcolm X came to represent the public face of Islam in the United States, scholars slowly began to note the presence of a new kind of Muslim on American soil. Called "orthodox Muslims" by Malcolm X, South Asian and Arab

---

[4]   Erdmann D. Beynon, "The Voodoo Cult among Negro Migrants in Detroit," *American Journal of Sociology* 43:6 (1938): 894–907.

[5]   C. Eric Lincoln, *The Black Muslims in America* (Grand Rapids, 1994 [1961]), pp. 43, 63.

[6]   Lincoln, *Black Muslims*, pp. 26, 43, 46, 210, 215.

American immigrants had planted roots and established local organizations during the first half of the twentieth century. But only in the 1950s
did their religious activities warrant major attention from scholars.

STUDYING THE ASSIMILATION OF "AUTHENTIC" MUSLIMS

As was the case with African American Muslims, it was sociologists who
first conducted research on the new Muslim American other. In 1966
Egyptian Abdo Elkholy, a sociologist at Northern Illinois University,
published a landmark comparative study of Muslim American mosques
in Toledo and Detroit. *The Arab Moslems in the United States*, as the
book was titled, was critical toward its Muslim subjects in Detroit,
whom Elkholy believed to be poorly assimilated into mainstream
American culture. Like Lincoln, he analyzed their failures as a problem
of working-class economic status: they worked "almost solely in the
auto factories" of Detroit, he explained. Elkholy also asserted that "these
Moslems live in a ghetto-like community in Dearborn. Besides delaying
the process of assimilation, the residential concentration of the Detroit
community has perpetuated the traditional conceptions of family and social relations, as well as of religion and of the sectarian conflict between
Sunnis and Shi'as."[7] By the 1980s, the construction of strong ethnic,
kin-based, and confessional enclaves (think Irish Roman Catholics and
East European Jews) would be understood as necessary precursors to or
even as expressions of successful assimilation into American culture.[8]
For Elkholy, however, such resources evidenced a lack of integration
into the American middle class.

Toledo was a different story. There, according to Elkholy, men,
women, and children reached across the generation gap to participate
equally in the life of the mosque regardless of their particular sectarian
background. Families attended Sunday school classes, contributed to
the public life of Toledo, and embraced the many interfaith (generally
Christian and Muslim) couples who were members of the mosque's
community. Elkholy argued that Muslims who were the most active in
the mosques' activities were also the most Americanized. This finding
dramatically questioned the idea, still popular among sociologists at the
time, that the ideals of "foreign" religions such as Islam conflicted with

[7]   Abdo A. Elkholy, *The Arab Moslems in the United States* (New Haven, 1966), p. 16.
[8]   Werner Sollors, *Beyond Ethnicity: Consent and Descent in American Culture*
(New York, 1987).

American norms. Elkholy showed that mosque participants were more likely to identify with the patriotic values of the white middle class than those who did not participate in the life of the mosque.[9]

Elkholy's vision of the mainstream, middle-class, "white" Muslim was never accepted as an important trope either in sociology or in media accounts because such an image did not complement popular notions of Islam as a symbol of protest. After 1965, the slain Malcolm X became a patron saint of Black power and Black consciousness movements, and there was no more effective symbol of protest against the Vietnam War than Muhammad Ali. The picture was further complicated by the presence of first-generation Muslim students, visitors, and immigrants from Africa and Asia. Coming in modest numbers to the United States first as students in the 1950s, this group began to challenge the older generation of "assimilated" Muslim immigrant leaders. As a result of the 1965 Immigration and Naturalization Act, perhaps more than 1.1 million new Muslims arrived in the United States before the end of the twentieth century.[10] They not only challenged but also displaced many of the older immigrant leaders. Not all of these immigrants were religious, but their significant educational and cultural capital (a large number were academics, physicians, and engineers) catapulted them into leadership positions among existing and newly established Muslim immigrant groups. In the 1960s, 1970s, and 1980s, they often presented themselves as the voice of authentic Islam, and for the most part, the media, academics, and the intelligence services, otherwise ignorant of diversity among Muslims abroad, took their word for it.[11]

Now that the so-called Black Muslims were declared to be inauthentic Muslims, some scholars began to search for the "real" Black Muslims. Unfortunately, they completely missed the phenomenon of Sunni African Americans, those Muslims not associated with the Nation of Islam who traced their lineage instead to interwar leaders such as Muhammad Ezaldeen, Wali Akram, and Daoud Ahmed Faisal and the heirs of these leaders.[12] Though Imam W. D. Mohammed, the son of Elijah Muhammad and heir to the Nation of Islam, received some scholarly attention, the focus was primarily on Black Muslim slaves. For a time, it was almost as if the only African American Muslims worthy of a

<hr/>

[9] Elkholy, *Arab Moslems*, pp. 17–18, 91–93, 102, 122–125, 129, 133–134.
[10] Mohamed Nimer, *The North American Muslim Resource Guide* (New York, 2002), pp. 24–25.
[11] Edward E. Curtis IV, *Black Muslim Religion in the Nation of Islam, 1960–1975* (Chapel Hill, 2006), pp. 35–65.
[12] Robert Dannin, *Black Pilgrimage to Islam* (New York, 2002).

book were the dead ones, figures like Kunta Kinte, so famously discussed in Alex Haley's *Roots* (1976).[13] Haley's book reflected the scholarly mood of the period. His personal search for a Muslim African ancestor was an attempt to weave African Americans into a larger story of American immigration; the middle passage became an immigrant crossing into the American homeland. A decade later, Terry Alford published the incredible tale of Abdul Rahman Ibrahima, the "Prince among Slaves" who returned to his native Africa, and Allan D. Austin compiled a sourcebook of antebellum documents pertaining to African American Muslim slaves, a book that remains the single best collection of primary sources on African American Muslims before the Civil War.[14]

At the same time, the study of Islam in America began to emerge as its own subfield, generally under the rubric of religious studies but shaped heavily by Islamic studies scholars teaching in other departments and in American seminaries. Most of the subfield's gaze was directed toward immigrants who had come to the United States after 1965. Even if the 1980s saw the academic embrace of various American ethnic populations in a narrative of multicultural inclusion, Muslims (i.e., the first-generation immigrants who were the focus of Islam in America studies) were seen as exceptional. American popular culture in the wake of the Iranian revolution of 1979 and the bombing of the Marine barracks in Beirut in 1983 refused to include Muslims as a piece of the American multicultural puzzle. The "Muslim" was transgressive and potentially dangerous. According to Melani McAlister, Muslims and Islam became important symbols in larger debates about U.S. military, economic, cultural, and political interests as U.S. foreign policy turned its attention to the Muslim world after the Soviet Union collapsed.[15]

Academic literature about Muslim American immigrants in the 1980s and 1990s tried to push back against increasing the easy association of Muslims with unjustified violence and other bad behavior by asserting that prejudices against Arabs and Muslims are as morally wrong as discrimination against other groups; that biased U.S. policy, especially concerning Israel, was rightly challenged by immigrants; and that, like earlier immigrants, Muslim immigrants suffered from a tension between their "traditional" cultures of origin and the "modern" and secularizing

[13] Alex Haley, *Roots* (Garden City, N.J., 1976).
[14] Terry Alford, *Prince among Slaves* (New York, 1986), and Allan D. Austin, ed., *African Muslims in Antebellum America: A Sourcebook* (New York, 1984).
[15] Melani McAlister, *Epic Encounters: Culture, Media, and U.S. Interests in the Middle East, 1945–2000*, 2nd ed. (Berkeley, 2005), pp. 198–265.

tendencies of mainstream culture.[16] The idea that Muslims faced challenges between assimilating into mainstream American culture and preserving their traditional Islamic values became the most salient theme in Islam in America literature.

Yvonne Y. Haddad emerged as the dean of this school of interpretation, writing and editing an incredibly varied and long list of publications about Muslims in North America. Her 1987 work, *Islamic Values in the United States*, coauthored with Adair T. Lummis, overlooked Elkholy's book to assert that "no other study has attempted ... to consider the role of the mosque/[Islamic] center in helping Muslims to integrate into American life and culture." Employing interviews and questionnaires, Haddad and Lummis demonstrated that "some Muslims are feeling at home and welcome assimilation into American life, while others are genuinely concerned that it will jeopardize the maintenance of Islamic values."[17]

This topic, the tension between Islamic values and assimilation into American culture, has had great staying power in the scholarly literature. John Esposito, in a 2000 introduction to *Muslims on the Americanization Path?* (coedited with Haddad), continued to defend its relevance as a central fact of Muslim American life: "Integral to the experience of Muslims, like all religious or ethnic minorities, is how to deal with the question of integration or assimilation.... The primary question facing Muslims in America is whether or not they can live Muslim lives in a non-Muslim territory."[18] Even if this theme was important for some Muslims in the 1980s and 1990s, identifying it as the "primary question" of Muslim American existence drew attention away from the ways that Muslim Americans were already assimilated. For most, the question was irrelevant.

Haddad's role in creating the subfield was much greater than the analysis she offered of Muslim American life. As the doyenne of the new field, she edited a number of scholarly volumes and convened groundbreaking academic conferences on Islam in America. Her 1991 edited book, *The Muslims of America*, emerged from a conference at the University of Massachusetts, and offered new scholarship on Muslim American political engagement, Muslim American women, Muslims

---

[16] Jack G. Shaheen, *The TV Arab* (Bowling Green, 1984); Yvonne Y. Haddad, ed., *The Muslims of America* (New York, 1991), pp. 217–235.

[17] Yvonne Y. Haddad and Adair T. Lummis, *Islamic Values in the United States* (New York, 1987), pp. 6, 171.

[18] Yvonne Y. Haddad and John L. Esposito, eds., *Muslims on the Americanization Path?* (Tampa, 1998), pp. 3, 5.

in prison, and more. Then, in *Muslim Communities in North America* (1994), Haddad and Jane Idleman Smith edited and published twenty-two chapters on a diverse array of Muslim communities and groups across North America.[19]

Both of these volumes included research on African American Muslims, which by the 1990s reemerged as a legitimate subject for study. Aminah McCloud and Richard Brent Turner led the way. McCloud wrote an overview of more than twenty different Black Muslim organizations; these groups had different Islamic doctrinal orientations, sometimes aligned more with Sunni Muslims than with the Nation of Islam.[20] Turner showed the pivotal role played by Pan-African thought and the Ahmadiyya movement in the creation of African American Islam and traced the evolution of the Nation of Islam.[21]

But along with the refereed scholarly work on Muslim Americans emerged a genre of Islamophobic literature that depicted American Muslims as potential enemies, a Trojan horse for Islamic extremism. *Militant Islam Reaches America!*, for instance, was penned in 2002 by professional jihad-watcher Daniel Pipes. Pipes, who later created the group CampusWatch.Org, argued in this book that militant Islam was the most potent threat to the West since Soviet communism. He declared that militant Muslims wanted to impose *shari'ah*, or Islamic law and ethics, in every nation, including the United States. He warned that these militants would use a variety of means, some cunningly nonviolent, to supplant the Constitution with the Qur'an. Perhaps surprisingly, Pipes refuted the notion that the United States was in the midst of a "clash of civilizations" with Islam. He claimed instead that there was an internal war within Islam between more "modern," secular views of the faith and militant Islam, an ideology that sought the destruction of American democracy and the reign of Islamic fascism.[22]

These polemics about the "Muslim threat" viewed Muslim Americans as outsiders, people whose essential foreignness had been unaffected by their life in the United States. In this story the Muslim protagonists were seen either as foreign agents or, in a more sympathetic light, as people fighting with themselves to square their "traditional" Islamic views with "modern" American culture. Pipes associated Americanization with

---

[19] Yvonne Y. Haddad and Jane I. Smith, eds., *Muslim Communities in North America* (Albany, 1994).

[20] Aminah Beverly McCloud, *African American Islam* (New York, 1995).

[21] Richard Brent Turner, *Islam in the African-American Experience* (Bloomington, 1997).

[22] Daniel Pipes, *Militant Islam Reaches America* (New York, 2003).

secularization, ignoring the conclusions of most U.S. historians that religion has been a formidable variable in American public life.

Such Islamophobic literature was the strange bedfellow of Islam in America studies. It posed some of the same questions as the more respectable scholars of Islam in America but gave different answers. If the question was whether Muslim Americans had been successful in becoming Americanized, the Islamophobic answer was that, regrettably, the Muslim could not do so by virtue of being Muslim. It was vulgar, but it did reverberate with Americans often inclined, because of their political and religious biases, to dislike Muslims.

THE PROLIFERATION OF STUDIES ABOUT AMERICAN ISLAM AFTER 9/11

In the final decade of the twentieth century and after 9/11, the study of Islam in America became an important academic subject. Monographs and articles multiplied, and scholars used data about Muslim Americans to weigh in on various questions in such fields as political science, social work, anthropology, religious studies, and gender studies. This scholarship more fully revealed the diversity of religious thought and practice among Muslim Americans, complicating the kind of overarching claims one could make about the Muslim American experience as a whole. Linda Walbridge studied the life of Twelver Shi'a Muslims in Greater Detroit, showing the dynamics of this group's attempt to maintain its religious traditions.[23] Marcia Hermansen wrote a helpful survey of different Sufi groups in the United States, and Frances Trix penned a more in-depth study of a Sufi community in Michigan.[24]

Barbara Metcalf's edited work, perhaps the most innovative of religious studies books on the subject in the 1990s, gathered a group of religious studies scholars to interrogate practices of "space-making" among Muslim Americans.[25] Chapters in the book uncovered the types of domestic, international, national, regional, gendered, and ritualized spaces that Muslims had invented in their homes, on the street, in their

---

[23] Linda S. Walbridge, *Without Forgetting the Imam: Lebanese Shi'ism in an American Community* (Detroit, 1997).

[24] Marcia Hermansen, "In the Garden of American Sufi Movements: Hybrids and Perennials," in Peter B. Clarke, ed., *New Trends and Developments in the World of Islam* (London, 1997), and Frances Trix, *Spiritual Discourse: Learning with an Islamic Master* (Philadelphia, 1993).

[25] Barbara D. Metcalf, ed., *Making Muslim Space in North America and Europe* (Berkeley, 1996).

mosques, and in or on their bodies. Scholars also examined the American mosque itself. Akel Ismail Kahera theorized about the aesthetics and gendered spaces of the mosque, while Ihsan Bagby's coauthored 2001 report on the American mosque became a much cited study that charted the demographics of Muslim congregants in the United States.[26]

No subject in the study of Muslim Americans was more popular than that of women and Islam, which was viewed both inside and outside academic circles as the mother of all topics, the hermeneutical key to comprehending Islam and Muslims as a whole. Muslim American women themselves created a great deal of scholarship on the topic. Generally progressive and activist in nature, the body of literature included Gisela Webb's *Windows of Faith: Muslim Women Scholar-Activists in North America*, which featured leading voices in American Islam, including Amina Wadud, Mohja Kahf, Aminah McCloud, Riffat Hassan, and Azizah al-Hibri.[27] Khaled Abou El Fadl, a scholar at UCLA, made the case for gender equality and pluralism from a shari'ah perspective.[28] Omid Safi's *Progressive Muslims: On Justice, Gender, and Pluralism* featured a section on gender justice, including a chapter on gay and lesbian sexuality in Islamic tradition.[29]

Anthropological literature portrayed the everyday life of Muslim Americans in far more ethnographic detail than had previously been available. Carolyn Rouse's important *Engaged Surrender: African American Women and Islam* depicted the lives of African American Sunni women in Los Angeles who employed the Qur'an and Islamic religious traditions in attempts to live more ethically.[30] These women utilized their own interpretations of Islamic texts to guide their decision making on everything from what they ate to how they lived with their husbands. Loukia Sarroub honored the efforts of Yemeni American schoolchildren to transform their public schools into places where they, along with their teachers, could negotiate competing religious and cultural identities.[31]

[26] Akel Ismail Kahera, *Deconstructing the American Mosque: Space, Gender, and Aesthetics* (Austin, 2002), and Ihsan Bagby et al., *The Mosque in America: A National Portrait* (Washington, D.C., 2001).

[27] Gisela Webb, ed., *Windows of Faith: Muslim Women Scholar-Activists in North America* (Syracuse, 2000).

[28] Khaled Abou El Fadl, *Speaking in God's Name: Islamic Law, Authority, and Women* (Oxford, 2001).

[29] Omid Safi, ed., *Progressive Muslims: On Justice, Gender, and Pluralism* (Oxford, 2003).

[30] Carolyn Moxley Rouse, *Engaged Surrender: African American Women and Islam* (Berkeley, 2004).

[31] Loukia K. Sarroub, *All American Yemeni Girls: Being Muslim in a Public School* (Philadelphia, 2005).

JoAnn D'Alisera illustrated the transnational and diasporic identities of Sierra Leonean Muslim Americans in the nation's capital.[32]

The flowering of academic literature after 9/11 also indicated how Muslim Americans, like Muslims more generally, had become increasingly popular sites for both the academic and popular gaze. As some non-Muslim Americans expressed anxiety over what they thought was the violent, woman-hating, intolerant, and generally backward nature of Muslims, many scholars, including Louise Cainkar, sought to protect the Muslim body from state detention, media manipulation, and mob violence.[33] Journalistic accounts about Muslim Americans often expressed greater concern than the academic literature about Muslim American radicals and fundamentalists, using subtitles such as the "Struggle for the Soul of a Religion."[34] Even as the administrations of both George W. Bush and Barack Obama aggressively pursued Muslim American radicals through the use of the state security services and various sting operations, both Bush and Obama hailed the contributions of Muslim Americans to U.S. society as part of foreign policy.[35]

By the end of the first decade of the twenty-first century, a new generation of Islam in America scholars was also challenging the journalistic and older scholarly accounts that cast Muslim Americans as victims of a conflict between Islamic and American values. Working separately but guided by many of the same historiographical themes, Kambiz GhaneaBassiri and Edward Curtis rejected old narratives of "Islam versus America" by producing sweeping chronicles about Islam *in* America. Integrating Muslims into the major questions, themes, and periods of U.S. history, GhaneaBassiri published a major monograph, and Curtis produced an encyclopedia, a short history, and a sourcebook of primary source documents.[36] One of the important methodological moves in this new scholarship was to ground Muslim Americans

---

[32] JoAnn D'Alisera, *An Imagined Geography: Sierra Leonean Muslims in America* (Philadelphia, 2004).

[33] Louise Cainkar, *Homeland Insecurity: The Arab American and Muslim American Experience after 9/11* (New York, 2009).

[34] Paul M. Barrett, *American Islam: The Struggle for the Soul of a Religion* (New York, 2007).

[35] See, for example, Barack Obama, "Remarks by the President on a New Beginning," Cairo, Egypt, June 4, 2009, http://www.whitehouse.gov/the_press_office/Remarks-by-the-President-at-Cairo-University-6-04-09/, accessed November 22, 2010.

[36] Kambiz GhaneaBassiri, *A History of Islam in America* (Cambridge, 2010); Edward E. Curtis IV, ed., *Encyclopedia of Muslim-American History* (New York, 2010); Edward E. Curtis IV, *Muslims in America: A Short History* (New York, 2009); and Edward E. Curtis IV, ed., *Columbia Sourcebook of Muslims in the United States* (New York, 2008).

in U.S. history, showing how larger political and social forces shaped and even constrained their behavior and how Muslim American protest and dissent (as much as Muslim American patriotism and consent) adopted American cultural forms. In addition, these works stressed how Muslim Americans could identify as U.S. nationals in both a legal and an ideological sense while also celebrating their ethnic loyalties and diasporic consciousness. Such multiple identifications were seen as Americanization, not alienation.

Finally, this new scholarship attempted to show how studying Muslim Americans could reveal new directions for the study of U.S. history. Using a Muslim American lens, it reconsidered major historical subjects such as antebellum social reform (including abolitionism and emigrationism), consumer culture in the Gilded Age, the development of domestic surveillance after World War I, domestic dissent during the Cold War, and U.S. foreign policy toward Muslim-majority nations in the post–Cold War era. In most cases, according to the new historiography, the symbolic and embodied presence of Muslim Americans has played a key role in inscribing religious, racial, ethnic, class, and gender norms in American life. Muslims have often provided a foil against which non-Muslims could define American identity. At the same time, images of Muslim Americans defy easy categorization in binary terms; it is not as simple as non-Muslims using stereotypes of Muslims to define what America is not. Instead, images of Muslims and the activities of Muslim Americans themselves have been part of three-dimensional social, political, and cultural domains in which the meaning and functions of American Islam have led in multiple directions.

As some scholars and a president wove Muslims into the larger story of America, however, Islamophobes continued to speak as if there were an inevitable clash between Islam and America, particularly in the discussions surrounding the proposal to build a Muslim community center near Ground Zero in lower Manhattan. The passage in 2010 of a referendum in Oklahoma to ban consideration of *shari'ah*, or Islamic law and ethics, in civil court and the continued physical attacks on Muslim places of worship throughout the country revealed just how foreign and threatening Muslim Americans were seen by many Americans. Whether the vision of Muslims as *part of* America would become the dominant narrative in both scholarship and popular discourse, as it had for so many other religious, racial, and ethnic groups, was by no means assured.

Further Reading

Curtis, Edward E., IV, *Black Muslim Religion in the Nation of Islam, 1960–1975* (Chapel Hill, 2006).

  ed., *Columbia Sourcebook of Muslims in the United States* (New York, 2008).

  ed., *Encyclopedia of Muslim-American History* (New York, 2010).

GhaneaBassiri, Kambiz, *A History of Islam in America* (Cambridge, 2010).

Haddad, Yvonne Y., and Jane I. Smith, eds., *Muslim Communities in North America* (Albany, 1994).

Lawrence, Bruce B., *New Faiths, Old Fears: Muslims and Other Asian Immigrants in American Religious Life* (New York, 2002).

Leonard, Karen, *Muslims in the United States: The State of Research* (New York, 2003).

Metcalf, Barbara, ed., *Making Muslim Space in North America and Europe* (Berkeley, 1996).

Moore, Kathleen M., *Al-Mughtaribun: American Law and the Transformation of Muslim Life in the United States* (Albany, 1995).

Smith, Jane I., *Islam in America* (New York, 2010).

2 African Muslim Slaves and Islam in Antebellum America

RICHARD BRENT TURNER

Signification, the issue of identity and naming, is the analytical key to understanding Islam in America from 1730 to 1860, and it is revealed through the interactions between the transnational self-identification of the influential West African Muslim slaves and the dominant culture's construction of hegemonic racial categories and stereotypes for people of African descent. Charles H. Long has examined the theme of signification in religious studies to refer to both the system, by which stereotypes, names, and signs were given to non-European peoples and cultures during the western exploration and conquest of the Americas that began in 1492 with Christopher Columbus, and the process by which the enslaved constructed subaltern resistance strategies in their liberation struggles against the racism of the majority community.[1] Although African Muslim slaves were stereotyped, stigmatized, and categorized for racial exploitation in the political economy of transatlantic slavery since the 1500s, their Islamic names and religious identities undercut this signification with a powerful self-signification, providing a counterconception to the hegemony of white American Christianity that enabled these Muslims to achieve independence from the dominant race and religion in the New World. Their fascinating stories and literacy in Arabic are a central theme for understanding how these slaves utilized intellectual resistance to signify themselves as the Muslims that they wanted to be. Their survival strategies of maintaining Arabic names, identifying with the universal Muslim community, reflecting on the Qur'an, praying, writing in Arabic, fasting, and wearing what they saw as Muslim clothing provide a sharp angle of vision to evaluate the complex inner struggles of African Muslims against Christian tyranny and the dehumanization of transatlantic slavery.

[1] Charles H. Long, *Significations: Signs, Symbols, and Images in the Interpretation of Religion* (Philadelphia, 1986), p. 3.

TRANSNATIONAL CONNECTIONS IN THE BLACK ATLANTIC WORLD

West African Muslims in the United States were part of a larger transnational context in the Black Atlantic world of enslaved African Muslims in the Caribbean, Latin America, and Brazil since the 1500s. The first Muslim slaves in the Americas came to Hispaniola in 1502 from Seville, Spain, where they had survived the Spanish Inquisition's policy to forcibly convert all Muslims to Christianity.[2] African Muslim slaves from Morocco who had also been enslaved in Spain, such as Estévanico from 1527 to 1539, were used to explore the areas in the Americas that are now the states of Arizona and New Mexico.[3]

Although the history and experiences of African slaves varied according to their location (the Caribbean, Latin America, and Brazil), in many cases these Muslim slave communities were well organized, highly visible, and involved in slave rebellions and bold plans to return to West Africa. In this early period, European Christians called the Berber and Arab peoples of North Africa, Moors.[4] Eventually, for white people in Europe and the Americas, the "Moor" signified Muslims wherever they came in contact with them in antebellum America. This term carried complex and historic, political, and religious significations for the communities that enslaved people of African descent in the Atlantic world. The Crusades initiated a long history of bloody battles between Muslims and Christians in the holy lands. Also, southern Italian, Portuguese, and Spanish Christians were politically dominated by North African Muslims for centuries before the dawn of the modern period. Thus, the signification of African Muslims as Moors placed these slaves in the realm of exotica about Islam as the enemy religion of Christianity in the modern world. Moreover, their powerful self-significations continued to prioritize their identification with their transnational African Muslim identities. Several outstanding examples of their resistance efforts follow. In 1522 Senegambian Muslims were part of a violent slave uprising in Santo Domingo, the capital of Hispaniola, which was governed by Christopher Columbus's son, Diego Columbus. Senegambians, including Muslims,

---

[2] Michael A. Gomez, *Black Crescent: The Experience and Legacy of African Muslims in the Americas* (Cambridge, 2005), pp. 12–14.

[3] Richard Brent Turner, *Islam in the African-American Experience*, 2nd ed. (Bloomington, 2003), p. 11.

[4] Kambiz GhaneaBassiri, *A History of Islam in America* (Cambridge, 2010), p. 11.

were also said to be the instigators of a slave revolt in San Juan, Puerto Rico, in 1527.[5]

In early nineteenth-century Trinidad, well-organized communities of African-born "Mandingo" Muslims and Muslim converts, with their own schools and imams in Quaré and Manzanilla, were led by free Mandingo Muslims who had been troops in the West India Regiments during the Napoleonic Wars. When these Muslim communities began to deteriorate because of the lack of state support, Muhammad Sisse, a member of the West India Regiments, moved to Port of Spain in the 1830s and worked unsuccessfully with a group of Black Muslims, led by Jonas Mohammed Bath, to persuade the British government to facilitate the Muslims' repatriation to Africa (in 1838 Sisse returned to West Africa through his individual efforts). In this transnational context, the enslaved Muslims' literacy in Arabic emerged as a central theme of intellectual resistance, to signify their religious identities and their plans to return to Africa. The Muslim repatriation efforts at Port of Spain included two petitions in 1833 and 1838, signed in Arabic and submitted to the king and queen of England.[6] Along the same lines, literate West African Muslim slaves in Jamaica in the 1820s and 1830s circulated a secret clerical document in Arabic, from Muslims in West Africa, supporting other enslaved Muslims to adhere to Islam.[7] Finally, in Brazil in 1835, hundreds of African Muslim slaves planned and carried out a major slave revolt in Bahia, clashing violently with civilians and soldiers in the streets of Salvador.

According to Michael A. Gomez, African Muslim slaves in Latin America, the Caribbean, and Brazil were so visible and so determined to transmit and preserve their religious practices and to be free that they were perceived as a threat to the state. Thus, political and military authorities stringently repressed Muslims in those contexts, and their religion emerged from slavery with little social or political power in the twentieth century. A different pattern of African Muslim slaves who complied with the state but who also signified themselves as Muslims prevailed in what became the United States. Islam quietly faded away for a brief period after enslavement and reappeared powerfully in African American communities in the early twentieth century. It is to the fascinating and complex life stories of West African Muslim slaves in the United States that we now turn.

---

[5]   Gomez, *Black Crescent*, pp. ix, 3, 18.
[6]   Gomez, *Black Crescent*, pp. 65–69; Sylviane A. Diouf, *Servants of Allah: African Muslims Enslaved in the Americas* (New York, 1998), p. 138.
[7]   Gomez, *Black Crescent*, p. 54.

LIFE STORIES, COMMUNITIES, AND PRACTICES

Political developments, including the disintegration of the Jolof Empire (in contemporary Senegal) in the 1500s and wars and raids between groups of Muslims and non-Muslims in the Gold Coast, Sierra Leone, the Bight of Benin, and Senegambia signaled the transformation of life on the Atlantic coast of West and West Central Africa. Among the thousands of Wolof, Yoruba, Mandingo, Hausa, Vai, Fulani, and Tukolor who were shipped as slaves to the United States, a significant portion consisted of Muslims, many of whom were prisoners of war from local conflicts who were sold to European and American slave traders. Of those captured between 1600 and 1800, an estimated 9.55 to 15.4 million Africans were transported across the Atlantic Ocean to the Americas,[8] and more than 2.3 million were forcefully moved across the Red Sea, the Indian Ocean, and the Sahara to suffer enslavement in the Muslim world. These figures do not include the people who died in the initial process of enslavement in Africa.[9]

Although slavery is a crime against humanity wherever it occurs, slavery in the United States and slavery in the Muslim world were quite different in scope and brutality. According to Walter Johnson's assessment of the slave trade by 1820, "Five times as many Africans traveled across the Atlantic as did Europeans. And those numbers do not include the dead – the five percent who died in crossings that took three weeks, the quarter who died in crossings that took three months."[10]

Although Portuguese, Spanish, French, Dutch, British, Arab, and West African elites (both Muslim and non-Muslim) participated in transatlantic slavery for profit, ultimately the European and white American mercantile and capitalist systems benefited more from this forced African migration in the Atlantic world (which included West Africa, Western Europe, Caribbean islands, and South and North America).[11] In the United States, especially in the American South, slaves of African descent did much of the work in the plantations, mines, transportation,

---

[8] Gwendolyn Midlo Hall, *Slavery and Ethnicities in the Americas: Restoring the Links* (Chapel Hill, 2005), pp. 27, 28.

[9] Paul E. Lovejoy, *Transformations of Slavery: A History of Slavery in Africa* (Cambridge, 1983), pp. 60–61.

[10] Walter Johnson, *Soul by Soul: Life Inside the Antebellum Slave Market* (Cambridge, 1999), p. 4.

[11] Paul E. Lovejoy, "The 'Middle Passage': The Enforced Migration of Africans across the Atlantic," in Howard Dodson and Colin Palmer, eds., *Origins* (East Lansing, 2008), pp. 43–90; 55.

and houses of the new world order of racial slavery and democracy, and they also brought Islam to America.[12]

In this context, European Americans continued the practice of signifying their Muslim slaves as Moors and constructed new racial categories (e.g., Negro) to objectify people of African descent in the United States. Allan D. Austin estimates that the total number of African Muslims in the United States was 40,000 out of the 4.5 million people enslaved by 1860;[13] Gomez argues that the paucity of quantitative data does not support a precise population estimate, but he admits there were thousands of Muslim slaves in the United States.[14] Sylviane A. Diouf hypothesizes that 15 to 20 percent, or between 2.25 and 3 million Muslims were enslaved in the Caribbean and North and South America.[15] Although there is no scholarly consensus about the number of Muslim slaves in the United States, several larger patterns and themes can be drawn from their life stories and communities. First-generation West African Muslim slaves continued to practice their religion in family networks and probably converted other slaves. Enslaved Muslims married non-Muslims and may have influenced Christian practices as well as class stratification and Black American identity in the slave community. Muslim slaves often occupied leadership roles in the jobs that slaves performed on plantations in the American South. Some Muslim slaves mentioned the superiority of their religion to Christianity and demonstrated their literacy in Arabic as a form of intellectual resistance to enslavement. Their names, dress, rituals, and dietary laws were perceived as powerful significations of Islamic identities in the slave community. Yet other African Muslim slaves and former slaves appeared to have converted to Christianity and constructed dual religious identities that included both Islam and Christianity. Here these Muslims, struggling to survive in hegemonic polyreligious communities, developed patterns of religious synthesis, similar to the adaptations of African diasporic Vodouists in Louisiana.[16] They reformulated and maintained their private African

---

[12] Lovejoy, "The 'Middle Passage': The Enforced Migration of Africans across the Atlantic," p. 55; Sylviane A. Diouf, *Dreams of Africa in Alabama: The Slave Ship Clotilda and the Story of the Last Africans Brought to America* (New York, 2007), p. 13.

[13] Allan D. Austin, *African Muslims in Antebellum America: Transatlantic Stories and Spiritual Struggles* (London, 1997), p. 22.

[14] Michael Gomez, *Exchanging Our Country Marks: The Transformation of African Identities in the Colonial and Antebellum South* (Chapel Hill, 1998), p. 60.

[15] Diouf, *Servants of Allah*, p. 48.

[16] Richard Brent Turner, *Jazz Religion, the Second Line, and Black New Orleans* (Bloomington, 2009).

religious identity of Islam through the presentation of a forcibly imposed public signification upon Christianity. African Muslim slaves in the United States sometimes successfully orchestrated campaigns to return to Africa, and arguably their plans for return could have been related to their self-identification with the Muslim ummah.

Diouf establishes the larger theme of transnational Islamic continuities between West Africa and American slave communities. Many West African Muslims enslaved in the United States had participated and were captives in religious-political wars in Bundu, Futa Jallon, Futa Toro, Kayor, central Sudan, the Gold Coast, and northern Dahomey. These men and women were often kidnapped from an elite group of educated and literate urbanites who were jurists, Qur'anic teachers, statesmen, merchants, and traveling scholars who lectured in Jenne and Timbuktu.[17] They were part of the West African ummah that took shape in eleventh-century Ghana and reached a high point in 1324, with the *hajj* (pilgrimage) to Mecca of Mansa Musa, the ruler of Mali who had diplomatic and cultural connections with Egypt, Tunisia, Algeria, and Morocco. Thus, transatlantic slavery brought cosmopolitan West African Muslims to the United States who had the intellectual skills to challenge the degrading racial significations of their times, to resist Christianization, and to practice Islam despite the brutality of slavery.

Austin's *African Muslims in Antebellum America: Transatlantic Stories and Spiritual Struggles* includes valuable information about seventy-five African Muslim slaves in America. The life stories of several of these Muslims stand out in the historical literature, because contemporary white Americans, though maintaining devastating racial and religious significations of Blacks, nonetheless noted their intellectual resistance, literacy in Arabic, and adherence to the religion of Islam.[18] Our discussion begins with the largest and most influential African Muslim communities in antebellum North America, located on the South Carolina and Georgia Sea Islands of St. Helena, St. Simons, and Sapelo. Here, Islam was part of a vibrant communal culture that was able to thrive in these isolated islands, known for their preservation of cultural and religious practices from West and Central Africa, because it escaped the attention of white authorities.[19]

Signification, the issue of identity and naming, sheds light on the resistance strategies that flourished among the Muslims in these

---

[17] Diouf, *Servants of Allah*, pp. 1, 35.

[18] Austin, *African Muslims in Antebellum America*, p. 5.

[19] Margaret Washington, *A Peculiar People: Slave Religion and Community-Culture among the Gullahs* (New York 1985).

contexts, where the retention of African names and literacy in Arabic presented a variety of threats to the social order of slavery. Gomez provides evidence from antebellum advertisements that "Muslim runaways" with names such as Moosa, Mustapha, Bocarrey, Bullaly, and Sambo and ethnic identities as Fula and Mandingo came primarily from the coastal areas of Georgia and South Carolina. He also discusses the cases of North African Muslim slaves from the Barbary Coast, such as Mahamut and Abel Conder, who submitted petitions in Arabic to the government of South Carolina in 1753 to challenge the legality of their enslavement. Moreover, in 1790 several former slaves from Morocco – Samuel, Hammond, Daniel, Sarah, Flora, and Fatima – "free Moors," who had bought their freedom in South Carolina, presented their petition to the state government to secure "the legal rights of whites."[20] According to John Hope Franklin and Loren Schweniger, newspaper notices about runaway slaves and petitions to courts and legislatures are some of the most accurate primary sources for understanding the familiarity of white people with the religious identities of their property and show that enslaved petitioners rose to the challenge of presenting themselves as Muslims to attain their freedom.[21]

Bilali and Salih Bilali were the West African leaders of the Muslim slave communities on Sapelo and St. Simons Islands. They led African and African American Muslims who were known for speaking an African language, for their devotion to Islam, and for their Muslim clothing and names. Bilali (d. 1859) was also called Bilali Mahomet, and Ben Ali was a Fulbe Muslim, born in Timbo, Futa Jallon, and initially enslaved in the Bahamas. Bilali, as the manager of Thomas Spaulding's plantation of five hundred slaves, exemplified the pattern of African Muslims as leaders in the occupational gradations of the slave community. He also signified Islam as superior to Christianity, when he referred to non-Muslim slaves as "Christian dogs."[22] This important aspect of Bilali's religious signification correlates with Osman and Forbes's analysis of other Muslim slaves – literate in Arabic and possessing a Qur'an, who also signified American Christians "as other."[23] Bilali wrote an Arabic manuscript on Sapelo Island that is difficult to translate and suggests the

[20] Gomez, *Black Crescent*, pp. 143, 146, 147, 149, 150.
[21] John Hope Franklin and Loren Schweniger, *Runaway Slaves: Rebels on the Plantation* (New York, 2000), p. 295.
[22] Austin, *African Muslims in Antebellum America*, pp. 89–92; Richard Brent Turner, "Islam and African Americans," in Dodson and Palmer, *Origins*, pp. 171–172.
[23] Ghada Osman and Camille F. Forbes, "Representing the West in the Arabic Language: The Slave Narrative of Omar Ibn Said," *Journal of Islamic Studies* 15:3 (2004): 331–343; 340.

deterioration of his language skills over time. His book, which is preserved in the University of Georgia Library, uses passages from Ibn Abi Zayd Al Qayrawani's *Risala*, a Maliki legal text popular in West and North Africa, to discuss Islamic law as a path to a healthy life. The manuscript discusses the call to prayer and ablutions.[24] Stories have survived that Bilali was buried with a prayer rug and Qur'an from Africa.[25]

Bilali's fame as a Muslim slave, in the public sphere in his lifetime and beyond, developed because of his literacy, his Arabic manuscript, and the signification of his race and religion in the context of the Sea Islands – "the most direct living repository of African culture to be found anywhere in North America,"[26] according to historian Joseph Holloway. Here, the Gullah Creole language flourished in the antebellum era, and Bilali's self-signification through "writing Arabic"[27] was perceived by nineteenth- and early twentieth-century scholars such as William Brown Hodgson, Lydia Parrish, Melville Herskovits, and Joseph Greenberg as additional evidence for the powerful African continuities on these islands.[28] Martin's translation of the "Bilali diary" shows that the Muslim slave wrote frequently: "O God, I bear witness that there is no God but God and Muhammad is the Messenger of God."[29] Thus, he preserved his Muslim identity in spite of his enslavement. Also, Bilali was involved in a transnational network of interactions with slaves in Charleston or the Bahamas who had access to materials from Africa; his manuscript was written on paper manufactured in Italy, exported to Tripoli, and then sent to Futa Jallon.[30]

Additional knowledge about Bilali and his antebellum Muslim community comes from the Savannah unit of the Georgia Writers' Project interviews with his descendants on Sapelo Island in the 1930s.[31] The interviewers were white Americans in the dangerous Jim Crow era, and their Black American subjects were probably reluctant to share any information that suggested their practice of Islam in the twentieth century (if it was going on). Shadrack Hall, his great-grandson, said that

---

[24] B. G. Martin, "Sapelo Island's Arabic Document: The 'Bilali Diary' in Context," *Georgia Historical Quarterly* 78:3 (Fall 1994): 589–601; 594.

[25] Austin, *African Muslims in Antebellum America*, p. 85.

[26] Joseph Holloway, ed., *Africanisms in American Culture*, 2nd ed. (Bloomington, 2005), p. 187.

[27] Austin, *African Muslims in Antebellum America*, backflap.

[28] Martin, "Sapelo Island's Arabic Document," pp. 593–594.

[29] Martin, "Sapelo Island's Arabic Document," p. 598.

[30] Martin, "Sapelo Island's Arabic Document," pp. 600–601.

[31] Savannah Unit of the Georgia Writers' Projects Administration, *Drums and Shadows: Survival Studies among the Georgia Coastal Negroes* (Savannah, 1986).

Bilali's wife, Phoebe, also came to St. Simons Island from the Bahamas and that the couple maintained Islamic traditions in their family for three generations. Bilali's daughters, Fatima, Medina, Margret, Chaalut, Beentoo, Hestah, and Yaruba, prayed daily at sunrise with prayer beads, while kneeling and bowing on a mat. Katie Brown, also a great-grand-child of Bilali, noted that her grandmother Margret wore the hijab during prayer and continued the West African custom of distributing *saraka* (rice cakes) to express the third pillar of Islam – almsgiving on Friday, the day of congregational prayer and sermon.

Finally, Cornelia Bailey remembered that her great-grandmother, Harriet Hall Grovner, practiced Islam on Sapelo Island and also became a member of the First African Baptist Church when it was founded in 1866. Gomez's interview with Cornelia Bailey in 1992 also indicates that, even before the establishment of the church, Sapelo Island Muslims were going to the "Tuesday, Thursday, and Sunday night" meetings in the Baptist prayer houses, and at the same time they were still practicing Islam in communal gatherings.[32] Analysis of these developments is very important because it provides valuable clues to understand how Islam began to decline in the islands and why it was surpassed by Christianity after the Civil War.

Little is known about African Muslim women enslaved in the ante-bellum era because the majority community signified them at the inter-section of America's most marginal identities, "as slaves, as women, as Africans, and as Muslims."[33] These significations rendered them almost invisible during slavery and beyond. There were also demographic struc-tures in slavery that hindered reports about Muslim women. Overall, West African male slaves outnumbered female slaves by more than 50 percent in the Black Atlantic world. In the eighteenth century, most Senegambian and Sudanese slaves in America were male. Thus, there were fewer Muslim women than Muslim men on U.S. plantations. In addition, among African-born slaves, including Muslims, there were high adult and infant death rates, and these factors often prevented the growth of African Muslim families. Some of the famous Muslim slaves either married non-Muslim women or did not marry at all. All of these demographic structures were barriers to the development of networks of West African Muslim women in antebellum America. The historical record does not provide evidence as to how they used Islam to navigate racist and sexist oppression, or how African Muslim women signified

[32] Gomez, *Black Crescent*, p. 160.
[33] Diouf, *Servants of Allah*, p. 66.

themselves through their religion to resist rape and the "mammy" and "jezebel" stereotypes that objectified them. How did their Muslim identities help these African women to negotiate marriages in which their husbands lived on neighboring plantations? How did they deal with the auction block, the sale of their children and husbands, and the destruction of their families by the white men and women who owned them? Finally, how did African Muslim women adapt to the female-slave networks that were dominated by non-Muslim women? These are several of the key questions about enslaved African Muslim women that the fragments of historical evidence do not answer. The lack of historical documentation may also be related to the fact that women enslaved in the Americas were not literate, a fate that they likely shared with most male slaves. Of the thousands of Muslim Africans who became slaves, only a small number left behind a written record attesting to their literacy and their knowledge of Arabic.

Salih Bilali was the overseer of the Couper family's St. Simons Island plantation from 1816 to 1846. He was born in 1765 into a significant Fulbe Mandingo clerical family and spoke the Fula language. He was kidnapped as a teenager, while traveling home from Jenne, the West African Muslim intellectual city. Like his counterpart Bilali, he, too was enslaved in the Bahamas around 1800.[34] However, his intellectual resistance strategies were not as rich as those of Bilali. His owner reported that Salih Bilali "reads Arabic, and has a Koran (which however, I have not seen) in that language but does not write it."[35] Although he was a devout Muslim, his owner signified him with a "Christian name," Tom, in the plantation documents. The plantation register provides evidence of additional Muslims – "six Fatimas, two Mahomets, and one Maryam." Valuable information about Salih Bilali's Islamic heritage comes from the WPA interview with his grandson, Ben Sullivan, in the 1930s. Ben Sullivan's father, Belali Sullivan, was enslaved as a butler on the Couper plantation until the end of the Civil War. He practiced Islam and also made saraka – to offer zakat on Fridays. Ben Sullivan also mentioned other practicing Muslims in the slave community, such as Daphne and Ole Israel, who used prayer mats, hijab, and a book during prayer. According to James Hamilton Couper, Salih Bilali's religious signification also included the fast, the fourth pillar of Islam. "A strict Mahometan: abstains from speritous liquors, and keeps the various fasts, particularly that of the

---

[34] Austin, *African Muslims in Antebellum America*, pp. 99, 106.
[35] William Brown Hodgson, *Notes on Northern Africa, the Sahara and the Soudan* (New York, 1844), p. 69.

Rhamadan,"[36] he wrote. The WPA also interviewed Alec Anderson and Rosa Grant on the Georgia Sea Islands in the 1930s, and they recalled nineteenth-century Muslims in their families who prayed daily, but especially every Friday.[37]

Ayuba Suleyman Diallo (1702–1773), another West African slave, was a member of an influential Fulbe Muslim family in Bundu. His enslavement occurred in 1731, on a trip to the Gambia River to sell slaves and to buy paper from a British ship. Instead, he was sold into slavery with another Muslim, Lamine Njai. In Maryland, he retained his Muslim beliefs and recited his prayers in Arabic in the woods. For some time, he was a runaway slave, but he was eventually recaptured. During Diallo's time in a Pennsylvania prison, he impressed white lawyers and ministers from Annapolis, Maryland, and an officer of the Royal African Company with a letter he wrote in Arabic to his family in West Africa and with his devotion to Islam. By March 1733, he sailed to London with his white American benefactors. In England, he wrote the Qur'an in Arabic, translated Arabic documents for the founder of the British Museum, and was freed by the Royal African Company and returned to Gambia as its assistant in trade in 1734. Although his American and British owners signified him as Simon and Job ben Solomon, Diallo's self-signification as a member of the West African Muslim elite, literate in Arabic and faithful to Islam, contributed to his eventual freedom. Also, his desperate effort to send a letter to his family in Bundu while he was incarcerated was another aspect of his intellectual resistance to enslavement that reflected his faith in the transnational power of African Muslim communities.

Yarrow Mamout, a Fulbe Muslim, former slave, and homeowner in Georgetown, Washington, D.C., may have been more than one hundred years old when Charles Willson Peale painted his portrait in 1819. The Historical Society of Pennsylvania owns this oil painting. The themes of religious signification in Yarrow Mamout's story come from Peale's diary and confirm that "he professes to be a Mahometan" and dresses in "Muslim style." Mamout was freed from slavery in 1807, continued to practice Islam, and is reported to have said, "It is no good to eat hog – and drink whiskey is very bad."[38]

The life story of Abd al-Rahman Ibrahima (1762–1829) is recounted in Terry Alford's book, *Prince among Slaves*. He was a Fulbe Muslim

[36] Hodgson, *Notes on Northern Africa*.
[37] Austin, *African Muslims in Antebellum America*, p. 110.
[38] Turner, *Islam in the African-American Experience*, pp. 26, 27.

prince, born in Futa Jallon to the prominent military leader Almami Ibrahima Sori, and he was educated in Jenne and Timbuktu. Ibrahima was captured by Mandinka merchants when he lost a military battle in West Africa in 1787 and was a slave on a plantation in Natchez, Mississippi, until 1828. He was a fugitive slave for a while. He married a Black Baptist woman but rejected Christianity, although his children were probably Christian. Ibrahima's freedom struggle began with a fateful encounter in Natchez with a white man whose life he had saved in Futa Jallon. Eventually he used his ability to write an Arabic letter to his family and a Qur'anic passage, which convinced the American consul in Morocco, a senator, the secretary of state, the president of the United States, and the king of Morocco that he was a citizen of Morocco who had been illegally enslaved. Ibrahima also convinced officials of the American Colonization Society that he would work on behalf of Christianity if they assisted his freedom from slavery and repatriation to Africa. When he was asked to write the Lord's Prayer in Arabic, he wrote the opening surah of the Qur'an. His Arabic manuscripts, which include his autobiography, are now housed at Yale University and the American Philosophical Society in Philadelphia. Before Abd al-Rahman Ibrahima and his wife departed for Liberia, they raised money to free some of their children, and the former prince traveled in the Northeast and met with important Black leaders. Abd al-Rahman Ibrahima continued to practice Islam when he arrived in Liberia in 1829, but he died later that year before he could reach Futa Jullon.

Signification and intellectual resistance are the major themes that elucidate Ibrahima's intriguing story. White Americans signified him both as an "unfortunate Moor" and as a "savage negro," depending on how individuals decided to interpret his fame in the context of the racial discourses of the antebellum era. The Muslim prince, of course, wanted to be free; so, to achieve his liberation, he signified himself both as a relative of the royal family of Morocco and as a "liminal" religious figure between Islam and Christianity.[39] In the final evaluation, Ibrahima was a Muslim who used the only form of intellectual resistance available to him in slavery, his literacy in Arabic, to signify and to manipulate powerful white Americans to return to Africa.

The Fulbe Muslim scholar, teacher, and trader Omar Ibn Said (1770–1864) from Futa Toro was brutally enslaved and beaten by his first owner in Fayetteville, North Carolina, in 1807. After a stint in prison for running away, he convinced James Owen, his second owner, that he had

---

[39] GhaneaBassiri, *A History of Islam in America*, pp. 20–29.

converted to Christianity and therefore was excused from hard labor until he died. He was baptized in the Presbyterian Church in 1821. For a long time, white Americans signified him as the docile, non-African Arabian "Prince Moro" with light skin color and straight hair, who loved white Americans and hated Africans. This signification supported racist stereotypes of slavery and Christian missionizing in the plantation South. His Arabic manuscripts (which are in libraries at Davidson College in North Carolina, Andover Newton Theological Seminary in Massachusetts, and North Carolina State Archives, Raleigh) include an autobiography, chapters from the Qur'an, the Lord's Prayer, and letters to a Muslim in Canton, China, and to the African Muslim slave Lamine Kaba. Omar Ibn Said's manuscripts support the possibility that he maintained dual religious identities as he secretly continued to practice Islam, while he read his Arabic Bible and his Qur'an and attended the Presbyterian Church in Fayetteville.[40] His 1831 narrative, *The Life of Omar Ibn Said Written by Himself* is the first Arabic writing in America and the only autobiography in Arabic written by a slave in the United States.[41]

Although Omar Ibn Said's life story shows that Christianity was imposed on him by slavery, Kambiz GhaneaBassiri suggests that in his case "Islam was evaluated and reconfigured to define common ground between both Christianity and Islam and other African religions in America."[42] Yet, Osman and Forbes's analysis of his slave narrative presents a very convincing possibility that he utilized intellectual resistance by constructing religious identities that allowed him to remain a Muslim and, at the same time, to engage with Christianity by signifying the religion in Arabic.[43] They conclude that "through the use of Arabic and Qur'anic references, Omar reveals an image of the 'West' and the 'Christian' not as that to which the African must aspire, but instead as an 'Other' in the realm of his enslaved Muslim African's world."[44]

Mahommah Gardo Baquaqua was born in Benin in 1830. He drank alcohol and was not serious about Islam. Enslaved in West Africa and Brazil, he escaped from a ship in New York City, was liberated through the help of Blacks in the New York Vigilance Society, and came to Boston in 1847. In Haiti, he struggled with alcohol and his mistrust of white missionaries, but he was baptized by William Judd, a white abolitionist and minister in the American Baptist Free Mission Society in 1849.

---

[40] Austin, *African Muslims in Antebellum America*, pp. 129–136.
[41] Osman and Forbes, "Representing the West in the Arabic Language," p. 331.
[42] GhaneaBassiri, *A History of Islam in America*, pp. 67, 93.
[43] Osman and Forbes, "Representing the West in the Arabic Language," p. 340.
[44] Osman and Forbes, "Representing the West in the Arabic Language," p. 343.

Baquaqua attended Central College – a school that was racially integrated and had Black professors in McGrawville, New York – for three years and then moved to Canada. His life story, *Biography of Mahommah G. Baquaqua*, was compiled by Samuel Moore and published in 1854. In 1857 he went to England and attempted to raise money for his repatriation to West Africa. Baquaqua's letters are available at the Amistad Research Center at Tulane University.[45]

His narrative, composed by a white abolitionist, exemplifies the mixed motives of African Muslim slaves and the white Americans who presented their stories in the nineteenth century. William Judd, Baquaqua's mentor in Haiti, signified him as a devout convert, with plans to recruit him as a missionary for Christianity in Africa, and Samuel Moore signified the African Muslim in the same light. Yet Baquaqua was never a devout Muslim or Christian. His first imposed conversion to Christianity occurred in Brazil as his owner "held a whip in his hand"[46] to force his slaves to participate in Catholic rituals. In Haiti, the United States, and Canada, he signified himself as a faithful Christian to use white Protestants and their abolitionist resources in order to survive in the realm of the ex-slave's hostile and racist world. In Baquaqua's final extant letters to his contacts in the Free Baptist Missionary Society in the 1850s, he struggled unsuccessfully to obtain resources from them to go back to West Africa as a missionary. Austin highlights a letter in 1853 in which Baquaqua expressed his disappointment with the racism and violence of Christians and wrote in Arabic, "Allah, Allah, most [or] ever."[47] Austin believes that these Arabic words indicate that the former slave may have reverted to Islam, although there is no conclusive evidence to support this possibility. In the final evaluation, his fame as an African Muslim ex-slave and convert to Christianity was trumped by institutional racism in America, and his conversion did not lead to his desired repatriation to Djougou in Benin.

Lamine Kebe, a West African teacher and scholar of the Qur'an from Futa Jallon was a slave on plantations in Georgia, South Carolina, and Alabama for almost forty years before he used his literacy in Arabic and an apparent conversion to Christianity to achieve his freedom from slavery and repatriation to Africa in 1835. Kebe was able to fascinate Theodore Dwight Jr. of Yale University with his descriptions of Muslim

---

[45] Austin, *African Muslims in Antebellum America*, pp. 158–171; Samuel Moore, comp., *Biography of Mahommah G. Baquaqua* (Detroit, 1854).

[46] Diouf, *Servant of Allah*, p. 53; Moore, *Biography of Mahommah G. Baquaqua*, p. 32.

[47] Austin, *African Muslims in Antebellum America*, pp. 168, 169.

education in West Africa (which Dwight published) and convinced him that he would distribute Arabic Bibles when he returned to Liberia. His manumission was related to the American Colonization Society's and a Philadelphia and New York company's plans to send ex-slaves to Liberia to Christianize the country. Kebe's owner and his white supporters in New York signified him as "Paul a professed believer in Christ." Yet the African Muslim slave told his life story and described himself as an intellectual, with many years of formal education in the West African Muslim world, and as an aristocrat who came from a family of distinguished clerics and teachers, including his aunt who was a well-known teacher. He described white Americans as people who "are very ignorant of Africa."[48] Kebe understood that it was necessary to establish his Christian credentials in order to return to his wife and family in West Africa, but Dwight doubted that his conversion was successful. Kebe's manumission was impacted by the interactions between missionary work for Christianity and the trade of American products in West Africa. White Americans had a vested interest in representing African Muslim slaves as malleable figures in their commerce.[49]

By the end of the Civil War in 1865, the Islam of African Muslim ex-slaves and their families was dormant in the American South for several reasons. Muslims of African descent on the South Carolina and Georgia Sea Islands had begun voluntarily to join Black Baptist churches by 1866, and this was also possibly the case for some of the Muslim former slaves in Africa Town in Mobile, Alabama.[50] Muslim converts to Christianity on Sapelo Island, such as Harriet Hall Grovner, might have also continued to practice Islam, and, according to some scholars, Islamic customs may have influenced Christian burial practices, the ring shout, and the blues.[51]

After slavery, white American hostility to African religions and the overwhelming Black preference for Protestantism prevented Muslims from establishing Islamic institutions and a missionary program for their religion, and their descendants did not practice Islam. Because the most important Muslim communities during slavery were located on isolated coastal islands, there was little opportunity for former slaves to spread Islam to new and larger constituencies in urban communities during Reconstruction. Moreover, the membership in Black churches might have offered ex-slaves who were Muslims a protective haven

[48] Austin, *African Muslims in Antebellum America*, pp. 115–125.
[49] GhaneaBassiri, *A History of Islam in America*, p. 33.
[50] Diouf, *Dreams of Africa in Alabama*, pp. 169, 170.
[51] Diouf, *Servants of Allah*, esp. chapter 6, pp. 179–210.

when the thousands of lynchings of the Jim Crow era began in the 1870s. Mohammed Ali Ben Said, a Muslim from Bornu and former slave in the Middle East and Europe, was a teacher in Michigan, South Carolina, Georgia, and Alabama and published his autobiography in 1873. Yet, he was a convert to Christianity.[52] We can only guess about the Muslim practices that endured in late nineteenth-century America, because those ex-slaves who knew did not tell, and scholars ignored these dynamics until the 1980s.

CONCLUSION: SCHOLARSHIP AND IDENTITY POLITICS

In the 1980s, African Muslim slaves became an important subject in the study of Muslim Americans. However, scholars unconsciously negotiated the artificial divide between African American and immigrant narratives in their research, and their discussions influenced Muslim American debates about identity politics and religious authenticity.

Austin's 1984 book *African Muslims in Antebellum America* led the way, by providing rich evidence in African American history, supporting Alex Haley's earlier explorations of the religious and cultural heritage of African slaves and their African American descendants in *Roots* (1976).[53] Haley traced the legacy of his own family and found evidence for the presence of Muslims among African slaves brought to America. For others, however, Islam's American history began only with Arab immigration in 1875. Scholarship on Muslims in America has tended to focus on immigrants from Muslim majority countries since the nineteenth century, and such scholarship has only recently been applied to research about the histories and legacies of African Muslim slaves. The politics of authenticity and signification are also at work in intra-Muslim debates about Muslim identity, Islamic practices, and American Muslim histories.

Historians of the African diaspora have negotiated the intertwined languages and narratives of West Africa, Islam, and the Americas, and their scholarship has advanced new identity claims for an African Muslim legacy in Black America. In her *Servants of Allah* (1998), Sylviane Diouf evaluated "Islamic survivals"[54] as central to the formation of African American culture after slavery. Michael Gomez in *Black Crescent* (2005), on the other hand, constructed an even bolder identity

---

[52] Precious Rasheeda Muhammad, *The Autobiography of Nicholas Said: A Native of Bornou, Eastern Soudan, Central Africa* (New York, 2000).
[53] Alex Haley, *Roots: The Saga of An American Family* (Garden City, N.J., 1976).
[54] Diouf, *Servants of Allah*, p. 184.

claim for a continuous Muslim presence from slavery into the twentieth century. He argued that African Muslim slaves could have been "founding mothers and fathers"[55] of African Americans: for example, African Americans with the surname Bailey may have been descendants of Bilali or Salih Bilali. What does all of this portend for the identity politics of recent Muslim American debates about religious authenticity?

One answer comes from a contemporary generation of African American Muslims, such as Precious Rasheeda Muhammad. She writes that the story of the Muslim ex-slave Nicholas Said resonates with the African heritage of her people and her personal identity claim as a descendant of slaves.[56] Finally, the divide between the preceding identity claims may have been bridged by the 2007 PBS film, *Prince among Slaves*. The project brought together artists, scholars, and the descendants of Abd al-Rahman Ibrahima (from the United States and Liberia) to present his powerful story about America's first Muslims, people of African descent whose lives were tragically intertwined with slavery and the larger struggles for racial justice, religious freedom, and democracy in the United States.

Further Reading

Austin, Allan D., *African Muslims in Antebellum America: Transatlantic Stories and Spiritual Struggles* (London, 1997).

Diouf, Sylviane A., *Servants of Allah: Africans Enslaved in the Americas* (New York, 1998).

GhaneaBassiri, Kambiz, *A History of Islam in America* (Cambridge, 2010).

Gomez, Michael A., *Black Crescent: The Experience and Legacy of African Muslims in the Americas* (New York, 2005).

Osman, Ghada, and Camille F. Forbes, "Representing the West in the Arabic Language: The Slave Narrative of Omar Ibn Said," *Journal of Islamic Studies* 15:3 (2004): 331–343.

Turner, Richard Brent, *Islam in the African-American Experience*, 2nd ed. (Bloomington, 2003).

---

[55] Gomez, *Black Crescent*, p. 143.
[56] Muhammad, *The Autobiography of Nicholas Said*, p. xx.

3 Laying the Groundwork for American Muslim Histories: 1865–1965

SALLY HOWELL

America's first mosque was built in 1893 on "Cairo Street" at the Columbian Exhibition in Chicago.[1] A close replica of the Mosque of Sultan Qayt Bey in Cairo, Egypt, the mosque was built to display Islam for American audiences. The Muslim workers and performers at the exhibition, including a trained imam, were encouraged to remain in their "native costumes" by the fair's organizers. But it was on their own initiative, and to the apparent delight of the public, that when the *adhan* (call to prayer) was made from the mosque's minaret five times a day, the visiting Muslims would duly gather inside and perform their obligations. At the exhibition's close, the mosque was torn down, and the staff and the performers at the "Cairo Street" exhibit, who had been imported to the United States as objects of spectacle, returned to their more prosaic lives in Egypt, Morocco, and Palestine, where the ritual of prayer would draw little comment.[2]

The second mosque to be built in the United States was completed in 1921, in Highland Park, Michigan. Built by Muslim migrants for use as a place of worship, this mosque, like the one on "Cairo Street," was intended to represent Islam to American observers, but the Muslims of Highland Park hoped to create a very different impression of their faith. The Islam to be practiced in the Moslem Mosque of Highland Park would not be exotic, foreign, or a thing of spectacle. It would be an American faith tradition not unlike those found in nearby churches and synagogues. It would attract worshipers who were American citizens.

---

[1] Of course this claim depends to some degree on how one defines mosque building. See Akel Ismail Kahera, Chapter 13 in this volume.

[2] Eric Davis, "Representations of the Middle East at American World Fairs, 1876–1904," in Abbas Amanat and Magnus Bernhardsson, eds., *The United States and the Middle East: Cultural Encounters* (New Haven, 2002), pp. 342–381; Adele Younis and Philip Kayal, *Coming of the Arabic Speaking People to the United States* (Staten Island, N.Y., 1995).

The history of Islam in the United States as it is practiced today begins effectively in the twenty-eight years that separated the construction of the Cairo Street and Highland Park mosques. The "Islam brought by the enslaved West Africans," Sylviane Diouf observes, "has not survived. It has left traces; it has contributed to the culture and history of the continents; but its conscious practice is no more. For Islam to endure, it had to grow ... through transmission to the children ... and through conversion of the unbelievers."[3] It was precisely these concerns – the transmission of Islam from one generation to the next, the conscious, everyday practice of the faith, and the conversion of non-Muslims to Islam – that motivated the construction of the Moslem Mosque of Highland Park and the mosques that followed. These priorities became especially urgent after 1924, when the U.S. Congress passed the National Origins Act, which restricted immigration from Asia and other Muslim-sending regions and thus stemmed the flow of new Muslim arrivals. They were also important among African Americans, who began to embrace Islam in the 1920s and 30s partially in response to the radical dislocations and racism they experienced prior to and during the Great Migration (the movement of disenfranchised southerners to industrial regions in the North). If they wanted Islam to survive, these new Muslims and new Americans would have to build viable communities and institutions, and between 1921 and 1965 scores of mosques were established across the United States in cities large and small. It was in these institutions that the process of creating distinctive Muslim American communities, identities, and practices, began in earnest.

NEW AMERICANS

When the performers at the Columbian Exhibition returned to their homes in the Levant, they told fanciful tales of "progress and opportunity" about their sojourn in North America. Their testimony added fuel to the emigration fervor that was already burning in many regions of the Ottoman Empire. By the first decades of the twentieth century, Muslim workers from Ottoman and former Ottoman domains began congregating in small mill towns, urban industrial centers, and on remote homesteads across North America, wherever work or trade could be found. South Asian Muslims also began to arrive in North America in this period. These Muslim populations were small and dispersed

---

[3] Sylviane Diouf, *Servants of Allah: African Muslims Enslaved in the Americas* (New York, 1998).

compared to the better-known European migrations of the same period, but unlike earlier populations of enslaved Muslims, they were free to practice their faith in the New World and to seek out communities of fellow believers. It is difficult to estimate the number of early Muslim migrants because U.S. immigration officials and the U.S. census do not collect data on religion. Furthermore, most of these migrants arrived from regions that were not exclusively Muslim. Syrian immigration, for example, was majority Christian; Indian immigration, majority Sikh and Hindu; and Turkish immigration, significantly Armenian Christian. Yet scholars have conservatively estimated that at least forty thousand Muslims had entered the United States by 1920.[4] These pioneers were a highly mobile group until the 1930s, moving from one city or work site to the next, seeking better pay, better working conditions, marriage partners, and the company of others who shared their native languages and religious traditions.

The earliest of these migrants, for the most part, did not envision settling permanently in the United States. They came to work, make money, and return home. This trend, coupled with legal restrictions on migration in both the United States and sending countries, produced sharp gender imbalances in most of these populations. The near absence of women and dependent children had significant consequences for the institutional development of the Muslim community. Populations made up primarily of young men were more likely to see themselves as sojourners, a self-image that facilitated their eventual return overseas and discouraged investment in mosque-building projects. Despite their status as temporary populations, by the early 1900s Muslim associations had begun to appear in cities like New York, Chicago, and Detroit, and in smaller communities in the Midwest and Great Plains states. These Muslim immigrants needed a place to perform communal prayers. They needed fellow Muslims to wash and pray over their dead in keeping with Islamic custom. And they longed for the company of their fellow countrymen, for conversation in their native languages, and for news of the families and friends they had left behind. These desires were as social as they were religious. They were also political. Many of the early Islamic associations doubled as nationalist organizations. Gradually, as Muslims gathered in the shadow of factories, in neighborhoods near railroad stations, and in the small towns that served as hubs along peddling routes, they began to build the infrastructure of a collective, Muslim American life.

---

[4] Kambiz GhaneaBassiri, *A History of Islam in America* (Cambridge, 2010), pp. 137–142.

Turkish and Kurdish Muslim enclaves were made up almost entirely of young peasant men who had left the Ottoman Empire circa 1900 to avoid conscription, political turmoil, and overall conditions of neglect in the countryside. Indians were a different matter. Excluded by the Barred Zone Act of 1917, and denied the right to naturalize in 1924, Indian Muslims arrived in the United States through undocumented channels. Bengali Muslims made up a large percentage of British maritime workers between 1900 and 1925, and many jumped ship or found other means of entering port cities like New York, Boston, and New Orleans.[5] Punjabi and other Indians entered the United States via similar routes or through Canada. Many made their way to the Imperial Valley in southern California to work in the newly irrigated agricultural districts that opened in the 1910s.[6] Lacking citizenship, Bengalis and other Indian Muslims were unable to sponsor the migration of spouses, or to travel back and forth between the United States and the subcontinent. The largest group of Muslim immigrants to arrive in this period was from the Ottoman Province of Greater Syria. In the 1890s, this group too was overwhelmingly male. Some reported not wanting to bring their families with them because they knew Islam was not practiced in the United States. By the 1910s, however, this community began to bring women and children to America.

The earliest social institutions to develop among the bachelor populations were the coffeehouse, the mutual aid society, and the national association or club. Coffeehouses were, in many ways, a surrogate for family life. In cities with diverse Muslim populations, they were organized loosely along linguistic and cultural lines, with Indians and Afghans meeting in one space, Turks and Kurds in another, Arabs in yet another. In locations with smaller populations, Turks, Armenians, Greeks, and Syrians would, sometimes reluctantly, share these institutions.[7] Coffeehouses gave men a place to relax and socialize when not working. They served "Turkish" coffee or tea and meals and provided patrons with a place to gather intelligence on work opportunities, learn of new arrivals and departures, observe religious holidays and communal prayer, and keep track of events taking place "back home." They were

[5] Vivek Bald, "Overlapping Diasporas, Multiracial Lives: South Asian Muslims in U.S. Communities of Color, 1880–1950," *Souls* 8:4 (2006): 3–18.

[6] Karen I. Leonard, *Making Ethnic Choices: California's Punjabi Mexican Americans* (Philadelphia, 1992).

[7] Isil Acehan, "Conflict and Cooperation: Diverse Ottoman Ethnic Groups in Peabody, Massachusetts," in Deniz Balgamis and Kemal Karpat, eds., *Turkish Immigration to the United States* (Madison, 2008), pp. 75–86.

also a lively context in which to organize ethnonational associations, religious mutual aid societies, and other clubs or societies. Communal organizations began to appear in 1906 and 1907 among Bosnian, Polish, Lithuanian, and Russian Muslims in Chicago and New York. Syrians, Turks, and men from the subcontinent followed in the 1910s and 1920s with Muslim associations opening in South Dakota, Pennsylvania, Indiana, Massachusetts, Ohio, and Michigan. Despite the great distances that separated these populations, they were frequently in contact, and often their efforts were coordinated. Sudanese immigrant and self-proclaimed "Sheikh of Islam in America" Satti Majid worked with communities in New York, Detroit, and Pittsburgh, establishing mutual aid societies and other Muslim associations.[8]

While coffeehouses were suitable for meetings and prayers in communities where few or no families were present, for the growing Syrian population, the male-centered world of the coffee shop presented a bar to the social and religious participation of women and children. Families often observed religious holidays, Friday prayers, mawlids, and other religious and social events at home. The better established Syrian families would host gatherings in their homes, enabling women to participate more directly in the affairs of the Muslim associations, hosting mawlids, Qur'an recitations, and other religious services. Basements were sometimes converted into classrooms for Arabic and Qur'anic instruction for neighborhood children. Like coffeehouses, the homes of American Muslims were important sites of religious and ethnic identity formation. But these private spaces could not accommodate large gatherings, nor were they welcoming to large parties of single men. As more families began to settle in towns and cities across North America, Syrian Muslims especially began to contemplate the construction of mosques in which they could teach Islam to their children.

At the close of World War I, Syrians set about building a mosque in Highland Park, Michigan, working together with local Turks, Kurds, Afghans, Albanians, and Indians. Their numbers had swelled when Henry Ford, hungry for men to keep his new assembly line in motion, began offering a five-dollar workday. The Moslem Mosque of Highland Park was established only a block away from the entrance to the Ford assembly plant. The opening-day celebration, held on Eid al-fitr, June 8, 1921, was led by imams Hussein Karoub, Kalil Bazzy, and Mufti Muhammad Sadiq. Karoub and Bazzy were Syrian immigrants, while Sadiq was an

[8] Rogia Rogaia Abusharaf, *Wanderings: Sudanese Migrants and Exiles in North America* (Ithaca, 2002).

Ahmadiyya missionary from Qadian, India. After breaking the fast
together, the three imams led a parade of "swarthy orientals, headed by a
band, and marching under the banners of America, Arabia, Syria, Mexico,
and Turkey."[9] Women were included in the procession, according to
the *Detroit Free Press*, in order "to show that they were Americans."[10]
Disputes over which imam should lead the institution, over how it
would be financed and supported, and over the controversial teachings
of Mufti Sadiq led to the closing and sale of the building in 1924, but a
second mosque was established in Detroit in 1925, followed by two in
Dearborn (one Shi'i and the other Sunni) in 1937 and 1938.[11]

Part of a national pattern of settlement and growth, Arabic-speaking
families opened mosques in Iowa, Indiana, North Dakota, Massachusetts,
Michigan, New York, Illinois, Ohio, and elsewhere by 1940. Many of
these mosques resembled the Highland Park mosque in their design, and
their congregations often maintained strong, crosscutting ties of marriage, kinship, and economic support. Detroit's Imam Hussein Karoub
visited many of these communities regularly and served as their spiritual
leader until they were able to attract imams of their own. The mosque in
Ross, North Dakota, was perhaps the most exceptional of these, having
sprung up on the prairie rather than in a city. In 1924 a congregation of
Grenadians, Arabs, and Indian seafarers also established a small mosque
on State Street in Brooklyn, and in 1931 East European Muslims bought
three buildings for use as mosques in New York City. Of these early
American mosques, only the one on State Street in Brooklyn was established by a primarily bachelor population, and even this mosque was
located near the city's Syrian community in the hopes that it would also
attract families.[12]

Although these institutions were scattered, Hussein Karoub, Kalil
Bazzy, Satti Majid, Mufti Sadiq, and the Ahmadiyya missionaries who
would follow Sadiq to the United States kept Muslims in touch with
one another. In the language of an earlier era, these early imams were
"circuit riders." They traveled from community to community, marrying the young and burying the dead, spreading the news of a mosque
opening here and a graveyard purchase there. They and the believers they
visited kept Islamic traditions alive in the United States by practicing

[9] "Moslems Celebrate Feast of Id-Ul-Fitr," *Detroit Free Press*, June 9, 1921.
[10] "Moslems Celebrate Feast of Id-Ul-Fitr."
[11] Sally Howell, "Inventing the American Mosque: Early Muslims and Their Institutions
in Detroit, 1910–1980" (Ph.D. diss., University of Michigan, 2009).
[12] Yvonne Haddad and Jane Smith, eds., *Muslim Communities in North America*
(Albany, 1994).

them, adapting them to local conditions, and passing them on to their American-born children.

NEW MUSLIMS

At the outbreak of World War II, Islam in the United States was practiced not only by immigrants and their children but by a growing number of Blacks and other converts who were working to practice and institutionalize Islam in their communities. The roots of this movement toward Islam by nonimmigrant Americans ran deep. They began with the importation of Muslim slaves in the colonial and antebellum eras, were augmented by the labor of several Muslim immigrants and missionaries to the United States, and firmly took hold when a confluence of early twentieth century spiritual and political leaders linked Islam to Black nationalism, Pan-Africanism, and the rejection of Christianity (as an ideological prop for slavery and other expressions of anti-Black racism). Nor is it a coincidence that Islam began to flourish among Black Americans at the same time (and often in the same neighborhoods) in which Muslim migrants were establishing themselves in the United States. The Columbian Exhibition of 1893 and the Moslem Mosque of Highland Park in 1921 are integral to this history as well.

One of the first documented white U.S. converts to Islam who took up proselytizing in the United States was Mohammed Alexander Russell Webb, who came to public attention in 1893 when he addressed the World's Parliament of Religions, which was convened alongside the Columbian Exhibition in Chicago. Like the exhibition itself, which displayed the world's cultures in a clearly delineated hierarchy of race, religion, and progress, the Parliament was intended to display world religions in a format that would allow (white, middle-class) Protestant Christianity to occupy a position of ultimate privilege.[13] Yet by allowing non-Christians to represent their own traditions, as they had in the Cairo Street Mosque, the event's organizers could not entirely control the outcome. Audiences were surprised, and many impressed, to hear non-Christians speak with such conviction about the traditions they represented. Webb, in particular, unsettled the audience by insisting that "there is not a Musselman on earth who does not believe that ultimately Islam will be the universal faith."[14]

---

[13] GhaneaBassiri, *A History of Islam in America*, p. 98.
[14] GhaneaBassiri, *A History of Islam in America*, p. 119.

Webb had recently organized the American Moslem Brotherhood in Brooklyn (1893) with a small group of followers and colleagues. This reading room and prayer space was created to capitalize on the Victorian spiritual restlessness and open-mindedness that had brought Webb and his colleagues to Islam.[15] A Theosophist preoccupied with the spiritualism and mysticism he found in Eastern religions, Webb eventually declared himself a Muslim while working as an American diplomat in the Philippines. While abroad, he met with many scholars and influential Muslim political leaders, including Said Ahmed Khan, an Indian Muslim reformer who was disturbed by Anglo-American efforts to convert Indians to Christianity, especially those who were acquiescent toward British colonialism. Khan and others agreed to underwrite Webb's mission to spread Islam and redress misconceptions about the faith in the United States.[16] Here then, at the first documented conversion of an American to Islam, three important intellectual threads were brought together: anticolonialism, an understanding of Islam as a universal religion, and a mystical-leaning orientalism.

In 1920 an important "foreign" missionary arrived in the United States with the explicit goal of introducing Americans to Islam: Mufti Muhammad Sadiq, who was also sent to the United States by an Indian reform movement tied to anticolonial campaigns there. Sadiq was an envoy of Mirza Ghulam Ahmad, the spiritual leader of the Ahmadiyya Movement of Islam based in Qadian, India. Mirza Ghulam Ahmad sent Sadiq to the United States, as he sent other missionaries to Europe, in response to the presence of Christian missionaries in India. Media reports of Sadiq's arrival and detention reached Detroit's Muslims, who were quick to invite this missionary and scholar to join their mosque-building campaign in Highland Park. Sadiq was an energetic agent of Islam in the United States, speaking at whatever public engagements he could arrange, writing frequently to local newspapers, and launching the *Moslem Sunrise*, the newsletter of the Ahmadiyya Movement in America. It was Sadiq who provided the English-language address on opening day at the Moslem Mosque of Highland Park:

> This is the first Moslem mosque built in this land and I am proud to have the first prayer in it, as the first imam therein. This mosque,

[15] Umar F. Abd-Allah, *A Muslim in Victorian America: The Life of Alexander Russell Webb* (New York, 2006).

[16] Mohammed Alexander Russell Webb, *Yankee Muslim: The Asian Travels of Mohammed Alexander Russell Webb*, ed. Brent D. Singleton (Rockville, 2007).

although built for the followers of Islam, will be open to the believers of all religions for a place of rest, prayer and meditation.

Mohammedans believe in worshipping but the one God. Mohammet, on whom be peace and the blessings of God, is a prophet of God who teaches us how to come into communion with Him. The religion of Islam treads underfoot all racial prejudices. Islam teaches its devotees that when they go to any other country they must peacefully obey the laws of the government of that country. Thus it is the sacred and religious duty of every Mohammedan here to be a good citizen of America and to learn the language of the country, without which we cannot understand each other rightly.[17]

Like Webb, Sadiq appealed to the universalism of the faith, yet Sadiq went a step further by describing Islam as an explicitly antiracist religion. In his writings, he was highly critical of Christianity on precisely these grounds. According to him, it had been used for the enslavement of Indians and Africans alike.

Sadiq's time in Detroit overlapped with that of another Muslim migrant-imam-missionary we have already mentioned, Satti Majid. Majid worked not only with Muslim immigrants but also with African Americans in New York, Pittsburgh, and Detroit. Sadiq too resided in areas where Muslim migrants and recently arrived Blacks from the Deep South lived in close proximity to one another and shared much in common. Each was adjusting to life and work in a rapidly industrializing, rapidly growing, and racially hierarchical urban environment. In this environment, Mufti Sadiq experienced success among Black Americans, who found his critique of American Christianity on racial grounds compelling and appreciated his insistence on self-discipline and respect. Yet Detroit's other Muslims considered Sadiq's Ahmaddiyya teachings to be heretical and withdrew his local sponsorship. Thus, in 1922 Sadiq moved to Chicago, where he opened a mission society and mosque of his own. Removed from the prevailing claims to orthodoxy of other Muslim leaders and institutions, he encountered rapid success, especially among Black migrants from the South.

African Americans who were drawn to Islam in the early twentieth century fell into many categories, but a synergy clearly existed between projects like those of the Ahmadiyya, with their antiracist, anticolonial message, and those of the newly emergent Black nationalist and Pan-African movements. For many, it was Marcus Garvey's *Negro World*, the newspaper the United Negro Improvement Association

[17] "Moslems Celebrate Feast of Id-Ul-Fitr."

(UNIA) established in New York in 1914, that first popularized the link between Pan-Africanism and Islam. By 1920 the UNIA had more than 100,000 members and 800 chapters worldwide. "Linking the entire Black world to Africa and its members to one another," Von Eschen writes, "Garvey made the American Negro conscious of his African origins and created for the first time a feeling of international solidarity between Africans and people of African descent."[18] Adopting the slogan, "One God, One Aim, One Destiny," and promoting the work of the Sudanese British Muslim activist, Duse Mohammed Ali, Garvey became an early advocate of Islam as an African religious tradition with the potential to link nonwhites in their opposition to European colonialism and racial oppression. Sadiq and Duse Ali were among those who hoped Garvey would eventually convert to Islam himself and lead the UNIA membership along with him.

Sadiq attended UNIA events, sometimes spoke at them, and had early success converting some of its members to Islam. He would train converts in the basic tenets of Islam, provide them with rudimentary Arabic skills, and then empower the adroit among them to proselytize and lead congregations of their own. In the 1920s, African American Ahmadiyya mosques sprang up in Cleveland, Pittsburgh, Cincinnati, Dayton, and smaller cities.[19] But in his brief time in the United States, and with a busy travel schedule and poor health, Sadiq was not able to instill a very deep knowledge of Islam in his followers. It was several years before an effective replacement could be found for him, and in these years many of Sadiq's converts sought religious training from immigrant Muslims. Wali Akram (born Walter Gregg) was perhaps the most influential of the early African American Ahmadiyya leaders. He organized and led the First Cleveland Mosque, beginning in 1927. His contact with the Arab and Turkish Muslim association in the city and his frustration over the financial obligations imposed by the Ahmadiyya Movement eventually led him to declare the group's independence in 1936 and to join the growing community of Sunni Muslims.[20]

Other African American leaders were quick to recognize the linkages between Islam and Pan-Africanism to build powerful movements of their own. Founded by Noble Drew Ali (born Timothy Drew), the Moorish Science Temple of America (MSTA) featured an array of

[18] Penny M. Von Eschen, *Race against Empire: Black Americans and Anticolonialism, 1937–1957* (Ithaca, 1997), p. 10.
[19] Robert Dannin, *Black Pilgrimage to Islam* (New York, 2002), pp. 87–116.
[20] Dannin, *Black Pilgrimage*, pp. 87–116.

teachings, which were appropriated from the symbols, texts, and traditions of both Islam and Freemasonry. Sections of the Qur'an, for example, were combined with mystical and other religious texts to form a new "Holy Koran." Drew Ali argued that Black Americans were not Negroes but Moors (from Morocco), and he encouraged them to think of themselves as "Asiatics," a term that linked their political status not simply to Africa, but to all of the world's nonwhite cultures. Like the UNIA, the MSTA promoted Black nationalism, but Noble Drew Ali went much further than Garvey by tying his movements explicitly to Islam and by proclaiming an Asiatic identity for Blacks. Both Garvey and Drew Ali encouraged their followers to wear the fez, turbans, and other garments associated with the "exotic" East. The MSTA was founded in Chicago, not far from Sadiq's Ahmadiyya mission, where Ahmadiyya converts also practiced sartorial Orientalism. Like Sadiq, Drew Ali also encouraged MSTA members to change their names from those provided by their "slave masters" to those which reflected their new identity as "Moors." In the 1920s MSTA chapters quickly spread to Detroit, New York, Philadelphia, Newark, and elsewhere.[21]

It was in Detroit, however, that the most influential of these movements, the Nation of Islam (NOI), was started in the early 1930s, only blocks away from the city's second mosque and the spiritual home of journalist, entrepreneur, stage actor, and staunch African nationalist Duse Ali during his sojourn in the city (1925–1927). Both of the movement's founders, Fard Muhammad (also known by several other names including Wallace D. Fard) and Elijah Muhammad (born Elijah Poole), had participated in UNIA chapters, and like the MSTA, the NOI appealed especially to newly arrived southern migrants and drew heavily on Islamic imagery and terminology in articulating a new Black nationalist ideology. It went much further, however, describing Fard Muhammad as God and Elijah Muhammad as his messenger, and constructing a human origins myth in which "white devils" had been engineered by an evil scientist intent upon interrupting the harmony of humankind (Blacks) and enslaving them. Like the MSTA, the NOI offered African Americans an alternative identity to that of the oppressed Negro. In so doing, it produced an effective model for self-help and "racial uplift," which accounts for much of the group's success. In its early days, however, which overlapped with the harshest years of the Great Depression, the NOI was beset by tremendous turmoil. One of its adherents committed a confused and much publicized act of human sacrifice, which drew

---

[21] Richard Brent Turner, *Islam in the African American Experience* (Bloomington, 2003).

the attention of law enforcement and the media. Troubling teachings in the group's new school, the University of Islam, also led to police intervention, and Fard was eventually expelled from the city and soon thereafter disappeared altogether. Despite this turbulence, the message of Fard Muhammad was a powerful one. The group included ten thousand dues-paying members across the country already in 1933. When Elijah Muhammad's leadership was challenged in Detroit, he too fled the city, moving the group's headquarters to Chicago, like Mufti Sadiq had a decade earlier. Muhammad too found it easier to operate in a city where other Muslims were less visible and had no mosques or imams to offer alternative readings of Islamic authenticity.[22]

From the perspective of migrant Muslims, their American-born children, and African American converts, the teachings of the MSTA and NOI were not recognizably Islamic and were exceedingly disturbing. Satti Majid, the Sudanese Muslim activist who had sought to educate Black Americans about Islam was so distraught by Noble Drew Ali's teachings that he confronted him directly. So too did many Blacks who had joined the Ahmadiyya movement or had become Sunni Muslims. Eventually, in 1929, Majid traveled to Al-Azhar University in Cairo on behalf of Muslim Americans to discuss the MSTA with scholars there, who quickly issued a *fatwa* (legal ruling) on the group's "errors."[23]

> This man of whom you asked [Noble Drew Ali] has established the clearest proof of his falseness, and the most shining demonstration that he is the greatest liar in the world and the man most [guilty of] perverting [the truth].... Cry out in the loudest voice that whoever gives credence to this liar in what he claims has repudiated the religion of God which He approved for His servants, and which he asked all folk of the earth to follow until God shall inherit the earth and those upon it, and has gone against what is known indisputably from the Mighty Quran, and deserves eternal and everlasting punishment in Hell.[24]

Majid, like other Muslim leaders in the United States, was also displeased with the Ahmadiyya Movement, which he described to the leaders in

---

[22] Turner, *Islam in the African American Experience*, pp.71–108.
[23] Ahmed Abu Shouk, J. O. Hunwick, and R. S. O'Fahey, "A Sudanese Missionary to the United States: Satti Majid, 'Shaykh al-Islam in North America,' and His Encounter with Noble Drew Ali, Prophet of the Moorish Science Temple Movement," *Sudanic Africa* 8 (1997): 137–191.
[24] "Fatwa from al-Azhar" translated in Abu Shouk, Hunwick, and O'Fahey, "A Sudanese Missionary to the United States," p. 170.

Cairo as heretical, emphasizing Qadiani reverence for Mirza Ghulam Ahmad as a living prophet of god. Neither their displeasure, their pleadings with the leaders of the MSTA (and later NOI), nor the fatwa Majid procured from Egypt succeeded at stemming the popularity of the MSTA or NOI teachings among African Americans.[25]

While MSTA and NOI teachings diverged significantly from those taught in American mosques of the 1930s and 1940s, these movements nonetheless continued to strengthen the links between Islam and the liberation, both spiritual and political, of African Americans first popularized by Garvey, Sadiq, Majid, and others. From his headquarters in Chicago, Elijah Muhammad developed a large, national organization with tens of thousands of members, an annual income in the millions, and an aptitude for promoting the economic independence of African Americans and their physical and spiritual health. Yet the number of Sunni Muslims in the Black community also grew significantly in the interwar period. Muhammad Ezaldeen, like Wali Akram, became an influential Muslim leader in this period. Ezaldeen had joined the MSTA in New Jersey in its early years and been an active supporter of Drew Ali. After traveling to Egypt in the late 1920s where he studied Islam for several years, he returned to the United States and became a powerful critic of the MSTA and NOI.[26] Men like Akram and Ezaldeen struggled to organize African American Muslims into national movements in the 1930s and 1940s, advocating for the same sense of racial uplift and economic security the other movements offered, while also adhering to Sunni Islamic practices and promoting the spread of this tradition among Americans. Akram initiated a Muslim Ten Year Plan in 1935, a social contract between believers that sought to ensure their spiritual and economic well-being during the Depression. Ezaldeen established the Adenu Islamic United Arabic Association in Buffalo, New York, in 1930, and an agricultural retreat, Jabul Arabiyya, in 1938 where the principles of shari'ah were to be applied to everyday life.[27] Similarly, a Caribbean migrant named Daoud Ahmed Faisal reopened the State Street mosque in Brooklyn as the Islamic Mission to America in 1939. This mosque provided *da'wah* (outreach) to African Americans while also serving as a spiritual home to the nearby Arabic-speaking population. It was one of several mosques and informal meeting spaces organized before the outbreak of World War II that brought together Black and other American Muslims.

---

[25] Abusharaf, *Wanderings*, pp. 27–31.
[26] Dannin, *Black Pilgrimage*, pp. 31, 46.
[27] Dannin, *Black Pilgrimage*, pp. 31, 46.

SYNTHESIS, EXPANSION, AND THE COLD WAR

In the aftermath of World War II, a new generation of Muslim scholars, formally trained in Islamic sciences and often possessing secular university degrees as well, was called to serve American congregations. Advocates of nationalism, economic development, and other modernist ideologies taking hold in their newly liberated homelands, these men were eager to revitalize the Muslim community for political and religious reasons. They were joined by a small cohort of new arrivals to the United States who migrated not as workers but as students attending American universities. These postwar arrivals, many of whom were from elite backgrounds, were frequently disturbed by the religious education they noted among the working-class and highly assimilated white ethnic Muslims they found scattered around the country. They were equally aggrieved by the separatist tendencies and, to them, the highly unorthodox, teachings of groups like the Nation of Islam. American mosques struck them as institutions that dedicated too much attention to social and political concerns and not enough to religious matters. They feared that the adaptations these mosques had made to their American context, such as hosting services on Sunday rather than, or in addition to, Friday or by sponsoring sock hops for the youth, meant that they had lost touch with the core values and tenets of Islam. The activists among these newcomers dedicated themselves to reforming the ethnoreligious institutions and identities American Muslims had created. They sought to align American Muslim practices with more critical and modernist interpretations of Islam that emphasized the example and sayings of the Prophet Muhammad. They found willing allies in this postwar revival among many young American Muslims, Black and white. Together these reformers built new mosques in communities across North America. They worked to link small, dispersed Muslim settlements to one another and to the larger Muslim world through two national organizations created in this period: the Federation of Islamic Associations of the United States and Canada (FIA) and the Muslim Students Association (MSA).

Abdullah Igram, of Cedar Rapids, Iowa, is credited with having founded the FIA. While serving in the Philippines during World War II, Igram had noted that Muslims who died in combat were not granted burial according to Islamic rites. Their religion was not recognized by the U.S. Armed Forces in a manner similar to Christianity and Judaism. After the war, he wrote President Truman to request that federal policies be amended to include Muslims. Denied accommodation, he called a meeting of midwestern Muslims to discuss the situation. Older attendees at this meeting had a very different concern. They were worried about how to identify potential Muslim spouses for their children and grand-children. Increasingly, young men and women were marrying outside the faith. They were also concerned by President Truman's support for the creation of Israel in 1948 and the ensuing Palestinian refugee cri-sis. Together, they convened a national meeting in 1952, to which they invited every Muslim organization they could identify. More than four hundred people, representing more than twenty congregations, attended. The Federation of Islamic Associations of North America and Canada was officially launched at this meeting, and the group was an immediate success, especially among those of Syrian, Lebanese, and Palestinian ori-gin. The FIA began hosting annual conventions that moved from city to city, attracting ever larger audiences. The group played a crucial role in reinforcing Muslim American identity, organizing communities at local and national levels, and bringing North American Muslims into more direct contact with Muslim institutions overseas. The FIA supported the development of new mosques across the country, and it encour-aged Muslim communities to help one another financially. It produced Sunday school materials and other educational tools for which dispersed Muslim congregations were hungry. The FIA published two periodicals, the *Moslem Life* (est. 1958) and the *Muslim Star* (est. 1960); one was a more scholarly quarterly that emphasized the basics of Islamic his-tory, beliefs, and practices, whereas the other was a newsletter for the association that covered announcements about mosque openings across the country, plans for *hajj* (pilgrimage) travel, the activities of FIA chap-ters and youth organizations, and news of the annual convention and its ancillary events. In 1958 the FIA was officially recognized by the Muslim World League and granted the opportunity to arrange the participation of American Muslims in the annual hajj in Saudi Arabia.

As this list suggests, the FIA gave Muslims in the United States a sense of forward momentum that was critical to the survival and growth of many mosques in the 1950s and 1960s. Their early successes encour-aged the FIA's primarily Arab organizers to reach out to member orga-nizations of Albanian, Pakistani, Iranian, African American, and other backgrounds, especially in cities like New York, Chicago, and Detroit, which had large, ethnically mixed Muslim populations. During this period the FIA began to facilitate the lecture tours of international Muslim activists, diplomats, politicians, and leaders who courted the support of American Muslims. These networks of patronage and poli-tics worked both ways. In 1959 the FIA was invited by Egyptian presi-dent Gamal Abdel Nasser to hold its convention in Cairo, Egypt. Abdel

Nasser also sent four Al-Azhar-trained imams to the United States and offered American students scholarships to Egyptian universities in order to meet the growing demand for Muslim preachers.

As the Cold War heated up in the 1950s, the Middle East, the Indian subcontinent, Africa, and Eastern Europe became frontlines of the conflict in both military and ideological terms. These regions were all points of origin and identification for American Muslims. The communist takeover of Albania in 1947 was of grave concern among Albanian Americans, many of whom had fled the new government. The Palestinian struggle for independence and self-determination was embraced by American Muslims of all backgrounds. Pakistan's independence and struggles with India were carefully observed in Michigan, Illinois, and California, as were events and movements throughout Africa. Muslim Americans frequently opposed American policies in their homelands and were increasingly outspoken on these matters in the 1950s and 1960s, which significantly increased their visibility to others. Similarly, as the civil rights movement gained momentum in the 1950s, African Americans were quick to link their struggle for rights in the United States to the struggles of nonwhites in the developing world for similar equality and justice. It was in this period that Malcolm X joined the Nation of Islam and became its official spokesperson. Serving congregations in Detroit, Boston, Philadelphia, and Harlem, Malcolm X revitalized and greatly expanded membership in the NOI with a strident critique of anti-Black racism in the United States and an equally harsh assessment of American global power. His notoriety increased the visibility of the NOI and by extension other American Muslims.

The 1950s and 1960s were also years of growth and prosperity at the local level for American Muslims, many of whom were now American-born and educated and lived solidly in the white middle classes. In some cities this new prosperity led to the opening of mosques for the first time. For others, it meant leaving behind immigrant ghettos and tired, converted mosque spaces to build grand mosques on main thoroughfares that could better represent the accomplishments, needs, and expectations of their congregations. Abdo Elkholy, a sociologist who conducted research in Toledo and Detroit in the 1950s, noted that mosques were emancipatory and affirming spaces for women, and he argued that without the participation of women, it was unlikely that the mosques he studied would have existed at all.[28] This pattern of increased

---

[28] Elkholy, *The Arab Moslems in the United States: Religion and Assimilation* (New Haven, 1966), p. 119.

influence for women in immigrant congregations (Christian, Muslim, and Jewish) was common in the United States at midcentury, often because these institutions were responsible for the social reproduction of entire ethnic communities and not just their religious beliefs. Women often ran the Sunday schools at mosques, organized community fund-raisers, saw to the administrative needs of imams and institutions, led youth programs, organized holiday celebrations, became spokespersons for Islam at interfaith events, and managed purchasing decisions. But the leadership and visibility of women in mosques also led to conflicts with the new imams and midcentury migrants, who were likely to judge mosques not by the standards then widely accepted in the United States but by the standards of their homelands where women's participation in mosques tended to be minimal. For the most part, these newcomers accommodated themselves to Muslim American norms and gradually became their champions.

Midcentury newcomers were also responsive to the revival of Islam among American Blacks. In particular, the Tablighi Jama'at, a South Asian missionary movement, began sending members to the United States on lengthy da'wah missions from Pakistan in 1952. Their missionaries frequently stayed in African American mosques and led study groups while they were in the country, greatly enhancing the educational offerings of these institutions and facilitating relations between American Muslims and foreign students studying at nearby universities. The State Street mosque in Brooklyn, for example, hosted Hafis Mahbub, a Tablighi missionary, for several years. He worked with Daoud Faisal at the mosque, teaching Arabic and exhorting his students to live Islam in all aspects of their lives. After three years of effort, his students felt strong enough to break off from this mosque and established the Yasin Mosque in nearby Brownsville, a more doctrinaire mosque where members sought to live according to the shari'ah. From this mosque, the Darul Islam (abode of Islam) movement was initiated, a da'wah project modeled on the work of the Tablighi missionaries within the United States.[29] In Detroit, Tablighi missionaries set up residence at Masjid al Mu'mineen, a small, Black congregation established in the late 1940s. There they provided Arabic and Qur'an classes for children and adults, led daily prayers, and transformed the institution into a welcome home away from home for foreign university students. These encounters were not without tension. Many members of the Mu'mineen congregation found the newcomers condescending, judgmental, and exceedingly conservative, but they also

---

[29] Dannin, *Black Pilgrimage*, pp. 65–67.

appreciated the depth of their scholarship and enjoyed being pulled into the life of the larger Muslim American community in the city.[30]

In 1963 a second national Muslim organization, the Muslim Students Association, was established by foreign students on the campus of the University of Illinois at Urbana. The group focused on providing religious support and a religious forum for Muslim students at a time when there were few mosques in the United States and campuses provided little accommodation to religious minorities of any stripe. The organization's leaders were explicitly political and identified with the Muslim Brotherhood in Egypt (a group that opposed Abdel Nasser's leadership and was violently suppressed by his regime), the Tablighi Jama'at (which received similar, if less harsh, treatment in Pakistan), and the Muslim World League (a Saudi-led and financed group that sought to consolidate and lead the Islamic reform movements of the period). They were adamantly opposed to socialism, communism, and much of American foreign policy. Like the FIA, the MSA included Muslims from diverse cultural backgrounds but was majority Arab.

This new intersection of Muslim politics and identities was reflected in the life of Malcolm X, who, as he rose to prominence in the NOI and gained a national reputation in the late 1950s, also drew the attention of Muslim and Muslim American activists. In the early 1960s, repeated efforts were made by Muslims to introduce Malcolm and his wife, Betty Shabazz, to Sunni Islam. Some of these efforts grew out of happenstance encounters he had with Muslim butchers or cab drivers in New York. Others were more concerted attempts at dialogue initiated by scholars and members of the Muslim World League. Finally, when Malcolm was expelled from the NOI because of a conflict with Elijah Muhammad, he was encouraged to make the annual hajj to Mecca. While on the pilgrimage he was treated as a special guest by the Saudi government, which was eager to facilitate his embrace of Sunni Islam. Struck by the sight of Muslims from all over the world worshiping together without rancor, Malcolm was challenged to rethink the separatist and explicitly antiwhite teachings of the NOI. While he did not abandon his activist support for Black nationalism, Malcolm X formally left the Nation of Islam in 1964.[31] He established a mosque of his own, the Muslim Mosque, Inc., a short time before his assassination. *Newly American* Muslims and *newly Muslim* Americans, who had worked together in the 1920s, began to do so again in the 1960s, joined now by

---

[30] Howell, "Inventing the American Mosque," pp. 250–263.
[31] GhaneaBassiri, *A History of Islam in America*, p. 245.

a generation of American- and Muslim-born children. The religious and political journey Malcolm X made in his final years was produced by this convergence of interests.

CONCLUSION

Between the 1920s and 1960s, Muslims in North America's small towns and in major cities set about creating an infrastructure for the practice and reproduction of Islam in a non-Muslim society. Some of this work was practical. It focused on identifying religious leaders and determining their role; on learning English or Arabic; on establishing mosques and determining their purpose and functions in their new American home; and on accommodating women and children in mosques and other Muslim spaces. This work was also political. It required Muslims to work together across racial, ethnic, national, and sectarian divides; to understand and frequently support one another's anticolonial aspirations; to represent their faith to an American population that was largely ignorant of Islam and frequently hostile; and to act together on a broad range of religious, social, and political issues.

In the early twentieth century, Muslims were new to each of these community- and identity-building activities (as are many new Muslim Americans today). More importantly, these new American Muslims also lacked models. Gradually, however, as their efforts succeeded and began to accumulate, their networks solidified and grew. They developed national institutions, beginning in the 1940s, that would eventually represent their interests on a larger, international stage. These early American Muslim institutions welcomed (and in many cases confronted) the new immigrants and new converts to Islam who joined the Muslim American community after U.S. immigration laws were liberalized in 1965. In an era of significant change – the civil rights and Black power movements, second-wave feminism, the Vietnam War, the rise of the Non-Aligned Movement, and anticolonial struggles in Arab and Muslim nations – newly arriving Muslims brought with them political and religious sensibilities frequently at odds with those of established Muslim Americans. They did not necessarily understand the long history of efforts and adaptations that had shaped the Muslim American institutions and identities they encountered. Yet the precedents set by the early Muslim Americans were there to be followed, improved upon, or indignantly rejected. Today American Muslims face related dilemmas of community building and cultural change, and the same cycles of adaptation and restoration are unfolding in mosques and Muslim communities across North America.

The great accomplishment of the early Muslim Americans was their creation of the institutions and communal spaces out of which new forms of Muslim identity can now emerge as faith traditions that are viably American and vitally connected to larger Muslim worlds.

Further Reading

Curtis, Edward E., *Muslims in America: A Short History* (New York, 2009).
Dannin, Robert, *Black Pilgrimage to Islam* (New York, 2002).
GhaneaBassiri, Kambiz, *A History of Islam in America* (Cambridge, 2010).
Gomez, Michael A., *Black Crescent: The Experience and Legacy of African Muslims in the Americas* (Cambridge, 2005).
Haddad, Yvonne Yazbeck, and Jane Idleman Smith, *Muslim Communities in North America* (Albany, 1994).
Howell, Sally, "*Inventing the American Mosque*: Early Muslims and Their Institutions in Detroit, 1910–1980" (Ph.D. diss., University of Michigan, 2009).
Jackson, Sherman A., *Islam and the Blackamerican: Looking toward the Third Resurrection* (New York, 2005).
Leonard, Karen, *Muslims in the United States: The State of Research* (New York, 2003).
Turner, Richard Brent, *Islam in the African-American Experience* (Bloomington, 2003).

4 American Muslims in the Contemporary World: 1965 to the Present

ZAIN ABDULLAH

AMERICAN MUSLIMS AND THE 1965 IMMIGRATION ACT

One Sunday afternoon in October 1965, hundreds took the boat to Liberty Island in New York Harbor. As the Statue of Liberty loomed in the background, President Lyndon Johnson addressed members of Congress, Vice President Hubert Humphrey, Ambassador Arthur Goldberg, governors, mayors, and a host of other guests. Still, no one expected anything momentous – including the president himself. "This bill we sign today," Johnson declared, "is not a revolutionary bill. It does not affect the lives of millions. It will not restructure the shape of our daily lives."[1] Yet in the ensuing years, the impact of the 1965 Immigration Act not only altered the country's demographics but also forever changed the religious fabric of American life.[2] This innovative piece of legislation was a crucial part of Johnson's sweeping civil rights reforms. So why did he try to minimize its effect? Perhaps because the bill was intended to extend America's influence in Cuba and parts of Europe, mostly beyond the three northern European countries from which 75 percent of immigrants entered the United States. While the expectation was that southern and eastern Europeans would migrate to America for jobs and family reunification, the greatest numbers of immigrants actually came from Latin America and Asia, which included a sizable population from countries such as India, Pakistan, and Bangladesh.

After their arrival in 1965, the treatment of Muslim Americans was shaped largely by a series of geopolitical encounters between the

[1] For a full copy of President Lyndon B. Johnson's speech, see online archives at http://www.lbjlib.utexas.edu/johnson/archives.hom/speeches.hom/651003.asp or *Public Papers of the Presidents of the United States: Lyndon B. Johnson, 1965* (Washington, D.C.: Government Printing Office, 1966), 2:1037–1040, entry 546.

[2] The 1965 Immigration and Naturalization Act is officially referred to as the Hart-Celler Act, since it was proposed by U.S. representative Emanuel Celler of New York and co-sponsored by U.S. senator of Michigan Philip Hart.

United States and various Muslim nations. In 1967 the Six Day War, a significant event in the ongoing Arab-Israeli conflict, brought negative portrayals of Arabs into the American media and fed into the worst stereotypes about Islam.[3] Media reports regularly associated Arabs with Muslims even though a significant percentage (some estimate the majority) of Arabs living in America were Christians. Arab Americans, particularly college students, who felt rejected in their efforts to integrate into the American mainstream reacted by emphasizing their ethnic heritage rather than their U.S. citizenship.[4] The 1970s oil embargo against the United States further exacerbated harsh views of Muslims and the Middle East. Long gas lines angered Americans, and Muslims in the United States felt the brunt of their rage. Major news outlets sketched caricatures of Arabs as rich oil "sheiks" bent on world domination. At the turn of the decade, the Iranian Revolution and the U.S. hostage crisis deeply upset the American public. The revolution, however, also inspired Muslim Americans across national, ethnic, and sectarian lines. They viewed the Shah's overthrow as a sign of hope for better foreign relations and democratic rule in the Middle East. The Iraqi occupation of Kuwait and in its wake the (First) Gulf War in the early 1990s were perceived as yet another act of aggression in the name of Islam, even though Saddam Hussein's socialist Ba'th Party never proposed an Islamic agenda and his regime had been supported by the United States in the Iran-Iraq War of the 1980s.[5] These conflicts (and U.S. military intervention in Kuwait) continued to generate negative portrayals of Muslims in the media and adversely influenced public opinion about Islam. Such portrayals included the representation of Muslims as militant, warmongering, and violent.[6]

This series of events, including their damaging impact on the attitudes of the American public towards Islam and Muslims, must be taken into consideration when assessing the public and media responses to the terrorist attacks of September 11, 2001. While hate crimes against American Muslims rose drastically after 9/11, the aftermath also produced many passionate pleas from outsiders for greater understanding and reconciliation. Muslims were forced to confront their complex attachments to and simultaneous alienation from the United States. Coexistence under

---

[3]   Sarah Gualtieri, *Between Arab and White: Race and Ethnicity in the Early Syrian American Diaspora* (Berkeley, 2009), p. 180.
[4]   Kambiz GhaneaBassiri, *A History of Islam in America* (Cambridge, 2010), p. 303.
[5]   The Persian Gulf War resulted in the deployment of a coalition force led by the U.S. code-named Operation Desert Storm in 1991.
[6]   See Nabil Echchaibi, Chapter 7 in this volume.

these conditions was no simple matter, and their successful integration into the U.S. mainstream has, in many respects, depended on their ability to negotiate multiple identities as Muslim immigrants, native-born converts, and American Muslims with foreign-born parents. But the persistence of a Muslim presence in the United States has also depended on other factors, such as the construction and maintenance of viable Muslim families. Before 1965, for example, Muslim immigrants tended to be young, uneducated or unskilled, and mostly male.[7] The period after 1965, however, granted greater access to a wider range of Muslim professionals, who brought their families to the United States or came to join relatives. Muslim women, more often than not, came as spouses and dependents, rather than on their own. This was especially true for Muslim families adhering to Islamic dictates regarding travel, particularly in the form of religious laws prohibiting women from traveling far unless accompanied by a *mahram* (adult male relative). This prohibition restricted the independent migration of Muslim women in larger numbers. Once Muslim couples wed (or previously married couples reunited) and had children, the decision to return to their countries would become much more difficult. This pattern of migration and identity formation in first and second generations is, of course, not limited to Muslim immigrants but rather a common pattern for migrants of at least the preceding century. "If you want to know whether you're going back home or not," Sulayman Nyang said about Muslim migrants, "just listen to the accent of your kids, and you'll know you're not going anywhere."[8] Even American-born Muslims would have had to rethink their integration into American society following their conversions, particularly if their spouses were not Muslim or if they became newly married and desired to raise Muslim children.

While the Census Bureau does not record religious affiliation, reports indicate that migrants entering the United States from Muslim-majority countries increased from just over 130,000 in 1960 to more than 800,000 in the 1990s.[9] Some estimate that the period between 1966 and 1997 witnessed the entry of nearly 3 million immigrants from countries with sizable Muslim populations.[10] As President Johnson spoke under the shadow of the statue he ennobled as "this grand old lady," he envisioned a new destiny for America. "And this measure that we will sign

---

[7] See Sally Howell, Chapter 3 in this volume.

[8] See the documentary film, *Dollars and Dreams: West Africans in New York*, directed by Jeremy Rocklin, color, 56 mins. (Watertown, Mass., 2007), cued at 48:23.

[9] GhaneaBassiri, *A History of Islam in America*, p. 293.

[10] Edward E. Curtis IV, *Muslims in America: A Short History* (New York, 2009), p. 73.

today," he announced, "will really make us truer to ourselves both as a country and as a people. It will strengthen us in a hundred unseen ways."[11] With over eighty different Muslim nationalities represented in the United States, Johnson's prediction about the one hundred ways the immigration bill would alter the country has virtually come true. Besides, not only did one report in early 2012 estimate the existence of more than twenty-one hundred mosques and Islamic centers throughout America,[12] scores of Buddhist and Hindu temples, Sikh gurdwaras, and African-inspired praise houses could likewise be found in cities and towns across the nation. What is most notable about Muslim immigration after 1965, however, is not the fact that it has added its own sacred pattern to America's religious mosaic. Rather, the dizzying array of Muslim identities and religious interpretations have also undergone their own peculiar transformations on U.S. soil, as each Muslim group is forced to grapple with the intricacies of America's social, economic, and political realities and struggles to navigate its status as a religious minority in a secular country.

AMERICANIZING ISLAM: THE 1970S AND BEYOND

Beginning in the 1970s, the civil rights era brought about a religious awakening and a new political awareness. It was a period Tom Wolfe, an American cultural critic of the time, dubbed the "'Me' Decade," alluding to a public shift away from the group marches of the 1960s and a move toward personal philosophies and self-help remedies.[13] This social shift affected both Muslim immigrants and converts. As social and political conditions declined overseas, Muslim immigrants were not so eager to return. Upheavals across the Middle East, Asia, and Africa forced many to reconsider their relationship with their adopted country. At the same time, African American and Latino Muslims looked for ways to reform their urban neighborhoods. Many started programs of community service and outreach. During this period, both long-standing Muslim immigrants and native-born converts sought Islamic solutions to redress what they believed were the ills of American culture, like rampant drug abuse,

---

[11] See reference for President Johnson's speech in note 1.
[12] See Ihsan Bagby, "The American Mosque, 2011," sponsored by Hartford Seminary and posted on the Web site of the Council on American Islamic Relations (CAIR) in January 2012, http://www.cair.com/Portals/o/pdf/The-American-Mosque-2011-web.pdf. Interestingly, the study did not include mosques associated with the Nation of Islam under the leadership of Louis Farrakhan.
[13] Tom Wolfe, "The 'Me' Decade and the Third Great Awakening," *New York Magazine*, August 23, 1976.

indiscriminate sex, and crass materialism. In many ways, the 1970s marked yet another step in the negotiation of Islam as an American religion. It was certainly a period when some form of the term "American" began to appear more frequently in the names of Muslim organizations.

Before the 1970s, many African American Muslim communities isolated themselves, attempting to protect their members from the adverse effects of racial discrimination. And although Muslim immigrants founded organizations with an American label of some sort in the early 1950s and 1960s, their primary focus was not integration or widespread assimilation. Rather, because of their prevailing intent to return to their respective countries after completing their education or acquiring enough wealth, they worked to establish facilities and services for cultivating and maintaining Islamic practices and Muslim identities.[14] After 1970, however, changes in the social and political climate in the United States and worsening conditions abroad forced both Muslim immigrants and native-born converts to deepen their concern for their own neighborhoods and the society at large. In 1971, for example, Black Sunni Muslims founded the Islamic Party of North America (IPNA), which became a multiaffiliate organization. Although the IPNA initially preached a separatist philosophy, the name of the organization speaks to its national or continental focus. And by 1975, it was heavily involved in civic engagement such as interfaith forums and community activism.[15] In Philadelphia, white middle-class Americans in search of spiritual fulfillment helped to found the Bawa Muhaiyaddeen Fellowship of North America in 1971. Leading them was a Sri Lankan–born Sufi named Bawa Muhaiyaddeen. His teachings appealed to many Americans in search of religious inspiration, spiritual practice, and an alternative to a world they perceived as mundane and materialistic.[16] Even the Nation of Islam (NOI) relinquished its religious and racial separatism, moving toward Sunni Islam and American integration after 1975. It was eventually renamed the American Muslim Society.[17] In 1975 Puerto Rican

[14] The original Muslim Students Association (MSA) of the United States and Canada, founded in 1963, was plagued by factional struggles and divisions along both Sunni-Shi'a lines and ethnic divides. See GhaneaBassiri, *A History of Islam in America*, pp. 265, 269; also see Liyakatali Takim, "A Minority with Diversity: The Shi'i Community in America," *Journal of Islamic Law and Culture* 10:3 (2008): 333–334.

[15] Khalid Fattah Griggs, "Islamic Party of North America: A Quiet Storm of Political Activism," in Yvonne Yazbeck Haddad and Jane I. Smith, eds., *Muslim Minorities in the West: Visible and Invisible* (Walnut Creek, 2002), pp. 77–106.

[16] See Gisela Webb, Chapter 11 in this volume.

[17] The Nation of Islam (NOI) under Imam Warith D. Mohammed was called the World Community of al-Islam in the West in 1976, the American Muslim Mission in 1980,

Muslims in East Harlem established Alianza Islámica, focusing on urban renewal, drug abuse counseling, and gang violence prevention.

During the same period, Muslim immigrants responded to the new political climate by planning activities to help them and their children manage the vagaries of American life. The Islamic Society of North America (ISNA), for example, was formed in 1982 as an umbrella group by the leaders of the Muslim Students Association in order to take its services beyond college campuses. They began organizing programs to promote Islamic education designed for a broader American Muslim audience. Both the American Muslim Alliance (AMA) and the American Muslim Council (AMC) worked to increase the political awareness and grass-roots activism of Muslims nationwide.[18] Institutions like the American Islamic College (AIC) started to work toward offering Muslims in the United States an alternative to the secular system of higher education.[19] Beginning in the 1970s, these organized efforts constituted a significant departure from earlier decades during which many Muslims attempted to separate themselves from the American mainstream. Before the 1970s, Muslims strategized to protect their Islamic values and identities until, as immigrants, they returned safely home to their countries of origin or, as native-born converts, they witnessed some form of social and racial redress in the United States. After the 1970s, however, they made concerted efforts to establish programs and institutions that addressed their immediate social and religious needs. With this change, American Muslims and their institutions underwent a much more deliberate process of mainstreaming in American society, a process that some have described as Americanization.[20] This is not to suggest that Muslim immigrants, their adult children, or converts to Islam abandoned concerns for the affairs of the global *ummah* (worldwide Muslim community). Rather, I would suggest that, during the 1970s and beyond, American Muslims began turning inward, expanding their views to encompass the U.S. homeland as well as the worldwide faith community abroad. In other words, many American Muslims were in the process of negotiating their American, transnational, and religious identities, and they continue to do so in the present.

the Muslim American Society in 1995, and finally the American Muslim Society in 2000. See Sally Howell, Chapter 3 in this volume, on American Muslim histories from 1865 to 1965.

[18] See Karen Leonard, Chapter 10 in this volume.

[19] For more on Islamic education in the United States, see Zareena Grewal and R. David Coolidge, Chapter 14 in this volume.

[20] See Edward E. Curtis IV, Chapter 1 in this volume, on conceptualizing the histories of American Muslims in the study of American Islam.

While Muslims in America may come from nearly one hundred different countries, the three largest communities today are African American, South Asian, and Arab.[21] Understanding American Islam, however, is not as simple as coming to know these three main groups, or the many smaller ones. While other Muslim communities are not as large, they do nonetheless diversify the whole, bringing together their different histories, religious practices, and interpretations of religious texts. They also augment the cause of Islam in America by their monetary contributions, religious devotion, and the various ways they support Islamic activities at their own and other religious institutions. Muslim immigrants from West Africa, for example, probably number around 200,000. But while this figure is small compared to other immigrant communities, they have had a major impact not only in New York City, their initial point of entry, but across the country as they resettle in places like Los Angeles, Chicago, Houston, and Atlanta. Moreover, the regular remittances and money transfers sent to their hometowns alter not only community life in these locales but also the gross national product of their respective countries. The West African Muslim population is small but rapidly growing, and increased attendance at nearby Arab and South Asian mosques has done much to enrich their services.[22] By the same token, navigating this type of ethnic diversity within a single faith tradition is extremely challenging. Many fault lines exist, dividing Muslim communities along not merely cultural but racial lines as well.

THE RACIAL DIVIDE

Race has been a constant in American life, and Muslims like others before them have been forced to grapple with its pernicious social and political effects. This does not mean, however, that their response to the consequences of race is similar to that of their predecessors. While racial

---

[21] See Amaney Jamal and Liali Albana, Chapter 6 in this volume. Also, several research centers have developed profiles on American Muslims. See Pew Research Center, "Muslim Americans: No Signs of Growth in Alienation or Support for Extremism," 2011, http://www.people-press.org/2011/08/30/muslim-americans-no-signs-of-growth-in-alienation-or-support-for-extremism/; Center for Race and Gender, University of California, Berkeley, and the Council on American-Islamic Relations, "Islamophobia and Its Impact in the United States: Same Hate, New Target," 2009–2010, http://www.cair.com/Portals/0/islamophobia2010.pdf; Gallup, "Muslim Americans: A National Portrait; An In-depth Analysis of America's Most Diverse Religious Community," 2009, http://www.gallup.com/strategicconsulting/153572/REPORT-Muslim-Americans-National-Portrait.aspx; Philippa Strum, ed., *Muslims in the United States: Identity, Influence, Innovation* (Washington, D.C., 2005).

[22] Zain Abdullah, *Black Mecca: The African Muslims of Harlem* (New York, 2010).

harmony has been an Islamic ideal, the reality continues to be much more complex. Post-1965 Muslim immigrants enter the United States imbued with their own colonial ideas about skin color and ethnic differences (where, very often, linguistic boundaries excluded outsiders). And while most Muslims would consider themselves to be religiously brothers and sisters and members of a universal faith group, American Muslims have rarely shared a life across these boundaries and have only reluctantly started to marry outside of their ethnic or racial communities.[23]

In October 2007, for example, Talib Abdur-Rashid, an African American imam of a predominately Black Muslim community in Harlem, visited the Islamic Center of Long Island in suburban Westbury. Later in the evening, he sat on the carpet chatting with a medical doctor, Faroque Khan, a South Asian Muslim immigrant who helped to found the center. Nearly thirty miles separated these two communities, but the distance between their social worlds is much wider. "The divide between Black and immigrant Muslims," states a *New York Times* article covering their meeting, "reflects a unique struggle facing Islam in America."[24] The reporter was correct in recognizing that the racial divide between African American and immigrant Muslims has often frustrated their ability to work together. And while their histories have been intertwined for much of the twentieth century, more could be done to rectify the problem. However, since the tragedy of the 9/11 attacks, individual efforts have been made to reach across the divide and build bridges on the basis of a common faith and civic concerns. In this case, Dr. Khan's chance reading of a 1968 book on Black rage helped to dispel his previous views of African Americans.[25] By the same token, African Americans often failed to appreciate the postcolonial baggage many immigrants carried, including the migrant realities they faced in their daily lives as "alien" outsiders in a new country.

After the 1960s, many African Americans, Latinos, and other Americans were afforded an opportunity to discover a renewed sense of personal freedom and religious choice. Some broke away from older Muslim communities and experimented with new forms of religious expression. Many Muslim immigrants, however, steered away from inner cities, where mostly African American converts and other minorities

---

[23] See Zareena Grewal, "Marriage in Colour: Race, Religion, and Spouse Selection in Four American Mosques," *Ethnic and Racial Studies* 32:2 (February 2009): 323–345.

[24] Andrea Elliott, "Between Black and Immigrant Muslims, an Uneasy Alliance," *New York Times*, March 11, 2007, late edition, Sunday final, sec. 1, col. 1, p. 1.

[25] Elliott, "Between Black and Immigrant Muslims, an Uneasy Alliance." The book on this topic was *Black Rage* by William H. Grier and Price M. Cobbs (New York, 1968).

lived. Their status as professional, technical, and kindred workers (PTKs) gave them access to suburban life, and their assimilation was accelerated if their complexion was light enough to pass as white. At times, Muslim first names were Anglicized to ease the process. The darker complexion of South Asian Muslims made assimilation more difficult. For them, it was their higher class standing and foreign-born status that allowed for the successful negotiation of a racial divide that had no fixed place for them.

At the same time, racial differences often mirror ideological or sectarian beliefs. Sufism, for instance, had since the early twentieth century attracted white converts and even non-Muslims. Marcia Hermansen argues that during the 1960s, Sufism appealed to "young, middle-class Americans [who] located the cause of racism, the Vietnam War, and the evils of technocracy in a spiritual sickness that establishment religions in America had not only failed to solve but had fostered."[26] But in recent years, there is less uniformity among its followers. "Characterizing 'Sufism' among white Americans in the 21st Century is challenging," says Alyson L. Dickson. "The range of Sufi groups and practices has varied significantly, from the most universalistic and New Age or metaphysical to those that strictly follow the *shari'ah*, the legal, ethical, and behavioral rules based on the Qur'an and Muslim tradition."[27] Still others, like most African American Muslims, adhere to more exoteric varieties of Sunni or Shi'i Islam. This fact highlights how race has structured and continues to shape religious orientations and identities in the United States.

In the first decade of the twenty-first century, most African American Muslims had embraced some form of Sunni Islam, although some Black Muslims have also identified with Shi'ism, particularly since the Iranian Revolution in 1979. For Black converts, however, embracing Sunni or Shi'i Islam more often than not resulted in a disavowal of their racial identities. For many Sunni Muslims, race consciousness was not only unnecessary but possibly heretical. Still, Black Sunni movements like Darul Islam, the Islamic Party of North America, and the Mosque of Islamic Brotherhood (MIB) established national networks and combined Sunni teachings with a concern for racial justice and Black pride.[28] With

[26] Marcia Hermansen, "Hybrid Identity Formations in Muslim America: The Case of American Sufi Movements," *Muslim World* 90 (Spring 2000): 159.

[27] Alyson L. Dickson, "White Muslim Americans," in Edward E. Curtis IV, ed., *Encyclopedia of Muslim-American History* (New York, 2010), p. 580.

[28] See Griggs, "Islamic Party of North America." Also see Robert Dannin, *Black Pilgrimage to Islam* (New York, 2002).

the exception of MIB, the other organizations disbanded, and many of
its former members joined other Muslim communities. Many African
American Sunnis became disenchanted with the rhetoric of a color-blind
fellowship in Islam, and they endeavored to form coalitions that could
more willingly speak to issues of race and other social problems facing American-born Muslims and their institutions. The formation of
the Muslim Alliance in North America (MANA), founded in 2005 by a
group of predominately Black Muslims, is an example of these efforts,
although their continued existence may be questioned.[29]

The tension between race and religion has been an ongoing issue
for many Americans, and it has been particularly vexing for Muslims in
the United States. However, few organizations have tackled this tension
as evocatively as the Nation of Islam. As a Muslim movement with a
Black nationalist agenda, the NOI began preaching about Islam as the
"natural" religion of the "Blackman" in the 1930s. Efforts to mainstream
the group began with the succession of Imam Warith Deen Mohammed
in 1975, which involved opening membership to whites and incorporating more Sunni doctrines and practices. As the son and heir of his
father, the Honorable Elijah Muhammad, Imam Mohammed continued
to preach about Black culture and identity, while his interpretations of the
faith increasingly departed from the NOI's original teachings. These and
other changes greatly upset Minister Louis Farrakhan, one of the group's
most prominent ministers, who left in 1978 to reconstitute the NOI,
based on Elijah Muhammad's lessons.[30] Even before, the NOI had begun
to splinter into several camps. The best known among them was perhaps
the Five Percenters.[31] What is worth noting, however, is how race and
religion intersected among Black Muslims. For some, religion trumped

[29] For more information on MANA, see its Web site at http://mana-net.org/.
[30] For the life and significance of Elijah Muhammad, see Claude Andrew Clegg III,
An Original Man: The Life and Times of Elijah Muhammad (New York, 1997); for
Warith Deen Mohammed, see Edward E. Curtis IV, *Islam in Black America: Identity,
Liberation, and Difference in African-American Islamic Thought* (Albany, 2002); for
Minister Louis Farrakhan, see Mattias Gardell, *In the Name of Elijah Muhammad:
Louis Farrakhan and the Nation of Islam* (Durham, 1996), and Amy Alexander, ed.,
*The Farrakhan Factor: African-American Writers on Leadership, Nationhood, and
Minister Louis Farrakhan* (New York, 1998).
[31] Although quite dated, two works on American Muslim sectarianism are *Mission to
America: Five Islamic Sectarian Communities in North America* by Yvonne Yazbeck
Haddad and Jane Idleman Smith (Gainesville, 1993) and *African American Islam* by
Aminah Beverly McCloud (New York, 1995). For work on the Five Percenters, see *Five
Percent Rap: God Hop's Music, Message, and Black Muslim Mission* by Felicia M.
Miyakawa (Bloomington, 2005) and *The Five Percenters: Islam, Hip Hop and the Gods
of New York* by Michael Muhammad Knight (Oxford, 2007).

race, at times creating distance between those who saw themselves as Muslim only and others who did not. On the other hand, some believed that race and religion were not mutually exclusive, realizing that any attempt to disregard race would only increase its relevance, allowing it to operate in Muslim settings unchecked. Many feared, then, that the acceptance of a color-blind Islam could easily allow for racist and other discriminatory practices to continue with impunity.

During the Park51 controversy in 2010, for example, when a firestorm erupted over what many believed was a mosque proposal at "Ground Zero" (the location of the Twin Towers attacks), African American Muslims (even those who were members of the sponsoring mosque) appeared to be excluded from the debate. Either by media design or by mosque selection, Black Muslims were conspicuously absent from a national debate on religious bias and Islamophobia, essentially a nationwide conversation about racism against Muslims. In fact, their outlier status precipitated the formation of a new group, the Coalition of African American Muslims, and a separate press conference was held at the National Press Club in Washington, D.C.[32] The exclusion and response clearly illustrate how race works in America, and how it continues to impact the lives of American Muslims.

THE QUEST FOR ISLAMIC AUTHENTICITY

During his 2010 presidential address at the Association for the Sociology of Religion (ASR), Rhys Williams spoke about the rise of an "American Islam" and observed that "Islam is coming to visibility, consciousness, and legitimacy within the general American public sphere and its religious pluralism – a dynamic that is the result of the numbers and resources of the post-1965 immigrants and their children."[33] While the visibility of Islam in the United States can hardly be debated, the Immigration Act of 1965 also reflects a new stage in the diversification of Islamic practice – but not only as a consequence of Muslim immigrants and their adult children. Rather, American converts as well as the descendants of Muslim immigrants to the United States have offered

---

[32] For Black Muslim exclusion, see Stephon Johnson and Orobosa Igbinedio, "Islam and Race: Black Muslims Left Out of National Conversation on Islam," *Amsterdam News*, September 2, 2010. And for the Coalition of African American Muslims' press conference, there were no major media outlets present, but there are several references to it on the Internet, and a ninety-minute video of the press conference can be viewed at http://www.noi.org/webcast/sep-02–2010/.

[33] Rhys H. Williams, "Creating an American Islam: Thoughts on Religion, Identity, and Place," *Sociology of Religion* 72:2 (2011): 128, and n. 1.

their own version of what it means to be Muslim in America. And this has complicated the notion of visibility, authority, and what one might consider an authentic representation of Islam.

African American, Latino, and other Muslims, for example, have popularized Islam in locales across the country, although they rarely receive adequate media attention. This lack of exposure for converts is obviously related to the stereotyping of Muslims as Arabs, with media producers often looking for images and representations their audiences can easily recognize. Since the end of the twentieth century, Muslim visibility has benefited from individual white converts including poet Daniel Abdal-Hayy Moore, and Ingrid Mattson, a former Hartford Seminary professor and past president of the Islamic Society of North America (ISNA). Still, Islamic visibility or authenticity often meant showing up on the evening news in prepackaged form for mainstream consumption. It involved a well-crafted selection of certain figures and personalities by media outlets, funding and governmental agencies, and other institutions. But Islam has entered the public arena in other complex ways. While the hijab or niqab have been perceived by outsiders as a sign of oppression and humiliation, a single reading of this sartorial practice misses the more subtle points for what it means to publicly wear religious clothing. The wearing of a black *jilbab*, for instance, can delineate the parameters of a Philadelphia neighborhood or infuse the downtown Center City district with religious meaning or an Islamic sensibility.[34]

The ethnic and religious diversity of American Muslims also means that there is no single source of Muslim authority or authenticity, no group to which all others can claim allegiance in matters of religion or public affairs. Who then has defined faith, religious practices, and their interpretations for Muslims in America? Can there be one American Islam? The answers to these questions are many and few, and this has made questions about Islamic authenticity so unsettling. Sulayman Nyang has argued that both American individualism and secularization have helped to prevent the rise of a single interpretation of American Islam.[35] Nyang's proposition rings true but also requires clarification. This American individualism (or, perhaps, American Islamic pluralism) speaks to the pluralization or expansion of women's rights, the increased presence of varying exegeses or textual analyses, and the recognition of

[34] See Zain Abdullah, "Culture, Community and the Politics of Muslim Space," *Journal of History and Culture* 1:3 (2010): 30.
[35] Sulayman S. Nyang, "The Muslim Community in the United States: Some Issues," *Studies in Contemporary Islam* 1:2 (1999): 67.

more complex sexualities. Secularization, within the American context, has also provided alternative spaces for Islamic practice, prompting Muslims to forgo visits to the mosque for time spent in Internet chat rooms or at spoken word venues.

Whether Muslim women see Islam as a force to liberate them or to affirm their traditional roles, their status continues to be in flux and, thus, challenges the prevailing views of an American Islam. At a time when women represent nearly half of the Muslim American population, male-dominated spaces in mosques, Muslim schools, and organizations have had to reckon with and make room for a growing cadre of talented and educated women. How can this religious playing field be leveled, altering restrictive gender relations that prevent women from access to spiritual enrichment and full mosque participation? This issue continues to be of great concern for Muslim Americans in the period from 2000 to the present. While the Pew Research Center stated that American Muslim men slightly outnumbered their female counterparts, the Latino American Dawah Organization (LADO) estimated that the opposite was true among Latino Muslims, where women had reached 60 percent.[36] Some have predicted that since "less than half of U.S. mosque leaders have received any type of formal Islamic studies education," women might increasingly challenge the religious parameters that maintain sexual inequality, especially when they are based on what men have defined as traditional dictates and authentic teachings.[37] These endeavors would fundamentally change their sense of Islamic authenticity, including the nature of Muslim visibility in America.

Both Muslim progressives and neoconservatives have weighed in on what constitutes correct belief in Islam. In the progressive Muslim movement, men and women have been active in various ways. While there is no single agenda, the overall thrust has been to encourage a historical rather than a literalist reading of Islamic texts, to foster multiple interpretations of Islamic sources and core principles, and to fight political corruption both within the United States and abroad. Groups like the Progressive Muslim Union (PMU), which operated from 2004 to 2006, and Muslims for Progressive Values (MPV) established a presence on the

[36] Pew Research Center, "Muslim Americans," p. 15; David W. Damrel, "Latina/o Muslim Americans," in Curtis, *Encyclopedia of Muslim-American History*, p. 335. Also see Hjamil A. Martinez-Vazquez, *Latina/o y Musulman: The Construction of Latina/o Identity among Latina/o Muslims in the United States* (Eugene, 2010).
[37] Edward E. Curtis IV, "Peril and Possibility: Muslim Life in the United States," in R. Michael Feener, ed., *Islam in World Cultures: Comparative Perspectives* (Santa Barbara, 2004), p. 302.

Internet. The LGBT (lesbian, gay, bisexual, and transgender) Muslim community has likewise become more visible and added their voice to the debate on Islamic authenticity. Its members have challenged the propensity to define Muslim family life in exclusively heterosexual terms. In 1998 the Al-Fatiha Foundation was set up in New York in response to the needs of a LGBT Muslim population. By contrast, American Muslim Salafis have called for a strict reading of Muslim texts, based on a return to premodern Islamic interpretations deemed to be more authentic. While this group did not typically form separate organizations, it established mosque communities and online sites such as salafipublications.com.

Besides these issues, a new set of concerns has emerged relating to the pervasive presence of technology and the influences of secular culture. The mushrooming of Muslim Web sites on an array of Islamic topics illustrates the emergence of a "Cyber Islam." Muslims overwhelmingly participate in social networking, personal Web pages for scholars or bloggers, and institutional or group debates, which includes consulting online fatwas for questions about Islamic sexual mores, dating, raising children, *halal* (permissible) job choices, sports, diets, and Islamic financing. American Muslim (and transnational) online activities point to the increasing significance of virtual networks for discussing Islam and meeting Muslims in the twenty-first century.[38] At the same time, other places have emerged as alternative sites for Muslim gatherings. They include street rallies, banquet halls for Islamic spoken word sessions, Muslim home study circles, or special eateries. And along with these new venues, Muslim Americans have envisioned new identities that may have previously appeared incongruous with traditional beliefs. American Muslims have also questioned the place of religion itself in the public sphere. Secular Muslims may have embraced Islam as their cultural or moral guide (or the label Muslim as an identity component) without practicing Islamic rituals in their daily lives. A *New York Times* journalist described the "silent, secular majority of American Muslims," adherents of a secular Islam, who look to retain a Muslim consciousness (a sort of best-practices approach) without the legalism of religion.[39]

The geopolitics that have shaped U.S.–Middle East relations, the 1965 Immigration Act, the "Me Decade" of the 1970s, ongoing racial and gender inequalities, and the rise of a technological and secular age have all played their part in impacting Muslim life in America. And

[38] See Gary R. Bunt, *iMuslims: Rewiring the House of Islam* (Chapel Hill, 2009); Curtis, "Peril and Possibility," p. 303.

[39] Quoted in Curtis, *Muslims in America*, p. 107. Also, see Zeyno Baran, ed., *The Other Muslims: Moderate and Secular* (New York, 2010).

there is no doubt that American Muslims with varying orientations, interpretations, and identities have made the American religious landscape much more pluralistic and diverse.

CONCLUSION: AMERICAN MUSLIMS IN THE AGE OF 9/11

The tenth anniversary of September 11 marked an important point in U.S. history. It was a day of mourning and remembrance. The victims of the attacks were people from numerous faiths and no faith at all, custodial workers and executives, men as well as women and children, members of various racial and ethnic groups, originating from ninety different countries. One face among the many lost that day was an American Muslim, Mohammed Salman Hamdani, a New York City Police cadet who rushed into the World Trade Center to help survivors. He was killed amid other Muslim first-responders.[40] Others became victims on the days following 9/11, as Muslims were assaulted along with Balbir Singh Sodhi, a Sikh man mistaken for a Muslim and gunned down at work, and Adel Karas, an Arab Christian murdered at his place of business.[41] Moustafa Bayoumi states that "hate crimes against Muslim Americans skyrocketed in the first six months after 9/11 (and still have not returned to pre-9/11 levels)."[42] So when the Day of Remembrance arrived in 2011, it could have been a day of reflection for the entire country and countless others around the world. Instead, the September 11th commemoration reflected decades of division and the rehearsal of old stereotypes. In the media, and not unlike in 2001, people lined up on one side charging that all Muslims were guilty by virtue of religious association, and that they were to be suspects because they shared the religion of the attackers. On the other side were those seeking reconciliation and better relations – although, even after ten years, few knew exactly what that meant. Even days after the original attack, government officials were sending mixed messages. President George W. Bush stood in the Islamic Center of Washington declaring that "the face of terror is not the true faith of Islam." At the same time, door-to-door searches were proposed by law

[40] For a video program on the case of Mohammed Salman Hamdani, see http://www.democracynow.org/2011/5/2/talat_hamdanI_mother_of_9_11. For a partial list of the Muslim victims killed at the World Trade Center that morning, see http://islam.about.com/od/terrorism/a/Muslim-Victims-Of-9-11-Attack.htm.
[41] For a list of other victims killed in the United States for being a Muslim or mistaken for one, see http://fateh.sikhnet.com/s/OtherHCVictims.
[42] Moustafa Bayoumi, "Between Acceptance and Rejection: Muslim Americans and the Legacies of September 11," *OAH Magazine of History* 25:3 (2011): 16.

enforcement targeting neighborhoods with large Muslim populations.[43] American preachers like Franklin Graham and Pat Robertson lined up to publicly excoriate Islam and its Prophet. The media ran one story after another that by and large presented a distorted view of Islam. Muslims had been portrayed as backward, intolerant, sexist, immigrant dodgers, and now terrorists. On the other hand, community residents around the country were reaching out to their Muslim neighbors. Interfaith dialogues were convened, and numerous events were held at churches, masjids, synagogues, and on college campuses nationwide.

While hate crimes drastically increased, there was also an unprecedented effort to understand Islam. Within days of the attacks, books on Islam, Muslims, or just the Middle East sold at surprising rates. Even large book chains like Barnes & Noble were sold out for days. This high level of curiosity itself constituted a watershed moment in relations between American Muslims and the larger public. At times, however, the information was skewed. But at other times it taught the public a great deal about what Muslims shared with Christians and Jews, since they all belong to the same Abrahamic tradition. Beyond matters of belief, a major issue that emerged after 9/11 was whether Muslims could be loyal and patriotic citizens while also maintaining their religious identities and practices. This negotiation of overlapping and conflicting loyalties is not unique to American Muslims but was also used as a tool for excluding Catholics and Jews in earlier periods of American history.

In 2011 the Pew Research Center published a national public opinion survey of Muslim Americans. The report revealed that nearly half of all Muslims in the United States considered themselves Muslim first and American second. While 26 percent of those surveyed thought of themselves as American first, a significant number or 18 percent described themselves as equally Muslim and American. These results were compared to a different study of Muslims living abroad. And while Muslims in America yielded a higher percentage for a Muslim-first identity than Egypt, Indonesia, Lebanon, Turkey (which equaled American Muslims), and the Palestinian territories, only Pakistan (94 percent) and Jordan (65 percent) were higher for people who placed a Muslim identity above their nationality. At the same time, the survey also showed that white American evangelicals at 70 percent were much more likely to identify as Christian first.[44]

---

[43] Eric Lichtblau, *Bush's Law: The Remaking of American Justice* (New York, 2009), p. 6.
[44] Pew Research Center, "Muslim Americans," 7, 35.

Although these data might be useful for designing more in-depth research, the findings do not tell us how the respondents understood the question. In other words, how did the participants understand what it means to be a Muslim or an American? Given the complexity of Muslim communities in America and their diverse social composition (e.g., their racial and ethnic composition; their status as immigrant, undocumented, or refugee; their gender relations and sexual preferences; youth and popular culture issues; and their social values and political views), these and similar questions would certainly produce a multitude of answers. Ultimately, however, whether one is Muslim first, American first, or views both as equally important, the presence of Muslims in America speaks to a much larger debate about how they collectively relate to the nation-state. The continuing presence of Muslims in the United States also speaks to an internal dialogue among Muslims themselves about their Muslim identity as Americans and their relationship with those Muslims living in other parts of the world. At an "Islam in America" conference at Chicago's DePaul University, for example, a presenter talked about her community activism in New York City.[45] She self-identified as a "Brooklyn born and raised Palestinian Muslim American," and then admitted her confusion about what constitutes a Muslim identity in America. "Can somebody tell me," she said, "what's the difference between a Muslim American and an American Muslim?" The question was an obvious one, but among an audience of Muslim and non-Muslim scholars and professionals, it received no reply. For many, the difficulty of reconciling one's religious belief and civic duty still rings true, particularly for Muslims in a post-9/11 world in which this questioning is rather relentless. More importantly, the answers may well have a real-life impact in the form of further discrimination, vilification, and hate crimes, or they may produce greater acceptance and inclusion in a society marked by debates over religion in the public sphere. For the United States, with its history of immigration, the question of how to blend old and new identities is not new and will continue to be of relevance for American Muslims. And as they continue to grapple with this question in diverse ways, American society, scholars of Islam in America, and American Muslims will be forced to rethink old assumptions about the contours of an American Islam and what constitutes Muslim life in the United States.

[45] The "Islam in America" conference was held at DePaul University in Chicago on September 23–24, 2011. See its Web site at http://tcoia.org/.

Further Reading

Abdullah, Zain, *Black Mecca: The African Muslims of Harlem* (Oxford, 2010).

Barrett, Paul M., *American Islam: The Struggle for the Soul of a Religion* (New York, 2006).

Bayoumi, Moustafa, *How Does It Feel to be a Problem? Being Young and Arab in America* (New York, 2008).

Cainkar, Louise A., *Homeland Insecurity: The Arab American and Muslim American Experience after 9/11* (New York, 2009).

Dannin, Robert, *Black Pilgrimage to Islam* (New York, 2002).

Karim, Jamillah, *American Muslim Women: Negotiating Race, Class, and Gender within the Ummah* (New York, 2009).

Mohammad-Arif, Aminah, *Salaam America: South Asian Muslims in New York* (London, 2002).

Takim, Liyakat, *Shi'ism in America* (New York, 2009).

Tate, Sonsyrea, *Little X: Growing Up in the Nation of Islam* (San Francisco, 1997).

Wolfe, Michael, ed., *Taking Back Islam: American Muslims Reclaim Their Faith* (Emmaus, 2004).

5 Converts and Conversions
MICHAEL MUHAMMAD KNIGHT

Strictly speaking, there is no Arabic term for conversion to Islam, apart from *aslama*, "to submit," the verb from which *islam* is derived. For Muslims in the United States, conversion is frequently described with the term *shahadah*, "bearing witness," signifying the moment at which a person becomes Muslim by testifying to the oneness of God and the prophethood of Muhammad. The term "conversion" is itself frowned upon by many Muslims, and alternatives such as "embracing Islam" or "taking shahadah" are often preferred. It is not uncommon for new Muslims to be described as "reverts," according to the notion that all human beings are born in a natural state of submission to God; for someone who had been raised in another tradition to embrace Islam later in life, therefore, is seen not as an act of "conversion" to something new but rather a "reversion" to his or her original state. For African American and Latino converts, becoming Muslim could carry additional meaning as the reclaiming of lost Islamic heritage, a "reversion" to ancestral identity. The term "conversion" may be problematized for both its assumptions regarding the new Muslim's past and his or her religious trajectory following the act of embracing Islam. As an alternative, Aminah McCloud suggests "transition," arguing that "conversion" unrealistically suggests a radical and absolute break from one's past. Amina Wadud chooses to use "transition" and "transformation" interchangeably to "determine that Islam does not start or stop with the *shahadah*, the declaration of faith."[1]

From a narrative theory perspective, such as that considered by Carolyn Moxley Rouse in *Engaged Surrender: African American Women and Islam*, "The power of conversion is the control one has over the recreation of a personal history."[2] For many converts, embracing Islam

---

[1] Amina Wadud, *Inside the Gender Jihad: Women's Reform in Islam* (Oxford, 2006), p. 263. Wadud reproduces McCloud's argument whither the term conversion and adds her own thoughts in an endnote to the introduction of the book.

[2] Carolyn Moxley Rouse, *Engaged Surrender: African American Women and Islam* (Berkeley, 2004), p. 133.

promises the reconstruction of a self through new narratives concerning identity, religious truth, and also the racialized and gendered body. This rewriting of personal history might also incorporate retellings of the social, cultural, and political contexts in which that history is embedded. Given the historically situated self that is to be reconstructed, therefore, it could be tempting to compartmentalize American conversions within experiences of "indigenous American Islam" and "immigrant Islam" as though these are fundamentally and self-evidently separate. However, the study of American converts and conversions reveals a richly interconnected history that calls these clearly defined categories into question.

NINETEENTH- AND EARLY TWENTIETH-CENTURY CONVERSIONS

Difficulties in naming the first American convert to Islam owe in part to the challenge of recovering Islam's history among African slaves and their earliest descendants. Certainly, the bringing together of diverse African populations by the transatlantic slave trade made interfaith encounters inevitable. Such encounters would have been informed by preexisting notions of religious difference among the captured slaves; for example, the use of Islamic prayers and verses from the Qur'an in magical amulets, which had been popular among Muslims and non-Muslims alike in West Africa, continued to provide a shared space between religionists in the Americas. As African Muslim slaves in colonial and antebellum America struggled to preserve their traditions and identities, it is not impossible that marriages and other encounters between Muslim and non-Muslim slaves led to conversions.[3] It can also be speculated that Islam's status as an Abrahamic monotheism and scriptural emphasis on literacy resulted in Muslims becoming somewhat privileged in the American slavocracy. This religious privilege, intersecting with constructions of racial difference between "Negroes" and "Moorish" Africans with perceived Arab ancestry, could have made conversion to Islam attractive as a means of social mobility.[4]

The first American convert for whom evidence exists is a "Reverend Norman," who traveled to Turkey as a Methodist missionary, embraced Islam in 1875, and returned to the United States to start his own Islamic propagation group.[5] He was followed about a decade later by Mohammed

3   Michael A. Gomez, *Exchanging Our Country Marks: The Transformation of African Identities in the Colonial and Antebellum South* (Chapel Hill, 1998), p. 60.
4   Kambiz GhaneaBassiri, *A History of Islam in America* (Cambridge, 2010), pp. 22–24.
5   Umar F. Abd-Allah, *A Muslim in Victorian America: The Life of Alexander Russell Webb* (Oxford, 2006), p. 71.

Alexander Russell Webb, who has been generally treated in popular and academic discourse as both America's first convert to Islam and Islam's first proselytizer in the Americas. Born in 1846 and raised in a Presbyterian family in Hudson, New York, Webb grew dissatisfied with Christianity as a teenager and spent years in search of spiritual truth. He moved from materialist philosophy to Buddhism and later joined the Theosophical movement, which advocated an esoteric perennialism and spiritual advancement through the comparative study of religion, particularly "Eastern" traditions. Founded in 1875, the Theosophical Society would boast thirty-four lodges in cities across the United States by 1890.[6]

Webb joined the Theosophical Society in 1881, initially focusing his studies on Buddhism. He later engaged in correspondence with Mirza Ghulam Ahmad, founder of the Ahmadiyya Movement. In his letters to Ahmad, Webb indicated that he believed in the divine missions of not only Muhammad and Jesus but also Buddha, Zoroaster, "and many others," and that he emphasized the shared truths of all religions over the differences in their "exoteric features."[7] In 1888, shortly after the end of his correspondence with Ahmad and around the time that he became American consul to the Philippines, Webb formally declared himself a Muslim. He found Islam resonating with the values that shaped his own world and drove his spiritual quest: Victorian morality, Protestant opposition to priestly hierarchy and divine intermediaries, scientific rationality, and the Theosophical belief in an esoteric wisdom that united the world's religions.

In 1892 Webb left the Philippines for India, where he would raise funds for the establishment of his own proselytization group, American Islamic Propaganda, to be headquartered in New York. One year later, Webb founded the American Moslem Brotherhood and the Moslem Publishing Company to print his own apologetic journals, and he also represented Islam at the Theosophist-heavy World's Parliament of Religions in Chicago. He established six study circles across the United States, beginning with "The Mecca Circle No.1 of New York City," at which both converts and sympathizers were addressed as "Brother" (it is not clear that women participated).[8] He was influenced in these efforts by the work of Abdullah William Henry Quilliam (1856–1932), a British convert whose Liverpool-based Moslem Institute established a New York branch, the American Moslem Institute, in 1895.[9] In his writings and

---

[6] Catherine L. Albanese, *A Republic of Mind and Spirit: A Cultural History of American Metaphysical Religion* (New Haven, 2007), p. 345.

[7] Abd-Allah, *A Muslim in Victorian America*, p. 65.

[8] Abd-Allah, *A Muslim in Victorian America*, pp. 178–179.

[9] Abd-Allah, *A Muslim in Victorian America*, p. 161.

lectures, Webb would promote Islam as harmonious with science and reason, compatible with the teachings of Christ, opposed to bigotry and violence, and advocating full equality between women and men. His mission, however, failed to attract many converts. Theosophists were resistant to his call, regarding Islam as fundamentally intolerant and hostile to the universalizing spirituality that they perceived in Buddhism and other Eastern traditions. Additionally, Islam was considered too insistent upon an absolute separation between humanity and the divine, while Theosophists held that "there can be no God different or separate from man."[10] In 1897, five years after the start of Webb's formal missionary work, his organizations closed their doors.

Although Webb supported Theosophy's mission of a "universal brotherhood" that would eliminate all forms of prejudice and presented Islam as antithetical to American racism, he also expressed racist views in his writings. He argued that assessments of Islam should allow for consideration of the "racial influences" impairing its adherents and described South Asians as "niggers" twice in his diaries.[11] Informed by the civilizational prejudices of his time, he bemoaned common Muslims as unsophisticated in their comprehension of Islam. "There are many professed Mussulmans who do not know that there is a philosophic side to their religion," he complained after unfulfilling encounters with Muslims in India. He excused what he saw as the inferior religion of average Muslims, fearing that more advanced intellectual pursuits would cause them to lose what "plain, safe and simple truths [were] already within their grasp."[12] He additionally derided South Asian Muslims who "deserted" Islam to become "Anglicized" as having also been feminized: "Why in the world can't these people have some manhood and independence, and cultivate a true manhood, instead of following the brutalizing habits and customs of their conquerors?"[13] Webb remained both a Muslim and a Theosophist until his death, but the spirituality of actual Asia did not correspond to the "metaphysical Asia" that he and other Theosophists imagined.[14]

The currents of alternative metaphysical discourses that influenced Webb's path to Islam also informed the teaching mission of Hazrat Inayat Khan, the earliest effort to spread Sufism in the United States. Arriving in San Francisco from India in 1912, Inayat Khan conceptualized Sufism

[10] GhaneaBassiri, *A History of Islam in America*, pp. 24–125.
[11] Abd-Allah, *A Muslim in Victorian America*, p. 139.
[12] GhaneaBassiri, *A History of Islam in America*, p. 118.
[13] Abd-Allah, *A Muslim in Victorian America*, p. 139.
[14] Albanese, *A Republic of Mind and Spirit*, p. 345.

as an expression of "universal wisdom" that was not contained within Islam but could be found in all religions. He deemphasized Muslim identity, positioned the "spiritual East" against the "material West," and acquired two hundred to three hundred followers in the United States. His message held particular appeal for women, to whom his mysticism offered the possibility of transcending the limits of sex within patriarchal religious frameworks.[15] Dismayed that America at large was not yet ready for his message, Inayat Khan left the United States in 1920; in later decades, however, the Sufi Order in America led by his son, Vilayat Khan, would attract thousands as initiated members, while multiple offshoots would also claim Inayat Khan's lineage.

The earliest missionary movement in the United States to emphasize Islamic identity was the Ahmadiyya movement, which had originated as a Muslim response to Christian missionaries in South Asia. The leading Ahmadiyya representative in America, Mufti Muhammad Sadiq, was awarded degrees from the College of Divine Metaphysics, a New Thought–oriented institution, and the Oriental University, which was affiliated with the spiritualist Universal Theomonistic Association. His successor, Sufi M. Bengalee, gave speeches with New Thought–inspired titles such as "The Supreme Success in Life" and "The Object of Life: Spiritual Progress and the Means of Accomplishing It" at Spiritualist churches in Chicago.[16] Comparable to Theosophy's esoteric perennialism, the Ahmadiyya newspaper, *Moslem Sunrise*, presented Islam as the fulfillment of the unity of religions and the culmination of an ongoing spiritual evolution that included not only Judaism and Christianity but also Hinduism, Buddhism, and Zoroastrianism.

The *Moslem Sunrise* regularly featured announcements of new conversions (listing converts by both their "American" and "Moslem" names), as well as articles and letters by converts. Several frequent themes in *Moslem Sunrise* would be featured in the Sunni apologetic discourse and pamphlet literature of later decades, including the status of women in Islam, Islamic contributions to science and philosophy, and presentations of Islam as the true religion of Jesus; a message of peace and equality; and the solution to color prejudice, with special significance placed on the story of Bilal ibn Rabah, Muhammad's Ethiopian companion and the first muezzin, as evidence of Islam's inherent antiracism.

---

[15] GhaneaBassiri, *A History of Islam in America.*

[16] Susan Nance, "Mystery of the Moorish Science Temple: Southern Blacks and American Alternative Spirituality in 1920s Chicago," *Religion and American Culture: A Journal of Interpretation* 12:2 (2002): 123–166.

Between 1921 and 1925, the Ahmadiyya reportedly attracted more than one thousand converts, most of them African Americans in cities such as Chicago and Detroit. In the 1940s and 1950s, converts included numerous notable jazz musicians, such as Art Blakely, Ahmad Jamal, and Yusef Lateef.[17] Tensions eventually developed, however, between the movement's South Asian leadership and its African American members, leading to breakaway, convert-led groups such as the First Cleveland Mosque and Shaykh Daoud Ahmed Faisal's Brooklyn mosque. These groups generally departed from loyalty to the Ahmadiyya movement and gravitated towards Sunni Islam.[18]

THE GREAT MIGRATION AND NEW ISLAMIC MOVEMENTS

For the early decades of the twentieth century, the major historical backdrop behind conversions to Islam was the Great Migration, beginning in 1915, during which upward of six million African Americans left the rural South for urban centers of the North. This mass exodus had a drastic impact on Black religious culture in cities such as Chicago and Detroit, as southern migrants commonly found their spiritual and social needs to be incompatible with the styles of worship and rhetoric in established northern churches. As a result, countless storefront churches and new religious movements emerged to appeal to the religiously displaced migrants. Additionally, urban environments exposed migrants to a vast array of new discourses about race, world history, and nationhood. As E. D. Beynon, a sociologist writing on the Nation of Islam in 1938, remarks, "The newer migrants entered a social milieu in which the atmosphere was filled with questions about the origins of their people ... they were wondering who they were and whence they came."[19] Many of the small churches and new movements developing during this period emerged as what have been called "messianic-nationalist sects," seeking to achieve cultural and political independence in part through the rejection of "Negro" identity as a pejorative label, the discovery of lost history and heritage, and reconstruction of the self and community through a new ethnic or religious identity. Among these movements were numerous Black Jewish groups such as the Star Order of Ethiopia, Beth

---

[17] Penny M. Van Eschen, *Race against Empire: Black Americans and Anticolonialism, 1937–1957* (Ithaca, 1997), p. 10.

[18] Robert Dannin, *Black Pilgrimage to Islam* (Oxford, 2002), pp. 92–96.

[19] Erdmann Doane Beynon, "The Voodoo Cult among Negro Migrants in Detroit," *American Journal of Sociology* 43:6 (1938): 894–907.

B'nai Abraham, the Royal Order of Ethiopian Hebrews, and the Moorish Zionist Temple, which argued that the original and "true" Hebrews were Black, and that African Americans must reclaim the Hebrew lineage that had been stolen from them. Parallel to these "Black Hebrew" discourses were movements claiming Islam as the lost or stolen heritage. The two most notable African American Islamic movements of the first half of the twentieth century, the Moorish Science Temple of America (MSTA) and Nation of Islam (NOI), both emerged in the postmigration urban North through the charismatic leadership of southern migrants. Noble Drew Ali, who led the MSTA in 1920s Chicago, is said to have been born in South Carolina; Elijah Muhammad, who assumed control of the Nation of Islam after 1934, had come to Detroit from rural Georgia.

Reportedly growing up near coastal South Carolina and Georgia, a region considered by Michael A. Gomez to be the "gravitational center of the antebellum Muslim community in North America," Noble Drew Ali (born Timothy Drew in 1886) would later claim to have traveled the world as a merchant seaman, during which time he received mystical initiation from an ancient priesthood at the Pyramid of Cheops. From this experience, he returned home with his new name and prophetic mandate, along with a revealed scripture, commonly known as the *Circle 7 Koran*. The volume's contents, extracted from New Thought texts, express Islamic theology and soteriology as Noble Drew Ali understood them: a conception of Allah as the human being's "higher self" with the devil as his or her "lower self," while heaven and hell are conditions in the present world. The underlying unity of religions was again affirmed, as Noble Drew Ali called upon his followers to honor all prophets, including non-Abrahamic figures such as Buddha and Confucius.[20] Answering the questions of lost origins and glorious pasts, Noble Drew Ali described African Americans as descendants of Moroccans, who were descended from the ancient Moabites, who were themselves a branch of the same Canaanite tree as pharaonic Egyptians and other ancient African peoples.[21]

Before his death in 1929, Noble Drew Ali's conception of Islam attracted a registered membership of at least three thousand converts, with temples established in a dozen cities nationwide.[22] One year later, southern migrants in Detroit began converting to Islam through the teachings of a mysterious individual who was known by more than fifty

---

[20] Gomez, *Black Crescent*, p. 253.
[21] Nance, "Mystery of the Moorish Science Temple," pp. 123–166.
[22] Nance, "Mystery of the Moorish Science Temple," pp. 123–166.

names, most notably W. D. Fard and Master Fard Muhammad. Initially, Fard Muhammad directed his message toward women, who would then spread his teachings to the men in their households.[23] He presented himself as a peddler of exotic silks; "In this way he could get into the people's houses," reported Danke Majied, an early convert, "for every woman was eager to see the nice things the peddlers had for sale."[24] According to Majied, Fard Muhammad told African Americans that his silks came from their "home country" and that he had been there. "So we all asked him to tell us about our own country."[25]

Fard Muhammad initially taught African Americans that his and their origin was Mecca and that Fard himself was descended from the Quraysh, the tribe of the Prophet Muhammad. Fard Muhammad's compelling tales would sometimes lead to his customers inviting him to stay for dinner; it is reported that he would eat whatever was offered to him but lecture his hosts after the meal: "Now don't eat this food. It is poison for you. The people in your country do not eat it."[26] As with the silks, Fard Muhammad's claims regarding proper diet provoked his hosts to ask more questions about their homeland.

These small dinners would evolve into basement gatherings and eventually rented banquet halls, during which Fard Muhammad preached against white supremacy and Christianity's role within it. He boasted a superior scientific knowledge that could discredit the Bible, as Challas Sharrieff recalls:

> The very first time I went to a meeting I heard him say: "The Bible tells you that the sun rises and sets. That is not so. The sun stands still. All your lives you have been thinking that the earth never moved. Stand and look toward the sun and know that it is the earth you are standing on which is moving." Up to that day I always went to the Baptist church. After I heard that sermon from the prophet, I was turned around completely.... Just to think that the sun above me never moved at all and that the earth we are on was doing all the moving. That changed everything for me.[27]

Contrary to the Theosophists' earlier charge that Islam was uniquely and absolutely opposed to the location of divinity within human beings, Fard Muhammad's vision of Islam emphasized the divinity of "original"

[23] Gomez, *Black Crescent*, p. 279.
[24] Beynon, "The Voodoo Cult."
[25] Beynon, "The Voodoo Cult."
[26] Beynon, "The Voodoo Cult."
[27] Beynon, "The Voodoo Cult."

people: "Now he taught us that the black people were the god," recalls Fard Muhammad's former secretary, Burnsteen Sharrieff Mohammed, "so when I would say my prayers, I'd shut my eyes and envision that great mass of people as god."[28] Within this deification of humanity, Fard Muhammad himself would later become the focus as the embodiment of the divine.

During the three and a half years that Fard Muhammad taught in Detroit and Chicago, the movement attracted roughly eight thousand converts, nearly all of them from southern migrant backgrounds.[29] Though Nation of Islam discourse included a vehement polemic against Christianity, the NOI echoed many mainstream Black churches in urban centers of the period through its rhetoric of economic advancement, calls to "buy Black," hard work, self-reliance, and conservative notions of race respectability, order, discipline, and what it meant to be "civilized."[30] This is particularly exemplified by the NOI's Muslim Girls Training (MGT) program, the female auxiliary to the all-male Fruit of Islam (FOI), providing instruction in home economics, health, and child care, similar to programs offered by some Black Protestant churches.[31]

Converts to Islam are not generally required to change their names, unless their pre-Islamic names signify explicitly anti-Islamic meanings, such as the worship of other gods. For Master Fard Muhammad, like Noble Drew Ali before him, the adoption of a new name expressed a restoration of religious, racial, and national identity. In the early years of the Nation of Islam, Fard Muhammad assigned "righteous" names to converts, such as Jam Sharrieff, Hazziez Allah, Anwar Pasha, Sharrieff Allah, and Elijah Muhammad.[32] After Fard Muhammad's disappearance in 1934, the Nation under Elijah Muhammad's leadership simply assigned "X" as a surname, signifying the convert's true identity that had been lost in the slave trade.

The Nation of Islam appealed to many potential converts through a promise of restoring the Black family, in part through what Edward E. Curtis IV calls "bodily discipline in decidedly gendered terms."[33]

---

[28] Burnsteen Sharrieff Mohammed, *I am Burnsteen Sharrieff Muhammad, Reformer and Secretary to Master W.D.F. Mohammed...and These are Some of My Experiences* (Detroit, 2011).

[29] Beynon, "The Voodoo Cult," pp. 894–907.

[30] Wallace D. Best, *Passionately Human, No Less Divine: Religion and Culture in Black Chicago, 1915–1952* (Princeton, 2005), pp. 75–76.

[31] Best, *Passionately Human*.

[32] Beynon, "The Voodoo Cult," pp. 894–907.

[33] Edward E. Curtis IV, *Black Muslim Religion in the Nation of Islam, 1960–1975* (Chapel Hill, 2006), p. 28.

Sherman Jackson writes that much of Islam's appeal in the United States has been its potential as a "haven of sorts for black manhood."[34] In NOI discourse, Black men were to achieve race respectability by reclaiming their rightful duties as provider, protector, and undisputed head of their households, while Black women achieved race respectability through dressing modestly, caring for the home, and recognizing the authority of the Black man as fundamentally divine. Sexuality factored significantly in the NOI message as it related to concerns for resisting genocidal white supremacy, regulating desire, and protecting Black women within Black patriarchy.[35]

As American Islam's most influential conversion movement, the Nation of Islam also produced what would become America's seminal Islamic conversion narrative, *The Autobiography of Malcolm X*, as told to Alex Haley. The *Autobiography* actually tells of two conversions to Islam: first, Malcolm's 1947 embrace of the teachings of Elijah Muhammad while in prison, followed by a second conversion in 1964, when he performed the pilgrimage to Mecca and relocated his Muslim selfhood within Sunni tradition. The NOI also inspired what could be seen as the most publicly witnessed conversion to Islam in world history, as Cassius Clay announced his conversion after winning the heavyweight championship, becoming Muhammad Ali, and immediately made headlines across the globe.

CONVERSIONS AND THE EVOLVING COMMUNITY

The 1970s and 1980s saw two major developments related to conversion. First, the passing of Elijah Muhammad in 1975 led to a process of reorientation within the Nation of Islam, as the community moved toward Sunni tradition under the direction of Warith Deen Mohammed. Second, in the decades after 1965's Immigration and Nationality Act, which enabled unprecedented immigration from Asian and African countries, Muslim immigrants began developing institutions to engage in *da'wah*, or propagation of Islam. The Muslim Students Association (MSA), which had been founded in 1963, became a significant means through which non-Muslim university students encountered Islam, and the Islamic Society of North America (ISNA), founded by MSA alumni in 1981, also supported da'wah work. Additionally, efforts to promote

[34] Sherman A. Jackson, *Islam and the Blackamerican: Looking toward the Third Resurrection* (Oxford, 2005), p. 20.
[35] Curtis, *Black Muslim Religion*, pp. 118–119.

conversion were influenced by global revivalist trends, as transnational da'wah organizations such as the World Assembly of Muslim Youth (WAMY) also supported propagation within the United States. Islamic publishing houses distributed works such as Hammudah Abd al-Ati's *Islam in Focus* (1978), aimed at attracting potential converts through arguments for Islamic conceptions of monotheism, morality, racial equality, and an honored status for women, as well as instructing the newly converted in basic practices such as prayer and ritual purity. It was also during this period that Khurram Murad, author of *Da'wah among Non-Muslims* (1986), influenced American Muslim discourse from his position at the Islamic Foundation of Leicester in Great Britain. It appears to have been Murad who first coined the term "revert" as an alternative to "convert," on the assumption that people who embrace Islam are not adopting a new way of life but rather "reverting" to their original nature.[36] In the 1980s and 1990s, Salafi da'wah networks flourished in the United States, driven largely by North American converts who obtained religious training in Saudi Arabia, such as Bilal Philips, Dawud Adib, and Abu Muslima.[37]

Through the 1980s and 1990s, what might be called the broader "Muslim world" became increasingly prominent in the American consciousness, owing to U.S. involvement in Afghanistan, escalating conflicts with Iran, controversy over *The Satanic Verses*, the Iran-Iraq War, the first Gulf War, and the 1993 attack on the World Trade Center. Meanwhile, Islam factored prominently in a resurgence of Black political consciousness, driven largely by the growing popularity of hip hop, which was dominated by Five Percenter artists and often peppered with Islamic references; a renaissance of interest in Malcolm X, due in part to the 1993 release of Spike Lee's epic biopic; and the rise to national fame of Louis Farrakhan, who led his Million Man March in Washington, D.C., in 1995. The growing attention paid to Islam in national discourses provided new possibilities for conversion. Despite the media's nightmare image of conversion to Islam in the story of the "American Taliban" John Walker Lindh, the events of September 11, 2001, actually inspired curiosity in Islam, a rise in Qur'an sales, and numerous conversions.[38]

[36] Karin van Nieuwkerk, "Islam Is Your Birthright," in Jan N. Brenner, Wout J. van Bekkum, and Arie L. Molendijk, eds., *Cultures of Conversion* (Leuven, 2006), pp. 151–164.

[37] Shadee Elmasry, "The Salafis in America: The Rise, Decline and Prospects for a Sunni Muslim Movement among African-Americans," *Journal of Muslim Minority Affairs* 30:2 (2010): 17–236.

[38] Akbar Ahmed, *Journey into America: The Challenge of Islam* (Washington, D.C., 2010), p. 305.

In the decades leading to and following 9/11, converts have increasingly appeared as "bridge builders" and community leaders.[39] In 1991 and 1992, convert imam Siraj Wahhaj and Warith Deen Mohammed became the first Muslims to offer prayers before the House of Representatives and the Senate, respectively.[40] In 2006, the Islamic Society of North America (ISNA) elected a convert, Ingrid Mattson, as its first female president. Hamza Yusuf and Zaid Shakir, leading figures in American Muslim communities and both converts, founded Zaytuna College in 2009. Convert scholar Amina Wadud, who in 2005 led a gender-integrated congregation in Friday prayer, has become an iconic figure for Islamic reform. The 2009 documentary *New Muslim Cool* tells the story of Hamza Perez, convert and hip hop artist, and provides a glimpse at the still inadequately studied phenomenon of Latino conversion to Islam in the United States.

The experience of conversion can be socially and personally disruptive, as converts often face difficulties relating to their non-Muslim families and social circles while simultaneously searching for their place in a new cultural setting. Patterns of Muslim converts experiencing "burn out," disillusionment, and culture shock within their adopted communities have inspired the emergence of institutions geared toward both mindful propagation of Islam and support for those who have converted. Ta'leef Collective, which began as a branch of Zaytuna Institute in 2002 but became an independent organization in 2005, provides "Convert Continuum of Care" (CCC), described as a "full-scale system providing step-by-step assistance from the point of a seeker's active interest, until the establishment of sustainable conversion and holistic practice of Islam, while facilitating a smooth integration into the community."[41] The CCC boasts professionally trained staff, religious instruction "specifically tailored for seekers," and a "welcome to the fold" program to nurture engagement with the community. According to Ta'leef's Web site, CCC has supported the conversions of more than two hundred new Muslims.[42] In addition to Zaid Shakir, who had converted in 1977, the leadership of Ta'leef includes three converts – Usama Canon, filmmaker Mustafa Davis, and David Coolidge – each of whom had become Muslim in the 1990s.[43]

[39] Ahmed, *Journey into America*.
[40] GhaneaBassiri, *A History of Islam in America*, p. 340.
[41] "Programs and Goals," *Ta'leef Collective*, Ta'leef Collective, 2010, https://www.taleefcollective.org/?page_id=37, accessed June 12, 2012.
[42] *Ta'leef Collective*.
[43] "About Us," *Ta'leef Collective*, Ta'leef Collective, 2010, http://www.taleefcollective.org/?page_id=26, accessed June 12, 2012.

CONCLUSION

The study of converts and conversions serves to undermine the division of American Muslims into "indigenous" (i.e., converts and their descendants) and "immigrant" experiences. Such a binary is of limited use for our understanding of American Muslim converts. Because "indigenous American Islam" is seen as essentially African American, such classification suggests that every African American convert discovers and practices Islam through a singular, monolithic "African American Islamic tradition" which contains no immigrant input. Meanwhile, the "immigrant" label suggests an Islam that is merely transplanted from another place, fully intact, self-contained, and isolated, unaffected by the American context and walled off from the influence of converts.

As has been shown here, these boundaries are not historical. For years, the leading presentation of Islamic conversion as a response to white Christian racism came through the transnational Ahmadiyya movement. Thus, an interpretation of Islam that originated from colonial Punjab became crucial to Islam's emergence in the United States as a discourse of Black empowerment. Similarly, the fortunes of the Ahmadiyya in the United States depended on those of Pan-African movements, as Michael Gomez argues that the rise and fall of the Ahmadiyya mission related closely to the career of Marcus Garvey.[44]

Master Fard Muhammad, founder of the Nation of Islam, was a South Asian immigrant, and thus further connects two American Islamic histories that are often imagined to be separate and unrelated. Additionally, the NOI's shift toward Sunni Islam in the 1970s does not occur in isolation from a new influx of immigrants to America from Muslim-majority countries. American Islam's definitive conversion narrative, *The Autobiography of Malcolm X*, has influenced the religious lives of not only converts but also born-and-raised Muslims of transnational backgrounds. The history of predominantly white converts reading Sufism through a New Age lens begins with a South Asian Sufi, Hazrat Inayat Khan, who presented his "Eastern spirituality" in a framework informed significantly by the interests of his Western audience. Finally, converts in the contemporary context who have risen to prominence as American Muslim thinkers, such as Hamza Yusuf, Zaid Shakir, Amina Wadud, Ingrid Mattson, and Sherman Jackson, do not exist in a convert bubble any more than their constituencies exist in convert or immigrant bubbles. The division of American Muslims into these neat and tidy "indigenous" or "immigrant" classifications betrays the

---

[44] Gomez, *Black Crescent*, p. 279.

extent to which each is deeply embedded within the other. It ignores the Western intellectual tradition behind Seyyed Hossein Nasr's perennialism, instead essentializing his thought as purely "traditional" Islam; likewise, it denies the transnationalism of a figure such as Siraj Wahhaj, who had first converted through the Nation of Islam but later studied in Saudi Arabia. To imagine Louis Farrakhan as completely outside the pale of the "Muslim world" ignores his outreach to Muslim-majority countries, including his relationship to Libya's government during the rule of Mu'ammar al-Gaddafi, and the ways in which Farrakhan's particular understanding of Islam engages not only American domestic racism but also U.S. foreign policy.

The indigenous-immigrant division problematically freezes American Muslims within categories that may no longer represent them. The "indigenous" label implies that even three generations after an African American embraced Islam in the 1940s, his or her grandchildren are still "converts" on some level, while a third-generation Pakistani American, the grandchild of immigrants, is still marked as belonging to the "immigrant community." Under these terms, an African American Muslim's Islam is deemed "indigenous" even if she follows the rulings of an ayatollah in Iran, and the Islam of a third-generation South Asian American remains "immigrant" even if his religious instruction comes from recorded lectures by Hamza Yusuf.

Finally, the questioning of these categories enables a challenge to notions of "conversion" itself. In American mosques, which are often shared spaces for Muslims of diverse ethnic and national backgrounds, immigrants can find their native beliefs and practices marginalized or even condemned as heretical innovations. The desire for a standardized, scripturally authenticated Islam, along with the belief in a clear distinction between categories of "religion" and "culture," leads many transnational Muslims toward what might be called "conversion" experiences, often at the hands of Muslim scholars and imams who themselves had been born into Christian homes. A new construction of "classical" and "authentic" Islam, itself unavoidably modern and arguably "indigenous" to America, becomes the Islam to which many immigrant Muslims convert.

Further Reading

Anway, Carol, *Daughters of Another Path* (Lee's Summit, 1996).
Dannin, Robert, *Black Pilgrimage to Islam* (Oxford, 2002).
GhaneaBassiri, Kambiz, *A History of Islam in America* (Cambridge, 2010).

Gomez, Michael A., *Black Crescent: The Experience and Legacy of African Muslims in the Americas* (Cambridge, 2005).

Knight, Michael Muhammad, *The Five Percenters: Islam, Hip-Hop, and the Gods of New York* (Oxford, 2007).

Nieuwkerk, Karin van, ed., *Women Embracing Islam: Gender and Conversion in the West* (Austin, 2006).

Rouse, Carolyn Moxley, *Engaged Surrender: African American Women and Islam* (Berkeley, 2004).

Turner, Richard Brent, *Islam in the African-American Experience* (Bloomington, 1997, 2003).

6 Demographics, Political Participation, and Representation

AMANEY JAMAL AND LIALI ALBANA

The factors that shape the political incorporation of Muslim Americans are multifaceted. They stem primarily from challenges in the mainstream political environment, an environment that is structured by a general climate of Islamophobia. Further, the vast multiethnic nature of Muslim Americans makes it more difficult to gain intracommunal consensus and political clout in the United States. In this chapter, we offer a general demographic overview of the Muslim American community and discuss general patterns of political participation among the Muslim American community. We consider individual patterns of political participation and also highlight the role of the mosque in structuring patterns of participation more broadly. Finally, we provide an overview of the external and internal challenges the community faces and continues to confront when it deals with issues relating to political representation.

DEMOGRAPHIC OVERVIEW

The American Muslim community stands at around 9–10 million individuals. The Pew Research Center estimates that the Muslim population is at 2.8 million. Muslim organizations like the Council on American Islamic Relations (CAIR) place the size of the community near 10 million. Most scholars who study the American Muslim community place the number at closer to 8 million. The actual number of Muslims generates significant political discussion because at the heart of the matter is the issue of political representation. Those who are skeptical of the higher number of Muslims, charge that community leaders are deliberately inflating their numbers for greater political representation.

Demographic data on the Muslim community have only more recently become available. Since 9/11, there has been a concerted effort to collect reliable data on the Muslim community. Scholars and community organizations are invested in collecting reliable data on the

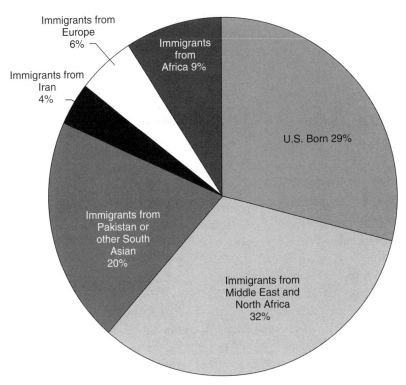

Figure 6.1. Muslim American demographics, 2011

Muslim American community in order to dispel existing stereotypes and misperceptions. Yet, other agencies are often linked to government surveillance.

According to a survey taken in 2011, 63 percent of the community are foreign born, while 37 percent were born in the United States. Muslim immigrants came from at least sixty-eight different countries. A regional breakdown shows 32 percent of the Muslim population emigrating from the Middle East and North Africa, 20 percent from Pakistan or another South Asian country, 4 percent from Iran, 6 percent from Europe, and 9 percent from Africa (see Figure 6.1). Of the Muslim population, 71 percent are relatively new, having arrived after 1990, and 40 percent arrived after 2000. Most American Muslims (81 percent) are U.S. citizens. Among native-born Muslims, more than half (59 percent) are African American: 20 percent of the community converted to Islam, whereas 80 percent were born into the faith. Muslims immigrated to the United States for a variety of reasons. Education and economic opportunities were cited by almost equal percentages of the population (26 percent and 24 percent, respectively); 20 percent of the Muslim population said that they came to the United States to escape conflict and persecution in their home country.[1] Of all Muslim immigrants, 70 percent are U.S. citizens. No single racial group constituted a majority among the Muslim American population: 30 percent described themselves as white; 23 percent, as Black; 21 percent, as Asian; and 21 percent, as mixed race. Thus, the Muslim American community is both racially and ethnically diverse.[2]

INCOME AND EDUCATION

Muslim Americans generally resemble the mainstream population when we examine their levels of education and income. More than a quarter (26 percent) of the Muslim population is enrolled in college or university classes.

Economically, family income among Muslim Americans is slightly lower than that of the general U.S. population. Among U.S. adults, 43 percent report household incomes of $50,000 or more annually, while household incomes of more than $50,000 are enjoyed by 35 percent of Muslim Americans. At the highest end of the income scale, Muslim Americans are about as likely to report household incomes of $100,000 or more as are members of the general public (14 percent for Muslims compared with 16 percent among the general public). Muslim Americans are more likely to be concentrated at the lower end of the economic spectrum. Close to half of the Muslim population (45 percent) reports household incomes below $30,000, while only a third (35 percent) of the general population reports similar household incomes.

Although American Muslims' economic status lags behind the general population, these levels of economic attainment stand in direct contrast to the experience of Muslims in Europe. Surveys of Muslim populations in Great Britain, France, Germany, and Spain conducted in 2006 as part of the Pew Global Attitudes Project found Muslims to fare much worse than their average European counterparts. For example, 53 percent of Muslims in Germany report family incomes of less

[1] Pew Research Center, "Muslim Americans: Middle Class and Mostly Mainstream," 2007, http://www.pewresearch.org/2007/05/22/muslim-americans-middle-class-and-mostly-mainstream/; Pew Research Center, "Muslim Americans: No Signs of Growth in Alienation or Support for Extremism," 2011, http://www.people-press.org/2011/08/30/muslim-americans-no-signs-of-growth-in-alienation-or-support-for-extremism.

[2] Pew Research Center, "Muslim Americans: No Signs of Growth in Alienation or Support for Extremism," 2011.

than 18,000 euros annually, compared to only 25 percent of Germans overall. A similar trend existed in France. In Great Britain, 61 percent of Muslims report incomes of less than 20,000 pounds annually, compared to only 39 percent of the general public. Among Spanish Muslims, 73 percent report incomes of less than 14,500 euros, compared with half of the Spanish public nationwide.[3] All in all, Muslim Americans are doing better than other Muslims in Western societies.

MUSLIM AMERICANS AND POLITICAL PARTICIPATION

The Muslim American community has seen a tremendous growth in its political organizations and institutions in the past century. In the mid-1920s, Muslim American representation was limited. By the early 2000s, there were more than two thousand organizations of all types representing Muslim Americans.[4]

Muslim political activism became more prominent in the 1980s and 1990s. In the 1990s, the American Muslim Council (AMC) was established with the mission to increase American Muslim political participation. AMC's goal was to increase awareness and recognition of the Muslim American community. It brought the community much needed political visibility. The AMC, for example, arranged for Imam Siraj Wahhaj of New York to deliver the first Islamic invocation before the House of Representatives, in 1991 and in 1992. Since 1996, Muslims have been invited to the White House to commemorate the Eid al-fitr holiday and feast. The Council of American-Islamic Relations (CAIR) was established in the mid-1990s to defend Muslims against discrimination and defamation. By the 2000s, CAIR was the chief defender of Muslim political and civil liberties across the United States. Having defended the rights of thousands of Muslims in the United States, it continues to be the most influential advocacy group on behalf of the Muslim American community.[5]

American Muslim community organizing often emerged from the efforts of dedicated leaders. Dr. Agha Saeed, for example, played an influential role in Muslim advocacy. Dr. Saeed had his first hands-on

---

[3] Pew Research Center, "Muslims in Europe: Economic Worries Top Concerns about Religious and Cultural Identity," 2006, http://www.pewglobal.org/2006/07/06/muslims-in-europe-economic-worries-top-concerns-about-religious-and-cultural-identity/.

[4] Mohamed Nimer, "Social and Political Institutions of American Muslims: Liberty and Civic Responsibility," in Philippa Strum and Danielle Tarantolo, eds., *Muslims in the United States* (Washington, D.C., 2003), pp. 45–61.

[5] Nimer, "Social and Political Institutions," p. 51.

involvement in U.S. politics in 1984 while working on the campaign of Democratic presidential candidate Jesse Jackson. This experience helped set the stage for the creation of the American Muslim Alliance (AMA) that he founded in October 1994.

By the end of its second year, the AMA had forty local chapters, and by 1997, this number had increased to seventy-five. The national board was diverse both geographically and in ethnic backgrounds. Board members, who must approve all important AMA decisions, represent the South Asian, Arab, Iranian, and Turkish Muslim immigrant communities as well as African American Muslims. This diversity helps assure access to mosques representing all branches of Islam.[6]

Muslim political participation in 1996 included a meeting with Bill Clinton to discuss implications of U.S. policy toward Bosnia. Clinton was seen as a pro-Muslim initiator for his recognition of Ramadan and for hosting the Eid al-fitr celebration at the White House. Hillary Clinton recognized the tremendous growth of the Muslim community and wished Muslims well. The first Muslim chaplains to the U.S. military were appointed during the Clinton administration.[7]

By 1999, nine major organizations had joined forces: Arab American Institute (AAI), Association of Arab American University Graduates (AAUG), American Arab Anti-Discrimination Committee (ADC), American Muslim Alliance (AMA), American Muslim Council (AMC), Council on American Islamic Relations (CAIR), Coalition for Good Government (CFGG), Muslim Public Affairs Council (MPAC), and National Association of Arab Americans (NAAA). Their main areas of cooperation included four major issues: the future of Jerusalem, civil and human rights, Arab and Muslim participation in the electoral process, and access and inclusion in political structures. The AMC assembled and mailed out voter registration kits. The AMA devoted its second annual conference in Detroit to political education and raising awareness in the minds of elected legislators of the presence of the Muslim community in America.[8]

National Muslim advocacy groups, such as CAIR, the Muslim American Society (MAS), and the Islamic Society of North America (ISNA) have carried out voter registration drives, encouraged mosque

---

[6]   Richard H. Curtiss, "Dr. Agha Saeed: Dynamic Leader of Expanding American Muslim Alliance," *Washington Report on Middle East Affairs*, December 1997, pp. 23–25.

[7]   Abdus Sattar Ghazali, *Chronology of Islam in America, 1178–2011* (January 2012), appendix V, pp. 2–3, http://www.amchronology.ghazali.net/AM_Chro_2012_Edition.pdf.

[8]   Ghazali, *Chronology*.

members to vote, and appealed to a wider constituency through mosque outreach campaigns. The coalition-building efforts of these Muslim organizations across mosques and Arab American groups were so effective that the unified Muslim bloc vote in 2000 is thought to have been significant in many states.[9] By and large, Muslim Americans threw their support behind George W. Bush. This was a departure from their previous two-to-one support for Bill Clinton in 1996. The American Muslim Political Coordinating Council Political Action Committee included several national Muslim organizations, including CAIR, the still functioning American Muslim Council, the American Muslim Alliance, and the Muslim Public Affairs Council. The American Muslim Political Coordinating Council endorsed President Bush.[10]

Muslim Americans see the American political system as a place where they can actively express their opinions and concerns. In a poll administered by the Muslims in the American Public Sphere (MAPS) project at Georgetown University in 2001, 93 percent of Muslims report that Muslims should participate in the U.S. political system, and 77 percent report that they were involved with organizations to help the poor, the sick and homeless, or the elderly.[11] There has been concern among Muslim communities, especially after September 11, that American Muslims do not participate enough in U.S. politics because of the secular nature of the United States. The Muslim Fiqh Council issued an extensive *fatwa* (Islamic legal edict) on the issue of participation in U.S. politics, basically stating that political participation in the United States was not only allowed but in fact a duty.[12] And patterns of civic engagement among mosque participants illustrate that this group of Muslims is actively engaged in American civic life through their local mosques.

While there are many issues that unify Muslim Americans, namely issues relating to civil and political liberties, there remain

---

[9] Analysts of Arab and Muslim political mobilization in the United States have suggested that the Arab vote and the Muslim vote have historically canceled one another. The 2000 elections witnessed a more unified stance between the two groups.

[10] *American Muslim Pac Endorses George W. Bush*, retrieved August 15, 2004, from http://www.amaweb.org/election2000/ampcc_endorses.htm.

[11] Muslims in the American Public Square (MAPS) Project, "American Muslim Poll," December 2001, http://www.islamicity.com/articles/Articles.asp?ref=MA0112-385, accessed January 28, 2012 (the Project MAPS Web site does not exist anymore).

[12] MAPS Project, "American Muslim Poll," 2001; *Fatwa Bank: Muslim Participation in the Political Science in the U.S.* (2004), retrieved October 15, 2004, from http://islam-online.net/fatwa/english/FatwaDisaplay.asp?hFatwaID=16542.

several underlying issues within the Muslim community that remain problematic and divisive. As Dr. Saeed highlights, "I also became aware that there was no internal cohesion or clarity within the American Muslim community. For a system to be created, the whole community has to be involved. There must be fundamental thinking by the community about its own mission and its own vision."[13] The multiethnic makeup of the American Muslim community, along with different aspirations of the various groups, may have been a factor that hindered political success and rendered the Muslim voice inaudible. While immigrants of Arab descent were mostly concerned with America's foreign policy in the Middle East, the African American community was primarily concerned with domestic social justice issues. Muslim immigrant populations increased substantially by the 1970s, and their immediate concern as an aspiring community was building mosques and schools. They were extremely concerned with U.S. foreign policy, with particular attention for the Palestine-Israel conflict, conflicts in Kashmir and Chechnya, and sanctions against Iraq. African American Muslim communities, on the other hand, were more concerned with domestic issues. Urban development, education, and economic and racial justice were among the concerns of their community. This internal friction in the community often stifles collective mobilization.[14]

Another factor that affected Muslim political involvement may have been the lack of endorsements by religious scholars and leaders. "Some have argued that American Muslims might be reluctant to participate and compete in American politics, perhaps for ideological reasons. While caustic debates on the merits and desirability of political participation among American Muslims were frequent up until the 1990s, the increase in the size of the American Muslim community, the realization that Muslims are here to stay, and increased infringements on civil liberties after 9/11 attacks have all but ended these debates."[15]

Before 1990, Muslims voted overwhelmingly Republican and had conservative tendencies on economic and social issues. They were strongly pro-family, fiscally conservative, opposed abortion, and did not oppose the death penalty.[16] However, in 1996, they set aside their conservative

---

[13] Curtiss, "Dr. Agha Saeed," *Washington Report on Middle East Affairs*, December 1997, pp. 23–25.

[14] Ghazali, *Chronology*, appendix V, p. 1.

[15] Abdulkader Sinno, "Muslim Underrepresentation in American Politics," in Abdulkader Sinno, ed., *Muslims in Western Politics* (Bloomington, 2009), pp. 69–95; p. 81.

[16] Imad-ad-Dean Ahmad, *American Muslim Engagement in Politics* (Washington, D.C., n.d.).

inclinations and endorsed Bill Clinton for the presidency. Muslims felt the xenophobic and stereotypical attitudes toward Islam at all levels of the Republican Party and thus felt unwelcome. The MAPS poll in 2001 showed that 46 percent of Muslims considered themselves Democrat, comparable to the general population at 39 percent Democrat; 16 percent of Muslims identified with the Republican Party as opposed to 34 percent of the general public; and 26 percent of Muslims and 27 percent of the general public were independent.[17]

BLOC VOTING

The 2000 presidential elections saw the first American Muslim bloc vote. In a postelection survey by CAIR, 72 percent of the respondents said they voted for Bush, 19 percent for Ralph Nader, and 8 percent for Al Gore. Of those surveyed, 85 percent indicated that the endorsement by AMPCC-PAC had influenced their decision. Paul Findley, author of *Silent No More*, estimated that 3.2 million Muslims voted that year. He states that 65 percent of the 70 percent of all Muslims eligible to vote voted for Bush. He believes that Bush owes his Florida victory to a 64,000 Muslim bloc vote.[18]

The determining factors for the 2000 Muslim bloc vote included civil rights issues, hopes for improved Middle East policies, and the endorsement by AMPCC-PAC. Bush's promise to halt the use of secret evidence in deportation hearings tilted the electorate scale in his favor. Salman Al-Marayati, director of MPAC, departed from his customary allegiance to the Democratic Party and had great influence on the Muslim bloc vote for Bush. However, the chief engineer of Muslim bloc voting was Dr. Agha Saeed.[19]

In the 2004 Presidential elections, Muslims supported Senator John Kerry not because of any political strategy but more out of frustration and disappointment with Bush. A Zogby International/Arab American Institute poll showed 78 percent disapproval with Bush's Middle East policy.[20] CAIR exit polls indicated 93 percent of Muslims voted for Kerry despite his support for Israel. Civil rights was still the main concern for 60 percent of Muslims polled.[21]

---

[17] MAPS Project, "American Muslim Poll."
[18] Ghazali, *Chronology*, appendix V, p. 6.
[19] Ghazali, *Chronology*, appendix V, p. 7.
[20] Ghazali, *Chronology*, appendix V, p. 10.
[21] Ghazali, *Chronology*, appendix V.

By 2004, the Muslim vote swung to the democratic campaign, a pattern that continued to 2008. According to James Zogby, in the past, Muslims and Arabs have voted along social and ethnic lines. "Many business-owning Arabs, for example, are Republicans, but African-American Muslims vote for Democrats,"[22] he said. In 2004 many predicted correctly that ethnic consciousness and conservative beliefs would take a back seat. The erosion of civil liberties and the unresolved Iraqi War and Israeli-Palestinian conflict were major issues unifying the community.[23]

According to a survey conducted by MuslimVotersU.S.A on November 4–5, 2008, 94 percent of Muslims voted for Obama while 3 percent voted for McCain. Results show that 17 percent of the voters were first-time voters and 25 percent did not vote in 2004. The Muslim vote has been overwhelmingly Democratic in the 2004 and 2008 elections, though most voters view themselves as politically moderate. Demographically, almost half of the voters were female.[24]

AMERICAN MUSLIMS AND 9/11

In the wake of September 11, American Muslims were quickly thrust onto the defensive and shared a feeling of estrangement as Islamophobia became an increasing threat. There emerged a common goal and an agreed-upon agenda from within the community to assuage American-Muslim relations. According to a poll released on September 10, 2003, by CAIR, American Muslims have increased their participation in political and social activities since 9/11. Of all American Muslims surveyed, almost half said that they increased their social (58 percent), political (45 percent), interfaith (52 percent), and public relations activities (59 percent) since the 9/11 terror attacks.[25]

The attacks on 9/11 exposed the deep misunderstandings that exist about Muslims and Islam. Mainstream America knew very little about the religion before 9/11. What little they did know was often based on the portrayals of the popular media – where Muslims were seen as terrorists well before 9/11. Through the lens of these types of portrayals, the American mainstream has come to learn about Islam and Muslims. A July 2005 Pew survey revealed that 36 percent of the American population

---

[22] Ghazali, *Chronology*, appendix V, p. 11.

[23] Ghazali, *Chronology*, appendix V, p.11.

[24] Farid Senzai, *Engaging American Muslims: Political Trends and Attitudes* (Washington, D.C., 2012), p. 76, http://www.ispu.org/GetReports/35/2457/Publications.aspx.

[25] Ghazali, *Chronology*, p. 11.

believes Islam encourages violence; another 36 percent report that they had unfavorable opinions about Islam, while 25 percent have no opinion about the religion. When asked whether they knew what Allah and the Qur'an stood for, only half of the U.S. population could identify "Allah" as the word Muslims use to refer to God and the Qur'an as their holy book. In fact, those Americans who knew what Allah and the Qur'an stood for were more likely to have favorable opinions about Islam and Muslims.[26]

Negative American attitudes about Islam in the United States emanate from decades-old misunderstandings about Islam and the Middle East. In fact, the July 2005 Pew poll found those Americans who know more about Islam are more likely to hold the most favorable opinions of American Muslims. The less informed Americans are about Islam, the more hostile they are to Muslims and the religion itself. In this post-9/11 period, one notes the continued growth of a startling pattern: an ongoing and mutually reinforcing relationship between government policies that target Muslims and tacit approval by mainstream America. The government continues to misrepresent Islam and Muslims in both domestic and international circles. The anti-Muslim rhetoric this nation consumes only increases levels of hate. Statements like those issued by Representative Peter King of New York are alarming. In 2004 King declared that most American Muslim leaders are "enemies living amongst us." He then added that he would say that 80–85 percent of mosques in the United States are run by "Islamic fundamentalists."[27] Since there has never been a comprehensive investigation of mosque leaders in the United States, these statements were astonishing, to say the least. Other U.S. political leaders, like Governor (and 2012 presidential candidate) Mitt Romney, have raised the prospects of wire-tapping U.S. mosques in order to prevent future terrorist attacks. Governing officials consistently asserted a direct and unsubstantiated link between U.S. mosques and terrorists abroad.

It is against this backdrop that Muslim Americans continue to strive to exercise their political rights and voices. When asked by the Pew survey of 2007 to identify the most important problem facing U.S. Muslims, 60 percent of response patterns among Muslims center on issues pertaining to discrimination, misunderstandings, and stereotyping.[28] Specifically, 19 percent report that discrimination, racism, and

---

[26] http://people-press.org/reports/display.php3?ReportID=252.

[27] "Congressman: Muslims 'Enemy Amongst Us,'" *WND (WorldNetDaily)*, February 13, 2004, http://www.wnd.com/2004/02/23257/.

[28] Pew Research Center, "Muslim Americans: Middle Class and Mostly Mainstream," 2007.

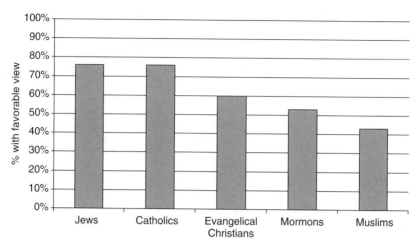

Figure 6.2. Favorability of U.S. religious groups: Pew 2009 (http://people-press. org/2009/09/09/muslims-widely-seen-as-facing-discrimination/)

prejudice are major problems; 15 percent report the major challenge centers on their image as terrorists; 14 percent indicate that ignorance and misconceptions about Islam continue to be problematic; and 12 percent add that generalizations and stereotypes about all Muslims are of great concern. In fact, 53 percent of Muslims believe that it is much more difficult to be a Muslim in the United States, after the events of 9/11. These concerns have remained stable and were expressed again in the Pew survey in 2011.

The Pew survey of 2007 also revealed that, specifically because of their faith, 37 percent of the Muslim population in the United States worry about job security, 31 percent about being monitored, and 51 percent that women who wear the hijab are subjected to unfair treatment. A full quarter of the Muslim population has fallen victim to acts of discrimination. Of those polled, 26 percent report non-Muslims acting suspicious of them; 15 percent had been called offensive names; and 9 percent had been singled out by law enforcement. Yet discrimination is not the only mode through which Muslims interact with mainstream society. A full third of the Muslim population report that they had been the recipients of support since the attacks from members of the mainstream population. Nevertheless, as the response patterns above indicate, American Muslims remain rather vulnerable to the ways in which the mainstream society views and treats them. In fact, as Figure 6.2 illustrates, Muslim Americans are the least favored religious group in the United States.

Thus, addressing this overall environment of Islamophobia continues to be a primary concern of U.S. Muslims. Unfortunately, in the last few years, especially after the election of Barack Obama as president in 2008, it appears to have become more publicly acceptable for the mainstream to disclose biases against Muslims.[29] Some of these tensions were heightened with accusations launched against President Obama that he may be Muslim. That the Tea Party and its supporters could use an Islamophobic platform to discredit the president was not only astonishing, but the response from the White House was equally frightening. The administration has consistently denied that President Obama is Muslim and has maintained that he is a Christian. Seldom has the White House questioned the accusation on its merits. What if President Obama were Muslim? The denials themselves have fed into the Islamophobic frenzy that dominated much of mainstream America. Polls taken after 2008 continue to show that Americans were biased against the religion. In 2010 the Public Research Institute found that 45 percent of Americans agreed that Islam is at odds with American values. A *Time Magazine* poll released in August 2010 found that 28 percent of voters did not believe that Muslims should be eligible to sit on the U.S. Supreme Court, and nearly one-third of the country thought adherents of Islam should be barred from running for president.[30] Further, in 2012, GOP candidates met in New Hampshire in a debate carried by CNN. Candidate Herman Cain maintained the he would treat Muslims differently from members of other faiths because he questioned their loyalty to the United States. These sentiments were echoed by other public officials like Newt Gingrich, who consistently maintains that shari'ah could replace the Constitution.[31]

Between 2010 and 2012, the Muslim American communities witnessed anti-Muslim bias spiral out of control and enter mainstream politics. Along with allegations that Obama is Muslim and political efforts to curb the influence of shari'ah law (when no such laws exist) in multiple states, the efforts to halt the expansion of the Park51 Mosque in fall of 2010 in New York gained widespread attention.[32] Further, Representative Peter King of New York conducted congressional hearings to determine whether elements in the Muslim youth population were becoming

[29] Mat Creighton and Amaney Jamal, "How it Became Acceptable to Publicly Reveal Bias against Muslims in America," *Huffington Post*, April 14, 2011.

[30] http://www.time.com/time/politics/article/0,8599,2011680,00.html.

[31] "Same Hate: New Target," CAIR, June 2011.

[32] See Rosemary R. Hicks and Akel Ismail Kahera, Chapters 9 and 13 respectively in this volume.

radicalized.[33] Many of the defamation campaigns against Muslims were mobilized by more conservative but mainstream political elements. It is no surprise, therefore, that in 2011, Muslim Americans were far less likely to identify as Republican; of the Muslim American population, 46 percent identified as Democratic, compared to 33 percent of the general population. Only 6 percent of Muslims – compared to 24 percent of the general population – identified as Republican.[34]

MOSQUE LIFE

The number of American mosques is almost as much a subject of debate as that of Muslim Americans. Often estimated at approximately 1,500, a 2011 survey counted 2,106 mosques in the United States.[35] Most mosques (87 percent) were built after 1970 and constituted a 62 percent increase since the 1980s. Within a four-year period, New York City itself witnessed a twofold increase in the number of mosques.[36] More than 20 percent of U.S. mosques are associated with Islamic schools, and mosque attendance has increased 75 percent in the past five years, with approximately 1,625 Muslims linked to each mosque.[37] U.S. mosques gather Muslims from all branches and generations, creating spaces for community and worship. Approximately 90 percent of contemporary U.S. mosques assemble congregations with mixed ethnic background. However, it is fair to say that specific ethnic groups – primarily African Americans, Arab Americans, and South Asians – dominate most mosques. Although segregated along ethnic lines, these mosques foster a sense of pan-ethnic Muslim identity. Political participation is a dominant theme within major Muslim-American organizations.

[33] Peter T. King is the U.S. representative for New York's Third congressional district and a member of the Republican Party. As chairman of the House Homeland Security Committee, King held hearings to discuss the radicalization of Muslims in America. He claimed that American mosques were breeding grounds for homegrown terrorists.

[34] Pew Research Center, "Muslim Americans: No Signs of Growth in Alienation or Support for Extremism," 2011.

[35] Ihsan Bagby, *The American Mosque, 2011* (Washington, D.C., 2012), http://faithcommunitiestoday.org/sites/faithcommunitiestoday.org/files/Thepercent20Americanpercent20Mosquepercent202011percent20web.pdf.

[36] In 1980, the five boroughs contained only eight or nine mosques, a number that expanded, according to Marc Ferris, to about thirty-seven in 1991. By 1994 there were more than seventy mosques; the number of mosques in New York City had doubled in three years. See Jerrilynn Dodds, *New York Masjid: The Mosques of New York City* (New York, 2002).

[37] Ihsan Bagby, Paul Perl, and Bryan Froehle, "The Mosque in America: A National Portrait," CAIR (2001), http://www.cair-net.org/mosquereport/Masjid_Study_Project_2000_Report.pdf, accessed January 11, 2007.

Patterns of civic engagement among mosque communities illustrate that this group of Muslims is actively engaged in American communal life through specific – and specifically mosque-authored – political avenues. The mosque, therefore, not only forms a crucial link between the Muslim community and mainstream political society; as an institution, it also serves as a civic community center, an educational facility, and a social hall. Within the walls of their mosques, Muslims gather to discuss, learn, engage, and exchange ideas. That the assault against Muslims has concentrated on mosques raises several points of inquiry about the mosqued participant's perspective on post-9/11 discrimination practices. Muslims who frequent the mosque are more likely to experience discrimination since 9/11, and it is they who feel most vulnerable. If the goal of law enforcement is to ensure that Muslim-Americans remain partners in the "War on Terror," then one would expect mosqued communities to feel the most reassurance, comfort, and safety in this post-9/11 era.

Approximately 40 percent of U.S. Muslims report attending mosque at least once a week. In many instances, the mosque remains a central vehicle of civic incorporation for the Muslim American community. Studies have found that mosques have a positive impact on political participation. In a study conducted in New York with the Muslims in New York Project (2003), Jamal found that Muslims who frequented a mosque were more likely to work with others to resolve a community problem and more likely to have contacted a local representative. In fact, mosques remain crucial to linking U.S. Muslims to the mainstream political process.[38]

AMERICAN MOSQUES AND 9/11

Ten years after 9/11, attacks on American Muslims and mosques were still on the rise. Each year since 9/11, acts targeting Muslims increased. The 2003 levels of hate crimes against Muslim Americans represented a threefold proliferation of cases of bias, harassment, and hate crimes since 9/11. And these numbers have steadily risen since 2003.[39] Because Islam is still a greatly misunderstood religion in the United States, representations of Islam and Muslims generated by the American media and entertainment industries continue to dominate conventional structures of

---

[38] Amaney Jamal, Mosques and Political Participation Project, 2003.
[39] CAIR, "Unequal Protection: The Status of Muslim Civil Rights in the United States," 2005, http://www.cair.com/civilrights/civilrightsreports/2005report.aspx.

cultural knowledge. This conventional wisdom has colored even political debate in highly ambivalent terms. U.S. politicians seem to acknowledge that Muslim Americans are a growing source of political power in the United States, and some extend their efforts to acquire Muslim votes. Congressman David Bonior, for instance, a Democratic representative from Michigan, reports, "It was once the kiss of death to be involved with that community. Now a large number of people seek their support."[40] Yet, other politicians have been less willing to accept the political support of the Muslim community. During the hotly contested Senate elections in New York, Rick Lazzio accused Hillary Clinton of accepting "blood money" when a member of the Muslim Public Affairs Council donated $50,000 toward her campaign. Leaving Muslim leaders exasperated and speechless, she returned the money to the generous donor.

Although the United States offers American Muslims unique forms of political expression and religious observance, the political climate surrounding this community remains overshadowed by the propagation of stereotypes and misperceptions. Community mobilization resources have been increasingly employed to alter the view of the American public toward American Muslims. Campaigns championed by CAIR like the "Not in the Name of Islam Petition" seem to have done very little to win over mainstream public support.[41] In addition to serving as sites for political incorporation and mobilization, mosques are increasingly becoming sites where Muslims attempt to bridge the gaps created by stereotypes between Americans and Muslim Americans. Open houses and interfaith dialogues have been initiated at many mosques across the country, as Muslims tried to reach out to members of other religious denominations and communities. When faced with local or national issues that concern the Muslim community, like the AMC call to support the USPS Eid stamp, mosque members initiate phone drives and petitions. Today, the American Muslim mosque is not only a house of worship or merely a community center; in many ways, it has also become a locus of advocacy work to address misconceptions and anti-Muslim discrimination.

ATTACKS ON MOSQUES

Attacks on mosques also appear to be on the rise. These attacks include vandalism, bombs, and assaults on congregants. Mosques across the

---

[40] Sam Afridi, "Muslims in America: Identity, Diversity and the Challenge of Understanding Islam," Carnegie Challenge (2001), Carnegie Corporation, New York (January 11, 2007), ERIC ED465008.

[41] Adopted in 2004, http://www.cair.com/ArticleDetails.aspx?mid1=777&&ArticleID=8761&&name=n&&currPage=1.

United States have become easy targets for hate crimes and often leave members of the Muslim community feeling vulnerable, insecure, unsafe, and unwelcome. Of more concern still is that the majority of the mosques are linked to full-time or part-time Islamic schools. Muslim children and youth, therefore, are often the witnesses of such acts of racism and discrimination.

Not only have hate crimes galvanized around mosques; mosques have also been singled out as government-targeted surveillance sites. In September 2005, it was disclosed that American mosques were being monitored by the U.S. government for radiation. In 2003, the FBI announced that it was counting the number of mosques within its jurisdictions in order to account for all Muslim centers. Illegal spying has taken place within mosques, and government officials do not deny that mosques are closely monitored in the United States. Some leaders have even gone so far as to accuse American mosques of harboring terrorists. Thus, the American mosque has become the focal point of both governmental and social hostility.

Unlike other religious institutions like churches and synagogues, American mosques are seen to hinder civic life in ways that undermine democracy. The mosque is seen as a threat, and the actions emanating from government officials reinforce the stereotype of mosques as security risks to American society. Mosque expansion projects are often met with fierce resistance from local neighbors. The debates surrounding the expansion of the Park51 mosque in New York during summer 2010 are but one example of the controversies shaping the institutionalization of the Muslim American presence. Opponents of the expansion project claimed that the site was too close to Ground Zero and therefore offensive to Americans. Muslim Americans responded that they as a community were not responsible for 9/11, and it was their right to have a community center to absorb the growing needs of the New York Muslim population. In the community, Muslim Americans worried about the consequences of these overt and public efforts to stifle the institutional needs of the community. If efforts to curb the Park51 expansion could gain such widespread acceptance, what would this mean for mosque expansion projects elsewhere? A CNN poll revealed that 68 percent of the mainstream American population was opposed to this project.[42] Thus, as the American Muslim community remains one of the fastest-growing religious communities in the United States, its communal needs are becoming increasingly difficult to accommodate

[42] CNN Opinion Research Poll, August 6–10, 2010, http://www.scribd.com/doc/35731051/Cnn-Mosque-Poll.

through mosque expansion frameworks. That these very vital and vibrant community organizations have emerged as key targets in the War on Terror poses great and conflicting challenges. The American mosque is not only an institution that links Muslim Americans to the mainstream but also one where the mainstream can and should reach out to Muslim Americans. Mediating mainstream attitudes toward mosques through the lenses of security and suspicion certainly hinders the pivotal role mosques play – or can play – in the civic and political incorporation of American Muslims.

MUSLIMS AND NATIONAL REPRESENTATION

The year 2000 saw at least 152 American Muslim candidates for various public offices get elected out of 700 who ran that year. Ninety-two were elected from Texas. The candidates were elected as members of precinct committees, delegates to Democratic and Republican Party conventions, city councils, state assemblies, state senates, and judgeships. Saghir Tahir, president of the New Hampshire chapter of the AMA, was elected to the State Assembly from the Thirty-Eighth District. Larry Shaw was reelected in North Carolina. Hassan Fahmy was elected to Prospect Park City Council in New Jersey. In 2002 there were only seventy American Muslim candidates running for office. Three were running for Congress: Syed Mahmood (Thirteenth District, California), Maad Abu Ghazalah (Twelfth District, California), and Ekram Yusri (Fifth District, New Jersey). There were also three candidates for state assemblies and three for state senates. Further, Dr. Mohammad Saeed was a candidate for governor in Washington State.[43]

In recent years, Muslim American groups and individuals have gained visibility as they continue to champion the rights of the community. Currently there are two representatives in Congress who are Muslim: Keith Ellison and Andre Carson. Ellison became the first Muslim member of the U.S. Congress. Both have been vocal about Muslim American issues, and in fact Keith Ellison gave moving testimony on behalf of the Muslim community during the King hearings of 2011. There are several other Muslim Americans in high-profile political positions. For example, Farah Pandith was appointed to head the Office of the United States Special Representative to Muslim Communities, Arif Ali Khan was appointed to serve as assistant secretary for the office of Policy and Development at the Department of Homeland Security, and Kareem

---

[43] Ghazali, *Chronology*, pp. 8–9.

Shohra was appointed to the Homeland Security Advisory Council, all in 2009; and Rashad Hussain has served as the United States' special envoy to the Organization of the Islamic Conference since 2010.

American Muslim candidates find a formidable opponent in politically dominant groups that have established roots and authority in the American government. Having overcome the internal debate, American Muslim political candidates have found that their patriotism was being questioned because of their proclaimed faith. Corey Saylor, legislative director for CAIR, with more than a decade of nonprofit political communications, legislative advocacy, and media relations experience, describes the challenges Muslims face when running for office as "Islamic Whackamole." He maintains that when Muslim candidates access power and begin to rise to higher positions, these candidates get attacked for their faith. This discourages many potential candidates from running for higher offices. Muslims that get elected or appointed to high offices get attacked and labeled as terrorists or terrorist sympathizers. Strong Christian-Zionist groups attack pro-Palestinian candidates, while neocons/Republicans/conservatives attack on the premise of national security issues, claiming that Muslims may want to overthrow the U.S. government if they grow in strength. In most cases, Muslims are attacked because it works. Candidates use Islamophobia and tie it to their pet issues like immigration to gain popular support. In a CNN interview, Saylor voiced concerns that "those who promoted Islamophobia poisoned our public discourse, appealing to fear and stereotypes. They promoted conspiracy theories such as the idea that Muslims are here to remove the Constitution or that our faith compels us to wage endless war against America."[44] Islamophobes have created hysteria and used fear mongering tactics to persuade the public that Muslims want to replace the Constitution with shari'ah. They claim that Islam and democracy are and always will be at odds.[45]

Conservatives have changed the tone of discussion about American Muslims. They have become harsher and increasingly more critical of Islam and Muslims. They have objected to mosques, banned shari'ah, and attacked passages in the Qur'an. American Muslims find themselves struggling for "self-preservation in the face of encroachments on their civil rights and liberties, of developing credibility as equal participants in the face of religious and cultural hostility, of defending themselves against

---

[44] CNN, "Corey Saylor: Concern That Islamophobia Is Trending toward Mainstream in the U.S.," June 23, 2011, http://coreysaylor.blogspot.com/2011_06_19_archive.html.

[45] Ghazali, *Chronology*, p. 390.

suspicions of double loyalty, of protecting labor rights from institutional ignorance or malice, and of attempting to support the rare sympathetic political candidate in the face of the formidable AIPAC-Evangelical alliance."[46] Muslims born in the United States are becoming more active as their numbers increase and they become more established and organized. The exact number of Muslims in elected positions has never been documented and is still difficult to estimate. The numbers could range anywhere from two hundred nationwide in various capacities to more than two thousand Muslims in elected offices in the United States today. There is a consensus that the numbers are increasing and Muslims are achieving higher positions in elected offices. Despite the apparent challenges facing the Muslim community in U.S. politics, American Muslims seem somewhat optimistic and united in their political goals.[47]

GENDER AND POLITICAL PARTICIPATION

Muslim women enjoy political opportunities in the United States and utilize their rights to represent their own and their community's interest. Several groups in the United States are designed to represent the needs of Muslim women specifically. These include organizations that seek to empower women within the spirit of Islam. The Women's Islamic Initiative in Spirituality and Equity (WISE) led by Daisy Khan seeks to advance equity among Muslim women and men through a more woman-friendly interpretation of the Qur'an and sunnah. There are other organizations in the United States that specifically address pressing problems like domestic violence. For example, Wafa House in Clifton, New Jersey, offers services to Muslim women in a culturally supportive environment.

A third of all American Muslim women work full time, with another 16 percent working part time. Half of American Muslim women are unemployed. This number is slightly below the U.S. national average which estimates that slightly more than 60 percent of women are in the U.S. labor force.[48]

Muslim women are as equally involved in American political life as are their male counterparts. According to the Pew study of 2011, 70 percent of women turned out to vote in the 2008 election. The same percentage of American Muslim men voted in that election as well. Muslim women were more likely, however, to vote for Obama than were

---

[46] Abdulkader H. Sinno, *Muslims in Western Politics* (Bloomington, 2009), p. 90.

[47] Ghazali, *Chronology*, p. 528.

[48] Pew Research Center, "Muslim Americans: No Signs of Growth in Alienation or Support for Extremism," 2011.

Muslim men. Although an overwhelming 88 percent of American Muslim men voted for Obama, women topped these numbers by lending 93 percent of their vote to the president. This is not so surprising, since according to the study Muslim women are more likely to identify as Democrats than are Muslim men (52 percent to 42 percent respectively).[49]

Muslim women are as devout as their male counterparts, with about a quarter showing a high level of religious commitment, measured by prayer, importance of God, and mosque attendance. They are active mosque goers and are vocal in addressing community problems.[50] A third of Muslim women wear the hijab on a regular basis.[51]

CONCLUSION

The attacks on 9/11 made the lives, political participation, and religious practice of Muslim Americans infinitely more difficult. However, the challenges facing them as a religious minority community under surveillance and suspicion has also created the need for the communities to come together on a similar platform – one that needs to address Islamophobia and the consequences of such policies and discrimination. Yet other challenges remain for the American Muslim community. First, although there are many Muslim national organizations, there is not one body that clearly represents the Muslim American community. In recent years, ISNA's efforts to institutionalize Ramadan and Eid dates have become more successful. Yet, on other matters – especially those linked to political representation – there remain multiple organizations and communities that are not in a tight coalition.

Second, although American Muslims have forged a tight consensus on domestic matters relating to the post-9/11 environment, they disagree on foreign policy matters. By and large the Muslim American community is sympathetic to causes like the Palestinian issue. However, there is disagreement within the community – especially between Asians and Arabs – as to how salient the Palestinian issue should be in matters relating to an American Muslim political agenda. In other words, some

---

[49] Pew Research Center, "Muslim Americans: No Signs of Growth in Alienation or Support for Extremism," 2011.

[50] Jamal argues that because Muslim women are more likely to be involved in mosques, they are more likely to have a stronger level of group consciousness than their male counterparts, and therefore they are more likely to vocalize their opinions when they perceive a discriminating act. See Amaney Jamal, "Mosques, Collective Identity and Gender Differences among Arab American Women," *Journal of Middle East Women's Studies* 1:1 (Winter 2005): 53–78.

[51] This is an estimate by the authors of this chapter.

in the Muslim community believe that this issue in particular can hold back the community and would rather have Muslim Americans focus on domestic issues.

Third, there appears to be a growing schism between first-generation immigrants and their second-generation children. The issues that divide the generation are not only related to matters concerning assimilation and acculturation. However, the second generation is far less likely to tolerate discrimination in the name of 9/11. Whereas, the immigrant generation accepted abuse as a way to cope and weather the 9/11 storm, the second generation has been less likely to do so and tends to be much more vocal about not tolerating discrimination and abuse.[52]

Fourth and finally, Muslims remain easy targets for attack. Given the general political and social environment – which sanctions Islamophobia and where mainstream public opinion which is very skeptical of Muslims – it looks like attacks on this population and its institutions and representatives will persist. To combat this Islamophobic tide, it will be imperative for other mainstream organizations, individuals, and government representatives to unequivocally denounce such acts against the community, which are not only injurious but hold the community back from greater political integration.

Further Reading

Ali, Tahir, *The Muslim Vote: Counts and Recounts* (Lima, 2004).

Bakalian, Anny, and Mehdi Bozorgmehr, *Backlash 9/11: Middle Eastern and Muslim Americans Respond* (Berkeley, 2009).

Bukhari, Zahid, Sulayman Nyang, Mumtaz Ahmad, and John Esposito, *Muslims' Place in the American Public Square: Hopes, Fears, and Aspirations* (New York, 2004).

Cainkar, Louise, *Homeland Insecurity: The Arab American and Muslim America Experience after 9/11* (New York, 2011).

Haddad, Yvonne, *Becoming American?: The Forging of Arab and Muslim Identity in Pluralist America* (Austin, 2011).

Khan, Muqtedar, *American Muslims: Bridging Faith and Freedom* (Herndon, 2002).

Sinno, Abdulkader, *Muslims in Western Politics* (Bloomington, 2009).

Strum, Philippa, and Danielle Tarantolo, eds., *Muslims in the United States* (Washington, D.C., 2003).

---

[52] Amaney Jamal, "Inside and Outside the Box: The Politics of Arab American Identity and Artistic Representations," in Paul DiMaggio and Patricia Hernandez-Kelly, eds., *Art in the Lives of Immigrant Communities in the United States* (New York, 2010), pp. 72–89.

7 American Muslims and the Media

NABIL ECHCHAIBI

> My ethnicity didn't faze me until I got to Hollywood, where they were like, "Hold this gun, take these people hostage?" I don't know how many terrorists there are in the world, but I'm guessing it's .000001 percent of the Muslim and Middle Eastern population. But in nine out of 10 films, those are the roles we're playing.... When I was first getting started, I was offered a part as an Afghan terrorist in a Chuck Norris movie [the 2002 made-for-TV *The President's Man: A Line in the Sand*], and I took it thinking that it would help me quit my day job. I felt awful playing that part.
>
> Maz Jobrani, Iranian American comedian

Iranian American comedian Maz Jobrani was often cast in stereotypical roles as a Middle Eastern terrorist in Hollywood films. The parts he played in blockbuster movies and popular shows like *24* and *NYPD Blue* were narrow and one-dimensional, largely reaffirming an old and relentless representational trope in which Muslims appear fundamentally different, threatening, and uncultured. One day, Jobrani decided to turn down similar roles and to focus instead on a career as a standup comedian writing his own material and parodying the place and perception of Muslims in American society. His popular comedy tours, like the *Axis of Evil* and *Brown and Friendly*,[1] have been critically appraised for their witty, self-deprecating humor and the perceptiveness of their social satire. But what is more revealing about Jobrani's career evolution is his transition from a marginal actor stuck in dull, prosaic roles to a mature artist who has somewhat more control over his image, complicating in the process the cultural frameworks that inform mainstream understandings of the Muslim American experience.

[1] In 2005, Maz Jobrani and other Arab and Muslim American comedians founded the Axis of Evil Comedy Tour based on George W. Bush's speech in which he designated Iran, Iraq, and North Korea as the axis of evil and the battlefront for the war on terror. The tour has been successful nationally and internationally playing in sold-out arenas in Dubai, Cairo, London, Los Angeles, Chicago, and Washington, D.C. In 2007 the group performed in a special on *Comedy Central*.

Kamran Pasha, a Muslim American novelist and screenwriter, also made his debut in Hollywood writing predictable roles for Muslims in the Showtime *Sleeper Cell* series, mostly as terrorists. Although such an overture made him the first Muslim writer in Hollywood, he still felt uncomfortable writing for a show where, he says, "the bad guys are constantly quoting the holy Koran," and he compared what he does to a "Christian writing a show where the only Christian lines were coming from people in the Ku Klux Klan."[2]

Jobrani and Pasha belong to a new generation of Muslim American artists who seek to challenge stale stereotypes about their communities on op-ed pages and in television news commentaries. For them, the discourse of Islam in America has been too linear and stubbornly linked to geopolitics, and the most creative way to purge it from the antagonism of politics is to weave fresh narratives about the experience of growing up as an American Muslim. Their arduous rise to fame, however, is as much about hard-fought gratifications as it is about tremendous setbacks. In 2009 Jobrani was cast for a principal role in *Funny in Farsi*, an ABC sitcom based on a comic memoir by Firoozeh Dumas that chronicles the coming of age of an Iranian American woman in California. Dubbed by Dumas as the "Muslim Cosby Show," the series never went into production despite a successful pilot episode and a Facebook page of twelve thousand fans from around the world. It is difficult to predict why ABC ultimately decided to shelve the series, but this is consistent with other recent examples of American networks equivocating about their role in bridging the gaping divide between Muslims and American audiences. In 2008 Fox bought the rights to *Little Mosque on the Prairie*, a popular Canadian television sitcom about a Muslim community in a fictitious prairie town but never produced it despite the series' international syndication in sixty-eight countries.

The mediation of Islam in America follows a tight, predictable script with timid risks and great hesitation to seek alternative stories and viewpoints. Thirty years after Edward Said's seminal book, *Covering Islam*, in which he denounced a belligerent rhetorical hostility against Islam in American mainstream discourse, the tendency to reduce Islam and Muslims to a hackneyed motif of violence, fundamentalism, and an intrinsic sense of anger endures fastidiously in contemporary media representations. The events of 9/11 and the ensuing "War on Terror"

---

[2] Eric Deggans, "One of Hollywood's Most Successful Muslim Writers Looks at Life beyond NBC's Kings," *Tampa Bay Tribune*, April 24, 2009, http://www.tampabay.com/blogs/media/content/one-hollywoods-most-successful-muslim-writers-looks-life-beyond-nbcs-kings.

further reinforced an almost static portrait of an imagined Islam that is hostile and antimodern; but amid the profound anxieties these events have invoked, they have also prompted an unprecedented public curiosity about Islam and its practitioners. This chapter focuses on the emergence of new Muslim American voices who seek to complicate mainstream narrow perceptions of Islam and streamline the Muslim presence as part of the collective American experience. Their creative response through old and new media is an ideal discursive site to interrogate the terms of Muslim media representations today and explore the transformative dynamics of Muslim media production. The cohesive narrative of the Muslim as a victim of media bias has begun to slowly fragment as more Muslims compete for the right to author their own stories and gain access to American audiences. This chapter cautiously argues that the reversal of roles in Muslim media productions like the one enacted by Maz Jobrani does not necessarily amount to a subversion of the symbolic power structure through which Islam is perceived in American society, but it certainly marks a turning point, one that not only calls into question the simplistic and uncritical classification of Islam but also ushers in an ambivalent process of negotiating American Muslim identities and experiences in a largely hostile political and cultural environment.

MEDIA SCRIPTS OF ISLAM AND MUSLIMS

In his 1981 edition of *Covering Islam*, Edward Said uses a 1979 *Time Magazine* cover story which catapulted Islam into American consciousness in the most ominous terms possible:

> The cover was adorned with a Gerome Painting of a bearded muezzin standing in a minaret, calmly summoning the faithful to prayer; it was as florid and overstated a nineteenth-century period piece of Orientalist art as one could imagine. Anachronistically, however, this quiet scene was emblazoned with a caption that had nothing to do with it: [Islam:], "the Militant Revival." There could be no better way of symbolizing the difference between Europe and America on the subject of Islam. A placid and decorative painting done almost routinely in Europe as an aspect of general culture had been transformed by three words into a general American obsession.[3]

---

[3] Edward Said, *Covering Islam: How the Media and the Experts Determine How We See the Rest of the World* (New York, 1997), pp. 16–17.

In 2010 a *Newsweek* cover showing a hazy and harrowing picture of the ruins of the World Trade Center asked whether a Muslim imam and his organization's plan to build an Islamic cultural center near the hallowed space of ground zero was an insensitive provocation. The cover story chronicled the remarkably churlish response that the idea of a Muslim building, largely perceived only as a mosque, had generated among some politicians, intellectuals, and ordinary Americans. Newt Gingrich led the charge against the building proposal, equating it with a creeping furtive plan whose sole purpose was Islamic triumphalism on American soil.

> They say they're interfaith, but they didn't propose the building of a mosque, church and synagogue. Instead they proposed a 13-story mosque and community center that will extol the glories of Islamic tolerance for people of other faiths, all while overlooking the site where radical Islamists killed almost 3,000 people in a shocking act of hatred. Building *this* structure on the edge of the battlefield created by radical Islamists is not a celebration of religious pluralism and mutual tolerance; it is a political statement of shocking arrogance and hypocrisy.[4]

Implicit in Gingrich's warning, which prompted slogans such as "Islam builds mosques on the sites of their conquests" and "All I need to know about Islam I learned on 9/11," is the imminence of the Islamic peril and the steadfastness of Muslims, including Muslim Americans, in their quest only to recreate an Islamic state in the United States.

While the 1979 *Time* cover image amalgamated the threat of Iran's "government of God" with the "powerful and compelling muezzin call to prayer," the 2010 *Newsweek* cover image, although rhetorical in its import, visually associated the proposal by a group of Muslim Americans to build an Islamic center in New York with an ideologically charged narrative that depicts Islam exclusively through the lens of destruction and intolerance. The *Newsweek* cover article, of course, did not endorse this narrative, but its highly sensational packaging of the "Ground Zero Mosque" debate joined and fed a stubborn discursive motif that interrogates the religious and cultural motives of Muslim Americans and exposes the confusion and frailty of their hyphenated identities. Even if the intention of *Newsweek* was to expose the fatuous nature of the debate around the mosque controversy, the image on the cover, much like the *Time* cover about the threat of Islamic revolution

---

[4]   Newt Gingrich, "No Mosque at Ground Zero," *Human Events*, July 28, 2010, http://www.humanevents.com/2010/07/28/no-mosque-at-ground-zero/.

in Iran, metaphorically constructed a representation that could be easily confused with reality. John Fiske points out that "denotation is what is photographed, connotation is how it is photographed."[5] The image of the ruins of the Twin Towers was recomposed to then trigger a suspicious association between the 9/11 tragedy and the motives of the builders of the Islamic cultural center.

This is not to argue that there have been no positive depictions of Muslim Americans in the news, but the frame of the Islamic peril has been largely more prevalent.[6] Of course, it would be unfair to conclude that there has been no progress in the coverage of Islam and Muslims in American news media in the three decades since the Iranian Revolution, but the label "Muslim" or "Islamic" still generates confusing caricatures and reductionist descriptions given the overall framing of the coverage of Islam, mostly around issues that show irreconcilable cultural differences. In addition to the major media event that was the 9/11 tragedy and the spate of stories it generated, including the ongoing wars in Afghanistan and Iraq and the global war on terror, consider these other prominent stories that have dominated American public opinion in the past few years: the veil ban in France in 2004; the Dubai U.S. ports management controversy and the Danish cartoons story in 2006; the runaway Muslim convert to Christianity in Florida, the Fort Hood shooting, and the arrest of a few Muslim Americans on charges of domestic terrorism in 2009; the "Ground Zero Mosque" controversy in 2010; and the congressional hearings about radical Islam and the move to ban shari'ah law by a dozen American states in 2011. At a time when alternative depictions of Islam and Muslims were few and far between, the imagery repertoire offered in mainstream media created a cohesive narrative that privileges a view of Islam as deviant and highly suspicious.

Even if Muslim Americans could speak, explain their positions, or distance themselves from acts of religious radicalism in much of this narrow coverage, their visibility in the media remained largely framed around a trope of the defensive Muslim who is only invited to react and whose lived experience as an American is perpetually perceived as in question. The same debate that surrounded the "Ground Zero Mosque" controversy also helped spawn a somewhat national discussion about the limits of religious tolerance, as in a *Time* cover article that wondered whether America is Islamophobic.[7] The article, accompanied by a photo

---

[5] J. Fiske, *Introduction to Communication Studies* (London, 1982), p. 91.

[6] Brigitte Nacos and Oscar Torres-Reyna, *Fueling Our Fears: Stereotyping, Media Coverage, and Public Opinion of Muslim Americans* (Lanham, 2007).

[7] August 30, 2010.

of the Muslim crescent adorned with the American flag, documented other less-mediated controversies around the building of mosques across the United States and asked whether suspicion and hostility of Muslims were growing in American society. "To be a Muslim in America now," the article said, "is to endure slings and arrows against your faith – not just in the schoolyard and the office but also outside your place of worship and in the public square, where some of the country's most powerful mainstream religious and political leaders unthinkingly (or worse, deliberately) conflate Islam with terrorism and savagery."[8] Citing 2009 and 2010 polls that had found that about 37 percent of Americans knew a Muslim American and 46 percent who believed that Islam was more prone to violence than other religions, the article identified a deep disconnect between ordinary Americans and their knowledge of the experiences of Muslims who live in the midst of their communities. Most probably, the suspicion of Islam and Muslims is also bred and animated by a media framework that reduces Muslims primarily to the role of the reactive, reinforcing thereby a perception of either complacency and indifference or powerlessness in the face of an overwhelmingly brutal religious force that is Islamic radicalism.

The study of Muslims in the media, however, is not concerned only with issues of representation and the shaping of public perceptions. Scholars have recently turned their attention to Muslims as agents of media production in a variety of platforms like Web blogging, social media, and film.[9] Studies of media representation, though of critical significance, tend to overemphasize the image of Muslims trapped in a structured system of signification that is impossible to overturn. While the power structure out of which public perceptions of Muslims emerge is indeed relentless, it is not necessarily static, and Muslims have become increasingly cognizant of the critical importance of media production as an effective mechanism to fight against their marginalization and otherization in public discourse. I started this section, however, with a cautionary argument to remind us of the unbaiting image of the Muslim in this discourse precisely to avoid oversimplifying our critique of the relationship between Islam and the media now that Muslims can produce competing images. The rest of this chapter addresses critical

---

[8] Bobby Ghosh, "Islamophobia: Does America Have a Muslim Problem?" *Time Magazine*, August 30, 2010.

[9] Gary Bunt, *iMuslims: Rewiring the House of Islam* (Chapel Hill, 2009); Dale Eickelman and J. Anderson, *New Media in the Muslim World: The Emerging Public Sphere* (Bloomington, 2003); Cemil Aydin and Juliane Hammer, special issue on Muslims and Media, *Contemporary Islam* 4:1 (2010).

questions emerging from the ongoing transition of Muslim Americans from objects in the media to actual producers of media narratives that challenge the terms and the ideological import of mainstream discussions of Islam and their experience in American society.

The examples discussed below are not meant to be exhaustive of the breadth of this active participation by Muslim Americans in the media, nor do they suggest that Muslim Americans never before produced their own media. In fact, the longest running Muslim publication was created in 1921 by Muhammad Sadiq, a prominent scholar and missionary of the Ahmadiyya movement who came to America in the 1920s from India. The *Moslem Sunrise*, a quarterly magazine that is still published today, featured articles on the missionary work of the Ahmadiyya leaders, introduced new Muslim converts to the proper performance of religious rituals, and defended Islam against misrepresentation in the American press.[10] Another important Muslim publication that served as a critical intrareligious voice for its readers was *Muhammad Speaks*, a newspaper created in 1961 by Nation of Islam leader Elijah Muhammad. It carried articles about Islam in the world and about the African American Muslim experience.[11] Muslim organizations in the United States also published newspapers, newsletters, and other periodicals to promote their work, including the Muslim Students Union, the Muslim American Society (MAS), the Muslim Public Affairs Council (MPAC), the Islamic Society of North America (ISNA), and a variety of educational and professional organizations. One such publication has been *Islamic Horizons*, ISNA's flagship magazine and arguably the most widely read Muslim magazine in America. Created in 1983, the magazine filled an important void in representing the religious and sociopolitical needs of a growing Muslim population in both Canada and the United States. Over time, *Islamic Horizons* grew from an organizational pamphlet into an important publication that advocated for a distinctly American brand of Islam encouraging Muslims to fully invest in American public life without forsaking their Islamic beliefs and practices.[12]

The publications I focus on in this chapter are not that different in their mission from the more official publications that preceded

---

[10] Richard Brent Turner, *Islam in the African-American Experience* (Bloomington, 2003).

[11] Yvonne Haddad, ed., *Muslims in the West: From Sojourners to Citizens* (New York, 2002).

[12] For more on the proliferation of publications among Muslims in America, see Edward E. Curtis, *The Columbia Sourcebook of Muslims in the United States* (New York, 2007); Kambiz GhaneaBassiri, *A History of Islam in America* (Cambridge, 2010).

them, but they represent some of the most prominent noninstitutional post-9/11 media productions that seek to interrupt the linear and uncritical understanding of the place and role of Muslims in American society. Their popularity today should not be seen as a radical departure from the themes and vision of earlier publications because they too are invested in a mission to help Muslims strike a healthy balance between their religious identities, American culture, and global modernity.

ALTMUSLIM: RESCRIPTING THE MUSLIM STORY

The relationship between the media and Muslims in the aftermath of 9/11 turned sour as newspaper articles and television shows precipitated an already biased image of Islam into a constant inquiry about the teachings of Islam and the loyalty of its adherents to the United States. The antagonism that accrued out of this checkered relationship meant that Muslims largely perceived the media as a trap of predictable paradigms or a powerful ideological apparatus Muslim minorities could never influence. As a Muslim American journalist based in Washington, D.C., Shahed Amanullah believed Muslims in post 9/11 America could not afford antagonizing mainstream media at a critical historical juncture when their Americanness was fiercely questioned. A few days after 9/11, he launched his blogging site, *AltMuslim*, both as an introspective voice to help Muslims critically address various faith and cultural issues and as a window to introduce non-Muslims to a new generation of well-trained Muslim commentators who do not fear or despise the media.

> There was a time when Muslims were very suspicious of the media, which is fine, but that suspicion turned into hostility: no I don't want to be interviewed; no I don't want to discuss certain issues with you; no I'm not going to answer certain questions. I wanted to create a different venue, one that didn't treat the media as an enemy. We'll treat it as a platform through which there could be an honest discussion in such a way that didn't compromise our community but elevated it and advanced it. And particularly with all Muslims, I wanted to create a venue that was equally accessible to Muslims and non-Muslims. The Muslims who were involved with the media at that time of pre 9/11 were doing so in such a way that didn't bring us dignity. It made us look like we were cowards, we didn't care about interacting with our neighbors. It made us look like we were on the defensive. We need to adopt a new position. It doesn't mean going around apologizing, coming up with excuses, or whitewashing

things, but it does mean having an honest discussion and owning up to things.[13]

Here Amanullah is articulating an elaborate philosophy of media activism that is not limited to denouncing the essentialism of mainstream media representations of Islam but is equally firm in its critique of Muslims whose media interventions prior to and after 9/11 had been rather formulaic and minimally impactful. Most revealing is Amanullah's exhortation to his fellow American Muslims to stop hiding behind a narrative of media victimization and start producing alternative discourses that would resonate with American audiences more effectively. *AltMuslim* developed over the years into a training ground for the cultivation of influential Muslim opinion leaders who could write well-argued articles about Muslim issues both for the site and for mainstream publications and also appear on television programs across the political spectrum. Amanullah and the site's associate editors in San Francisco, Toronto, and London indeed appeared on high-profile television networks such as CNN, Fox News, BBC News, National Public Radio, and the site's commentators have contributed op-ed pieces for publications such as *Newsweek, San Jose Mercury News, New York Times, Washington Post, BeliefNet, Los Angeles Times, Christian Science Monitor*, and *San Francisco Chronicle*. Since 2001 *AltMuslim* has produced more than two thousand articles and dozens of podcasts on a variety of issues, many of them on topical news events, as well as others generated from the community of writers who contribute to the site.

The editors of *AltMuslim* were keen on praising their ability not simply to follow and react to the news agenda set up by mainstream coverage of Islam. While the comment section directly addressed leading news stories, other sections on visions, reviews, and newsmakers featured new books, films, and music by or about Muslims, which might have received little or no attention in other media. Many of the articles in 2011, for example, were devoted to the analysis of the Arab Spring events, the congressional hearings on the radicalization of American Muslims, and the proposed state ban on shari'ah law in the United States. Other sections of the site reviewed films written or made by Muslim directors, such as *Mooz-lum*, a film about the coming of age of a Muslim African American as he straddles a strict religious household and a deeply polarized post-9/11 society, or books such as *Green Deen*, which details how Islamic principles of consumption and preservation

[13] Author's interview, by phone, April 6, 2011.

could contribute to the protection of the environment, or music such as the 2011 album of Malaysian-born and New York-based female singer and songwriter Yuna, who is described as a rising artist who "manages to dispel scores of stereotypes about Muslim women – their independence, their creativity, and their ability to fashion a comfortable hybrid of cultures at peace with their religiosity."[14]

Highlighting the cultural production of Muslims in general and Muslim Americans in particular has been a primary mission for *AltMuslim* that is also reflected in the work of its own staff. Wajahat Ali, the site's San Francisco associate editor, is also a successful playwright who received accolades for his play *The Domestic Crusaders*, which tells the story of a Pakistani American family as it grapples with the pressures of tradition, modern life, and the tensions of a post-9/11 America. The play premiered off-Broadway in New York at the Nuyorican Poets Café and broke the venue's box office records during a five-week run. In an article on "The Power of Storytelling: Creating a New Future for American Muslims," Ali urged Muslims to search for compelling stories in their Muslim and American heritage in order to rescript the narrative of Islam and also spoke to those who complain about victimization but do not move beyond such complaints:

> It is not surprising that African Americans and Jewish Americans, two groups who have suffered tremendously in past centuries, have arguably been some of America's most influential cultural creators. Both groups created stories drawing upon their unique experiences, tragedies, languages, and histories, which eventually became infused with the larger American narrative. If Muslim Americans can learn from the struggles of minority groups before them, we will realize the best ways to escape "our shadow" is by finally telling our own stories in our own voices and using art and storytelling as a means of healing and education. The future of Islam in America has to be written by Muslim Americans who boldly grab hold of the conch and become heroes of our own narratives. We can no longer exist in culturally isolated cocoons or bury our heads under the sand waiting for the tide to subside on its own.[15]

[14] Zahed Amanullah, "Singer Yuna: From Malaysia, with Guitar," *Patheos,* March 16, 2011, http://www.patheos.com/blogs/altmuslim/2011/03/from_malaysia_with_guitar/.

[15] Wajahat Ali, "The Power of Storytelling: Creating a New Future for American Muslims," *Patheos,* August 17, 2010, http://www.patheos.com/Resources/Additional-Resources/Power-of-Storytelling-Creating-a-New-Future-for-American-Muslims, accessed March 10, 2011.

Much like Amanullah, the founder of *AltMuslim*, Ali firmly believes that the tone of the debate on Islam in American public discourse can change only when the hyphen in the label "Muslim-American" becomes a source of storytelling inspiration. To prove his point, Ali uses the example of taqwacore, a Muslim punk scene inspired by the novel of a white American convert in which Muslim suburban kids "are just as comfortable citing hadiths of the Prophet as they are reciting Sex Pistol lyrics – all while styling their mohawks."[16] Ali also mentions the work of Sahar Ullah, an American Muslim who was inspired by Eve Ensler's *Vagina Monologues* to write and perform her own version, *Hijabi Monologues*, in which veiled women tell humorous and deeply emotional stories about their experiences as Muslim Americans. The rescripting in this case is most effective when the veil, a public issue that generates endless discussion, is privatized again and owned by the personal narrative of the veiled woman who has a unique opportunity to diffuse clichés.

AltMuslim is not the only media site that seeks to document and orient the Muslim American experience. Since 2006, *Illume Magazine* has served a similar purpose by promoting Islam and Muslims through news and the arts.[17] Other like-minded magazines, such as *Islamica* and *Muslim Girl Magazine*, had a shorter life span because of financial constraints and the lack of advertising revenues. The Internet, however, remains an ideal space for the proliferation of alternative Muslim voices like *AltMuslim* and *Muslimah Media Watch*, another blogging site where a group of feminist Muslims critique the representation of Muslim women in popular culture and advocate for a greater visibility of their voices in the discussion of Islam in America and abroad. It is difficult to assess the impact these Muslim media interventions have on the larger discourse on Islam in the United States, and it would be an exaggeration to argue that they have a definitive bearing on that discussion. But these alternative media, despite their limited overall exposure, are critical sites to understand not only how Muslims react to their marginalization but also how they imagine and define the terms of their assimilation and belonging in a sociocultural context that is not readily embracing their differences. In doing so, Muslims are self-reflexive about how to streamline Islam in the American context and mitigate those differences, but their efforts can also be perceived by non-Muslims as an unsettling reminder of the unboundedness of the established norms of consensus. In other

---

[16] Ali, "The Power of Storytelling."

[17] *Illume* was honored at the National Press Foundation Annual Awards Dinner in 2010 for "journalistic quality, balance and fairness of its work in covering the Muslim-American community." Other recipients of the honor included CNN, MSNBC, and NBC.

words, Muslim Americans are at the heart of an intense cultural debate that constantly questions the limitations of pluralism and tolerance and expands the boundaries of what it means to be American. Much like other minorities before them, Muslims have become the current, to use Derrida's concept, "constitutive outside" for many Americans despite a cultural heritage of diversity and heterogeneity that has been at the foundation of American society. Increasingly, Muslims are perceived as an alien cultural force that threatens the stability of American cultural and religious identity. Their mounting visibility in public discourse can therefore cause much angst and anxiety as it forces an edgy debate on difference and contests the conventional logic of cultural inclusion and exclusion.

MUSLIMAH MEDIA WATCH: MUSLIM WOMEN'S VOICES

Founded in 2007 as a personal blog by Fatemeh Fakhraie, a Muslim American woman of Iranian heritage in the Bay Area, *Muslimah Media Watch* quickly grew into a group site animated by a team of twenty-one women bloggers of various nationalities who self-identified as Muslim feminists weary of their unidimensional representation in the media. The site describes the bloggers' mission as one of locating and critiquing "misogyny, sexism, patriarchy, Islamophobia, racism, and xenophobia as they affect Muslim women." They declare that "we believe in equal opportunities, equal respect, equal freedom, and equal value – regardless of gender, race, ethnicity, sexual orientation, nationality, religion, and ability." In addition to commentaries, *Muslimah Media Watch* offers a weekly roundup of relevant links to anything related to Muslim women from small local newspapers and national publications to books, films, and international media. The blogging team is made up of an eclectic group of women, many of them graduate students who share Fakhraie's aspiration to counteract the stereotypical and simplistic depiction of the Muslim woman as oppressed and defenseless. The biographies of the site contributors introduce well-educated and "emancipated" women whose voices are not often heard. Among the contributors is Diana, an American convert with a political science university degree:

> Her interests include gender and sexual politics in Muslim societies and the experiences of women within post-colonial societies of the Muslim world. After converting to Islam in early 2008, her desire to learn about the religion from a more traditional perspective grew. Since graduating college, she has been studying Arabic, hadith and

fiqh, and Islamic law and methodology through an online Islamic Academy. She also enjoys reading, writing, and watching medical dramas with her soon-to-be doctor husband.[18]

One of Diana's articles in 2011 was a critique of a 2010 *Law and Order* episode loosely based on the story of "Jihad Jane," the Muslim American convert who was arrested in 2010 for her involvement in a conspiracy to aid terrorists. In it she laments how *Law and Order* joins a chorus of stereotypes where "Muslim women were depicted by the media either as being coerced by Muslim men to take part in terrorist acts or as victims of entrapment, enslaved by a religion that calls for jihad. Whatever story viewers believed, the media made sure it was one that would stir up feelings of sympathy for Muslim women, even those suspected of engaging in terrorist acts."[19]

Another prolific blogger for *Muslimah Media Watch* is Sana, a Master's student in Islamic Studies. She is described this way: "In terms of writing, she knows no bounds – topical or ethical. She is interested in issues relating to western Muslim identity formation, shari'ah in the modern context, civilizational wardrobe wars, everything hip hop, skin-bleaching and state-citizen relations. When she's not at *Muslimah Media Watch*, she's blogging at the ever-irreverent KABOBfest.com." In an article entitled "Zehra Fazal's Shock-n-Schtick," Sana reviews *Headscarf and the Angry Bitch*, an award-winning one-woman show by Muslim performer and playwright Zehra Fazal about growing up Muslim in America. Sana is both fascinated by the comedic quality of Fazal's performance and repulsed by the "shock and schtick" style of her comedy. "While the video showcased in this post is quite funny," Sana writes, "it's part and parcel of really shticky comedy, particularly with the use of the *hijab*, which Fazal does not wear off the stage.... While Fazal is ostensibly a funny person, her over-clichéd adornment of oxymoronic imagery (e.g., beer in hand, bacon strip in mouth, hijab on head) will attract only a limited audience, pulled in by the novelty and not by her humor. It will undercut what is indeed a creative mind."[20]

In similarly critical posts, many *Muslimah Media Watch* contributors challenged established discursive practices about Muslim women

---

[18] Diana, "Law and Order's Lovesick Jihad Jane," *Muslimah Media Watch*, February 24, 2011, http://www.patheos.com/blogs/mmw/2011/02/law-orders-lovesick-jihad-jane/, accessed March 20, 2011.

[19] Diana, "Law and Order's Lovesick Jihad Jane."

[20] Sana, "Zehra Fazal's Shock-n-Schtick," *Muslimah Media Watch*, April 14, http://www.patheos.com/blogs/mmw/2011/04/zehra-afzals-shock-n-schtick/, accessed April 20, 2011.

as is often the case with their critique of the symbol of the veil as a nonmodern sign of female subjugation. While they all denounce gender discrimination where it exists among Muslim men, both in the United States and elsewhere, *Muslimah Media Watch* bloggers are careful about nuancing veiling as a matter of an educated choice that is not opposed to the modern ideals of rationality or individual emancipation. The visibility of veiled and unveiled women on a blog where women speak to claim their voices suggests a different narrative where unveiling is not seen as a prerequisite for the projection of a modern identity. In a post entitled "What Not to Write: More on Bad Veil Headlines," Krista, a blogger and a Ph.D. student from Montreal, denounces the hackneyed use of headline puns like "behind the veil," "under the veil," and "beyond the veil." "It [the headline] de-legitimizes the role of the veil as part of a woman's experience," Krista writes.

> There really isn't anything all that interesting behind the veil anyway. You really want to know what's behind it? Often there's hair, there's usually a head, and occasionally a face. It's not that exciting. For those who were hoping that the veil was there to conceal superhuman beauty, Medusa-like snake hair, or secret alien antennae, I'm sorry to disappoint."[21]

As indicated in the title of the blog and in these brief examples, *Muslimah Media Watch* both monitors the failures of mainstream media in their facile depictions of Muslim women and locates the successful examples of Muslim women as narrators of their own stories in the media and in the arts. As such, the site offers not only a critique of the established narrative of the Muslim woman experience but also new images and subjectivities – a new way of imagining the Muslim subject no longer at the margin but at the center of American society. On this and many other sites of marginalized voices, Muslims elaborate not only a counter-image of themselves as both critical consumers and producers of media messages but also a rival view of American identity by calling for the appropriation of their differences and the inclusion of their social imaginary in a renewed version of the American experience. This, of course, presents some jarring implications as ordinary Americans are confronted with an emerging generation of Muslim Americans who are deeply engaged in an intellectual exercise of how to reconcile their religious

---

[21] K. Riley, "What Not to Write: More on Bad Veil Headlines," *Muslimah Media Watch*, July 22, 2010, http://www.patheos.com/blogs/mmw/2010/07/what-not-to-write-more-on-bad-veil-headlines/, accessed September 2, 2010.

values with a secular modernity. The implications are jarring because in this new self-construction of the American Muslim, which refutes a mimetic relation to Western culture, other Americans are called upon to expand their social imagination and to question their value system. Islam becomes threatening for some because its visibility is ascending in public spaces, which might explain the recent anxieties around mosque building and shari'ah law in the U.S. context. Muslims are threatening when their symbols and values are rendered public, which in turn explains why Muslim Americans have very restricted spaces where they can speak for themselves other than on the free and unregulated forums of the Internet. Perhaps there is no other space where this alternative visibility is denied than in mainstream entertainment media, which some Muslims believe is the ideal ground to invert a distorted mediated reality and restore some reason to their perception in American society. As indicated at the outset of this chapter, multiple efforts in this direction have been aborted, and much like *AltMuslim* and *Muslimah Media Watch*, Muslim comedians and writers resort once again to alternative spaces to intervene in an alienating and divisive social order.

MUSLIMS IN ENTERTAINMENT MEDIA

In a *New York Times* column entitled "Liberties: Cuomos versus Sopranos," Maureen Dowd deplores how years of feminist critique, diversity, and political correctness campaigns have failed to wipe out the most dehumanizing stereotypes about minorities in public discourse. In describing a new musical, *The Producers*, Dowd describes the comical exploitation of revived stereotypes about Irish, gays, Jews, Germans, southerners, and elderly women.[22] One could easily add another category to Dowd's archetypal pairs: that of Muslim men as terrorists or bad guys and Muslim women as oppressed and voiceless.

Stereotypes, though shallow and reprehensible, "got box office ba-da-bing," as Dowd says. While it is easy to find more complex depictions of the minorities Dowd lists in her column, one would be hard pressed to find representations of Muslims other than those of the pervasively threatening cultural "other." As Jack Shaheen demonstrates in his comprehensive review of more than nine hundred Hollywood films, the caricature of the Arab and the Muslim "has prowled the silver screen.

---

[22] Maureen Dowd, "Liberties: Cuomos versus Sopranos," *New York Times*, April 22, 2001, http://www.nytimes.com/2001/04/22/opinion/liberties-cuomos-vs-sopranos.html, accessed March 19, 2011.

He is there to this day – as repulsive and unrepresentative as ever."[23] Citing film after film where persisting caricatures add up to a neat undisturbed portrait, Shaheen builds a strong case for the archetypal "celluloid Muslim" average Americans have been exposed to over a long period of time. Even if his survey stops in 2001, it is not difficult to find continuities in representations of Muslims as suspicious enemies, perverted sheikhs, and eroticized maidens in more recent Hollywood productions. In fact, some of the stereotypes Shaheen encountered in films like 1921's *The Sheikh* and 1923's *The Tents of Allah* are strikingly retraceable in the orientalist palooza of the 2010 blockbuster film *Sex and the City 2*, which grossed close to $300 million worldwide. Here a trip to Abu Dhabi in the United Arab Emirates by four American women, who look more like colonial Barbies, is turned into a phantasmagorical time travel to a land of hidden desires, unexplainable differences, and female exploitation. Never mind that at times the words used by the actors are Punjabi, not Arabic, or that the word *niqab* pronounced ni'ka:b in Arabic is repeatedly mispronounced as ni'kwa:b. It's all an incomprehensible, exotic world where all women eat their French fries behind a veil and follow the rigid orders of their conservative men. Riding limos and camels in the desert and spending lavishly on designer clothes, the four American so-called feminist women never take time to talk to a local woman, and when that encounter accidentally takes place at the end of their trip, it is full of shallow assumptions about the real women who reside beneath that thick black garb: in a moment of climactic truth, a group of niqab-wearing women take off their veils and reveal stylish Western clothing and shoes just like models in a New York City fashion show. Here again, Muslim women are made to speak only when they remove their veil and blend with their Western non-Muslim counterpart, as if to insinuate that modesty and emancipation are mutually exclusive. The heavily orientalist iconicity of the film has been widely criticized in mainstream American media, but despite the outcry it has provoked, Muslims continue to be denied a favorable visibility on entertainment television and on the silver screen. As absent others or threatening others, Muslim Americans stand no chance in their desire to narrate their own stories and make a case for their Americanness.

Beside the typical image of the Muslim in film, the Muslim archetype on television has not been much different. It is the terrorist on the Fox hit series *24* who detonates a bomb on U.S. soil leading to the internment of

---

[23] Jack Shaheen, *Reel Bad Arabs: How Hollywood Vilifies a People* (New York, 2001), p. 2.

seven million Muslim Americans; it is the Palestinian or Somali terrorist on the NBC hit show *NCIS*; it is the American Muslim convert on NBC's *Law and Order* whose misogyny leads him to kill a woman, associating conversion to Islam with some pathologies; and it is Faris Al-Farik, the deceitful leader of a terrorist group on Showtime's series *Sleeper Cell*. While *Sleeper Cell* does not follow the typical Hollywood frame of the Muslim as the villain (one of the writers is Muslim, and the lead role in the series is of a loyal Muslim FBI agent who infiltrates a terrorist sleeper cell to prevent looming attacks), the series is still about a clichéd pattern of associations that views Muslims only in connection to the grave problem of violence and terrorism. Muslim Americans still anxiously await a more prominent and nuanced representation that reflects more accurately their lived experience within American society.

The CW Television Network came the closest to a Muslim playing a prominent role, but the writing remained mired in trite caricatures. *Aliens in America* aired in 2007 as a sitcom about Rajah, a Pakistani exchange student, and his awkward adjustment to his white host family in a small Wisconsin town. Rajah's goofiness is revealed through his difference, his frequent prayers, his traditional Pakistani dress, his accent, and his food restrictions. He evokes, as Ellen Seiter writes, the African American butlers and Latina maids.

> [Rajah] joins the long line of ethnic others who are neutralized and made "positive" by displaying their deep love and willingness to sacrifice for the hero.... To deepen the character, by adding a flaw to his unbelievable saintliness, the writers introduced challenges to his outlook on women. (He is surrounded by scantily clad cheerleaders and porn in his host home.) But Rajah softens the hearts of the conservative, consumerist family with his geekiness, his cheerfulness, and even his willingness to do housework.[24]

But perhaps the biggest damage *Aliens in America* inflicts on its audience is its insistence on denying the role of Rajah to a culturally assimilated Muslim American. Instead, the writers of the sitcom prefer to make the story of Islam an alien one where Americans are introduced to Muslims only through the character of a geeky traditional Pakistani who speaks English with an accent and requires deep initiation to the rituals of one of America's most hallowed experiences, the high school. The message

---

[24] Ellen Seiter, "A Place at the Table: *Aliens in America* and U.S. Policy in the 'Islamic World,'" *FlowTV*, February 27, 2008, http://flowtv.org/2008/02/a-place-at-the-table-ali ens-in-america-and-us-policy-in-the-islamic-world/, accessed January 4, 2010.

here is that Muslims are cultural strangers who accidentally come to America (Rajah was supposed to be a white Australian exchange student, but the exchange student agency mixed up the files) only to face insurmountable, albeit hilarious, challenges in cultural translation.

The failure of American television to broach the Muslim story through a Muslim American perspective further alienates this minority, as is clear in the example of *Aliens in America* and the backing out from producing the series *Funny in Farsi* and *Little Mosque on the Prairie*. While they wait for mainstream television to cease thinking of the Muslim story as an edgy topic, Muslim Americans are slowly reshaping their image and reclaiming their humanity through comedy. Stand-up comedians like Maz Jobrani, Azhar Usman, Ahmed Ahmed, Dean Obeidallah, and Maysoon Zayid have enjoyed a privileged position as cultural mediators of the Muslim experience to mainstream American audiences. Ethnic comedy magnifies senseless stereotypes on both sides because, as Mucahit Bilici argues, "the comic stands uneasily on the fault line, yet by standing there he becomes a sort of a stitch that holds together the two sides of the cultural rift."[25] Muslim comedy can invert stereotypes by questioning their common sense and rendering them laughable, turning fear and anxiety into humor. Dean Obeidallah, an American of Palestinian Sicilian origin who describes himself as a comic missionary, often uses a routine about his father's Arabic accent:

> I grew up in Northern Jersey in a little town called Lodi, New Jersey. Let me tell you about ethnic diversity in Lodi. You were either Italian or you were my dad. And my dad has an accent. He was born in Palestine and the Jersey kids have an accent too. So they come see my dad and they go: [Italian Jersey accent] "hey Mr. Obeidallah, what's goin' on, how are doin', what's goin' on?" And my dad is like, "I don't know. What is going on? Dean: is something on and I don't know?" And the Jersey kid says "Your dad has a weird freaking accent. Where's he from?" I'm like "He's born in Palestine" and they're like "Oh, Southern Jersey?" And I say, "No the Middle East" and they say, "Oh like Ohio?"[26]

This routine is a good example of how comedy is used not only to comment on the irrationality of stereotypes but also to bridge the cultural

[25] Mucahit Bilici, "Muslim Ethnic Comedy: Inversions of Islamophobia," in Andrew Shryock, ed., *Islamophobia/Islamophilia: Beyond the Politics of Enemy and Friend* (Bloomington, 2010), pp. 195–208; p. 196 for quotation.
[26] Dean Obaidallah, "Dean Obeidallah on The View," May 18, 2007, http://www.youtube.com/watch?v=uzRqEzhy4So, accessed March 10, 2011.

divide between Muslims and the majority society by highlighting their discordant views about each other and anchoring the experience of the comedian growing up in Jersey as an ordinary happening. Muslim comedy abounds with routines like these, which seek to minimize suspicions and play up commonalities, but despite its popularity in small theater circles, most Americans remain unexposed to this important effort by Muslims to deamplify their otherness and affirm their Americanness.

CONCLUSION

This overview of the representation of Muslims in American media and the production of Muslim media provides a perfect illustration of the cultural and political patterns that inform the relationships between Muslim Americans and their majority society. This, of course, is not an exhaustive view of the range of media that Muslims produce, nor is it necessarily representative of the ideological spectrum that informs how Muslims view their integration in American society. But the examples used in this chapter indicate that some Muslim Americans have a creative desire and ability to mitigate persisting incongruities at a time when cultural and religious tensions flare up. They also reveal a remarkable hesitation on the part of mainstream media to arbitrate this uneasy encounter as they keep reinforcing the view that Muslim Americans, at least until now, can only be spoken for by others. The breakthrough for Muslims in writing their own stories, however, should not be reduced to producing Islamophilic accounts of Muslims as good Americans or whitewashing problems that might affect this cultural encounter. As Andrew Shryock put it, we need to go beyond the "politics of enemy and friend" in our discussion of Islam.[27] This means that media depictions of Muslim Americans should capture the complexity of their experience by showing its ups and downs, its fears and aspirations, its accomplishments and its failures, and, above all, its human frailty.

Further Reading

Aydin, Cemil, and Juliane Hammer, "Muslims and Media," *Contemporary Islam* 4:1 (2010): 1–10.
Bunt, Gary, *iMuslims: Rewiring the House of Islam* (London, 2009).
Gottschalk, Peter, and Gabriel Greenberg, *Islamophobia: Making Muslims the Enemy* (Lanham, 2009).

[27] Andrew Shyrock, ed., *Islamophobia/Islamophilia: Beyond the Politics of Enemy and Friend* (Bloomington, 2010), p. 18.

Nacos, Brigitte, and Oscar Torres-Reyna, *Fueling Our Fears: Stereotyping, Media Coverage, and Public Opinion of Muslim Americans* (Lanham, 2007).

Said, Edward, *Covering Islam: How the Media and the Experts Determine How We See the Rest of the World* (New York, 1997).

Shaheen, Jack, *Reel Bad Arabs: How Hollywood Vilifies a People* (New York, 2001).

Shryock, Andrew, ed., *Islamophobia/Islamophilia: Beyond the Politics of Enemy and Friend* (Bloomington, 2010).

Siapera, Eugenia, "Theorizing the Muslim Blogosphere: Blogs, Rationality, Publicness, and Individuality," in A. Russell and N. Echchaibi, eds., *International Blogging: Identity, Politics, and Networked Publics* (New York, 2009), pp. 29–46.

8 Muslims in the American Legal System
KATHLEEN M. MOORE

The American Muslim community is said to be the fastest-growing faith community in the United States. Muslims in the United States can be of any ethnic, racial, or geographic origin; immigrants from many different countries, native-born Muslims, and converts to the faith constitute the diverse nature of the Muslim American community. Given this wide range, it is not surprising that the historical experience with the law among Muslim Americans is also highly varied. Such diversity with respect not only to ethnic or racial identity and national origins but to rituals, doctrines, and observances as well has resulted in a mixed record of encounters with the law.

APPROACHES TO THE STUDY OF LAW AND THE AMERICAN MUSLIM EXPERIENCE

Although people have offered many accounts and theories about Muslim presence in the United States, research focusing specifically on sociolegal inquiry has become more prominent only very recently. Among sociolegal researchers today we find at least three different approaches to the underlying questions that undergird the production of knowledge: the legal positivist, constitutive theory, and the social constructionist.

The Legal Positivist Approach
The legal positivist approach takes as its object of study the state and federal laws laid down by legislatures, courts, and bureaucracies, by which Muslims are affected. These studies argue that what is "the law" is determined only by those recognized institutions and authorities that have the validity to posit and enforce it. Legal positivism reminds us of the core principles of the liberal legal order – the rule of law, due process, procedural justice, and legal formality – and maintains that "the law" must meet certain procedural requirements so that the individual is able to obey it. In this line of inquiry, "the law" is narrowly conceived of as

rules and procedures, and justice is understood as rules compliance. In its critique of the law, the legal positivist approach sometimes demonstrates that these commitments have not always led to just outcomes. How is the law being implemented? Is the law itself consistent with its declared values? As a final point, legal positivism also emphasizes law's aspirational side – its effort to create safety through regulation, to redress inequalities, and to police abuses of governmental power.

Political scientist Michael Suleiman provides an illustration of this perspective when he writes about the days immediately after the Oklahoma City bombing of the Murrah Federal Building in 1995. In the media coverage, speculation abounded that we would soon discover the perpetrator to be Middle Eastern, Arab, or Muslim. This generated a backlash. "Seven mosques were burned down or vandalized" within three days of the blast, according to Suleiman, yet "local police authorities at times refused to call (or refrained from calling) such activities 'hate crimes,' and occasionally even used the incident to investigate the victims themselves."[1] His skepticism about the fairness and objectivity of law enforcement in this situation – mentioning the use of the incidents as a pretext to "investigate the victims themselves" – reflects the legal positivist approach, a view that persists in seeing the law as an apolitical institution that can be reformed so that legal needs (e.g., protection) are more effectively met. His are openly normative questions that presume that the disclosure of contradictions – in other words, the highlighting of shortcomings – will result in pressures toward reform in order to restore the congruence between law and values and, optimistically, to render law more fair and effective.

It is not surprising that the numerous experiences of prejudice and surveillance shared by Muslims (and those presumed to be Muslim) in the United States, over the past two decades in particular, have aroused considerable scholarly interest and have generated research that documents a gap between law's promise and delivery or, in other words, a divergence between "the law on the books" and "the law in action."[2] Many of these studies demonstrate how Muslims *are faring* in the face of official and

---

[1]   Michael W. Suleiman, "Islam, Muslims and Arabs in America: The Other of the Other of the Other ...," *Journal of Muslim Minority Affairs* 19:1 (1999): 33–47; citation on p. 40.

[2]   Sociolegal studies of the "gap problem" – studying the gap between the ideal of the law and the actual practices flowing from it – originated in the 1960s and 1970s out of the powerful dialectic between two kinds of knowledge, one in a renewed interest within the academy in decoding appellate decisions and other indicia of legal doctrine (e.g., the Critical Legal Scholars), and the other in behavioral research, which tries to understand the attitudes and conditions under which legislation or judicial decisions effectively guide behavior or result in desired social change. The concern is that there

societal discrimination and focus less on how they engage in a dialectic that builds institutions and channels political action. Typically, positivist or reformist studies of this type divert us from thinking about the structural factors that stimulated the research in the first place and are likely to frustrate its aims (e.g., greater justice). Generally, the greatest strength of the legal positivist approach lies in its quest for definitions, coherent propositions, and explanations based on the best available evidence, because this helps us to see whether and under which conditions access to justice materializes in practice and whether formal law affects behavior. However, little guidance is provided for thinking about the social and historical roots of power and politics in framing the very categories the law uses to differentiate by proclaimed diversities of race, ethnicity, and creed. The power of positivism is in knowing *that* something exists, but it does little to help us to know *how* something exists – the purview of the next two lines of inquiry discussed in this essay.

Legal positivism fails to ask what it is about the social order that makes problems of injustice more likely. Throughout the 1980s and 1990s, this approach underwent post-structural and postmodernist challenges in the academy and debates among activists. Although it is impossible to be exhaustive, it helps to contrast the positivist approach with the application of postmodernist thought to the study of law and religion in order to clarify and critically engage certain elements of the most common methodological approaches. The next two lines of inquiry I outline owe a considerable amount to the climate of postmodern thinking that has become widely in evidence in sociolegal study.

Constitutive Theory

The second focus of sociolegal inquiry is called *constitutive* because it seeks to understand how expectations, responsibilities, and constraints

is only a loose coupling between legal rules and social behavior. See Austin Sarat, "Legal Effectiveness and Social Study of Law: On the Unfortunate Persistence of a Research Tradition," *Legal Studies Forum* 9:1 (1985): 23. For examples of the positivist approach vis-à-vis Muslims, see Kathleen M. Moore, *Al-Mughtaribun: American Law and the Transformation of Muslim Life in the United States* (Albany, 1995); Ian F. Haney Lopez, *White by Law: The Legal Construction of Race, Revised and Updated* (New York, 2006 [1995]); Muneer I. Ahmad, "A Rage Shared by Law: Post September 11 Racial Violence as Crimes of Passion," *California Law Review* 92:5 (2004): 1259–1330; Leti Volpp, "The Citizen and the Terrorist," *UCLA Law Review* 49 (2009): 1575–1600; John Tehranian, *Whitewashed: America's Invisible Middle Eastern Minority* (New York, 2009); Anny Bakalian and Mehdi Bozorgmehr, *Backlash 9/11: Middle Eastern and Muslim Americans Respond* (Berkeley, 2009); Louise A. Cainkar, *Homeland Insecurity: The Arab American and Muslim American Experience after 9/11* (New York, 2009); and Detroit Arab American Study Team, *Citizenship and Crisis: Arab Detroit after 9/11* (New York, 2009).

are shaped (constituted) vis-à-vis the law and legal statuses, which in turn help to create the cultural meaning of those statuses.[3] This approach goes well beyond the courtroom or the police precinct to reveal how legal doctrine requires cultural narrative to give it meaning in everyday contexts. Social life is considered too irreducibly complex, overflowing with multiple and fluid determinations of both subjects and structures, to make fixed categories anything but oversimplifications that produce inequalities in the process of producing differences. The constitutive approach emphasizes the value of and methods for excavating the "ways of knowing" for persons who are subject to the law or, in other words, are *exposed* to and by the law through surveillance, harassment, and intimidation. Legal statuses (e.g., immigrant, citizen, suspect) and their attendant rights and duties are *co-produced* from the mutually constitutive relationship between institutions and the communities attentive to those institutions. Legal subjects are conceived of as active agents, and the law's meaning is not entirely beyond their control. As Pierre Bourdieu and Loic Wacquant put it, according to constitutive theory, legal subjects are "knowing agents who, even when they are subjected to determinisms, contribute to producing the efficacy of that which determines them in so far as they structure what determines them."[4]

Here accounts are of the legal subject as situated and embodied, and the purpose becomes one of seeing how individuals and groups participate as agents in the construction of their own social reality. The focus on the agency of the Muslim subject allows us to ask a variety of questions about intentionality, relations with others, and how differently "raced" bodies imbue subjectivities differently. At its deepest level, the constitutive focus attends to the role of ideas and practices in regulating social life and thus in constituting the law's subjects, and this displays an acute sensitivity to the role of language. Language is viewed as always deployed in the service of some social function (i.e., there is no neutral method of generalization or categorization), and so constitutive scholars must interrogate the boundary-making and boundary-defining significance of language itself. It is helpful to ask of any system of meaning what special purpose is being served by this particular description of the world, and in what way is the creation of categories in this form an exercise of power? The constitutive approach is sensitive to past exercises of power

---

[3] Alan Hunt, *Exploration in Law and Society: A Constitutive Theory of Law* (New York, 1993); John Brigham, *The Constitution of Interests* (New York, 1996); Roger Cotterrell, "Law in Culture," *Ratio Juris* 17:1 (2004): 1–14.

[4] Pierre Bourdieu and Loic J. D. Wacquant, *An Invitation to Reflexive Sociology* (Chicago, 1992), pp. 167–168.

that shape our contemporary vocabulary and social arrangements, as it acknowledges the stable and even durable relationships that social categories represent at any given point in time. However, it also maintains a critical stance toward categories. This approach requires that scholars provisionally adopt existing analytical categories in order to document and critique relationships of inequality and changing configurations of inequality along multiple dimensions. Constitutive scholars tend to focus on particular social groups at neglected points of intersection in order to reveal the complexity of lived experience within such groups.[5]

We can see this illustrated in early twentieth-century California. In 1913 California adopted the Alien Land Law to bar "aliens ineligible for citizenship" from leasing or owning agricultural land, ostensibly to be directed primarily against Japanese farmers. But the law's application actually discriminated against not only the Japanese but all Asians, because of the widespread perception that "Asian" farming practices presented unfair competition for "white" landowners and agribusiness. California lawmakers drew the category "aliens ineligible for citizenship" from a federal immigration law enacted in 1875, which classified "all Asians" as persons ineligible for citizenship because of their race. Nevertheless, federal courts continued to grant naturalized citizenship to *some* Asian applicants, with judges determining for themselves who counted as "white" for the purposes of citizenship. Asian Indian applicants for naturalized citizenship often were successful because they argued to the federal courts' satisfaction that they were of the same "Aryan" origins as white Europeans and were thus members of the Caucasian "race." In 1908, with respect to Abdul Hamid and Bellal Houssain, two Asian Indian Muslim applicants for U.S. citizenship, the federal district court in New Orleans, Louisiana, accepted this line of reasoning over the objection of the U.S. attorney general's office.[6]

It is crucial to note from a constitutive standpoint that the state itself produced the terms of its own contestation by forming an "Asian" identity with deep political resonance at that historical moment. Distinct practices and markers became the basis for social categories. In 1917, when the U.S. Congress enacted an immigration law that delineated a "barred Asiatic zone," immigration from seventeen countries was restricted. The consequences of this for Asian Indians already in the United States were profound. The federal government challenged the naturalization of individuals from British colonial India, arguing that

---

[5]   Leslie McCall, "The Complexity of Intersectionality," *Signs* 30:3 (2005): 1771–1800.
[6]   Moore, *Al-Mughtaribun*, p. 57.

persons who now belonged to a class ("Asiatics") barred from entry into the United States should no longer be considered acceptable as citizens, even if they already had been legally accepted as such. Renewed efforts to exclude Asian Indians steered the government toward rescinding the legal status of those already naturalized. This led to the 1923 landmark decision by the Supreme Court of the United States, *United States v. Baghat Singh Thind*, in which the Court reviewed the federal government's claim that Thind, who had previously characterized himself as a "high caste Hindu" in his successful petition for naturalized citizenship, was no longer suitable as a citizen.[7] The Court agreed with the attorney general and revoked Thind's U.S. citizenship, which had been granted by a federal court in Oregon some years before. The basis for the decision was that while Thind's contention was plausible that Asian Indians were of "Aryan" origins, this did not make them "white" for the purposes of the law. Asian Indians were marked as being outside the popular understanding of what it meant to be a "white person." Further, while immigrants from Greece and Italy may be "dark eyed and swarthy," they would, in the Court's opinion, assimilate into the popular category of whiteness within a generation or two. Yet, for a reason the Court never explains, the descendants of "Hindus [would] retain the clear evidence of their ancestry," bounded by their ethnicity as a fact of birth that one cannot imagine will ever change. Simply put, "Hindus" as a category could not ever become "white persons."[8]

In its decision, the *Thind* Court quoted the Barred Zone Act of 1917 to defend its logic, arguing:

> It is not without significance ... that Congress ... has now excluded from admission to this country all natives of Asia ... including the whole of India. This ... is persuasive of a similar attitude towards Asiatic naturalization as well, since it is not likely that Congress would be willing to accept as citizens a class of persons whom it rejects as immigrants.[9]

As a consequence, not only did Thind lose his citizenship, but the decision triggered litigation that stripped many others of their naturalization, and the legal status of a class of persons previously accepted under the law was profoundly altered. Federal courts began to rely on the *Thind*

---

[7] See *U.S. v. Baghat Singh Thind*, 261 U.S. 204, 1923.
[8] See Moore, *Al-Mughtaribun*, pp. 57–59.
[9] Kathleen M. Moore, "Pakistani Immigrants," in Ron Bayor, ed., *Multicultural America: An Encyclopedia of the Newest Americans*, vol. 3 (Santa Barbara, 2011), p. 1666.

ruling in cases involving Arab, Syrian, Persian, and Afghani applicants for citizenship.[10] These subjects of the law where mobilized to counter their exclusion but never *the terms* of their exclusion. Many challenged their personal exclusion because they could in fact be construed as "white by law," but in so doing, they sustained the very logic of exclusion and selective inclusion along racial and ethnic lines. This shows the precarious position many immigrants from the Muslim world were found in in the first decades of the twentieth century. In the United States, "Hindu" was a racial appellation and not a religion, part of the Western colonial discourse on race, religion, civilization, and empire. Terms such as "Mohammedan," "Turk," and "Moor" were similarly used to consign persons to an inferior status.[11] Including questions of religion, caste, geography, and descent as part of the assessment of Thind's legal "whiteness" – whatever its inaccuracies, complexities, and implications – reaffirms the sociohistorical embeddedness of racial categorization.[12] The consequences of the decision were widespread and affected Muslims in the United States at least until Congress effectively reversed the *Thind* decision by legislation in 1946 and allowed immigration and naturalization from Asia to resume.[13]

Social Construction

The third line of inquiry is the constructionist school of thought.[14] This kind of study considers how certain phenomena or objects of

[10] See Moore, *Al-Mughtaribun*, pp. 43–67.

[11] An interesting aside is related by Thomas S. Kidd in *American Christians and Islam: Evangelical Culture and Muslims from the Colonial Period to the Age of Terrorism* (Princeton, 2009) about late nineteenth-century American Christian evangelicals and observers of Islam, who "made a pseudo-science of discerning the ostensible intellectual and moral characteristics of the world's races" (p. 44). As to the Middle East, for example, Joel Hawes, a pastor in Hartford, Connecticut, thought it was relevant to distinguish the Turks' race from their religion. The Turks were in his estimation "naturally" a noble race and Islam was "a dreadful curse" upon their empire (ibid.).

[12] See Lopez, *White by Law*, p. 62.

[13] For example, in 1942 a district judge in Michigan ruled that a Yemeni Muslim named Ahmed Hassan was ineligible for naturalized citizenship because of the combination of race and religion: "Apart from the dark skin of the Arabs, it is well known that they are part of the Mohammedan world and that a wide gulf separates their culture from the predominantly Christian peoples of Europe." Furthermore, dark skinned Muslims were not among the people living in the United States who were recognized as "white persons" at the time of the adoption of the Naturalization Act of 1790. *In re Ahmed Hassan*, 48 F. Supp. 843 (1941).

[14] See Erik Love, "Confronting Islamophobia in the United States: Framing Civil Rights Activism among Middle Eastern Americans," *Patterns of Prejudice* 43:3–4 (2009): 401–425; Sherene H. Razack, *Casting Out: The Eviction of Muslims from Western Law and Politics* (Toronto, 2008).

consciousness develop from larger historical practices, within particular contexts of time and place. From this perspective, because the Muslim legal subject is not a *fixed* category, it must be established and continuously maintained and confirmed by social interactions in order to persist. So, for instance, the eighteenth- and nineteenth-century perception of the Muslim (or, more commonly, the "Mahometan") as Turk, Saracen, or Moor is just as much a product of the social intercourse of its time period as the twentieth- and twenty-first-century construction of the Muslim as Arab, extremist, or jihadi, though there is a discontinuity between these more or less related but strongly contrasting forms, which are indexed to the problem of order. In this general framework, around the theme of social order, both constructions require, and perform, considerable ideological work to make and maintain their significance. In the constructionist approach, the legal subject is studied not only or primarily through material experience but through *discourse*. The legal significance of "Muslim" is incessantly renegotiated through the discursive dynamics that define everything from legal and racial categories to the criteria used to assign people to constructed categories and the characteristics attributed to those racialized groups.

Both the constitutive and the social constructionist approaches owe an intellectual debt to postmodernist thought. Because both developments can be traced to what arguably has been the defining characteristic of research in this area, it is important here to draw some distinctions, at the risk of overstating the difference. Postmodernism in the mid-1980s had us question the unitary nature of any particular subjectivity and the concepts of autonomy, choice, and freedom, arguing instead that factors of race, geographic location, historicity, class, sexuality, and gender, among others, contribute in multiple and contradictory ways to the creation of a subjectivity and the meaning of the subject's activity. Postmodernist writings had quite an impact in shaping legal inquiry about the social nature of power, positing that the individual subject acts in a discursive field only within a complex, historically delimited set of options. Power is supple and has a productive role in shaping consciousness and subjectivity. Relations of power emanate not from a substantive and invasive source (e.g., domination) but in the procedures by which people's conduct is governed. And, relatedly, forms resistant to governmentality are multiple and operate contingently, inscribed in relations of power as an irreducible opposite.[15] Thus, Michel Foucault famously posits that

---

[15] Michel Foucault, *The History of Sexuality*, vol. 1: *An Introduction* (New York, 1978), p. 96.

power and resistance oscillate, functioning only when they are a part of a chain in which the subject both submits to and can exercise power.[16]

When American Muslim inmates demanded the right to communal prayer in prison,[17] or to have access to clergy from outside organizations,[18] they were organizing important relations within a captive network in ways that allowed them to imagine the possibility of religious liberty. In the prisoners' rights movement of the 1960s and 1970s, in which various Muslim inmates achieved significant victories, certain shifts in the discursive field – in the techniques and tactics of domination – permitted the articulation of demands that previously would not have been intelligible. These claims resisted the state's denial of freedom while operating within the reality of incarceration. Muslim prisoners' resistance of the conditions of their confinement led them to gain access to the courts, where inmates could challenge their treatment at the hands of prison authorities. According to this perspective, the juristic doctrine resulting from the Muslims' active participation emerged from a certain type of speech (a civil rights discourse) and reaffirmed the authority of the very institutions in position to control and distribute rights. Here we can see that the political instantiation of liberal philosophy (the autonomy of a rights-bearing citizen) and power (authority to limit freedoms in prison) are coterminous.[19] The discursive forces that allow the onset of rights claims are the same forces that create the justifying and explanatory authority to do so.

As demonstrated in the prisoners' rights cases fought on behalf of Muslim inmates, Otherness exists along both racial and religious grounds, and an important way to understand the highly varied experiences of American Muslims with the law is to examine the normative racial stratification system in the United States. The social constructionist approach holds that Muslim identity is racialized because it is constructed by the state as a form of *alterity* – an inassimilable other. In this line of sociolegal inquiry, the focus is on how the Muslim subject narrates her or his experiences into the framework of racial hierarchy and interprets various religious understandings and practices in

---

[16] Michel Foucault, *"Society Must Be Defended": Lectures at the College de France, 1975–76* (New York, 2003), p. 79.

[17] *O'Lone v. Shabazz*, 107 S.Ct. 2400, 1987.

[18] *Walker v. Blackwell*, 411 F.2d 23, 5th Cir., 1969.

[19] Michel Foucault, *Discipline and Punish*, trans. Alan Sheridan (New York, 1979), p. 201. See also discussion in Joshua Foa Dienstag, "Postmodern Approaches to the History of Political Thought," in George Klosko, ed., *The Oxford Handbook of the History of Political Philosophy* (New York, 2011), pp. 36–46.

relation to the dominant institutional arrangements that have shaped American society throughout the years. As such, this *relational* argument requires investigating the ways in which American Muslims (a fragmentary identification), in describing themselves as Muslim, have coped with racial classification and racial oppression. Their subjectivities have been transformed through their engagement with certain ways of knowing and being.

Nowadays, of course, it is highly controversial to think of racialized groups as biologically inferior. Yet dominant groups often perceive of minority groups as possessing *cultures* that are inferior. For instance, Islam is often viewed as overly patriarchal and invariantly a violent religion.[20] To take a small example, consider how Islamophobia operates as a pattern in which skin color, attire, and other physical markers become the basis for stereotypes and discrimination. This is not just a fear of Muslims or Islam but a phenomenon that is tied to American racism, even though it is not often identified as a racial problem at all. How do American Muslims respond to Islamophobia? How organizers may provisionally utilize their popularly recognizable, type-casted, and marginalized identity to increase unity and strength in numbers is a key element to understanding the varied experiences of American Muslims with the law. The theoretical and analytical frameworks shaping the research in this area draw on sociolegal concepts to explain phenomena such as discrimination, identity formation, and culture and legal consciousness linked to agency in order to account for how American Muslims simultaneously construct, inhabit, and move between different groups and contexts and their apparently "different" and "contradictory" behavior in this process.

Islam's increasingly public presence during the twentieth century became both a source of irritation and a challenge to popular ideas of American national identity when American Muslims began to point out the race and class divisions in society and to suggest Islam as the solution. Historian Thomas Kidd tells us that G. H. Bousquet, a scholar of Muslim law and Christian evangelist, warned in the pages of the *Moslem World*[21] in 1935 that Islam in the United States could "play here a magnificent trump: namely, the far greater *real* equality of races in Islam than that existing in Christian America."[22] This was a perceptive observation, as

---

[20] For a discussion of the culturalization of racism in North America, see Razack, *Casting Out*, pp. 171–180.

[21] Founded in 1911, this was the leading periodical in the United States devoted originally to the evangelization of Muslims around the world, though its objective has changed over time.

[22] Cited in Kidd, *American Christians and Islam*, p. 96.

African American advocates of Islam in the 1930s progressively featured the proclaimed race blindness of Islam as a means to critique dominant white Christian society. Islam was framed as a suitable alternative a religion benefiting the oppressed races and superior in terms of the aims of Black nationalism. Seen most notably in the career of Malcolm X, Islam could feed alternatively into a racial separatist mode of thought (when a disciple of the Minister Elijah Muhammad) or an inclusive mode (as expressed after Malcolm's transformational hajj).[23]

The process of racial formation, of "whitening" or "blackening," is not yet completely understood as it relates to many Muslim immigrants to the United States and their native-born offspring, not to mention converts of various ethnic and racial backgrounds. Increasing numbers of scholars have debated whether "being Muslim" in the United States constitutes a new racial formation.[24] For instance, Nadine Naber argues that historically Arab Americans have been simultaneously classified as white and nonwhite and have been racialized by religion (Islam) instead of biology.[25] Other scholars have examined the experiences of South Asians,[26] Iranians,[27] and others[28] and have consistently found that, in the case of Islam, religious identity serves as a malleable and important means of structuring systemic inequality. In many situations those identified as Muslims experience discrimination in ways that are comparable to the experiences of racial minorities. Assaults on the civil rights of Muslims after September 11 are just one example of the subordination of Muslims *as Muslims*, and it would seem that "being Muslim"

---

[23] Kidd, *American Christians and Islam*, p. 98.

[24] For instance, Love, "Confronting Islamophobia in the United States"; Michelle D. Byng, "Complex Inequalities: Muslim Americans after 9/11," *American Behavioral Scientist* 51:5 (2008): 659–674; and Lori Peek, "Becoming Muslim: The Development of a Religious Identity," *Sociology of Religion* 66:3 (2005): 215–242.

[25] Nadine Naber, "Ambiguous Insiders: An Investigation of Arab-American Invisibility," *Ethnic and Racial Studies* 23:1 (2000): 37–61.

[26] For instance, Nazli Kibria, "Not Asian, Black or White? Reflections on South Asian American Racial Identity," *Amerasia Journal* 22:2 (1996): 77–86; Nazli Kibria, "The 'New Islam' and Bangladeshi Youth in Britain and the U.S.," *Ethnic and Racial Studies* 31:2 (2007): 243–266; and Sunaina Maira, *Missing: Youth, Citizenship, and Empire after 9/11* (Durham, 2009).

[27] For instance, Nilou Mostofi, "Who We Are: The Perplexity of Iranian-American Identity," *Sociological Quarterly* 44:4 (2003): 681–703; and Kambiz GhaneaBassiri, *Competing Visions of Islam in the United States: A Study of Los Angeles* (New York, 1997).

[28] For instance, M. Shoeb, H. M. Weinstein, and J. Halpern, "Living in Religious Time and Space: Iraqi Refugees in Dearborn, Michigan," *Journal of Refugee Studies* 20:3 (2007): 441–460; and Pamela A. De Voe, "Symbolic Action: Religion's Role in the Changing Environment of Young Somali Women," *Journal of Refugee Studies* 15:2 (2002): 234–246.

is a significant factor in positioning subjects within the U.S. racial stratification system.

CONCLUDING REFLECTIONS

Sociolegal inquiry into the American Muslim experience with American law is a relatively new endeavor though a remarkably rich one. Interrogations of criminal justice and prisoners' rights, immigration and naturalization, and equal opportunity have been the staples of critical examination. Whether popularly perceived at the turn of the twentieth century as a Turk, Moor, or Hindu; at mid-twentieth century as a Black separatist; or a jihadist in the twenty-first century, the Muslim as legal subject has been construed differently across time, according to the discursive practices at the root of social life in a particular time and place.

After September 11, the field of study has been widened to take into its scope significant developments in national security law and women's rights. These areas are considered here in turn.

Domestic Counterterrorism and Preemptive Punishment

Though the "War on Terror" was officially inaugurated by George W. Bush, the number of indictments for jihadist-related offenses in the United States nearly doubled in the first two years of the Barack Obama Administration.[29] This would suggest that the problem of "homegrown terrorism" is on the rise and has led law enforcement, intelligence, and homeland security officials to anticipate and intervene early against alleged terrorist conspiracies. The task of addressing "the ascendancy of homegrown terrorism" took center stage shortly after an uptick in terrorist plots executed in late 2009 to early 2010 and prompted the White House to release the National Security Strategy in May 2010 to "underscore the threat to the United States and our interests posed by individuals radicalized at home."[30]

[29] Center on Law and Security, "Terrorist Trial Report Card: September 11, 2001–September 11, 2011," New York University School of Law, 2011, retrieved on September 2, 2011, from http://www.lawandsecurity.org/Portals/0/Documents/TTRCpercent20Tenpercent20Yearpercent20Issue.pdf.
[30] White House, National Security Strategy (2010), p. 19, retrieved on May 19, 2011, from http://www.whitehouse.gov/sites/default/files/rss_viewer/national_security_strategy.pdf. It is noteworthy that, in spite of its disparate impact on persons who are deemed to be Muslim, Arab, or Middle Eastern, the document maintains that U.S. national security strategy "is not a global war against a tactic – terrorism or a religion – Islam" (ibid.).

The preemptive approach the government has adopted for its national security program has relied on questionable tactics to identify domestic terrorist threats. One tactic has been racial profiling, and another has been the reliance on "religious speech" to signal the intention to commit or abet violence. An example of the latter is the so-called *throat note* found in the wallet of Hamid Hayat, a Californian of Pakistani descent, who was convicted of material support for terrorism because the note – which the prosecution translated from Arabic as reading, "Lord, let us be at their throats, and we ask you to give us refuge from their evil" – could be read in only one way. According to the prosecution's expert witness, this was a prayer "used by Muslim fanatics and extremists that consider themselves to be in a state of war with the rest of the world or their own government." On the basis of this scant evidence of his intent to commit a future offense, the prosecution summarized the case against Hayat by invoking the throat note to show that he had "a jihadi heart and a jihadi mind" and "the requisite jihadist intent." The note and other religious speech in Hayat's possession at the time of his arrest persuaded the jury to convict him in 2006. In fact, after the trial the jury foreman explained that the throat note and related expert testimony had been "quite critical" in convincing the jury of his guilt.[31]

The increasing prospect of homegrown terrorism has legitimized the views of several national security experts and task force members who since September 11 have advised a restrictive approach in spite of the costs to civil liberties generally and for American Muslim communities in particular. For instance, several expert reports of this type argue that until recently American Muslim communities have been relatively resistant to the kind of homegrown forms of terrorism that have troubled Western Europe, owing to American Muslims' greater integration into mainstream society. But by 2009, the impact of Al-Qaeda's argument that the global war on terror (GWOT) is actually a war on Islam began to "bear fruit" in the form of domestic sources of jihadist-related offenses (e.g., the arrest of Najibullah Zazi, an airport shuttle driver in Colorado, for conspiracy to use weapons of mass destruction, and of U.S. Army major Nidal Malik Hassan for an attack on Fort Hood, killing thirteen and wounding thirty). Similarly, Congressman Peter King (R-NY), chair

---

[31] For citations and further discussion, see Aziz Z. Huq, "The Signaling Function of Religious Speech in Domestic Counterterrorism," *Texas Law Review* 89:1 (2010): 833–900, at pp. 842–844.

of the House Homeland Security Committee, held controversial hearings called "Radicalization of Muslim Americans" in 2011, using unsubstantiated claims that 80 to 85 percent of the mosques and Islamic centers in the United States are controlled by Islamic fundamentalists to justify his political aims.[32]

Contrary to this perspective, however, a study by the Triangle Center on Terrorism and Homeland Security disputes these figures, arguing instead that homegrown terrorism is a serious *but limited* problem. Moreover, the practices of American Muslim communities – namely, self-policing, public denunciations of terrorist violence, civic engagement, and community building – help to prevent and address instances of radicalization. Moreover, the Triangle Center on Terrorism and Homeland Security has shown that documented cases of homegrown terrorism have declined of late, resulting in twenty arrests in 2011, down from twenty-six in 2010.[33] The problem with instances of domestic terrorism is the massive publicity that they engender, provoking fear and anti-Muslim sentiment in the American public.[34]

A productive line of sociolegal inquiry lies at the intersection of reports provided by a range of think tanks and research centers on domestic counterterrorism. In 2007 a homeland security official told the House Intelligence Committee that domestic "radicalization challenges" had prompted the creation of a new unit in the Department of Homeland Security specifically focused on homegrown terrorist threats, which might explain the increase in the number of jihadist-related indictments reported in the first two years of the Obama administration.[35] Scholars and analysts are gaining a better understanding of this correlation between institutional efforts to ramp up the prosecution of terrorism in the criminal justice system and the Muslim American lived experience with the law.

[32] See House Committee on Homeland Security, Rep. Peter T. King Holds a Hearing Entitled: "The Extent of Radicalization in the American Muslim Community and That Community's Response," March 10, 2011.

[33] Charles Kurzman, "Muslim-American Terrorism in the Decade Since 9/11," Triangle Center on Terrorism and Homeland Security, 2011, retrieved on April 20, 2012, from http://sanford.duke.edu/centers/tcths/documents/Kurzman_Muslim-American_Terrorism_in_the_Decade_Since_9_11.pdf.

[34] David Schanzer, Charles Kurzman, and Ebrahim Moosa, "Anti Terror Lessons of Muslim-Americans," Triangle Center on Terrorism and Homeland Security, 2010, p. 1, retrieved on July 15, 2011, from http://sanford.duke.edu/centers/tcths/documents/Anti-TerrorLessonsfinal.pdf.

[35] See Huq, "The Signaling Function of Religious Speech in Domestic Counterterrorism," p. 841.

Women's Rights

Muslims in the United States are confronted with the dominant paradigm in liberal democratic theory, which is based on modern rationality and the privatization of religious practice. This paradigm maintains that family law, including the personal status of women, is an aspect of private religion and is constitutive, categorically, of *the* (monolithic) Muslim way of life. So, for instance, when women seek to dress in accordance with what they interpret to be Islamic prescriptions about modesty and solidarity, they find themselves to be caught between the prevailing standards, which require greater conformity with a secular vision of America, and their personal convictions.[36]

Contests such as these are nowhere more apparent than in American courts of law. There are divergent views among Muslims about whether Islam requires women to dress in a particular way, and those views are especially pronounced in a religiously diverse and publicly secularized society such as the United States. Many issues about dress codes and similar bans on wearing hijab in public have resulted in court trials. Since September 11 in particular, women in hijab have become focal points for anti-Muslim sentiment, ranging from hate crimes to discrimination in employment, education, and transportation, as illustrated in several court cases. To name just a few, a landmark ruling was reached in the appeals case of Bilan Nur, who sued her employer, Alamo Rent-a-Car, because she was denied permission to cover her head during the month of Ramadan only after 2001 (she had been permitted to do so before the September 11 attacks). The court ruled in Ms. Nur's favor, setting an important precedent for working women who dress in particular ways for religious reasons. Another highly publicized trial that also went to an appellate court was the case of Sultaana Freeman, the Florida resident who wished to have a photo-less driver's license. One had been issued to her before 2001, but the Florida Department of Motor Vehicles suspended this license and required Ms. Freeman to replace it with a license affixed with a photograph showing her face for security purposes. The trial court judge ruled in favor of the state, ruling that while Freeman "most likely poses no threat to national security, there likely are people who would be willing to use a ruling permitting the

---

[36] Like the problem of overstating the popularity of jihadist ideology and violence among American Muslims, the phenomenon of wearing hijab is problematic not for its numbers but for what it symbolizes. Most Muslim women, in the United States as elsewhere, do *not* wear the headscarf. But the matter has become one of freedom for public displays of religiosity and faith that goes beyond the question of "how many" are affected by legal constraints.

wearing of a full-face cloak in a driver's license photo by pretending to ascribe to religious beliefs in order to carry out activities that would threaten lives."[37] The court of appeals affirmed the judge's ruling, stating that national security concerns outweigh the individual's interest in religious liberty when it comes to Islam. Civil cases such as these, which affect women in the workplace, in transportation, education, and the military, and in marriage and divorce cases, among others, are investigated by sociolegal scholars and are important because of the cultural generalization that Islam is irremediably patriarchal.

To summarize, no single narrative can capture the varied American Muslim experience with the law. Recent studies of this experience take three general approaches: the legal positivist, the law-as-constitutive, and the social constructionist. Sociolegal scholars concerned with doing research that would reduce inequality first asked, Does the law as it is applied square with the law on the books? But soon the question became, How do our theories and ways of doing research change if we assume the legal subject has the capacity to do more than resist? The task for the scholar is to see what lies underneath different lived experiences and legalities – to expose the ways in which law and policy, which often appear neutral or rational, contribute to a particular, normative representation of social reality. Such an exploration draws attention to the ways that the law produces and shapes the meaning of race and religion and its role in making such identities politically salient.

Further Reading

American Civil Liberties Union, *Blocking Faith, Freezing Charity: Chilling Muslim Charitable Giving in the "War on Terrorism Financing."* Retrieved November 15, 2009, from http://www.aclu.org/human-rights-national-security/blocking-faith-freezing-charity.

Amnesty International, *Threat and Humiliation: Racial Profiling, Domestic Security, and Human Rights in the United States*, U.S. Domestic Rights Program of Amnesty International (New York, 2004). Retrieved August 18, 2011, from http://www.amnestyusa.org/pdfs/rp_report.pdf.

Cole, David, *Enemy Aliens: Double Standards and Constitutional Freedoms in the War on Terrorism* (New York, 2005).

Constitution Project, *Report on Post-9/11 Detention*, Georgetown University Public Policy Institute (Washington, D.C., 2004). Retrieved June 4, 2010, from http://www.constitutionproject.org/pdf/57.pdf.

Fournier, Pascale, *Muslim Marriage in Western Courts: Lost in Transplantation* (Surrey, 2010).

[37] Cited in Kathleen M. Moore, *The Unfamiliar Abode: Islamic Law in the United States and Britain* (New York, 2010), p. 134.

Freedland, Richard, "The Treatment of Muslims in American Courts," *Islam and Christian-Muslim Relations* 12:4 (2001): 449–463.

GhaneaBassiri, Kambiz, *A History of Islam in America: From the New World to the New World Order* (Cambridge, 2010).

Ghori, Safiya, "The Application of Religious Law in North American Courts: A Case Study of Mut'a Marriages," *Journal of Islamic Law and Culture* 10:1 (2008): 29–40.

Gualtieri, Sarah M. A., *Between Arab and White: Race and Ethnicity in the Early Syrian American Diaspora* (Berkeley, 2009).

MacFarlane, Julie, *Islamic Divorce in North America: A Shari'ah Path in a Secular Society* (New York, 2012).

Moore, Kathleen M., *The Unfamiliar Abode: Islamic Law in the United States and Britain* (New York, 2010).

Peek, Lori, *Behind the Backlash: Muslim Americans after 9/11* (Philadelphia, 2011).

Razack, Sherene, *Casting Out: The Eviction of Muslims from Western Law and Politics* (Toronto, 2008).

9 Religious Pluralism, Secularism, and Interfaith Endeavors

ROSEMARY R. HICKS

PRESSURES UNDER SECULAR PLURALISM TO MAKE INTERFAITH ALLIES

On Wednesday, October 13, 2010, Brooklyn Orthodox Rabbi Yehuda Levin called a press conference to announce that he was withdrawing his support from New York Republican gubernatorial candidate Carl Paladino. The decision was due to what Rabbi Levin described as Paladino's political flip-flopping, or, in his exact words, to Paladino having "folded like a cheap camera." In a speech to Levin's congregation the week prior, Paladino had spoken against gay marriage and homosexual "brainwashing" but later apologized to his gay constituents and to his gay nephew and staff member for his insensitivity. In response, Levin called a press conference, though not at his synagogue, Brooklyn's City Hall, or even in the state capitol. Instead, Levin made his announcement on the steps of St. Patrick's Cathedral in Manhattan with the hopes that doing so would spur Catholic Archbishop Timothy Dolan to join him in creating a more politically weighty interreligious alliance.[1]

Neither Archbishop Dolan nor Paladino responded to Rabbi Levin's proposals on that occasion. However, both weighed in on another controversial issue of the 2010 election cycle: Park51, a proposed Islamic Center modeled on the YMCA and JCC (Jewish Community Center) that Imam Feisal Abdul Rauf of the Cordoba Initiative, Daisy Khan of the ASMA Society, and Sharif el-Gamal of Soho Properties planned to build in lower Manhattan. Paladino had intended to highlight his opposition to Park51 when he addressed Levin's synagogue, as well, but was asked not to use the word "mosque" in that forum.[2] The political theater surrounding these issues, along with other developments related to

---

[1] Elizabeth A. Harris, "Rabbi Breaks with Paladino over Apology," *New York Times*, October 13, 2010.

[2] Reuven Fenton and Jeremy Olshan, "Paladino Goes on Anti-Gay Rant, Warns against 'Brainwashing,'" *New York Post*, October 10, 2010.

Park51, reveal some of the limits of American secularism and pluralism and illuminate how marginalized religious groups, especially Muslims, have increasingly attempted to navigate such limits by participating in interfaith endeavors.

Like matters of gay rights, around which interreligious coalitions have also mobilized, the Park51 debate was an unanticipated but unsurprising part of the 2010 midterm elections. Significantly, although both the *New York Times* and Fox News first covered the planned Islamic Center in December of 2009, it did not become a topic of larger debate until six months later. During the following summer, Tea Party candidates and others attempted to create a national platform plank out of the otherwise local matter. By the fall of 2010, coverage of Park51 and (sometimes violent) protests over it and other mosques and centers across the country made international news. Suddenly, however, after the tragic death of Rutgers University student Tyler Clementi on September 22, 2010, gay rights became the focal point of the New York gubernatorial election. While politicians and media outlets elsewhere moved on to other subjects, questions about the status, safety, and future of Muslims in the United States did not disappear. That November, for example, Oklahoma voters approved an amendment to their constitution preemptively prohibiting the use of Islamic or any other international law in that state's courts. The measure demonstrated, according to Roger Cohen of the *New York Times*, that "shari'ah is the new hot-button wedge issue, as radicalizing as abortion or gay marriage, seized on by Republicans to mobilize conservative Americans against the supposed 'stealth jihad' of Muslims in the United States and against a Democratic president portrayed as oblivious to – or complicit with – the threat. Not since 9/11 has Islamophobia been at such a pitch in the United States."[3]

Muslims around the country redoubled their efforts to build connections with their non-Muslim neighbors during 2010. These various endeavors included a week of "open house" outreach similar to that started by the Council of American Islamic Relations in 2001 and extended nearly a decade of Muslim Americans' efforts to counteract the backlash caused by the September 11 attacks and ongoing U.S. wars in Muslim-majority countries.[4] The Islamic Society of North America (ISNA), the largest Muslim organization in the United States, again encouraged mosques around the nation to participate in community

---

[3] Roger Cohen, "Shari'ah at the Kumback Café," *New York Times*, December 6, 2010.

[4] For histories and types of Muslim interfaith engagement, see Jane I. Smith, *Muslims, Christians, and the Challenge of Interfaith Dialogue* (Oxford, 2007).

service and interfaith outreach in 2010, while numerous Muslim New Yorkers worked even harder to demonstrate their pluralist sentiments and openness to interfaith engagement. That December, many participated in a weekend of events to promote "tolerance, peace, and love" that the New York City Council co-organized after an imam involved in local interfaith endeavors was assaulted.[5]

While interreligious engagements like these (efforts at dialogue and political coalition building) had gradually grown more common during the twentieth century, as had invocations of pluralism, both continued to involve uneven power dynamics that place Muslims at a disadvantage. This is, in part because secularism and pluralism in the United States are not neutral. Rather, they carry the imprint of Protestant traditions and thus privilege specific (sometimes secularized) Protestant practices and understandings of religion instead of creating an even space in which various groups interact. While some Jewish, Catholic, Protestant, and other groups have achieved measures of inclusion in the United States, early twenty-first-century developments raised new questions about the limits of secularism and pluralism, as well as about the kinds of tolerance and inclusion interreligious activities offered American Muslims.[6]

PLURALISM: PROMISES AND PROBLEMS

Appeals for pluralism were not new to the American landscape in 2010. Nevertheless, American understandings of pluralism as a mechanism that guarantees social equality had a rather short history. As sociologists Courtney Bender and Pamela Klassen described, pluralism, "defined as a commitment to recognize and understand others across perceived or claimed lines of religious difference," was often taken to be an unequivocal social good and a requirement for living in a liberal democracy. However, they explained, pluralism is a mode of controlling for difference, based on *particular* interpretations of religion that

---

[5]   New York City Council, "Love-Love Interfaith Weekend," available on the Council's Web site at http://council.nyc.gov/html/action_center/love-love-interfaith-weeekend.shtml, accessed December 9, 2010.

[6]   For debates and contests involved in forming recent "interfaith" and earlier "Judeo-Christian" coalitions, see Jodi Eichler-Levine and Rosemary R. Hicks, "As 'Americans against Genocide': The Crisis in Darfur and Interreligious Political Activism," *American Quarterly* 59:3 (September 2007): 711–735, and J. Terry Todd, "The Temple of Religion and the Politics of Religious Pluralism: Judeo-Christian America at the 1939–1940 New York World's Fair," in Pamela E. Klassen and Courtney Bender, eds., *After Pluralism: Reimagining Religious Engagement* (Columbia, 2010), pp. 201–222.

are assumed to be *universally* shared. This understanding was common to those who endeavored to create "harmonious interfaith coalitions," to "secular detractors who decried both evangelical Christians and Muslim terrorists as equally religious zealous," and to others.[7] Crucially, although most people assume they mean the same thing when speaking about "religion," questions of *how* what counts as authentic religion gets defined and regulated, by whom, and through which institutions are rarely discussed. Edward E. Curtis IV's chapter (in this volume) on the historiography of Muslims in the United States provides a case study of how Americans' preexisting notions of what religion is (in that case, the Protestant and secularized Protestant ideas about religion held by FBI agents and sociologists) can prevent them from recognizing some practices as truly religious (namely, those of Muslims, especially working-class Muslims and Muslims of nonwhite ethnicities). Similarly, those in dominant social positions, however well intentioned they may be, use preexisting frameworks to set the terms of pluralist, "interreligious," or "interfaith" engagement in various ways.[8]

Pluralism as understood in 2010 began to take shape in the 1970s and 1980s, somewhat coinciding with the growth of multicultural philosophies in the United States. These movements followed the ecumenical and "interfaith" movements of the early twentieth century.[9] Liberal Christian leaders emphasized cooperation between Protestant denominations and sometimes with Catholics, Jews, and other groups during the first decades of the 1900s. Simultaneously, some Muslim leaders argued for a universal brotherhood of humankind that would unite Muslims of all racial backgrounds and, perhaps, all religious practitioners worldwide.[10] These ecumenical and interreligious movements were

---

[7] Pamela E. Klassen and Courtney Bender, "Introduction: Habits of Pluralism," in Klassen and Bender, *After Pluralism*, pp. 2 and 5, respectively.

[8] While "interfaith" is a common description for engagement, several academics and practitioners caution that this description stresses faith, or belief, over action, which reveals the Protestant bias in the term. On these and related issues, see also Talal Asad, *Genealogies of Religion: Discipline and Reasons of Power in Christianity and Islam* (Stanford, 1993), and Winnifred Fallers Sullivan, *The Impossibility of Religious Freedom* (Princeton, 2007). On Protestant underpinnings of toleration in the United States, see Wendy Brown, *Regulating Aversion: Tolerance in the Age of Identity and Empire* (Princeton, 2008).

[9] See William R. Hutchison, *Religious Pluralism in America: The Contentious History of a Founding Ideal* (New Haven, 2003).

[10] For information on some of these groups, including Ahmadiyya missionaries, Pir Inayat Khan's Sufi Order of the West, and the African American Moorish Science Temple of America, see Edward E. Curtis IV, *The Columbia Sourcebook of Muslims in the United States* (New York, 2009).

not exactly egalitarian and waned in popularity during World War I and World War II, but they gained momentum again in the 1950s and 1960s, just as new legislation afforded civil rights to Black Americans and permitted greater Asian immigration to the United States. These combined social changes greatly influenced debates about religion, race, and citizenship in the United States, a country governed by what one historian has described as an enduring "Protestant establishment."[11]

Contrary to many twenty-first-century assumptions, in the 1950s President Dwight Eisenhower and many others viewed Islam as *complementary* to American values and Middle Eastern allies as essential to American interests.[12] During this time and after, however, the global influence of both the United States and independent Muslim-majority nations increased greatly, and conflicts between Muslim populations and representatives of U.S. political or economic activities garnered ever more space in the media. Consequently, several advocates of pluralism in the United States started to describe Islam as a possible problem for liberal democracies and for American interests. In response, various Muslim intellectuals countered that pluralism is supported by the Qur'an and historically evident in Muslim societies.[13] Importantly, several of those intellectuals who wrote more recently also emphasized that American pluralism involved uneven power dynamics. They noted especially the challenges posed to pluralism and to American Muslims' lives and well-being when U.S. militaries and media depicted Muslims as inherently dangerous. Many of these Muslim intellectuals also stressed connections between pluralism and other issues of social and economic justice.[14]

Interfaith dialogue became a popular method for creating a more pluralist population during the 1980s and 1990s. Because of long-standing American misperceptions of Islam as one static entity, however, both defenders and detractors of Islam ignored the diversity of Muslims' beliefs and practices. Consequently, those searching for representatives to participate in interfaith dialogue overlooked Muslims of diverse ethnic backgrounds or practices. Worse, detractors who regarded Islam as monolithic sometimes defined Muslims as entirely opposed to pluralism. In such cases, the language of "religious freedom" and "American values"

---

[11] Hutchison, *Religious Pluralism in America*, pp. 3 and 209–213, especially.

[12] See Richard Bulliet, *The Case for Islamo-Christian Civilization* (New York, 2004).

[13] See, for example, Khaled Abou El Fadl, *The Authoritative and Authoritarian in Islamic Discourse* (Austin, 1997).

[14] These include Farid Esack, *Qur'an, Liberation, and Pluralism* (Oxford, 1997); Abdul Aziz Sachedina, *The Islamic Roots of Democratic Pluralism* (Oxford, 2001); and after 2001, Sherman Jackson, *Islam and the Blackamerican: Looking toward the Third Resurrection* (Oxford, 2005), and Omid Safi, ed., *Progressive Muslims: On Gender, Justice, and Pluralism* (Oxford, 2003).

was used to oppose Muslims' free practices and exclude Muslims from interreligious alliances. This also happened during the Park51 debate. Pamela Geller first drew negative attention to the Islamic Center in 2010 by labeling it a "victory" mosque for terrorists. Following Geller's lead, the *New York Post* inaccurately described Park51 as a "WTC [World Trade Center] Mosque" in May and referred to it as the "Ground Zero Mosque" thereafter. In 2009 Geller and Robert Spencer assumed leadership of the American Freedom Defense Initiative (also known as "Stop Islamicization of America") from Anders Gaves, the Dutch founder of Stop Islamicization of Europe. That year, they also sponsored Dutch anti-Islam activist Geert Wilders's venture to address members of the U.S Conservative Political Action Conference. Collectively, these figures used the language of freedom to make Islamophobia (which Gaves calls "the height of common sense") a platform plank for political parties in the United States and to restrict Muslims' practices and activities.[15]

Imam Feisal Abdul Rauf and Daisy Khan, who cofounded the ASMA Society in 1997 with Ahmed Kostas, trusted that the protections of U.S. law were robust and applied evenly to all religious groups. Still, Abdul Rauf sought to build greater cultural capital for Muslims after 2001 by expanding the tolerance afforded Jews and Catholics in the United States. Over the following ten years, he and John Bennett of the Aspen Institute established the Cordoba Initiative, a specifically interfaith, or "multifaith" organization dedicated to informing policy makers about issues facing Muslim communities domestically and internationally and to highlighting "Abrahamic" (not just "Judeo-Christian") commonality.[16] Simultaneously, several theorists of U.S. law and secularism urged caution about such narratives of commonality, which can hide political and economic issues, including the various levels of marginalization non-Protestants continue to face within U.S. secular institutions.

SECULARISM IN THE UNITED STATES: PROTESTANT HERITAGE AND PRACTICE

The Park51 issue underlines a point Janet Jakobsen, Ann Pellegrini, and other theorists have made: that secularism in the United States

[15] Anne Barnard and Alan Feuer, "Outraged and Outrageous," *New York Times*, October 8, 2010. On the *New York Post*, see Justin Elliott's *Salon.com* article, "How the 'Ground Zero Mosque' Fearmongering Began," August 16, 2010, http://www.salon.com/2010/08/16/ground_zero_mosque_origins/.

[16] Rosemary R. Hicks, "Creating an 'Abrahamic America' and Moderating Islam: Cold War Political Economy and Cosmopolitan Sufis in New York after 2001" (Ph.D. diss., Columbia University, 2010).

has never been neutral or antireligious but accommodates particular kinds of Protestant practices more than, and sometimes to the exclusion of, Catholic, Jewish, Muslim, and other traditions (such as Native Americans') that were not originally considered "religious" or relevant to First Amendment protections.[17] This situation of Protestant privilege has certainly changed over time, and the United States is a more multicultural and pluralist nation than in previous centuries but is still marked by clear limits. For example, many speak of the United States as a Judeo-Christian nation that includes Protestants, Catholics, and Jews. Archbishop Dolan, Rabbi Levin, Pamela Geller, and Chief Justice Antonin Scalia were among them in 2010, despite the fact that the narrative of an inclusive Judeo-Christian America was primarily a twentieth-century product and, like pluralism, more of a complicated ideal than an accomplished fact.[18]

Tapes from the 1970s revealing Quaker President Richard Nixon's disparaging dialogues about Irish and Italian Catholics, Blacks, and Jews, for example, demonstrate that many elites only thinly tolerated these groups, despite changes brought by immigration reform, civil rights legislation, and thirty years of popular references to the "Judeo-Christian" tradition.[19] Moreover, as many less affluent Americans have argued since (especially those defined as non-Protestant or non-"white"), having equal rights before the law does not guarantee that legal protections are *applied* evenly or that full inclusion is inevitable. Narratives of American identity and structures of secularism privilege certain kinds of Protestant practice over others. Because of this, cultural historians Laura Levitt and Tracy Fessenden argue, Jews, Catholics, and minoritized groups of various ethnic backgrounds whose practices resemble or conform to Protestant templates are the ones most able to achieve the status of Americanness and to avoid the kinds of frictions produced by being too different or too in need.[20]

Debates over Park51 highlighted how the challenges of Protestant privilege were even more difficult to navigate for less affluent

---

[17] Janet R. Jakobsen and Ann Pellegrini, eds., *Secularisms* (Durham, 2008).

[18] See Deborah Dash Moore, *GI Jews: How World War II Changed a Generation* (Cambridge, Mass., 2004), and Mark Silk, "Notes on the Judeo-Christian Tradition," *American Quarterly* 36:1 (Spring 1984): 65–85.

[19] Adam Nagourney, "In Tapes, Nixon Fails about Jews and Blacks," *New York Times*, December 10, 2010.

[20] Laura Levitt, "Impossible Assimilations, American Liberalism, and Jewish Difference: Revisiting Jewish Secularism," *American Quarterly* 59:3 (September 2007): 807–832, and Tracy Fessenden, *Culture and Redemption: Religion, the Secular, and American Literature* (Princeton, 2006).

practitioners. For example, when President Obama addressed the Park51 issue at a White House dinner during Ramadan of 2010, he argued that Muslims, like other Americans, have First Amendment rights to build houses of worship on private property.[21] This commonly evoked connection between private wealth and religious freedom illuminated an issue central to liberalism in the United States: those already propertied are frequently better able to actualize or defend their rights when pressed. Crucially, though, private property was not an unconditional guarantee of free practice in New York City, and secularism, which many assumed involved separating religious institutions from other institutions, was not absolute.

Irrespective of Mayor Michael Bloomberg's support of the center and the Manhattan Community Board's approval, Democrat governor David Patterson suggested using state financing to move Park51 out of lower Manhattan. He appealed to the notion of propriety in what became a rather common refrain: building the community center downtown is a *legal* thing to do but perhaps not an *appropriate* thing to do.[22] Others questioned the legality and appropriateness of using state funding to move the project. Why, some wondered, was Patterson's proposal not considered a violation of the separation between church and state? Importantly, the phrase "separation of church and state" does not appear in the U.S. Constitution. Practices of secularism in the United States have instead evolved out of judicial opinions about the First Amendment, which the Fourteenth Amendment and later case law applied to state governance. Despite federal and state prohibitions against making laws that privilege one establishment of religion over another, the questions of how to define religion and matters of free practice continue to bedevil the courts.

Regarding free practice, Protestants involved in creating and executing laws for most of U.S. history did not usually wear items marked as religious in ostensibly nonreligious settings like the workplace, for example, nor did most refrain from eating particular things (e.g., pork). While other practitioners did and requested protection of such practices, courts did not always view these diverse traditions as authentically "religious"

---

[21] "Remarks by the President at Iftar Dinner," White House Office of the Press Secretary, August 13, 2010, http://www.whitehouse.gov/the-press-office/2010/08/13/remarks-president-iftar-dinner-0.

[22] Rosemary R. Hicks, "Whose Hallowed? Ground Zero, Mosques, and American Questions," *Washington Post/Newsweek* blog "On Faith," August 18, 2010, http://onfaith.washingtonpost.com/onfaith/guestvoices/2010/08/whose_hallowed_ground_zero_mosques_and_american_questions.html.

and deserving of defense. Further, practitioners of other traditions may not have refrained from ingesting certain items but did ingest others (e.g., peyote) outside the purview of what courts and legislators considered "religious." Similarly, some held that particular tracts of land were sacred and deserving of protection only if kept *vacant* of built houses of worship. The Protestant dominance that prevented such practices and traditions from being considered authentic has led one widely cited legal scholar to label religious freedom in the United States a practical "impossibility."[23]

In New York, proposals made by contenders for the Republican gubernatorial nomination also prompted questions about the uneven use of law and about U.S. secularism. Both Rick Lazio and Carl Paladino promised during their campaigns to use eminent domain, the municipality's or state's ability to seize private property in pursuit of a compelling public interest, to relocate Park51. Such efforts would have tied up the project and the developers, who were already enmeshed in two lawsuits, in additional years of expensive court cases.[24] Thus, questions about how free religious practice is in the United States and for whom arose again in the Park51 case. For other American Muslims, the pressure to distinguish "good" or "real" religion from "bad" or "political" religion sometimes took precedence over issues of free practice, especially when Muslims participated in interfaith coalitions where the agenda was already set. In 2007, for example, senator and presidential candidate Barack Obama defined what constituted proper religious practice and interfaith projects: dealing with social problems, AIDS, and countering the "genocide" (a designation the United Nations denied) committed by Muslims in Sudan.[25]

INTERFAITH ENDEAVORS: BUILDING ALLIANCES IN TIMES OF CRISIS

While formally orchestrated dialogue is one mode of interfaith engagement, other kinds have been less formal. Interfaith marriages, for example, have a long history among African American Muslims, as well as

[23] Sullivan, *The Impossibility of Religious Freedom.*
[24] These involve one suit brought by a former New York City firefighter alleging pain and suffering due to the memories reignited by the controversy, and the developers' countersuit to recoup the lawyers' fees necessary for their defense.
[25] See Rosemary R. Hicks, "Saving Darfur: Enacting Pluralism in Terms of Gender, Genocide, and Militarized Human Rights," in Klassen and Bender, *After Pluralism,* pp. 252–276.

among late nineteenth-century immigrant laborers from Asia and the Middle East. Official programs for interfaith dialogue involving Muslim intellectuals (academics and religious leaders) took root in the 1960s. Among the most notable in the United States were those efforts led by Palestinian refugee and scholar Isma'il al-Faruqi, who earned graduate degrees at Harvard and Indiana universities, as well as from Al-Azhar University in Cairo, and who founded the Islamic Studies program at Temple University in the 1960s.

Al-Faruqi traveled extensively to lecture on interreligious relations, Islamic economics, and Islamic education and at Temple mentored a young Catholic scholar of Islam, John Esposito. According to Esposito, who later founded the Georgetown University Center for Muslim-Christian Understanding (1993) and Center for the Study of Islam and Democracy (1999), 1967 was the beginning of al-Faruqi's ecumenical career. During the latter part of that decade, al-Faruqi began to participate in the interfaith programs Protestant organizations had developed after World War II. In the 1970s, al-Faruqi also played a leading role in meetings sponsored by the National Council of Churches, the Inter-Religious Peace Colloquium (for which he served as vice president from 1977 to 1982), and the Vatican. His involvement in diverse venues made him not only "a leading Muslim spokesperson for Islam" but perhaps "the most visible and prolific Muslim contributor to the dialogue of world religions."[26]

The year 1967 was also the beginning of another Muslim leader's interfaith career – that of Egyptian intellectual Muhammad Abdul Rauf. While serving as director of the New York Islamic Center Abdul Rauf initiated meetings with other leaders and appeared formally for the first time alongside an Orthodox rabbi to urge "reconciliation" after the 1967 war in Palestine.[27] Further, he encouraged both Muslims and non-Muslims to attend the center's educational classes. In 1979, after Abdul Rauf had moved to Washington, D.C., to direct the Islamic Center there, al-Faruqi invited him to represent Islam at that year's American Academy of Religion meetings. During the multiple-session "Trialogue of the Abrahamic Faiths" (and in a message his son, Feisal Abdul Rauf, would later popularize), Muhammad Abdul Rauf outlined what united Jews, Christians, and Muslims. Yet, with his opening remarks, he addressed some of the foremost issues on attendees' minds and

---

[26] John Esposito, "Ismail R. Al-Faruqi: Muslim Scholar-Activist," in Yvonne Yazbeck Haddad, ed., *The Muslims of America* (Oxford, 1991), p. 76.

[27] Irving Spiegel, "Islamic Leader and Rabbi Agree Their Faiths Need Closer Ties," *New York Times*, November 17, 1967.

condemned as anti-Islamic the taking of hostages in Iran or elsewhere. Although these formal endeavors did increase some Americans' familiarity with Muslims, they mainly involved Sunni elites until the late 1970s (Seyyed Hossein Nasr, a professor and Iranian expatriate, contributed to knowledge of some Shi'i and Sufi traditions thereafter) and rarely involved Black American Muslims.[28]

Because of the growth of Muslim-led institutions and networks in the United States during the latter decades of the twentieth century, non-Muslims had little difficulty locating Muslim spokespersons for interfaith dialogues in 2001 and after.[29] Crucially, though, insufficient awareness of the diversity of Muslims in the United States and of the issues facing different groups sometimes created tensions between Muslims and others and among Muslim communities. For example, Imam Abu Namous, the Palestinian American leader of the New York Islamic Cultural Center, was initially in high demand as a speaker. However, his continual criticism of Israeli activities, such as in a tense conversation with Rabbi Marc Shneier at an interfaith event in 2005, elicited negative attention. In November 2007, Abu Namous and Shneier met again at a larger national gathering of Jewish and Muslim leaders in New York that, notably, did not include Christians. Talk of Palestine was specifically disallowed at that event.[30] In the meantime, against the specter of Muslim terrorism, some Black spokespersons emphasized their longer histories within the United States and their more established "American" credentials. Moreover, several criticized affluent Muslims (those who enjoyed greater resources and greater access to various American elites) for affording their needs more attention than others.

These pressures and intra-Muslim tensions do not indicate that Muslims' attempts to build connections with other religious groups were ineffective in garnering tolerance. To the contrary, the response of many political and religious leaders after 2001 was a testament to the success of Muslims' organizing efforts throughout the 1990s. Likewise, the responses of the religious and political figures who gathered at the

[28] See Jane I. Smith, "Seyyed Hossein Nasr: Defender of the Sacred and Islamic Traditionalism," in Haddad, *The Muslims of America*, pp. 80–95.

[29] See Mohamed Nimer, "Social and Political Institutions of American Muslims: Liberty and Civic Responsibility," in Philippa Strum and Danielle Tarantolo, eds., *Muslims in the United States* (Washington, D.C., 2003), pp. 45–61.

[30] Marc Perelman, "With Certain Topics Kept Off Table, Rabbis and Imams Find Common Ground," *Forward*, November 14, 2007.

Islamic Society of North America's Washington, D.C., Interfaith Press Conference in September of 2010 testify to the success of post-2001 outreach efforts, including those of Feisal Abdul Rauf and his wife and colleague, Daisy Khan. In 2006, in fact, the Interfaith Center of New York awarded Abdul Rauf and Khan its James Park Morton Interfaith Award, which the couple shared with, among others, actor Richard Gere and former Supreme Court Justice Stephen Breyer (the latter of whom railed against the "ignorance" demonstrated in some Americans' intolerance of Park51). Nevertheless, continuing controversies of 2010 prompted Muslims and others to question the bases and limits of such tolerance and inclusion.

While Abdul Rauf and Khan received a measure of support from various elites and media outlets during 2010 and after, other Muslim communities from Staten Island to California experienced less-commonly reported backlash and even violence.[31] Further, research conducted during those years revealed that minoritized groups, especially ones that lacked capital and had more difficulty securing protections and provisions than Muslims who had funding and connections, often engaged in interfaith endeavors established by Protestants so as to meet basic civic and social needs.[32] These complicated legal, economic, and social dynamics demonstrated that the tensions between Muslim groups and between Muslims and non-Muslims that had arisen during the early twentieth century were similar to those which other non-Protestant groups historically experienced while navigating pressures to conform and assimilate to the larger Protestant-secular society of the United States.

---

[31] Plans to build mosques and community centers in locations ranging from Staten Island to California were challenged and canceled while the Park51 debate unfolded. Further, Muslims' lives and property were threatened and damaged: a few of the incidents include a mosque site in Tennessee vandalized by arson, a New York cab driver stabbed, and a mosque in Florida bombed. See Paul Vitello, "Church Rejects Sale of Building for a Mosque," *New York Times*, July 22, 2010; AOL News, "FBI Finds Pipe Bomb Used in Blast at Fla. Mosque," May 12, 2010, http://www.aolnews.com/crime/article/fbi-finds-pipe-bomb-used-in-blast-at-fla-mosque/19475001, accessed October 16, 2010; Phil Willon, "Planned Temecula Valley Mosque Draws Opposition," *Los Angeles Times*, July 18, 2010; Lucas L. Johnson II, and Travis Loller, "Tennessee Mosque Site Fire Was Arson, Police Say," *Huffington Post*, August 30, 2010, http://www.huffingtonpost.com/2010/08/30/murfreesboro-mosque-fire-arson-acceleran t_n_699696.html, accessed October 16, 2010; John Eligon, "Hate Crime Charges in Stabbing of a Cabdriver," *New York Times*, August 30, 2010.

[32] Matt Weiner, "Interfaith in the City: Religious Pluralism and Civil Society in New York" (Ph.D. diss., Union Theological Seminary, 2009).

CONCLUSION: INSTITUTIONALIZING INTERFAITH
SERVICE IN THE NEW MILLENNIUM

In a June 4, 2009, speech at Cairo University in Egypt, President Barack Obama lauded the "proud tradition of tolerance" exemplified in the medieval Muslim city of Cordoba and in his childhood home of Indonesia. Stressing the imperative of religious freedom, he then pledged to protect Muslims' practices in the United States. "We can't disguise hostility towards any religion behind the pretense of liberalism," the President remarked. "In fact, faith should bring us together. And that's why we're forging service projects in America to bring together Christians, Muslims, and Jews." Obama praised the interfaith efforts of Saudi Arabian and Turkish leaders, and promised, "we can turn dialogue into interfaith service" around the world "so bridges between peoples lead to action."[33] One year later, and building on the work of the prior Republican administration, the White House Office of Faith-based and Neighborhood Partnerships and the White House Office for Social Innovation and Civic Participation co-sponsored a half-day symposium designed to increase interfaith dialogue and community service at colleges and universities. Isma'ili Muslim American Eboo Patel, a member of the President's Advisory Council and Executive Director of the Interfaith Youth Core, helped plan the event.

It is perhaps not surprising that like Catholic, Jewish, and other groups marginalized from "public" provisions in previous decades, Muslims formed independent organizations to provide social services. In Daisy Khan's view, the process of transitioning from service provision for co-religionists to providing interreligious cultural programming is a trajectory all religions in the United States follow. "All religions Americanize over time," Khan told reporter Christiane Amanpour in an August 22, 2010, episode of ABC's *This Week*. "They go from a place of worship to a place of service, and community centers have been developed by Christian communities like YMCA, and the Jewish community has developed the JCC. And [the] Muslim community is inevitably going to also develop such a [cultural] center." Indeed, as revealed when local New York Muslim groups supported the Park51 project but criticized its lack of social services, interfaith activities and contests over them promised to be an enduring aspect of the power dynamics produced by Protestant secularism and pluralism in the twenty-first century.

---

[33] "Remarks by the President on a New Beginning," White House Office of the Press Secretary, June 4, 2009, http://www.whitehouse.gov/the_press_office/Remarks-by-the-President-at-Cairo-University-6-04-09/.

Further Reading

Brown, Wendy, *Regulating Aversion: Tolerance in the Age of Identity and Empire* (Princeton, 2006).

Hicks, Rosemary R., "Between Lived and the Law: Power, Empire and Expansion in Studies of North American Religions," *Religion* 43:2 (June 2012): 409–424.

Hutchison, William R., *Religious Pluralism in America: The Contentious History of a Founding Ideal* (New Haven, 2003).

Smith, Jane I., *Muslims, Christians, and the Challenge of Interfaith Dialogue* (Oxford, 2007).

Wilson, John Frederick, and Donald L. Drakeman, *Church and State in American History: Key Documents, Decisions, and Commentary from the Past Three Centuries* (Boulder, 2003).

10 Organizing Communities: Institutions, Networks, Groups

KAREN LEONARD

American Muslims are developing institutions, networks, and groups with social, economic, and political as well as religious power. An overview of the historical and contemporary American Muslim landscape precedes discussion of the many organizational forms. Institutions include mosques, schools, religious organizations, and political organizations in the United States. Networks include diasporic or transnational movements and less formal associations that also tend to be transnational. Groups include voluntary associations and groupings based on ethnicity, national origin, or gender in the United States.

OVERVIEW

Indigenous African American Muslims were arguably the first in the United States to mobilize on the basis of Islam, in the early twentieth century, as they looked for new identities in "Asiatic" origins and Islam. As African Americans moved north in the late nineteenth and early twentieth centuries and tried to establish themselves economically, they sought alternatives to white and Christian domination by founding several religious and political movements based on Islam. Of the two early African American Muslim movements (see the Appendix at the end of the chapter), the Moorish Science Temple of America (1913) and the Nation of Islam (1930), the second, more powerful NOI encouraged the rejection of American citizenship, voting, and service in the military. The MSTA, while providing cards identifying members as Moorish citizens, did not deny U.S. citizenship or reject participation in American politics. Although in both movements contact with Arab Muslim immigrants furnished some impetus and provided some content, little significant interaction occurred between indigenous African American Muslims and Muslim immigrants until the arrival of a few dedicated Ahmadiyya missionaries from British India in the 1920s. The Ahmadis, followers of a charismatic late nineteenth-century teacher in northwestern India whose movement sent missionaries abroad, gave these African American movements access to the Ahmadiyya English-language translation of the Qur'an and some of the "Old World" teachings.[1]

Arab immigrants were next to mobilize as Muslims in North America. Arab Muslims, along with larger numbers of Arab Christians, came to the United States in the late nineteenth century. These first- and second-generation Muslim immigrants established mosques in Detroit, Michigan, starting in the 1920s,[2] and, along with newly arrived foreign students, they initiated broader organizations in the 1950s and 1960s.[3] The leaders of these – the Federation of Islamic Associations and the Muslim Students Association organizations[4] – mobilized to maintain and transmit their religion in Canada as well as the United States. Not only was their focus directed toward members of their families and communities; they also sought to change American misconceptions about Islam and influence foreign policies, especially regarding Palestine. As immigrants from South Asia arrived and Arab immigrants continued to arrive, new religious organizations formed, the most recent initiated by American Shi'a Muslims.

After the 1965 Immigration and Naturalization Act that spurred immigration to the United States by Muslims from all over the world, American Muslims increased their efforts to form political coalitions on the basis of religion. South Asian Muslims, characteristically well-educated professionals from India and Pakistan, constituted a third major group of American Muslims,[5] and they and other post-1965

[1] Yusuf Nuruddin, "African American Muslims and the Question of Identity: Between Traditional Islam, African Heritage, and the American Way," in Yvonne Haddad and John L. Esposito, eds., *Muslims on the Americanization Path?* (Tampa, 1998), pp. 215–262; Ernest Allen Jr., "Identity and Destiny: The Formative Views of the Moorish Science Temple and the Nation of Islam," in Haddad and Esposito, *Muslims*, pp. 163–164; Edward E. Curtis IV, *Islam in Black America: Identity, Liberation, and Difference in African-American Islamic Thought* (Albany, 2002).

[2] Sally Howell, "Inventing the American Mosque: Early Muslims and Their Institutions in Detroit, 1910–1980" (Ph.D. diss., University of Michigan, 2009).

[3] Arab Muslims mobilized first on the basis of language, culture, and national origin, together with Arab Christians, forming the Arab-American Anti-Discrimination Committee (ADC). American notions of race initially complicated their citizenship, but early court decisions that Arabs were Asiatic and therefore could not be citizens were reversed, and they were classified as Caucasian and white. Suad Joseph, "Against the Grain of the Nation – the Arab," in Michael Suleiman, ed., *Arabs in America: Building a New Future* (Philadelphia, 1999), pp. 257–271.

[4] See the appendix at the end of the chapter for a list of organizations mentioned here.

[5] These new Muslim immigrants arrived after the Luce-Celler Act of 1946 set aside the 1923 decision to bar Asian Indians from citizenship as nonwhites: Karen Leonard, "American Muslims, Before and After September 11, 2001," *Economic and Political Weekly* 37:24 (2002): 2292–2302.

Muslim immigrants gradually moved to become citizens. Muslim national political coalitions sprang up from the 1980s: the American Muslim Alliance, the American Muslim Council, the Muslim Public Affairs Council, and the Council on American-Islamic Relations. Arab and South Asian leaders engaged some African American Muslims in these coalitions. The Nation of Islam led by Warith Deen Mohammed, son of Elijah Muhammad who died in 1975, was moving closer to mainstream Sunni beliefs and practices. Mohammed participated in some coalition activities, notably as a member of the Islamic Society of North America's governing council; he was also recognized by leaders in Saudi Arabia as the representative of American Muslims. However, relations between the diverse American Muslim communities remained weak. For example, in 1997 Warith Deen Mohammed renamed his community the Muslim American Society, although an immigrant-based Muslim American Society had been founded in 1992 (Mohammed's previous names for his community were, successively, World Community of al-Islam in the West, American Muslim Mission, and Ministry of W. D. Mohammed). After 9/11, Mohammed renamed his community yet again, this time as the American Muslim Society, to emphasize its foundation in American history and culture. Before his death in 2008 the community was renamed again and remains The Mosque Cares.[6]

At the end of the twentieth century, African American Muslims constituted from 30 to 42 percent of the American Muslim community, while Arabs constituted from 12.4 to 33 percent and South Asians from 24.4 to 29 percent.[7] These three major groups of American Muslims were developing converging constructions of race, religion, and the nation as well as converging religious and political trajectories.[8] Moves to citizenship and participation in mainstream politics characterized the major organizations, although issues of race, class, and gender divided the "community." Muslim immigrants tended to be, as the Pew Research Center survey of 2007 found, "middle class and mostly mainstream,"[9] although this was not true of refugees. African Americans continued to

---

[6] Precious Rasheed Mohammad, "Mohammed, W.D. (b. 1933)," pp. 422–426, and Gwen McCarter, "Muslim American Society," pp. 446–447, both in Jocelyn Cesari, ed., *Encyclopedia of Islam in the United States* (Westport, 2007).

[7] Karen Isaksen Leonard, *Muslims in the United States: The State of Research* (New York, 2003), p. 4.

[8] Karen Leonard, "American Muslims: Race, Religion, and Nation," *ISIM Newsletter* 14 (April 2004): 16–17.

[9] Pew Research Center, "Muslim Americans: Middle Class and Mostly Mainstream," http://www.pewresearch.org/2007/05/22/muslim-americans-middle-class-and-mostly-mainstream/.

differ from immigrant Muslims in many respects, their mosques more often located in poorer downtown areas with segregated congregations, and they stressed *'asabiyyah* or community interest and solidarity more than *ummah* or the international community of Muslims. Women played prominent roles in the earlier Arab Muslim communities, but many of the newer immigrant groups (post-1965) have imported more patriarchal cultures; African American Muslims generally continued more egalitarian traditions but have also adopted gendered practices, and there are some among them who justify polygyny (multiple wives) as a response to conditions in the African American community.[10]

For American Muslims, 9/11 changed the political situation dramatically. Major national Muslim organizations had been optimistic about the role of American Muslims both in America and in the Muslim ummah, talking about the three Abrahamic traditions constituting Western civilization. The aftermath of 9/11 put American Muslims on the defensive, despite the vigorous repudiation of the terrorists by national organizations and leading spokespersons.[11] Another consequence of 9/11 was increased participation in mainstream politics by American Muslims and more open recognition, by Muslims and others, of the differences among Muslims.[12] Leading African American Muslims now stress their Americanness, contrasting themselves to immigrants whose cultural baggage constrains their full citizenship. The immigrants, who earlier talked of being simultaneously American and members of an international Islamic ummah and envisioned American leadership of that ummah, now stress their status as American citizens and emphasize the universal principles of Islamic law and its areas of agreement with generalized American notions of social justice.[13] Arab Muslims in particular face challenges to enjoyment of full citizenship rights. Scholars have

---

[10] Sherman A. Jackson, "Islam(s) East and West: Pluralism between No-Frills and Designer Fundamentalism," in Mary L. Dudziak, ed., *September 11 in History* (Durham, 2003), pp. 112–135; Debra Majeed, "Polygyny: An African American Muslim Response of Resistance and Hope," *Pakistan Journal of Women's Studies* 13:1 (2006): 31–44.

[11] ISNA's Fiqh Council of North America condemned the destruction and violence committed against innocent people on 9/11 from 2001 on, calling it contrary to Islam, but the national media only highlighted the fatwa issued in 2005.

[12] Leonard, *Muslims*; Katherine Pratt Ewing, ed., *Being and Belonging: Muslims in the United States since 9/11* (New York 2008); Louise A. Cainkar, *Homeland Insecurity: The Arab American and Muslim American Experience after 9/11* (New York, 2009); Detroit Arab American Study Team, *Citizenship and Crisis: Arab Detroit after 9/11* (New York, 2009).

[13] Karen Leonard, "Finding Places in the Nation: Immigrant and Indigenous Muslims in America," in Pierrette Hondagneu-Sotelo, ed., *Religion and Social Justice for Immigrants* (New York, 2006), pp. 50–58.

written about "disciplinary inclusion" as Muslims try to balance their experiences of inclusion against ones of stigmatizing discipline.[14]

INSTITUTIONS: MOSQUES, SCHOOLS, AND RELIGIOUS AND POLITICAL ORGANIZATIONS

The number of mosques has grown steadily over the decades. First among immigrant mosques was one in Highland Park, Michigan, in 1921, although a mosque founded in 1934 in Cedar Rapids, Iowa, also claims to be first.[15] Mosques and cultural centers have been started by the various strands of Islam in the country, from Sunni, Shi'a, and Sufi (the last a mystical path that can be either Sunni or Shi'a) to groups like the Ahmadiyya and Druze, whose status as Muslims is sometimes questioned (most scholarly treatments of American Muslims include the last two).

Mosques vary a great deal and change over time. Mosques that were Ahmadiyya have seen African American membership decline as Pakistani immigrants arrived, having left Pakistan after its government's 1974 decision that Ahmadis were not Muslims. Mosques that were affiliated with the Nation of Islam moved toward Sunni Islam through Warith Deen Mohammed's reforms, and new NOI mosques were founded with Louis Farrakhan's revival of the movement.[16] At least one African American mosque that followed Sunni practices has become more Sufi-oriented as leadership changed, while others remain anti-Sufi or more legalistic.[17] Mosques or Islamic spaces have been founded in prisons and on campuses, with African American Muslims mounting the legal battles to secure Islamic worship spaces and halal food in prisons.[18] Mosques in Dearborn and Detroit that had adopted American cultural practices (such as holding dances or card games) became more conservative as new immigrants dominated the congregations in the 1970s and

---

[14] Wayne Baker and Andrew Shryock, "Citizenship and Crisis," pp. 3–32, and Andrew Shryock and Ann Chih Lin, "The Limits of Citizenship," pp. 265–286, both in Detroit Arab American Study Team, *Citizenship and Crisis.*

[15] See Sally Howell, Chapter 3 in this volume.

[16] Linda Walbridge and Fatimah Haneef, "Inter-ethnic Relations within the Ahmadiyya Muslim Community in the United States," in Carla Petievich, ed., *The Expanding Landscape: South Asians and the Diaspora* (Delhi, 1999), pp. 123–146.

[17] Darul Islam, founded and led from 1962–1983 in New York by African American Sunnis, was renamed Fuqra, through the influence of a South Asian Sufi; see Aminah Beverly McCloud, *African American Islam* (New York, 1995), p. 72.

[18] Kathleen M. Moore, *Al-Mughtaribun: American Law and the Transformation of Muslim Life in the United States* (Albany, 1995).

1980s but are now beginning to return to earlier practices.[19] When limited by funds or conversion of existing buildings, earlier mosques were sometimes inconspicuous, but now they often proudly assert Islamic identities in public space.[20]

The roles of American Muslim women in mosques have changed over time. Women were instrumental in establishing early mosques in Detroit, Michigan; Michigan City, Indiana; Cedar Rapids, Iowa; and Toledo, Ohio.[21] Segregation of women (by barriers like walls and curtains) in some American mosques has increased in recent years, especially in some immigrant Sunni mosques.[22] Gender segregation is generally less practiced in African American Muslim mosques, especially those of Warith Deen Mohammed.[23] Exactly how women should be participating in mosques across America is being taken up locally in mosque after mosque.[24]

Issues of mosque governance and religious decision making are institutional ones. Muslim immigrants, shaped by the American context, find new ways of governing mosques and new sources of religious authority as *shari'ah* or religious law is interpreted by laypeople rather than specialists in *fiqh* (Islamic jurisprudence). African American mosques typically are led by one charismatic and powerful imam (historically, Black churches in America were led by one preacher or minister).[25] Immigrant mosques more often turn to "congregationalism," to governing models that qualify religious institutions for tax exemption.[26] This means writing constitutions, making lists of dues-paying members, and electing boards of directors, organizational features new to many

[19] Nabeel Abraham, "Arab Detroit's 'American' Mosque," in Nabeel Abraham and Andrew Shryock, eds., *Arab Detroit: From Margin to Mainstream* (Detroit, 2000), pp. 279–309.

[20] See Akel Ismail Kahera, Chapter 13 in this volume.

[21] Abraham, "Arab Detroit's 'American' Mosque"; Abdo A. Elkholy, *The Arab Moslems in the United States: Religion and Assimilation* (New Haven, 1966).

[22] Ihsan Bagby, Paul M. Perl, and Bryan T. Froehle, *The Mosque in America: A National Portrait; A Report form the Mosque Study Project* (Washington, D.C., 2001), pp. 9, 11, 56.

[23] Ihsan A. Bagby, "A Profile of African-American Masjids: A Report from the National Masjid Study, 2000," *Journal of the Interdenominational Theological Center* 29:1–2 (2001–2002): 205–241.

[24] For views about female prayer leadership, see Imam Zaid Shakir, Laury Silvers, and Ingrid Mattson in Edward E. Curtis IV, ed., *The Columbia Sourcebook of Muslims in the United States* (New York, 2008), pp. 240–262.

[25] Fredrick C. Harris, *Something Within: Religion in African-American Political Activism* (New York, 1999).

[26] Discussion of Bagby, Perl, and Froehle's 2000 survey reviews these clear differences among American Muslim mosques; Leonard, *Muslims*, pp. 76–78.

immigrants.[27] The governing boards are dominated by middle-class professional men (doctors, engineers, lawyers, and IT professionals), while the imams, employees of the governing boards, are generally imported from abroad. The imams lead prayers and teach about Islam but are often hindered by inadequate linguistic or cultural knowledge from playing more important roles in their new settings.[28] As the congregants learn and practice organizing skills, religion becomes a political resource, encouraging Muslims to participate in local and higher levels of politics.[29] A path-breaking Detroit Arab American Study and other recent studies reinforce the point with respect to Arab Americans, a slight majority of whom are Christian.[30]

Women's services on the governing boards of mosques and as imams are contested issues. Women participate prominently in the institutions and activities of the transnational Nizari Isma'ili and Ahmadiyya movements. Among the Twelver Shi'a, allegiance to religious and judicial authorities (maraji') in Iran, Iraq, and Lebanon remains strong, so when closed-circuit television was introduced to allow women seated separately to watch a male religious speaker, opposition in some Shi'a centers in North America was overcome by the ruling of a marja'.[31]

The exercise of Islamic religious authority in the United States raises institutional questions, because (save for some movements) there is no centralized authority structure in Islam. There are many imams but fewer scholars of fiqh in the United States. Muslim immigrants can continue to turn to authorities in their former homelands, or they can recognize those becoming established in the United States, many of them academics teaching Islamic law in institutions of higher education. Professor Khaled Abou El Fadl at UCLA has argued that "new spokesmen" without traditional legal schooling have stepped forward,

[27] In many Muslim homelands, the government maintains mosques and pays clerics.
[28] In Bagby, Perl, and Froehle's 2000 survey, 49 percent of the imams were Arabs and 29 percent were South Asian; Leonard, *Muslims*, p. 77.
[29] Harris argues that African American Protestant churches with their charismatic pastors, like Catholic and megachurch structures, discourage participation by congregants; Harris, *Something Within*.
[30] Detroit Arab American Study Team, *Citizenship and Crisis*. This face-to-face survey of more than one thousand Arabs and Chaldeans in Wayne, Macomb, and Oakland counties, Michigan, used complex sampling techniques and quantitative methodologies. See also Amaney Jamal and Nadine Naber, eds., *Race and Arab Americans Before and After 9/11* (Syracuse, 2008), and Philippa Strum, ed., *American Arabs and Political Participation* (Washington, D.C., 2006).
[31] Abdulaziz Sachedina, "A Minority within a Minority: The Case of the Shi'a in North America," in Yvonne Haddad and Jane I. Smith, eds., *Muslim Communities in North America* (Albany, 1994), pp. 11–12.

professional doctors and engineers who read the Qur'an and hadith and dispense opinions about religious issues.[32] Furthermore, the governing boards and imams of mosques seem to have little respect for the traditional schools of Islamic law: respondents to a 2000 national survey of mosques placed the schools of law at the very bottom of the list of sources of authority for worship and teaching.[33] This suggests that legal interpretations from former homelands are not determining beliefs and behaviors in the United States and that "new spokesmen" are having an impact. Many of these "new spokesmen" are less feminist, less helpful to the "gender jihad" underway among American Muslim women, than fiqh and Qur'an scholars like Khaled Abou El Fadl, Amina Wadud, and Kecia Ali.[34]

Increasing American Muslim participation in politics has led to the establishment of organizations above the congregational or local level to further and defend religious and political goals. The appendix to this chapter lists the major religious and political movements, beginning with efforts by African Americans to mobilize on the basis of Islam in the early twentieth century and moving to the religious and then the more political organizations. Arab and South Asian immigrant Muslims currently lead the major Muslim religious and political coalition efforts, although American-born leaders are stepping forward in some organizations.

The earliest national (actually binational) association to organize on the basis of Islam was the Federation of Islamic Associations of the United States and Canada, or FIA, in 1953. Second-generation Lebanese and Syrians and foreign students and new immigrants worked together to educate Muslims and non-Muslims about Islam, connect Muslim Americans to each other and to the global community of Muslims, and seek accommodations from mainstream North American institutions. By the 1970s, internal conflict over political and religious goals drained the FIA's support; although it functioned into the 1990s, it was eclipsed by other organizations, particularly the Islamic Society of North America

---

[32] Khaled Abou El Fadl, "Striking a Balance: Islamic Legal Discourse on Muslim Minorities," in Haddad and Esposito, *Muslims*, p. 41.

[33] Respondents to the 2000 national mosque survey who deemphasized the traditional schools of Islamic law included imams but even larger numbers of mosque presidents and members of governing boards: Bagby, "A Profile of African-American Masjids," p. 28.

[34] Khaled Abou El Fadl, *Speaking in God's Name: Islamic Law, Authority, and Women* (New York, 2001); Amina Wadud, *Qur'an and Women: Rereading the Sacred Text from a Woman's Perspective* (New York, 1999); Kecia Ali, *Sexual Ethics and Islam: Feminist Reflections on the Qur'an, Hadith, and Jurisprudence* (Oxford, 2006) and *Marriage and Slavery in Early Islam* (Cambridge, 2010).

(ISNA).[35] ISNA developed out of the Muslim Students Association (MSA), inaugurated by Arabic-speaking foreign students in the United States in 1963. As these students grew older, they established ISNA in 1982, head-quartered in Plainfield, Indiana. ISNA's goal was primarily religious: to further education about Islam and to maintain commitment to the faith. In the twenty-first century, ISNA has taken on political goals as well, bringing together Muslims across lines of affiliation, race, and gender and participating in interfaith events. It established the Fiqh Council of North America, which issues *fatawa*, or legal opinions on issues: for example ISNA and the Fiqh Council issued a fatwa against terrorism in 2005.[36]

National organizations with similar religious goals were founded later by new South Asian and newer Arab immigrants. The Islamic Circle of North America (ICNA) was founded in North America in 1971 by Pakistani members of a political party in Pakistan, the Jamaat-i Islami.[37] In 1992 chiefly Arab immigrants founded the Muslim American Society (MAS), and in 2002 Shi'as of the (largest) Twelver branch founded the Universal Muslim Association of America (UMAA).[38]

In the late 1980s and 1990s, American Muslim organizations formed to engage in mainstream politics. Officially first was the Muslim Public Affairs Council (MPAC), founded in 1988 by leaders of the Islamic Center of Southern California in Los Angeles; this organization works to "en-rich America" through education and political outreach activities.[39] Next was the American Muslim Council (AMC), started by Eritrean-American Abdurahman Alamoudi in Washington, D.C., in 1990; this organization ended in 2009. The American Muslim Alliance (AMA) was developed by Pakistani American educator Agha Saeed in northern California from the late 1980s and was officially incorporated in 1994.[40] Saeed went on to organize two national Muslim coalitions aimed at mobilizing bloc votes for the 2000 and 2004 elections, the American Muslim Political Coordinating Committee (AMPCC) and the American Muslim Taskforce

---

[35] See Sally Howell's article in Edward E. Curtis IV, ed., *Encyclopedia of Muslim-American History I* (New York, 2010), pp. 192–193.

[36] See Shariq A. Siddiqui's article in Curtis, *Encyclopedia I*, pp. 296–300.

[37] See Saeed A. Khan's article in Jocelyn Cesari, *Encyclopedia of Islam in the United States I* (Westport, 2007), pp. 354–355.

[38] McCarter, "Muslim American Society."

[39] See Sarah Eltantawi's article in Cesari, *Encyclopedia I*, pp. 452–453.

[40] A failed merger with the AMA in 2002 and the jailing of its founder in 2003 for illegal business dealings and a false citizenship application contributed to the AMC's demise; see articles by Edward E. Curtis IV and Marcia Hermansen, both in Curtis, *Encyclopedia I*, p. 52.

(AMT); the latter continues as the American Muslim Taskforce on Civil Rights and Elections.[41] Finally, the Council on American-Islamic Relations (CAIR) was founded in Washington, D.C., in 1994 by chiefly Arab American leaders and has become the largest Muslim civil rights and advocacy organization in North America.[42] Like AMPCC, CAIR is a lobbying organization. All of these organizations enthusiastically engage in democratic politics, using skills partially learned in American-styled mosques and sometimes interfaith politics as well. Muslims increasingly contend for political offices all across the country, although 9/11 set back such efforts significantly.

Several organizations have worked to further knowledge production by and about American Muslims. The African American Institute for Islamic Research, founded in 1990 in Newark, New Jersey, by Amir Al Islam and Zain Abdullah, convened two national conferences, and The Conference on Islam in America (in 2011) (TCOIA) brought together scholars, community and civic leaders, and members of the media for educational goals.[43] The Institute for Social Policy and Understanding (ISPU), a post-9/11 organization founded in Detroit but now headquartered in Washington, D.C., brings together scholars conducting empirical research and offering policy analysis on issues relating to American Muslims and Muslims around the world.[44]

Islamic schools, pioneered by the Nation of Islam as alternatives to the segregated and inferior schools available to African Americans, are being established by middle- and upper-class immigrant Muslims. Many started out as part-time or weekend classes at mosques, but full-time Islamic schools, most accredited by the relevant regional and national educational associations, attract some Muslim parents throughout the country. Early ambitions to establish higher educational institutions of Islamic learning have not succeeded. In Herndon, Virginia, the International Institute of Islamic Thought (IIIT) was founded in 1981 and has offices and branches in the United Kingdom, Bangladesh, Pakistan, Nigeria, and elsewhere. Its "Islamization of Knowledge" project aimed to apply a reformed version of Islamic thought to global problems. In the 1990s it established the Graduate School of Islamic Social Sciences, which trained imams and Muslim chaplains (many were employed in

---

[41] See the AMT Web site, www.americanmuslimtaskforce.net/contactus.html.

[42] Articles by Nada Unus and Emily Tucker in Cesari, *Encyclopedia I*, pp. 163–168, and Edward E. Curtis IV in Curtis, *Encyclopedia I*, pp. 128–129.

[43] http://www.mpac.org/events/inaugural-conference-on-islam-in-america-to-be-held-at -depaul-university-in-chicago.php#.UP7wKfLFook.

[44] See the organization's Web site www.ispu.org/portal/7/WhoWeAre.aspx.

the American military and in prisons); this was reorganized after 2001 and renamed the Fairfax Institute. Also after 2001, an FBI investigation and public scrutiny led to more outreach and education programs for non-Muslims.[45] In Chicago, the American Islamic College established in 1981 experienced financial difficulties by 1986 and never achieved accreditation. After a court case over control of the property, it was reconstituted in 2006 and was still operational in 2010.[46] There are scattered reports of seminaries training students to be American imams: Darul Uloom al-Madania in Buffalo, New York, Darul Uloom in Chicago, the American Islamic University in Detroit, the Islamic Association of North Texas in Dallas, and Hartford Seminary in Connecticut. An Imam Ali Seminary reportedly trains women as well in Medina, New York. The Zaytuna Institute in San Francisco, founded in 1996 by the charismatic white Islamic scholar Hamza Yusuf, has started Zaytuna College, which enrolled a freshman class in the fall of 2010.[47]

NETWORKS: ALUMNI ASSOCIATIONS, TRANSNATIONAL MOVEMENTS

Networks include less formally established groupings, such as voluntary associations for the graduates of predominantly Muslim schools and universities, political parties based overseas with networks in the United States, and Sufi or other movements based overseas with members in the United States. In the first alumni category one finds the Old Boys and Girls of India's Aligarh Muslim University and Pakistan's Karachi University.[48] While there are analogous networks from other Muslim-majority countries like Yemen (the Yemeni Students Association Abroad or YSAA), Arab immigrants have tended to form secular associations with both Christian and Muslim members. Some hometown or place-of-origin associations, such as Hyderabad associations for people from Hyderabad, India, or the Beit Hanina Social Club for Palestinians, showcase languages and cultures that can be called Muslim (in terms

---

[45] See Juliane Hammer's article in Curtis, *Encyclopedia I*, p. 269.

[46] See Zareena Grewal and R. David Coolidge, Chapter 14 in this volume; also Marcia Hermansen's article in Curtis, *Encyclopedia I*, pp. 51–52.

[47] See al-Husein N. Madhany's article on Zaytuna in Cesari, *Encyclopedia I*, pp. 646–647.

[48] My major finding in a study of emigrants from Hyderabad, India, in seven new settings (Pakistan, the United Kingdom, Australia, Canada, the United States, Kuwait, and the United Arab Emirates), was that the old school tie was most meaningful for them: Karen Isaksen Leonard, *Locating Home: India's Hyderabadis Abroad* (Palo Alto, 2007).

of civilizational heritage) if not Islamic (religious). The Association of
Muslim Social Scientists of North America and the Islamic Medical
Association of North America both developed from the MSA and are
clearly identified as Muslim. Other associations based on occupation or
national origin, like the Association of Pakistani Physicians of North
America (AAPNA), the Pakistani American Public Affairs Committee
(PAKPAC), or the American Association of Yemeni Scientists and
Professionals (AAYSP) are often thought of as Muslim organizations.

Diasporic religious movements and political parties, like the
Tablighi Jamat from South Asia and the Jama'at-i-Islami party from
Pakistan, focus on reviving and maintaining faith abroad. Possibly more
political would be the Ikhwan or Muslim Brotherhood, based in Egypt,
and Deobandis, comprising graduates of the Dar ul Ulum Deoband seminary in northern India.[49] These last two movements have triggered interest from American intelligence agencies. The Muslim Brotherhood has
attracted more attention because of its history of political opposition to
the regimes in Egypt and Syria and because some of its factions abroad
have justified the use of violence against the state and citizens. However,
while many Arab foreign students coming to the United States from the
1960s were members of the Muslim Brotherhood, no American branch
of the organization has ever been established. Some of the students who
established the MSA and then ISNA, as well as some of the scholars from
Arab countries and Malaysia who founded the International Institute
of Islamic Thought in 1981, were inspired by the Brotherhood. But by
helping to establish these American Muslim organizations and institutions, Muslims with ties to the Brotherhood differentiated themselves
from followers of Wahhabism in America, choosing instead to relate to
the non-Muslim majority and mainstream politics. Muslim American
political organizations such as the AMC, MAS, and CAIR have also
been allegedly influenced by the Brotherhood. Lorenzo Vidino tries to
make a case for what he terms "the new Muslim Brotherhood in the
West" as a transnational Islamist organization supportive of terrorism,
while admitting that this "network" has relatively few members and
no clear indication of significant support among American Muslims.[50]
Also, he finds those with ties to the Brotherhood disagreeing with each

[49] The encyclopedias edited by Cesari and Curtis have entries for the Tablighi Jamat and
the Jama'at-i-Islami party, and one has an entry for the Muslim Brotherhood, but neither had an entry for Deoband or Deobandis (or for the Hizb-ul-Tahrir, which opposes
democracy and advocates establishment of an Islamic system of government and rein-
stitution of the Caliphate).
[50] Lorenzo Vidino, *The New Muslim Brotherhood in the West* (New York, 2010), p. 16.

other as they and other Muslim activists develop American Muslim political organizations.[51] Finally, Vidino states that "a new generation of American-born activists is slowly replacing the foreign-born founders of the network and their views cannot be exactly the same as their predecessors."[52]

The term "Deobandi" seems to have no political resonance in the United States, although there is probably an "old boys' network" of graduates from India's Dar ul Ulum Deoband. Web sites feature competing Islamic messages and networks that claim "orthodoxy" in various ways, Deobandi ways among them, and various Tablighi Jamat or Deobandi Sufi spinoffs can be located in Chicago and elsewhere. But does online communication equal a "virtual community," and, further, does a "virtual community" equal an offline community in any meaningful way? Research remains to be done on this question.[53] Deobandi movements have pragmatically adapted to the countries in which they find themselves.[54] Internet articles on Deobandis in the United Kingdom and in Pakistan do not provide insight into Deobandis in the United States (or in India).[55] In any case, recent activities and pronouncements by the Dar ul Ulum Deoband in India disassociate Islam and Muslims from terrorism and exhort Muslims to abide by the laws of the states in which they reside.[56]

Transnational Islamic charitable organizations like the Holy Land Foundation were major recipients of American Muslim *zakat*, charitable donations, before 9/11, and such funds were sent primarily abroad. However, as the FBI and the Department of Justice began to investigate

---

[51] Vidino, *New Muslim Brotherhood*, pp. 168, 176–177.

[52] Vidino, *New Muslim Brotherhood*, p. 198.

[53] See Doris Jakobsh's exploration of such questions in her review of five recent books on religion and cyberspace: Doris R. Jakobsh, "Understanding Religion and Cyberspace: What Have We Learned, What Lies Ahead?" in *Religious Studies Review* 32:4 (October 2006): 237–242.

[54] Metcalf points to the very different history of Deobandis in Pakistan; see "'Traditionalist' Islamic Activism: Deoband, Tablighis, and Talibs," on the Immanent Frame, http://blogs.ssrc.org/tif/2011/09/07/traditionalist-islamic-activism/, and in Barbara D. Metcalf, *Islamic Contestations: Essays on Muslims in India and Pakistan* (New York, 2004), pp. 265–284.

[55] Most Deobandis in the United Kingdom are working-class immigrants from Pakistan and loom large partly because South Asians (and splits among them) dominate the Muslim population there (as in Canada and South Africa). In the United States, African Americans, South Asians, and Arabs produce a very different sociopolitical constellation.

[56] In February 2008, 'ulama of various schools of thought convened for an All-India Anti-Terrorism Conference in Deoband to declare that terrorism was un-Islamic. In June in New Delhi, some 200,000 Muslims gathered to hear and cheer a fatwa signed by the grand Mufti of Deoband, Maulana Habibur Rahman, stating that Islam was against terrorism.

and indict Islamic charities as possible supporters of foreign terrorist organizations, American Muslims have looked more to charities based in the United States like the Life for Relief and Development in Michigan, now the largest Muslim-led charity headquartered in the United States.[57]

The final category of transnational networks among American Muslims includes minority religious movements within Islam like the Twelver Shi'as, Isma'ili Shi'as (Nizaris and Bohras), the Ahmadiyyas, the Druze, and Sufi movements. Very diverse, these movements look to specific recognized leaders who are often abroad (*maraji‘* or religious scholars, the Aga Khan, a *da'i* or head, and other authoritative designations).[58] They are not always recognized as part of the American Muslim community: surveys taken by American Muslim immigrant leaders to define and describe Muslims in the United States have omitted some of these organizations, as well as the Nation of Islam and the Moorish Science Temple of America.[59] Twelver Shi'as[60] are now usually included, as American Muslims try to work together.

The Sufi orders headed by pirs and shaykhs teach mystical and meditative techniques and often invoke poetry, music, and dance to achieve higher levels of spiritual awareness. These movements are not always specifically Islamic, and some have been labeled "pop" Sufism.[61] Both Sunni and Shi'a, Sufi movements have produced many offshoots and recombinations in the United States, and women are arguably more prominent in Sufism.[62] The charismatic leaders of early movements came from both immigrant and Euro-American backgrounds, and most early followers were white; the tomb of Samuel Lewis in New Mexico may be America's first Sufi shrine.[63] Most notable among Sufi orders in the United States are the Chishtis, the Bektashis, the Bawa Muhaiyaddeen Fellowship, the

---

[57] Sally Howell, "(Re)Bounding Islamic Charitable Giving in the Terror Decade," *Journal of Islamic and Near Eastern Law* 10:1 (2011): 35–64.

[58] See Leonard, *Muslims*, for overviews and further references, pp. 33–41, 54, 84–85, 108; Liyakat Takim's article in Cesari, *Encyclopedia I*, pp. 574–582; and, in Curtis, *Encyclopedia I*, articles by Brannon Ingram, pp. 32–34; Ali Asani, pp. 303–304, and Edward E. Curtis IV, pp. 160–161.

[59] See Leonard, *Muslims*, pp. 21–22.

[60] Linda S. Walbridge, *Without Forgetting the Imam: Lebanese Shi'ism in an American Community* (Detroit, 1997).

[61] See Gisela Webb, Chapter 11 in this volume; Peter Lamborn Wilson, "The Strange Fate of Sufism in the New Age," pp. 179–109, and James Jervis, "The Sufi Order in the West and Pir Vilayat 'Inayat Khan: Space-Age Spirituality in Contemporary Euro-American," pp. 211–260, both in Peter B. Clarke, ed., *New Trends and Developments in the World of Islam* (London, 1997).

[62] Leonard, *Muslims*, pp. 40–41, 95–96.

[63] Marcia K. Hermansen, "In the Garden of American Sufi Movements: Hybrids and Perennials," in Clarke, *New Trends and Developments*, pp. 155–178.

Halveti-Jerrahi Order of Dervishes, the Mevlevis, the Nimatullahis, and the Naqshbandi-Haqqanis. The Chishti musician and pir Inayat Khan came from India in 1910, and he and his son Vilayat Inayat Khan built a following featuring *qawwali*, the singing of religious songs as *dhikr*.[64] The Bektashi pir Baba Rezheb came from Albania to Michigan in the early 1950s.[65] The Sri Lankan teacher Bawa Muhaiyaddeen founded a fellowship in 1971 in Philadelphia.[66] Muzaffer Özak, sheikh of the Halveti-Jerrahi Order of Dervishes, came from Turkey in 1977; his order is headquartered in New York.[67] The Mevlevis, who trace their founding to the poet Mevlana Jalal al-Din Rumi in thirteenth-century Anatolia, have three branches in the United States.[68] Shaykh Muhammad Hisham Kabbani moved from Lebanon to the United States in 1991 and links the American branch of the Naqshbandi-Haqqani Sufi order to its head in Cyprus.[69] West African orders, the Tijaniyyah and the Murids, arrived with immigrants at the end of the twentieth century, and Cheikh Amadou Bamba (of the Murids) Day is celebrated in New York City annually.[70]

The Gülen movement from Turkey focuses on education, religious piety, and philanthropy. Influenced by Sufism and Anatolian culture, it was founded in the late 1970s by followers of preacher and teacher Fethullah Gülen. This mission, now global, emphasizes education and interfaith dialogue, and Gülen himself moved to the United States in 1999.[71]

GROUPS

Under this imprecise heading, one finds national-origin groups, such as South Asian Muslims, Palestinian Muslims, and African American

---

[64] See articles in Curtis, *Encyclopedia I*, by Erik S. Ohlander, pp. 327–329, and Natalia Slain, pp. 114–115.

[65] See Natalia Slain's article in Curtis, *Encyclopedia I*, pp. 82–83.

[66] See Natalia Slain's article in Curtis, *Encyclopedia I*, pp. 81–82.

[67] See Juliane Hammer's article in Curtis, *Encyclopedia I*, pp. 230–231.

[68] The Mevlana Foundation was established in 1976 by a shaykh from London who studied under Vilayat Khan; the Mevlevi Order of America was established in 1978 by the son of the shaykh of the order in Turkey; the Threshold Society was established by an appointee of Dr. Celalettin Celebi, descended from Rumi and the late head of the international Mevlevi order. See Natalia Slain's article in Curtis, *Encyclopedia II*, pp. 369–370.

[69] See articles by Erik. S. Ohlander in Curtis, *Encyclopedia I*, pp. 319–320, and Joseph Shamis in Cesari, *Encyclopedia I*, pp. 365–366.

[70] Zain Abdullah, *Black Mecca: The African Muslims of Harlem* (Oxford, 2010).

[71] See articles by Marcia Hermansen in Curtis, *Encyclopedia I*, pp. 221–222, and Emily Tucker in Cesari, *Encyclopedia of Islam*, pp. 271–272.

Muslims.[72] There are voluntary associations, like the Muslim Boy Scouts and Muslim Girl Scouts, with all-Muslim chapters established officially in the 1970s for Boy Scouts and in the 1980s for Girl Scouts (although Muslims participate in other chapters).[73] American Muslims have formed local, regional, and national associations for specific purposes, for example, the Latin American Dawa Organization (LADO) founded in New York in 1997 for Spanish-speaking converts.[74] Certainly the Muslim Alliance in North America (MANA) with its strong focus on African American Sunni Muslims (those not associated with W. D. Mohammed) and other American-born Muslims (Euro-American converts and the children of immigrants) has become increasingly relevant and sees itself as supplementing ISNA (if not eventually replacing that immigrant-dominated organization). MANA's first elected leader, Siraj Wahhaj and others, like Hamza Yusuf, appeal to younger American-born Muslims.[75]

The Progressive Muslim Union (PMU), though short-lived, was founded in 2004, and formulated as its goal the development of an independent, spiritually and intellectually sophisticated Islamic discourse that was distinctly North American, while remaining true to the teachings and values of Islam, but internal dissension (much of it centered on the war in Iraq) led to resignations of leaders like Omid Safi, Hussein Ibish, Laury Silvers, and Sarah Eltantawi, and eventually to its demise in 2006.[76] Muslims for Progressive Values (MPV) headed by Zuriani 'Ani' Zonneveld and Pamela Taylor, constitutes a continuation of PMU's goals and promotes a progressive American Islam.[77]

American Muslim women are increasingly influential. *Islamic Horizons*, ISNA's major publication, started a series on its own history by focusing on the Muslim women who nurtured the MSA and helped develop ISNA.[78] In 2007 young Muslim women swept the polls in the MSA national elections, resulting in a female president heading an all-women executive board.[79] Muslim women are being appointed to national leadership positions. Most significant was Dr. Ingrid Mattson's

72 See entries from the two encyclopedias already extensively cited.
73 See Konden R. Smith's articles, pp. 91–92 and 217–218, in Curtis, *Encyclopedia I*.
74 See Hjamil A. Martinez-Vasquez's article in Curtis, *Encyclopedia I*, p. 330.
75 See Edward E. Curtis IV's article in Curtis, *Encyclopedia II*, pp. 406.
76 See Shabani Mir's article in Cesari, *Encyclopedia I*, pp. 515–516; Omid Safi, ed., *Progressive Muslims: On Justice, Gender, and Pluralism* (Oxford, 2003), for the goals of PMU. Saleemah Abdul-Ghafur, ed., *Living Islam Out Loud* (Boston, 2005), features personal essays by American Muslim women.
77 See the Web site, www.mpvusa.org.
78 *Islamic Horizons*, May–June 2003.
79 "Women Sweep MSA Polls," *Islamic Horizons*, September–October 2007, 11.

election in 2006 to head ISNA, the largest Islamic organization in the United States and one generally viewed as conservative rather than progressive by both Muslims and non-Muslims.

Muslim women's groups are prominent locally and regionally, such as American Muslims Intent on Learning and Activism (AMILA) founded in San Francisco in 1992[80] and the Muslim Women's League or MWL established in 1992 in Los Angeles.[81] Readers of the glossy magazine *Azizah*, with its stylish contents and hijab-wearing models on the cover,[82] or of the (short-lived) *Muslim Girl Magazine* aimed at teenagers started in 2007, may constitute groups, like the followers of the many Islamic or Muslim hip hop groups or of the many Web sites and blogs on the Internet.

American Muslim women scholars are establishing themselves in the field of Qur'anic studies and jurisprudence, and their work has ranged from attacks on the very foundations of Islamic marriage and family law to more limited attempts to reinterpret Islamic law.[83] These Muslim feminists include indigenous and immigrant Muslim women, with academics Leila Ahmed, Amina Wadud, and Kecia Ali (an Egyptian American, an African American convert, and a white convert, respectively) leading the way. They call for a rethinking of the Qur'an and hadith, asserting that much now considered divine and immutable is the result of a long, male-dominated intellectual process. Amina Wadud, an Islamic studies professor, published *Qur'an and Woman* in the 1990s in several countries and languages, evidence of the global reach of the U.S.-based "gender jihad."

North American Muslim women from many national and sectarian backgrounds are increasing women's roles in Islam, with early twenty-first century groups supporting mosque participation and mixed-gender congregational prayers led by women imams. Patriarchal practices in mosques have been challenged: a "walk-in" in Morgantown, West Virginia, in 2004 involved six Muslim women (African American, South Asian, and Arab American) who entered by the front door and seated themselves in the main area. In a widely reported event, Dr. Amina Wadud gave the sermon and led men and women in Islamic prayer in New York in 2005.[84]

---

[80] See Andrew O'Brien's article in Curtis, *Encyclopedia I*, pp. 53–54.
[81] See Emily Tucker's article in Cesari, *Encyclopedia I*, pp. 455–456.
[82] See Jamillah Karim's article in Curtis, *Encyclopedia I*, pp. 75–76.
[83] See Juliane Hammer, Chapter 19 in this volume.
[84] Pamela Taylor, co-leader of Muslims for Progressive Values, led men and women in prayer in a mosque in Toronto in 2007.

Trying to generalize about all American Muslims at this time, one turns to Andrew Shryock. He writes that for Arab and Muslim Americans a "structure of feeling" is firmly in place, characterized by "the sense of marginality, the ambivalence about inclusion in (or exclusion from) the cultural mainstream, desires for greater political influence in the United States, the fear of being scrutinized, spied on, and judged a threat to security."[85] Leading American Muslims have not hesitated to express dissatisfaction with American foreign and domestic policies that affect them: MPAC, AMA, and CAIR have been especially strong critics, before and after 9/11. The Detroit Arab American Survey shows that church and mosque attendance have provided members with skills, confidence, a sense of civic culture, and a desire to work for change, leading to the development of an "oppositional" culture or "engaged resistance" based on a perceived lack of respect by other Americans.[86] Such oppositional or engaged resistance is historically justified and a legitimate, productive way to engage in politics. The British Muslim sociologist, Tariq Modood, defines political mobilization in a way that legitimates a vigorous American Muslim oppositional culture: "interaction and participation in the political system to register protest, win or support allies, defeat opponents, influence political processes, initiate, modify, or prevent policies, win public resources, or seek to achieve some other political goal, including the basic goals of gaining legitimacy for one's presence in the country and for one's existence as a collective presence of a certain sort."[87] Many immigrant American Muslims are clearly developing an oppositional culture or a culture of engaged resistance, similar to that of African American Muslims in the past and present, of Black Protestant churches and Arab American churches, and of contemporary American Muslim feminists. American Muslims may feel marginalized and disrespected, yet their engagement with mainstream politics has become deep and ongoing.

[85] Andrew Shryock, "The Moral Analogies of Race: Arab American Identity, Color Politics, and the Limits of Racialized Citizenship," in Amaney Jamal and Nadine Naber, eds., *Race and Arab Americans Before and After 9/11* (Syracuse, 2008), p. 81.

[86] See especially Ronald Stockton, "Arab-American Political Participation," in Amaney Jamal and Nadine Naber, eds., *Race and Arab Americans Before and After 9/11* (Syracuse, 2008), pp. 61–64, and Shryock, "The Moral Analogies," pp. 91–92. See also Ewing, *Being and Belonging*; Cainkar, *Homeland Insecurity*; Nabeel Abraham, Sally Howell, and Andrew Shryock, eds., *Arab Detroit 9/11: Life in the Terror Decade* (Detroit, 2011).

[87] Tariq Modood, "Ethnicity and Political Mobilization in Britain," in Glenn C. Loury, Tariq Modood, and Steven M. Teles, eds., *Ethnicity, Social Mobility, and Public Policy: Comparing the U.S.A. and UK* (Cambridge, 2005), pp. 457–474; p. 457 for quotation.

Appendix: Muslim American Organizations

Name	Founding Date and Information	Initial Location
I. African American Islam		
Moorish Science Temple of America (MSTA)	1913, Noble Drew Ali	East Coast, Midwest
Nation of Islam (NOI)	1930, Wallace Fard Muhammad, Elijah Muhammad	Detroit, Chicago
	1975, leadership assumed by Elijah Muhammad's son Warith Deen; renamed many times, ultimately as The Mosque Cares	
	1977, Louis Farrakhan split off, reclaimed NOI name in 1978	
II. Islam in America		
Federation of Islamic Associations (FIA)	1953, Lebanese immigrants	Midwest, Canada
Muslim Students Association (MSA)	1963, Arabic-speaking foreign students in the United States	
Islamic Society of North America (ISNA)	1981–1982, roots in MSA	Plainfield, Indiana
Islamic Circle of North America (ICNA)	1971, Pakistani Jamaat-i Islami party	New York
Muslim American Society (MAS)	1992, Arab Americans	Falls Church, Virginia
Universal Muslim Association of America (UMAA)	2002, Twelver Shi'a	East Coast
III. American Muslims		
Muslim Public Affairs Council (MPAC)	1988, Islamic Center of Southern California	Los Angeles
American Muslim Council (AMC)	1990, Arab Americans, ended 2009	Washington, D.C.
American Muslim Alliance (AMA)	1994, South Asians	Fremont, California
Council on American-Islamic Relations (CAIR)	1994, Arab Americans	Washington, D.C.
American Muslim Political Coordinating Council (AMPCC)	1998, AMA, AMC, MPAC, CAIR	Youngstown, Ohio
American Muslim Taskforce (AMTF)	2004, 11 organizations	Fremont, California

Further Reading

Abraham, Nabeel, Sally Howell, and Andrew Shryock, eds., *Arab Detroit 9/11: Life in the Terror Decade* (Detroit, 2010).

Abraham, Nabeel, and Andrew Shyrock, eds., *Arab Detroit: From Margin to Mainstream* (Detroit, 2000).

Esposito, John L., ed., *Oxford Encyclopedia of the Islamic World* (New York and Oxford, 2009).

Haddad, Yvonne Yazbeck, Jane I. Smith, and Kathleen M. Moore, *Muslim Women in America: The Challenge of Islam Today* (New York, 2006).

Jackson, Sherman, *Islam and the Blackamerican: Looking toward the Third Resurrection* (Oxford, 2005).

Leonard, Karen, *Muslims in the United States: The State of Research* (New York, 2003).

Safi, Omid, ed., *Progressive Muslims: On Justice, Gender, and Pluralism* (Oxford, 2003).

11 Negotiating Boundaries: American Sufis
GISELA WEBB

ISLAM, MUSLIMS, AND SUFIS

The term "Sufism" (tasawwuf) refers to a variety of modes of spirituality that developed in the Muslim world, including ascetic, sociocritical movements, esoteric interpretations of the Qur'an, and spiritual confraternities. Sufis were major transmitters of Islamic belief and practice to regions beyond the religion's "Middle" Eastern origin – Central Asia, Africa, the Indian subcontinent, the Malay-Indonesian world – and Sufis continued that tradition in North America. Before the 1960s, little scholarly attention was given to Sufism in America, mainly because American-bred Sufi groups were dismissed as part of New Age religions or as cults.[1]

The historical legacy of Sufism itself complicated the issue of understanding the relationship of modern Sufi movements to traditional Islamic and Sufi practice. Some modernist and conservative elements in Muslim revivalist discourses saw Sufism as tied to precolonial and colonial situations of backwardness, pacifism, and societal decay in Muslim societies, which they in turn blamed for the success of the colonial takeover of large territories inhabited or ruled by Muslims. Nevertheless, the role of the *wali Allah* (friend of God) remained a central focus of popular religious and devotional life throughout Muslim-majority societies.[2] In addition, some Americans involved in Sufi movements emphasized historical Sufism's language and goal of "the transcendent unity of God beyond *all* distinctions" (including religious distinctions)

---

[1] Gisela Webb, "Sufism in America," and "Subud," in Timothy Miller, ed., *America's Alternative Religions* (Albany, 1995), pp. 249–259; Gisela Webb, "Tradition and Innovation in Contemporary Islamic Spirituality: The Bawa Muhaiyaddeen Fellowship," in Yvonne Haddad and Jane Smith, eds., *Muslim Communities in North America* (Albany, 1994), pp. 75–108.

[2] See James Morris, "Situating Islamic Mysticism: Between Written Traditions and Popular Spirituality," in Robert Herrera, ed., *Mystics of the Book: Themes and Typologies* (New York, 1992), pp. 293–334.

in a way that denied any "essential" connection of "Sufism" with the *religion* of Islam. Despite the contested boundaries of Sufism, American Sufis have remained major contributors to Islamic religious beliefs, as well as Muslim cultural values and practices in the United States. They created alternatives to Islamist discourses on Islam and Sufism as they uncovered, analyzed, and appropriated historical as well as contemporary Sufi practices and ethics (including sexual ethics). The works of contemporary women scholars of Sufism such as Sachiko Murata, Sa'diyya Shaikh, Laury Silvers, and Kecia Ali contributed such approaches.[3] Seyyed Hossein Nasr, William Chittick, Michael Sells, and others have demonstrated the multivalency of the language of gender in studies of Islamic mysticism and philosophy.

Sufism had its historical origins in the eighth century C.E., as a number of Muslims began to criticize the accumulation of wealth and power and concomitant "forgetfulness of God" that the early Umayyad conquests had brought to Muslim societies. Many of these Muslims devoted themselves to ascetic practices such as nightly vigils, fasting beyond religious requirements, giving away worldly possessions, and wearing simple cloaks of wool (Arabic *suf*, from which the word "Sufi" derives). By the tenth century, Sufis were developing a lexicon of Islamic mystical concepts derived from, and legitimated in, Qur'anic language and exegesis. Early figures of Sufism included Hasan al-Basri of Iraq (d. 728 C.E.); Rabi'a of Basra (d. 801 C.E.); al-Muhasibi, a teacher in Baghdad (d. 857 C.E.); Dhu'-Nun, a Nubian in Egypt (d. 859 C.E.); and Al-Tustari (d. 896 C.E.).

By the twelfth century, formal religious orders (*tariqas*) began to crystallize around revered teachers. Each order was headed by a spiritual master (*shaykh* or *pir*) whose lineage was claimed to go back to the original founder of the order and, ultimately, to the Prophet Muhammad, through a chain of transmission (*silsilah*). There was a close bond between shaykh and disciple (*dervish* or *murid*), with the dervish vowing obedience to the shaykh. The shaykh was teacher and guide (*murshid*) for the disciple on his or her inward journey of the soul to God. Disciples met in lodges (*khanaqah*) for their rituals and often lived close to the compound (*zawiyyah*, or *dergah*) of the shaykh. Sufis married and only occasionally took vows of celibacy in becoming a member of a tariqa.

Sufi orders developed their own particular communal rituals and practices (based on the teaching of the shaykh) to complement and

---

[3] Sa'diyya Shaikh, "In Search of al-Insan: Sufism, Islamic Law, and Gender," *Journal of the American Academy of Religion* 77:4 (November 2009): 781–822.

deepen the fundamental requirements of Islamic worship. Perhaps the most central Sufi practice to develop was the *dhikr* (or *zikr*), the ritual of "remembrance of God," which included the invocation of the name or attributes of God. Some tariqas developed a silent dhikr, such as the silent, rhythmic repetition of the first part of the Islamic testimony of faith *La ilaha illa Allah* (There is no God but God). Other tariqas practiced a vocal dhikr, in which blessings on the Prophet and some of the ninety-nine beautiful names of God were repeated hundreds of times, often with the aid of a *tasbih* (rosary-like counting beads). Many tariqas came to utilize both types of dhikr, silent and chanted.

Some tariqas developed the use of rhythmical instruments to accompany singing and movement. The spiritual concert (*sama'*) became an important practice in many parts of the Muslim world. The "dance" became the part of some Sufi orders' practices, such as the Mevlevis (the Whirling Dervishes). Sufi gatherings utilized poetry, recitation, and musical compositions, which were intended to express and cultivate a certain *hal* (spiritual state). Sufi piety came to include the practice of making pilgrimages to the shrines or tombs (*mazar*) of Sufi teachers. The veneration of saints was discouraged in some areas of the Muslim world, such as Saudi Arabia, but the "friend of God" (or saint) became a central focus of popular religious and devotional life in many parts of the Muslim world.

Traditional Sufi orders were most often named after their founders, with Sufi aspirants seeking to emulate the qualities and teachings of the founder. Among the earliest of Sufi orders was the Qadiriyya order, based on Abdul Qadir al-Jilani of twelfth-century Baghdad, with members from West Africa to Indonesia. The Naqshbandiyyah order was important in Central Asia and India. The Chishtiyyah order emerged in India, the Shadhiliyyah order in North Africa. The Mawlawiyyah (the Mevlevis, or Whirling Dervishes), the Khalwatiyyah, and the Bektashiyyah orders represented some of the living spiritual orders of what was to become Turkey in the twentieth century. The Nimatullahis have had a long history in Iran; the Tijaniyyah order was prominent in West Africa. All of these traditional orders, and others, took root in North America.

SUFISM COMES TO AMERICA

The development of Sufism in America corresponded to distinct periods of interaction between the Euro-American and Asian worlds in the twentieth century. The first (documented) period, beginning in the early 1900s, was characterized by the interest of Americans and Europeans in

"Oriental wisdom," which grew from European contact with Asia during the colonial period. Along with the negative aspect of the "Orient as other" that characterized the period, the interaction of cultures produced a number of Sufi teachers trained in "traditional wisdom" and in European institutions. These teachers spoke of a spiritual lack and longing in "the West," and some brought their teachings there as well. Islam and Sufi traditions were also brought to the United States from West Africa during the transatlantic slave trade, which was well underway by the 1700s. These traditions were suppressed in America, but there is increasing evidence of secret transmission of Islamic traditions among African slaves before the nineteenth and twentieth centuries.[4]

Hazrat Inayat Khan, who in 1910 founded the Sufi Order in the West, is the best-known representative of the early period of Sufis in America. He was trained in both classical Indian and Western music and was initiated into the Chishtiyyah order by Khwaja Abu Hashim Madani. His teachings had elements characteristic of Chishtiyyah Sufism, in particular the melding of Indian or "Hindu" Advaita Vedanta and Islamic *wahdat al-wujud* (unity of being) philosophical perspectives, as well as the use of sacred music to elevate and "attune" the soul to the unitive structures of reality. Hazrat Khan believed that he had been given the mission of spreading the "Universal Message of the time," a teaching that could unite East and West and lead to universal brotherhood, love, and peace. However, he taught that this "Sufi" message was not essentially tied to historical Islam, that the universal truth of Sufism lay at the core of all religions, and that he was called to develop new forms of "universal worship" for his followers.[5] His autobiographical writings provide a glimpse of the attitudes and social structures underlying early twentieth-century American spiritual "searching." Hazrat Khan lamented how in the West "there are no disciples, only teachers"; how prejudice and scorn pervaded attitudes toward Islam, people of color, and people from "the East"; and how his audiences were (only) of the artistic and wealthy elites.[6] Hazrat Khan married an American, Ora Meena Ray Baker Noor, and after

---

[4]   See Richard Brent Turner, Chapter 2 in this volume.

[5]   This is an example of Marcia Hermansen's "perennial" designation; see Marcia Hermansen, "Literary Productions of Western Sufi Movements," in Jamal Malik and John Hinnells, eds., *Sufism in the West* (London, 2006), pp. 28–48.

[6]   See Gisela Webb, "Third-Wave Sufism in America and the Bawa Muhaiyaddin Fellowship," in Malik and Hinnells, *Sufism in the West*, pp. 86–102. See also Pir-O-Murshid Inayat Khan, *Biography of Pir-O-Murshid Inayat Khan* (London, 1979), p. 107. Given Hazrat Khan's articulation of Americans' aversion to things "Islam," one must consider to what extent Hazrat developed his "universal" teachings and dances – and distancing himself from Islamic *religion* – as a pedagogical necessity given the political and social realities of his host country.

initiating a number of disciples in the United States, he briefly returned to India, then came back to the United States to establish the first Sufi Order lodge in Fairfax, California: the "Kaaba Allah." Hazrat Khan died in 1927, leaving small groups of disciples to propagate "the Message," but disagreement among the murids regarding leadership, property, and philosophies resulted in the decline of the order. The late Meher Baba (d. 1969) attained some of the Sufi Order properties, adapted many of the order's teachings, and created "Sufism Reoriented."

SECOND-WAVE SUFISM: TRADITION AND INNOVATION

A second wave of Sufi activity in the United States coincided with the 1960s and 1970s countercultural movement in which larger numbers of (mostly) young middle-class (mostly) white Americans identified the source of racism, the Vietnam War, and the evil of technocracy as a spiritual sickness that establishment religions in America not only had failed to solve but had fostered. It was an era of seeking teachers of traditional, usually "Hindu" wisdom from the "East," often with little knowledge of or concern for the historical foundations of practices such as Zen, Yoga, or Sufism. It was a time of growth in comparative religious studies departments in the United States, interest in religious mysticism (fostered by Mircea Eliade, William James, Thomas Merton, Huston Smith, Seyyed Hossein Nasr, Rabbi Zalman Schachter, and D. T. Suzuki), and cross-pollination of cultures and religions. Jewish and Christian Americans studied "Eastern" wisdom traditions and attempted to revivify the mystical traditions of their own religions (albeit in new adaptations).[7] It was the era of acknowledging that the roots of Martin Luther King's civil rights movement were not only in the Bible but in Gandhi and Black Jewish and Black Muslim movements that sought to revive elements of a lost legacy in the "Asiatic" world. Teachers from the "East" were associated with therapeutic approaches to individual and global transformation.

Several Sufi teachers and organizations emerged in this era. Some used Sufism to designate a universal teaching that transcended institutional Islamic religious doctrine and practice. These universalistic, "perennial"-oriented groups adopted some elements of traditional Sufi practice but tended to avoid overt affiliation with institutional Islam.

---

[7] See the film *The Jew in the Lotus* for Rabbi Zalman Schachter's discussions with the Dalai Lama, directed by Laurel Chiten (1998). See also Bawa Muhaiyaddeen, *Questions of Life, Answers of Wisdom* (Philadelphia, 1991), pp. 17–22, for a record of Rabbi Schachter's discussions with Bawa Muhaiyaddeen.

The best-known example of this model is the Sufi Order of America, which was rejuvenated under the leadership of Pir Vilayat Inayat Khan, son of Hazrat Inayat Khan and his American-born wife Ora Begum. Pir Vilayat was educated in Europe and served in the British Royal Navy during World War II. After World War II he sought spiritual training from a number of masters of religious traditions in India and the Middle East. Through him and other persons associated with the order, notably Shahabuddin Less and Sam Lewis, the West Coast Sufi, Zen, yoga, Hassidic master of the late 1960s, thousands of people were introduced to "the Message," and the Sufi Order of America became associated in popular American culture with "Sufi Dancing" (later "Dances of Universal Peace"). Membership increased as the order began to cosponsor events (with other universalistic groups like the Temple of Understanding), such as the "Cosmic Masses" at St. John the Divine Cathedral in New York, organized in 1975 as part of the Spiritual Summit marking the thirtieth anniversary of the United Nations.

During the 1970s, the Sufi Order of the West had purchased land previously part of a Shaker village in the Berkshire Hills of upstate New York, naming it "the Abode of the Message." The Abode became a major host site not only for Sufi Order lectures, Universal Worship Services, and Sufi Dancing but for holistic health retreats and workshops, with the Sufi Order shifting its focus to the bridging of world spiritualities, psychology, alternative medicine, and ecological concerns, which, together characterized an important aspect of postmodern spirituality in contemporary America. Some of those inspired by Hazrat Inayat Khan's teachings gravitated to other Sufi groups that had a more traditional Islamic shaykh-disciple and communal relationship, particularly as waves of non-European immigrants changed the religious landscape of North America to a religiously pluralistic one.

The 1970s also saw the development of branches of Sufi orders that had originated in Muslim cultures and were transplanted into the American milieu.[8] The Turkish Halveti-Jerrahi Order of America was an example of tariqas in the United States that derived from larger traditional orders of Sufism, some of whose living masters did not live in the United States. Spiritual guidance and authority were provided by local shaykhs. These groups had long established silsilahs as well as traditional Islamic practices and *adab* (etiquette), reflecting their regional

---

8   Marcia Hermansen discusses "hybrid models" in "Literary Productions of Western Sufi Movements," in Malik and Hinnells, *Sufism in the West*, pp. 28–48, and includes Jerrahi, Nimatullahi, and Naqshbandi communities.

origins. The late Shaykh Muzaffereddin (Ozak) al-Jerrahi al-Halveti came to the United States from the main Jerrahi lodge in Istanbul and established the first Jerrahi order in the United States in Spring Valley, New York. He appointed Tosun Bayrak, Turkish-born but longtime resident of the United States (and well-known 1960s New York artist), as shaykh of the Spring Valley mosque community with more than seventy dervishes. The community built a mosque to accommodate not only the dervishes but also the increasing number of "non-Sufi" Muslims of the surrounding New York area who attended Friday prayers but not necessarily Sufi rituals, such as the regular dhikrs. This Sufi mosque became the choice of those Muslim immigrants who wanted a community that was culturally heterogeneous, conservative in morality, and traditional in Islamic practice. Religious education classes were developed for children, and the community maintained a conscious appreciation and appropriation of classic Sufi teaching and practice as well as a commitment to the traditional arts and translation of traditional Sufi texts. Shaykh Tosun Bayrak, Rabia Terri Harris, and the late Mukhtar Holland provided English translations and publication of Arabic and Turkish Sufi literature, including works of Ibn 'Arabi, al-Sulami, al-Qushayri, Abdul Qadir al-Jilani, and al-Ghazali.[9] For the American Jerrahis, Sufism was identified with Islamic spirituality. In going back to traditional Islamic sources, the Jerrahi scholars located precedents within the Islamic tradition itself for renewed interpretation of sacred texts, law, and traditional arts, using the tools of *fiqh* (Islamic jurisprudence), *ijtihad* (interpretation), and *tafsir* (Qur'anic commentary) as living traditions for addressing new social realities. The Jerrahi order became particularly active in international charitable activities in the last decades of the twentieth century and beyond, raising money and collecting supplies for victims of political crises and the war in Iraq, Bosnia, and Afghanistan. The Jerrahis also contributed to educational and other social services for the economically disadvantaged in the Spring Valley area. Such local and international engagement in relief efforts in countries with Muslim populations became a characteristic of the 1990s and the beginnings of the third wave of American Sufism.

---

[9]   See Rabia Terri Harris, "Reading the Signs: Unfolding Truth and the Transformation of Authority," in Gisela Webb, ed., *Windows of Faith: Muslim Women Scholar-Activists in North America* (Syracuse, 2000), pp. 172–194; Ibn al-Husayn al-Sulami, *The Way of Sufi Chivalry*, trans. Tosun Bayrak al-Jerrahi (Rochester, 1983); Muhyiddin Ibn 'Arabi, *What the Seeker Needs*, trans. Tosun Bayrak and Rabia Terri Harris (Putney, 1992).

NEGOTIATING BOUNDARIES: SUFISM IN THE ERA OF GLOBALIZATION

The period between the twentieth and twenty-first centuries has been called the "third wave" of Sufism in the United States. The term corresponds to types of activities and challenges that Sufi groups in America experienced in that period, as they addressed issues of authority and tradition that all religious communities faced (if they were to survive) and new issues related to globalization. Those issues include how to remember the founding story; the transmission of major teachings during the life and after the death of the founder; defining communal identity within the larger religious landscape; and continued leadership, interpretation, and relations with other communities in changing contexts.

Globalization has had its impact on the development of Sufi communities in North America as they responded to the increased number of immigrants coming to the United States from predominantly Muslim countries, global Islamic revivalism, and heightened religious and political self-consciousness in Muslim immigrant communities. The turn of the century also saw a proliferation of intercommunity, interfaith discussions and forums (not only interdenominational but inter-Sufi, between Sufi and non-Sufi Muslim, between Sufi and non-Muslim, and between Muslim and non-Muslim), particularly in response to September 11, on terrorism and radicalism in Islam, the Middle East crisis, and the development of Web sites to bring access to histories and literatures of Sufism, past and present.

THE BAWA MUHAIYADDEEN FELLOWSHIP: NEGOTIATING BOUNDARIES OF ISLAM AND SUFISM

The case of the Bawa Muhaiyaddeen Fellowship, a Sufi community in Philadelphia founded by the Tamil-speaking teacher from Sri Lanka, Muhammad Raheem Bawa Muhaiyaddeen, offers insight into these developments. The community had its American origins during the "second wave" of Sufism in the 1970s,[10] but it gradually reflected a closer identification with "normative" Islam during the 1980s and 1990s. Despite some tensions that emerged in relation to its Sufi or Islamic identity, the

---

[10] Bawa Muhaiyaddeen took members of his group to visit Pir Vilayat Khan at the Abode of the Message and had numerous dialogues with Shaykh Tosun Bayrak and other members of the Halveti-Jerrahi order, including the late Lex Hixon, who established a somewhat less traditional branch of the Jerrahiyyah in New York City.

community created an environment that attracted and served part of the growing multiethnic Muslim community in the United States.[11]

This community united a variety of interpretations of Sufism's relation to Islam – "Sufi-Muslim," "Sufi–not Muslim," and "Muslim–not Sufi" – under the umbrella of the "Bawa Muhaiyaddeen Fellowship and Mosque." With his arrival in Philadelphia from Sri Lanka in 1971, Bawa Muhaiyaddeen became an influential exemplar and transmitter in America of the legacy of Sufi teachings developed in South Asia. The content and form of his teachings, as well as his role as shaykh, presented a contemporary example of traditional mystical theories about the nature and function of the wali Allah and the *qutb* (spiritual pole of the age).[12] The translation and publication in 2001 of a volume of Bawa's discourses, songs, and dialogues, *The Resonance of Allah: Resplendent Explanations Arising from the Nur, Allah's Wisdom of Grace*,[13] was an example of the transmission of "wisdom teachings" to his American audiences that he had long shared with his Sri Lankan audiences. Studies of Bawa's teachings, as well as their appropriation and ongoing dissemination after his death in 1986, shed light on the dynamics of the transmission of Sufism in the context of developments in Islam, diaspora religion as well as interfaith and intrafaith relations in the United States.

SRI LANKAN ORIGINS: QUTB IN THE MALDIVES

Bawa Muhaiyaddeen's public career began in Sri Lanka in the early 1940s, when, as his Sri Lankan disciples recall, he emerged from the jungles of northern Sri Lanka and was approached by some pilgrims of local shrines, who recognized him as a "holy man." The pilgrims asked Bawa to teach them. Older members of the community described dreams or mystical encounters with Bawa before they met him physically. Most of his earliest followers were Hindus from the Jaffna area. Bawa rarely spoke about his personal history and journeys, but in an early publication from the 1940s, he described travels throughout "Serendib" before coming to Jaffna, spending several years in Kataragama, "a jungle shrine in South Sri Lanka, in Jailani," a shrine dedicated to Abdul Qadir Jilani

---

[11] This discussion of the Bawa Fellowship is based on archival materials of the fellowship, including audio and video recordings of Bawa's discourses, songs, and community events.

[12] *Qutb* refers to the highest spiritual authority in the hierarchy of saints: the pole, or "axis" that anchors the connection of the mystical disciple to God.

[13] Bawa Muhaiyaddeen, *The Resonance of Allah: Resplendent Explanations Arising from the Nur, Allah's Wisdom of Grace*, trans. K. Ganesan (Philadelphia, 2001; originally published in Tamil in Sri Lanka in 1969 under the title *Allahvin Mulakkam*).

of Baghdad, and other pilgrimage sites across Sri Lanka.[14] His early Jaffna audiences looked to him as a healer of medical and spiritual ailments and as one who could cast out demons. To accommodate the growing number of people that sought guidance and healing from him, he founded an ashram in Jaffna. As their numbers increased, he applied to the government for land and leased farmland south of Jaffna. The farm became the beginning of his teaching through service. Farming also became the metaphor for inner purification, knowledge, and growth. Life processes became symbols for the spiritual life and the processes of growth therein.

Several Muslims from the area of Colombo encountered Bawa's teachings on their travels to the Jaffna area and invited him to Colombo to teach. In 1955 Bawa laid the foundation for a mosque in Mankumban, north of Jaffna (which he attributed to a spiritual experience with Mary, the mother of Jesus). The building itself would not be built by Sri Lankans, but by American followers whom Bawa would bring to Sri Lanka in the 1970s. In 1967 the "Serendib Sufi Study Circle" was inaugurated and became a place of study and publication of Bawa's teachings in Colombo.[15]

Bawa's teaching stories utilized imagery from Hindu sources (Puranas, Upanishads) as well as Islamic sources, including hadith and *Qisas al-Anbiya* (Tales of the Prophets). These stories included figures such as Muhammad, Fatima, Gabriel, Ali, Rabi'a al-Adawiyyah, Hasan al-Basri, Uways al-Qarani (used by Bawa to identify his own spiritual lineage as not silsilah-bound), Moses, Khidr, Abraham, Jesus, Mary, and Abdul Qadir al-Jilani. Neither the followers of Bawa who came from Hindu background in Sri Lanka nor the early followers of Bawa in America who tended to be more familiar with Hindu and yoga imagery immediately recognized the preponderance of Islamic and Sufi images in Bawa's teachings.

THE AMERICAN COMMUNITY

Between 1969 and 1971, Bawa received letters from a young woman seeker from Philadelphia, who, like many young Americans, was disenchanted by the wave of gurus who had come through America in the 1960s.

---

[14] There are accounts and photos of Bawa Muhaiyaddeen going back to the early 1900s, putting Bawa at perhaps near one hundred when he died in 1986, but Bawa's followers are hesitant to speculate on his chronological age.

[15] The series of volumes entitled *Wisdom of the Divine* (vols. 1–6) has been published through the Serendib Sufi Study Circle, and reflects Bawa's commentaries and teachings on traditional Sufi doctrines, such as the transcendent unity of religions, the Sufi understanding of particular hadith, the spiritual stations, and the heart as the seat of wisdom.

She learned about Bawa Muhaiyaddeen from an anthropology student from Sri Lanka studying in Philadelphia. On the basis of an "inner experience," she began a correspondence with Bawa, urging him to come to the United States. Others followed and eventually a small group of seekers sponsored Bawa's first trip to the United States. This early group included both white and Black Americans, Christian and Jewish, mostly middle class, with a background in the "spiritual seeker" and yoga circuit in Philadelphia. African Americans in particular had hopes in Bawa as someone who, as a person of color, might help in healing the racial divide in America. Bawa arrived in Philadelphia on October 11, 1971. His American teaching began in small discussion groups at a home in Philadelphia. Growing numbers of followers and visitors necessitated larger spaces and the burgeoning group purchased a former synagogue in the Overbrook area that would become (and remains) the central location of the Bawa Muhaiyaddeen Fellowship. Most of the early members say they did not see Bawa as a teacher of Islamic religion, or even as a Sufi. He was identified more as a counselor-teacher with no formal spiritual practices and an ascetic. Bawa emphasized Islam as a state of unity and trust in God, an inculcation of the qualities of God, and as a discarding of distinctions of race, caste, and religion. Despite the lack of background (or intention) on the part of the Americans to recognize traditional Sufi themes and imagery, themes such as the mystical doctrine of the origin of creation, the "Inner Qur'an" as the essence of God's revelation in humankind, letter symbolism, the role of the true spiritual guide and leader, the journey to God through invocation, and the presence of saints in the world were part of his discourses from the 1970s onward. Bawa used the term *qutb* to signify the state or faculty of qutb or *qutbiyyat*, the eternal capacity or presence in the human heart of God's own power, grace, or illumination, the presence of which existed in the walis and qutbs of the past, including Abd al-Qadir al-Jilani, the twelfth-century Baghdadi preacher who was called *muhyi ad-din* (reviver of the faith). Bawa also used the term to signify that presence in the historical and inner reality of himself, Bawa Muhaiyaddeen, in the present era.[16]

TOWARD "IMAN-ISLAM": THE MOSQUE AS BOUNDARY AND BRIDGE

Between 1971 and 1986 there emerged a stronger identification of the Bawa Muhaiyaddeen Fellowship with traditional Islamic practice, not

---

[16] Bawa Muhaiyaddeen, "The One Who Rules Baghdad," Tape 5-Songs, elucidates this teaching. Bawa's followers consider Bawa a living presence, still the qutb of the age.

only when Bawa taught the salat (daily prayers) the members with attention to their outer formal requirements and their interior "Sufi" meaning, or when he taught a silent and an audible invocation,[17] but most profoundly when he announced his plan to build a mosque. That mosque, which was built by fellowship members and completed in 1984, was open to persons of any religion for private prayer except during the times of the Muslim liturgical prayers (as had been the case in the "house of God" in Mankumban, Sri Lanka). Liturgical prayers were conducted in strict adherence to Hanafi practice (the Islamic legal school of Sri Lanka), and any Muslim could join the congregation in daily and Friday prayers. The mosque would bring traditional gender distinctions in use of social space, with men in the front and women behind them, a lace curtain separating them. Members say that in consolation for this new separation, Bawa designed the space so the transparent dome would be over the women's area. In Bawa's discourses until this time, men and women were in the same room, though one can see from videos that although there is no barrier between men and women, and no "hierarchy of proximity," the women and men are generally in different spaces in the room.[18]

The building of the mosque was a public articulation of Islam that brought into high relief the question of the relationship of Bawa's teachings to Islamic practice. Did Bawa intend a gradual movement toward Islamic religious practices (such as salat) as an outer manifestation of inner maturity and discipline, or did he intend it as a concession to the human need for unifying cultural forms and rituals, despite the "illusory" quality of religious distinction, or was it both? With the building of the mosque, several members left the fellowship because of an overt identification with Islamic religion they did not want. Others attempted to challenge or distance themselves from the Bawa Fellowship because of an identification with an expression of Islam they, for different reasons, did not accept. The building of the mosque affected the legitimacy and

---

[17] For a more detailed description of the dhikr Bawa taught, see Webb, "Tradition and Innovation," pp. 82–85 and 94–95. The silent dhikr includes the process of ablutions, recitation of the Qur'anic chapters Fatiha, Nas, Ikhlas, and Falaq, practicing a rhythmic recitation of the "La ilaha illa Allah" (there is no God but God) while focusing on left and right body/breath until "there is no other." The traditional association of the "left" with the negative pole and first part of the shahadah (*La ilaha*) and the "right" with the positive pole of the shahadah (*illa Allah*) can also be seen in Sufi poetry, especially of the Qadiriyyah Sufi order. The loud dhikr consists of repetition of traditional formulae, such as the attributes of God, and the "La ilaha illa Allah."

[18] Women have had leadership roles in the fellowship – teaching and administration – from the beginning, including president and secretary of the fellowship. The mosque imams appointed by Bawa were always male. Many Fellowship women have participated in national Sufi women gatherings.

acceptance of the Bawa Muhaiyaddeen Fellowship within the larger religious community in Philadelphia and beyond, nationally and internationally, Muslim and non-Muslim. It became a symbol of Muslim identity for many communities in America. The number of individuals and families of Turkish, Indian-Pakistani, and "Middle Eastern" origin increased. Those families in turn transmitted Bawa's teachings abroad. Articles on Bawa's teachings appeared in Turkish religious journals, and there began an interchange of discussions and formal visits among Sufi-oriented Muslims in Turkey and members of the Philadelphia fellowship. Many in the American Muslim community did not see themselves as followers of Bawa but nevertheless participated in mosque activities, especially the traditional Muslim celebrations, such as Ramadan and the two Eid festivals. The mosque also gained membership from the African American Muslim community. Finally, the mosque became for many individuals of the early community, from diverse backgrounds, the locus and anchor point of their journey, with their guide, toward Islamic practice.

Over the years there have been a gradual negotiation and accommodation of the variety of perspectives on the meaning and function of the mosque, with members affirming that Bawa would have been able to embrace such diversity, pointing to his earlier inclusive Sri Lankan "ministry" to both Hindus and Muslims. Three major orientations have characterized the fellowship: those who came for Bawa's wisdom teachings on the interior, "universalist-core" experience of Islam alone (focusing on acquiring Islam as a state of purity and unity that transcends religious forms); those who came for the mosque and (non-Sufi) Islamic religious practices and celebrations; and those who came for both the mystical teachings and exoteric practices of Islam, the latter of which are seen as an exteriorization of the inner experience and an important means of fostering community life and continuity. The symbolic move toward a more recognizable exoteric Islam through the building of the mosque has contributed significantly to the inclusion of the fellowship in inter-Islamic and inter-Sufi communication and solidarity as well as in civic interfaith communication and dialogue in the Philadelphia area.

DEVELOPMENTS IN COMMUNITY LIFE: THE FARM AND THE MAZAR

As in Sri Lanka, Bawa used a variety of forms to teach subtle mystical and philosophical doctrines to his American followers, including formal discourses,[19] devotional teaching songs, and artwork as a visual access to core teachings. Among the community activities Bawa instituted were the practices of the daily prayers, Friday prayers, observances of Ramadan, *zakat al-fitr* (charitable giving) at the end of Ramadan, the Eids, mawlids in honor of the Prophet and of the Qutb/Muhaiyaddeen, and devotional visitation to Mecca (*'umrah*). While he did give many public talks outside of Philadelphia, most of his discourses took place in the meeting room of the fellowship house in Philadelphia; many were given in his bedroom, particularly as his health declined.

Bawa did not appoint a shaykh to succeed him. Since his death in 1986, the transmission of his teachings has been continued through the "elders" of the community,[20] who use the vast archives of Bawa's videotapes and published discourses. He had appointed two imams to lead Friday prayers, one from Sri Lanka and one American (now others may lead prayers), instructing them "not to use the *khutbah* to beat people, but to melt their hearts."[21] Among the weekly activities of the fellowship are Sunday meetings (led by a wide range of the fellowship's elders, but sometimes by the children who were raised in "the Fellowship," which focuses on Bawa's wisdom teachings), Friday prayers, salat and early morning dhikr in the mosque, children's meetings, Friday night dhikr instruction and practice, and regular readings and discussion of Bawa's work. Women have held leadership positions from the beginning, including translator (of Bawa's Tamil into English), president, and secretary of the fellowship. Ritual congregational prayers, however, maintain separate spaces for men and women.

Beyond the mosque in Philadelphia, fellowship activities are also held at the community's farm in Unionville, Pennsylvania, which Bawa

[19] The titles of the discourses and songs are telling of their contents and their function in the community, for example, on the meaning of the Quran and the Mi'raj experience: "The Stages of Ascendancy," "The Meaning of the Suras" (8.26.76 APT7608–03); devotional songs: "Eternal Prayer" (9.1.74. ARS 7409–01), "First Muhammad Song" (11.9.77 ARS 7711–04), "The Qalb, the Island of Serendib" (10.11.75 ARS-74–0802); on Bawa's teachings on his vision of the meaning and building of the mosque: "Bawa Muhaiyaddeen's vision of building the mosques in Mankumban and Philadelphia" (08/24/79), "Laying the cornerstone: God gives his Rahmat according to the age and maturity of each being. Learn *'ilm* and know the taste of prayer, worship, and ibadat" (11.14.83. [Tape 1 of 8, 790824–01 MOSQ]. The audio tapes are in the process of being transferred to CD's in the archival work of the fellowship.

[20] Administrative decisions are made according to bylaws set up by Bawa in 1973, which defined duties and functions of an executive committee, board of trustees, and general council. There have been discussions in the community about the need to integrate new members, new approaches, and new leadership into meetings and other functions in the community.

[21] *Khutbah* is the Friday sermon delivered before the congregational Friday prayer.

had directed the community to purchase for three functions: a farm for community life and teaching, a burial site for Muslims, and a mazar for Bawa Muhaiyaddeen.

As in Sri Lanka, Bawa used farming and cooking to teach community skills, service, and charity as members were instructed in the parallel spiritual work of cultivating the spiritual virtues, the divine names and attributes, and the remembrance of God with every breath. Instructions on the characteristics and qualities of food (physical and spiritual) became another focus of discourses. The farm also became a venue for outdoor family camp weekends and retreats. Thus, on a given "unity weekend" the community would perform the cycle of daily prayers, attend to the needs of the farm and the cooking and serving of food, engage in practice of silent or loud dhikr as taught by Bawa, and organize discussion groups on Bawa's spiritual teachings. Some fellowship members live near the farm and have organized a branch community in that area.

Bawa had also directed the purchase of the farm in order to provide a burial site for fellowship members and for the shaykh himself. Since Bawa's death in 1986, the traditional, simple mazar has become not only the center for prayers on the anniversary of his death, songs, and Qur'anic recitation in honor of Bawa but also a pilgrimage site for Sufis from other tariqas. The mazar has increasingly become a pilgrimage and family gathering site for Muslim immigrants, including Turkish, South Asian, and Iranian Muslims. These recent immigrants did not know Bawa, but they brought with them cultural traditions from their homelands where family gatherings – picnics, songs, and prayers – are often shared near the site of a saint.

The cemetery has provided a burial site for "Bawa's children," and several of the earliest members of the community have died. With increasing numbers of immigrant Muslims in the United States, Muslims who are not students of Bawa have become members of the mosque community so that they may have an Islamic burial and site for themselves and their families. Women and men from the community participate in the traditional Islamic rituals of washing and burial of the deceased members of the community.[22]

OUTREACH – LOCAL AND GLOBAL, SACRED AND POLITICAL

Since the late 1980s, the Bawa Muhaiyaddeen Fellowship has been regularly invited to participate in a variety of interfaith and international

---

[22] See Gisela Webb, "When Death Occurs: Islamic Rituals and Practices in the United States," in Lucy Bregman, ed., *Religion, Death and Dying* (London, 2010), pp. 111–126.

activities: citywide commissions, local church and synagogue interfaith relations, and meetings with formal representatives from major faith communities: Catholic, Episcopalian, Lutheran, Methodist, Jewish, and others. This was the beginning of the fellowship's inclusion in formal interfaith dialogue in Philadelphia and the United States. The larger Philadelphia religious community began to see fellowship representatives as articulate spokespersons of traditional Islam (as opposed to its "cult" or "New Age" status of the early 1970s). The fellowship regularly sent members to schools, churches, temples, and community gatherings to speak about Islam and interfaith relations and to host university student groups wishing to visit the Islamic Friday prayers or events at the Fellowship Farm. The media has utilized the fellowship when events relating to Islam called for reportage, with an increase in interest and coverage after the 1993 World Trade Center bombings and again after 9/11.

However, the relationship between the fellowship and the media had its beginnings during the late 1970s with the Iranian Revolution and the taking of American hostages. Fellowship members recall Bawa's response to Khomeini's presentation of Islam and his role in the taking of American hostages. Bawa began a letter writing campaign to several world leaders involved in the 1979–1981 crisis. Bawa had always emphasized the internal human forces driving greed, violence, injustice, and disunity in the world, but his engagement in the political realm was a new turn. His criticism of Khomeini was quoted (and pictured) in *Time Magazine*. His letters were compiled in a 1980 publication, *The Truth and Unity of Man* (now out of print);[23] they included strong criticism of Khomeini for damaging Islam and a plea to return to the compassion and brotherhood of "true" Islam and to the nobility of early Islamic figures, such as Muhammad and Ali.[24] In his now famous *Islam and World Peace*,[25] Bawa not only defined Sufi understanding of terms such as *salam* (peace), *jihad* (struggle), and the Inner Qur'an but presented an outline of the history of the most famous example of strife among the children of Abraham: Jerusalem. While maintaining that establishing inner peace (salam) within oneself is the only effective road toward world peace,[26] he nevertheless made an appeal for an "outer" United Nations Peace Force to be sent to maintain border security between "the

---

[23] Bawa Muhaiyaddeen, *The Truth and Unity of Man: Letters in Response to a Crisis* (Philadelphia, 1980).

[24] Bawa Muhaiyaddeen, *The Truth and Unity*, pp. 8–23, 45–61.

[25] Bawa Muhaiyaddeen, *Islam and World Peace* (Philadelphia, 1987).

[26] Bawa Muhaiyaddeen, *Islam and World Peace*, especially the final chapter, "Everyone Is Speaking about Peace."

two lands."²⁷ While Bawa's focus was on teachings to heal and transform the "inner self," his concern for "God's justice" prompted involvement in the global arena and became a precedent for a number of fellowship members since Bawa's death. The community refrained from taking on political commitments as a group, owing to varying political perspectives and commitments; however, there has been involvement and leadership in various international peace and justice organizations and activities by individual members. Examples include the Muslim Peace Fellowship, the Global Dialogue Institute, Global Security Institute, Fellowship of Reconciliation, the 2001 International Conference on Racism in South Africa, Muslim women's rights work, and environmental justice work. A particularly important legacy of this peace and justice outreach component of Bawa's work that has continued since his death is the visitation of prisoners and the Free Book Program for Prisoners. The fellowship has been in contact with more than eight thousand prisoners through the years, many of whom have communicated their reflections on their studies of Bawa's discourses through letters.

The 1990s saw the emergence of nationwide inter-Sufi gatherings (including Sufi women's gatherings)²⁸ in which fellowship members participated. Some fellowship members have become participants in inter-Sufi and inter-Islamic online networks. An example of inter-Sufi, intercommunity support took place in the winter of 2001 as a public benefit event was held at the University of Pennsylvania to raise funds for the publishing of Bawa Muhaiyaddeen's *Resonance of Allah*. Rumi poetry recitation and musical concerts have brought together performers from various Sufi groups as well as audiences from Sufi groups on the East Coast and the public at large. The young adults, children of the first and second generation of Bawa's "family," now participate in activities and speak at meetings.

The Bawa Muhaiyaddeen Fellowship has been a microcosm of the dynamics of Sufism in America. Bawa Muhaiyaddeen was a twentieth-century example of the tradition of popular Sufi teachers in South Asia who taught the mystical dimension of Islam to regions well beyond the geographic origins of the religion. Bawa brought to both his Sri Lankan and American followers the Sufi tradition of the *qutb*, which he identified as the ongoing cosmic process of divine illumination through the prophets, qutbs, and saints and his own role as qutb and re-viver of the faith (*muhyi ad-din*) of this era. His legacy of oral and literary

²⁷ Bawa Muhaiyaddeen, *Islam and World Peace*, p. 22.
²⁸ Maryam Kabeer Faye, *Journey through Ten Thousand Veils* (Somerset, N.J., 2009).

traditions of wisdom contributed to the development of a long-standing community of American Sufis. The community went through stages in negotiating its relationship to other Sufis and to the larger community of Islam. Ultimately it accommodated members from a variety of orientations of Sufism as well as the non–Sufi Muslim community that saw the fellowship mosque as a culturally integrated expression of Islam. The number of members in Philadelphia who defined themselves as Bawa's students has held steady at about one thousand, with several smaller groups of members around the country (and Canada). The community has continued to attract and interact with Muslim populations in the United States that increased through conversion and immigration. While Bawa gave many directives in terms of leadership and established a board of directors and an executive committee (with a woman president) to vote on policies, the future will inevitably pose the question of transference of leadership, power, decisions, and interpretation of Islam and Bawa's teachings beyond the first generation of the Bawa Muhaiyaddeen Fellowship and Mosque.

Further Reading

Hermansen, Marcia, "The Academic Study of Sufism at American Universities," *American Journal of Islamic and Social Sciences* 24:3 (Summer 2007): 24–45.
"Hybrid Identity Formations in Muslim America: The Case of American Sufi Movements," *Muslim World* 90:1–2 (March 2000): 158–197.
Malik, Jamal, and John Hinnell, eds., *Sufism in the West* (London, 2006).
Nasr, Seyyed Hossein, *The Heart of Islam* (San Francisco, 2002).
Renard, John, ed., *Windows on the House of Islam* (Berkeley, 1998).
Webb, Gisela, "Tradition and Innovation in Contemporary Islamic Spirituality: The Bawa Muhaiyaddeen Fellowship," in Yvonne Haddad and Jane Smith, eds., *Muslim Communities in North America* (Albany, 1994), pp. 75–108.
Westerlund, David, ed., *Sufism in Europe and North America* (London, 2004).

12 Religious Normativity and Praxis among American Muslims

KAMBIZ GHANEABASSIRI

When, in 1920, Muhammad Sadiq arrived in the United States as a missionary of the Ahmadiyya Movement in Islam, immigration officials refused him entry because he adhered to a religion that permitted polygamy. The Immigration Act of 1891 had deemed "polygamists; or persons who admit their belief in the practice of polygamy" inadmissible, along with a host of other undesirables such as anarchists, "idiots," insane persons, paupers, felons, and "persons with a dangerous contagious disease." Sadiq challenged his deportation by requesting a hearing where he argued, "I have not come here to teach plurality of wives. If a Moslem will ever preach or practice polygamy in America he will be committing a sin against his religion."[1] To make his case, Sadiq highlighted the distinction in Islamic law between permissible (halal) and obligatory (fard) acts. He explained that the practice of polygamy is not an obligatory duty for Muslim men. It is a permissible act, "and that permission is taken away under the commandment that I must obey the Law of the Ruling Government of the country."[2] Sadiq's explanation satisfied immigration officials, and he was admitted to the United States.

Sadiq's experience with U.S. immigration regulations resulted from a common misconception of religion. Immigration officials denied Sadiq entry on the assumption that religious laws are doctrinaire. The Immigration Act of 1891 assumed that anyone who adhered to a religion that legally permitted men to marry up to four wives must believe in the normativity of polygamy and therefore will seek to practice or preach polygamy in the United States.

In his appeal, Sadiq demonstrated that in practice Islamic laws are not dogmatic prescriptions for behavior; rather, they provide a hermeneutical framework through which religious teachings are interpreted

---

[1] Richard Brent Turner, "Islam in the United States in the 1920's: The Quest for a New Vision in Afro-American Religion" (Ph.D. diss., Princeton University, 1986), p. 142.

[2] Muhammad Sadiq, "No Polygamy," *Moslem Sunrise* 1:1 (July 1921): 9.

and applied to new circumstances. His explanation showed that the Islamic legal system does not impose norms regardless of circumstances but allows for religious norms to be established in relation to varying circumstances. The determination of what is legally permitted in Islam, he argued, has to take into consideration the laws of the land where one lives.

It is noteworthy that Sadiq himself did not argue for a dynamic understanding of Islamic law. He did not base his appeal on the fact that the practice of polygamy is subject to varying interpretations. By arguing that the commandment to follow the laws of the ruling government in the United States stripped Muslim men of their permission to marry multiple wives,[3] he simply interchanged one Islamic precept for another in order to demonstrate that his religion would not violate American social and legal norms. This shows that while in practice Islamic laws are interpretive and adaptive, ideally they are believed to be universal and normatively binding. Examining Islamic praxis thus allows one to see how Islamic ideals and traditions are negotiated and implemented in varying contexts. Central to this assertion is the contention that Islamic laws and practices have not been shaped solely by the Qur'an, *hadith*, and principles of jurisprudence developed by Muslim scholars to discern God's will but also by popular traditions, local customs, and historical circumstances.

NORMATIVITY AND DIVERSITY IN ISLAM

Muslim-majority societies span the rim of the globe from West Africa to Southeast Asia, and in each successive region Islam has been adapted to local cultures. The regional and cultural diversity encompassed by "the Islamic World" has historically resulted in a variety of understandings of Islam. Indeed, the diversity of Islamic beliefs and practices has been a central problem of Islamic studies. Scholars of Islam, just as scholars of ritual and practice in general, have debated whether religion is best understood through its textual sources (scriptures, legal and theological writings) or through its practice in local contexts. In discourses on Islam in America, this debate is animated in regard to the framing of Islam within an American context. Is American Islam best understood

---

[3] This is a reference to Qur'an 4:58, "O those who have faith obey God and obey the Messenger and obey those who have authority to command among you." Sadiq seems to have interpreted this verse to mean obey the laws of the ruling government wherever one is.

as the latest episode in a long history of expansion, this time into "the West," or as a "new religion" or minority religion amid the plurality of religions in the United States?[4] Should we study Islamic praxis in terms of analytical framings developed within the Islamic tradition, such as *fiqh al-aqalliyyat* (Islamic laws for Muslim minority communities), or those used in American studies, such as race, gender, assimilation, and class?

There is no obvious right and wrong side to these scholarly debates because there is something to be learned about Islam in America from each of these framings. Nonetheless, approaching diversity within Islam as a problem seems wrongheaded. Diversity becomes a problem only when we begin from the assumption that unity is the norm in religions and that religious beliefs and laws are formative of religious behavior irrespective of varying sociohistorical contexts. Empirically, religion constantly interacts with local contexts and is variously adapted and reinterpreted in light of local circumstances. In view of the diverse environmental and cultural conditions that shape human experiences, diversity should be seen as the norm rather than the problem that requires explanation. This is as true for global Islam, given the cultural and geographic diversity of the regions in which Islam is practiced, as it is for American Islam, given that Muslims from all over the world have immigrated to the United States and that there are also movements formed in the name of Islam that are native to this land (e.g., the Nation of Islam and the Moorish Science Temple).

If we begin with the premise that diversity rather than unity is to be expected in the way in which religions are practiced, then to understand Islamic praxis in the United States we need to ask how certain practices and beliefs are signified as Islamic and not how a unified understanding of Islam is diversified by its practice in the United States. Put differently, we need to approach Islamic normativity not so much in terms of orthodoxy and orthopraxy but in terms of the means or structures by which Muslims deem certain beliefs and performances as Islamic. This approach allows us to move beyond reified or idealized understandings of Islam to inquire into how religious authority and normativity are practically negotiated in relation to changing circumstances.

---

[4] Of course, there is a flip side to this question. How we frame Islam in America does not depend solely on how we approach Islam but also on how we conceptualize America. Is America fundamentally a Protestant nation where Islam is an outsider religion or is America a religiously pluralistic society in which Muslims could practice their religion as they see fit?

THE RELIGIOUSLY AUTHORITATIVE IN ISLAM

The assertion that the religiously authoritative has to be negotiated demands qualification. After all, religiously speaking, there are no established negotiating parties or entities to which one could point to describe how a particular belief or practice is determined as Islamic. There is no equivalent to the Vatican in Islam that could pass judgment on orthodoxy and orthopraxy or to determine membership within the Muslim community (*ummah*). The most universally accepted authoritative sources in Islam, namely the Qur'an and hadith, are both subject to interpretation and cannot themselves be said to "negotiate" what is properly Islamic in a given context.

Taken to its logical conclusion, the notion that the religiously authoritative has to be negotiated posits orthodoxy and orthopraxy as products of the activities of some agent. There has to be a subject that carries out the act of negotiating. This has led some scholars to define orthodoxy and orthopraxy as products of power relations. Talal Asad has made perhaps the most influential articulation of this view in recent years. Addressing the dichotomy between universal and local conceptualizations of Islam, Asad argued that "the most urgent need for an anthropology of Islam is a matter not so much of finding the right scale but of formulating the right concept." The influential concept he put forth was "a discursive tradition." As a discursive tradition, Islam has to constantly be negotiated. As Asad explained,

> A tradition consists essentially of discourses that seek to instruct practitioners regarding the correct form and purpose of a given practice that, precisely because it is established, has a history. These discourses relate conceptually to *a past* (when the practice was instituted, and from which the knowledge of its point and proper performance has been transmitted) and *a future* (how the point of that practice can best be secured in the short or long term, or why it should be modified or abandoned), through *a present* (how it is linked to other practices, institutions, and social conditions). An Islamic discursive tradition is simply a tradition of Muslim discourse that addresses itself to conceptions of the Islamic past and future with reference to a particular practice in the present.[5]

Discourse alone, however, does not authoritatively define proper belief and practice. Orthodoxy and orthopraxy are products of "a relationship

---

[5] Talal Asad, *The Idea of an Anthropology of Islam* (Washington, D.C., 1986), p. 14.

of power," according to Asad. "Wherever Muslims have the power to regulate, uphold, require, or adjust *correct* practices, and to condemn, exclude, undermine, or replace *incorrect* ones, there is the domain of orthodoxy." Anthropology of Islam, thus, should concern itself with "the way these powers are exercised, the conditions that make them possible (social, political, economic, etc.), and the resistance they encounter (from Muslims and non-Muslims)."[6]

From this perspective, social, political, and economic power relations reveal the entities negotiating orthodoxy and orthopraxy in Islam. As welcome as the visibility of social, political, and economic forces is in determining proper religious belief and practice, the notion that orthodoxy and orthopraxy result from power relations is not fully satisfactory because it neglects to address the role individual cognitions, emotions, experiences, and intuitions play in understandings of God and the hereafter. Orthodoxy and orthopraxy are just as dependent on individual understandings of the normative as they are on the power relations enforcing correct belief and practice.

I do not mean here to posit a theological understanding of religion against a social scientific one or to pit individual agency against social structure. The fact that the social, the political, and the economic play a role in negotiating religious authority is undeniable. Rather, I wish to draw attention to the fact that an understanding of orthodoxy and orthopraxy as products of power relations locates the determinant of orthodoxy and orthopraxy within the social rather than the individual and, as such, harkens back to idealized and unifying conceptions of religion rather than diversity of religious practice.

Theory is as valuable as the context to which it is applied. In the U.S. context, where individuals or small groups have often practiced Islam in isolation from other Muslims, a social theory of proper Islamic practice is not particularly instructive. Even when Muslims come to be a sizable minority in the United States during the second half of the twentieth century, given the absence of established Islamic traditions in this country and the plurality of understandings of Islam, the individual – her religious understandings, intuitions, experiences, and desires – continues to play a formative role in understandings of proper Muslim belief and practice. As such, a theory of proper religious belief and practice that does not adequately address the way in which normativity is determined by the individual (in relation to the social, the political, the economic,

---

[6]   Asad, *Anthropology of Islam*, p. 15.

the Islamic tradition, etc.) does not adequately illuminate the practice of Islam in America.

CONCEPTUALIZING ISLAMIC PRACTICE IN THE UNITED STATES

For a more illuminating understanding of Islamic praxis in the United States, it is useful to examine the structure of Islamic acts of worship. Such an approach is particularly constructive because for much of the early history of Islam in America the only evidence we have of the practice of Islam is isolated accounts of Muslims performing acts of worship by themselves. Structurally, Islamic acts of worship embody a triangular relationship between God, individual, and community. This point, I think, is best demonstrated through concrete examples. Take the proverbial Five Pillars of Islam. The first pillar, *shahadah*, for example, comprises an attestation in one's heart and by one's tongue that "there is no deity but God and that Muhammad is His messenger." This individual attestation of belief in God and the prophethood of Muhammad ibn 'Abd Allah establishes the principle of faith through which Muslim community (ummah) is conceived. It is the means by which individuals affirm belonging to the ummah and in the case of converts, the means by which other Muslims accept one as part of the ummah. The shahadah triangulates the individual, God, and community by establishing the notion of a universal Muslim community through individual Muslims' profession of faith in God and His messenger.

A similar triangular relation between individual, community, and God is established through the second pillar – daily ritual prayers (*salat*). The ritual prayer itself is an act of worship commanded by God for individuals to perform, but individual Muslims are obligated to perform these prayers within set intervals during the day, facing the shortest direction to Mecca. The content of the prayer – its liturgy and physical movements – is also more or less set. Individuals may choose a section of the Qur'an they wish to recite following a recitation of the Fatiha (the first chapter of the Qur'an). They may also embellish their prayer with supererogatory praises of God. Short of these, the content of the prayer, the physical movements performed during the prayer, and the rules of ritual purity to be observed during the prayer are relatively uniform regardless of the individual performing the prayer. These consistencies in the act of worship itself, in addition to the common spatial and temporal orientation that the salat requires, all embody in the individual a sense of community even if one performs the act in solitude. For example, when Ayuba bin Sulayman (anglicized as Job Ben Solomon), an enslaved Fulbe Muslim, retreated into the woods in Maryland in the early 1730s to perform the salat, he was not simply fulfilling an individual religious obligation but also reaffirming his connection to a larger Muslim community and disassociating himself from his contemporary circumstances as a slave.[7] Through his performance of the salat, he singularly extended the ummah to colonial America.

Fasting from dawn to dusk during the lunar month of Ramadan, another of the Five Pillars of Islam, is an individual act of worship commanded by God that, like the daily ritual prayers, provides a common orientation for individual Muslims in the same region, thus reinforcing the relationality of God, individual, and community in Islam. The act of abstaining from food and drink during daylight hours creates a common bodily experience, which Muslims throughout the world generally celebrate by coming together with family and friends in the evenings to break the fast. The communal dimension of the fast is also reinforced by the obligatory communal prayer that accompanies the holiday of Eid al-fitr, which marks the end of the month of fasting. In the United States, this communal prayer is usually organized by a conglomeration of mosques within a region, and many Muslims who may not attend mosque or regularly observe other Muslim acts of worship typically attend this holiday.

Zakat, which is an obligatory alms usually calculated at 2.5 percent of one's discretionary income, also relates individual, God, and community. Zakat in Arabic connotes purification. This payment of alms purifies wealth and at the same time reinforces individuals' moral and religious obligations to the needy in the larger Muslim community.

Finally, the *hajj* (pilgrimage) is the embodiment of the triangular relationship between individual, God, and community articulated by the shahadah. All Muslims who are financially and physically capable of making this pilgrimage to the House of God – the Ka'aba – in Mecca during the month of Dhu al-Hijja on the lunar Islamic calendar are obligated to do so. During the pilgrimage, Muslims of varying backgrounds come together to perform a common set of rituals as a result of their individual belief in God and the prophetic mission of Muhammad ibn 'Abd Allah.

How does the relationality of individual, God, and community embedded in the structure of Muslim acts of worship affect conceptions of normativity in Islam? By relating individual, God, and community,

[7] Thomas Bluett, *Some Memoirs of the Life of Job* (London, 1744), pp. 19–20.

Muslim acts of worship make these three entities inherently dependent on one another. They, in a sense, check one another in order to establish normative understandings of belief and practice. God relates to both the individual Muslim and the Muslim community through God's commands as they are articulated in the Qur'an and the hadith. The Qur'an and the hadith are subject to individual interpretation since, in Islam, God holds humans individually responsible for their behavior.[8] Individual interpretations of how to worship God are in turn checked by communal traditions, customs, and public understandings, which needless to say are subject to social, political, and economic forces. Communal consensus, or *ijma'*, limits individual interpretations within a historical context in order to prevent individual understandings of Islam from becoming idiosyncratic or factional.[9] Conversely, individual experiences and understandings of God's will, when articulated within the discursive tradition of Islam, allow for translocal and transtemporal articulations of Islam to develop which could ethically or politically challenge communal consensus, local customs and practices, and those who are in power. The triangular relation (between individual, God, and community) embedded in the structure of Muslim acts of worship thus shapes normativity by harmonizing the tension between particular understandings of Islam, local traditions and consensus, and divine commands and prohibitions derived from the Qur'an and the hadith.

Such an understanding of Islamic practice (in contrast to the one to which Sadiq was subjected) allows us to see how Islamic norms are not doctrinaire ideals but a product of a process through which Muslims, both individually and communally, put their beliefs into practice in varying contexts.

Given the role of local communities in determining proper Islamic beliefs and practices, there has been much discussion both in the academy and in the public square as to whether it is possible to practice Islam among non-Muslims. Questions are asked about Muslims' ability to

---

[8] See Qur'an 7:172–173 and 75:12–15.

[9] It goes without saying that there are numerous examples of religious factionalism throughout Muslim history. Generally speaking, such factions form when particular interpretations of Islam are not in accord with the communal consensus, and their emergence poses a challenge to conceptions of normativity. Consequently, either the general consensus changes to accommodate these individual interpretations, in which case the challenge is framed by later generations as a reformation, or the consensus remains in opposition, in which case the interpretation is deemed factional. Whether factional beliefs and practices come to be regarded as a basis for exclusion from the Muslim community depends on the degree to which they pose a threat to the makeup and the self-understanding of the community itself.

assimilate into American society.[10] Some even suggest that the practice of Islam in the United States necessarily demands the conversion of American society because it is impossible for Islam to be practiced under non-Muslim rule.[11] As we have seen, however, such understandings of Islam are based on idealized conceptions of Islam and not on Islam as it is actually practiced. Moreover, definitions of Islam and proper Islamic praxis have differed on the basis of individuals' backgrounds, desires, needs, and levels of understanding. In short, the ways in which the relationship between individual, God, and community could be normatively configured are as diverse as Muslims' varying understandings of what God demands of them individually in different communal settings.

Does this mean that to understand Islamic praxis in the United States we would have to talk to every American Muslim? Chances are that if we asked individual Muslims about their understandings of Islam and Muslim acts of worship, as one anthropologist did in a small village in Iran in the 1970s,[12] we would find, as he did, widely different answers, losing sight of the forest for the trees. While individual Muslims may have different understandings of Islam, not all individual understandings of Islam affect communal norms or reshape how individuals participate in their communities religiously. To understand the sociohistorical significance of religious practice, we need to focus our attention on understandings of Islam and Islamic practices that effect community building. In the next section, I identify four "ideal types" of Islamic praxis that have shaped the way in which Muslims have conceived communal ties in the United States. These ideal types are heuristic and not mutually exclusive. Nonetheless, they each identify how American Muslims, through their practice of Islam, have defined their place in the United States and have sought to affect normative communal relations.

IMPROVISATIONAL PRACTICES

Muslims in the United States have, under varying circumstances, improvised religious practices. Improvised practices entail practices that are meant to be temporary adaptations, which make do with what is

---

[10] See, for example, Yvonne Haddad and John Esposito, eds., *Muslims on the Americanization Path?* (Tampa, 1998), p. 3.

[11] See, for example, David Horowitz, *Unholy Alliance: Radical Islam and the American Left* (Washington, D.C., 2004), p. 124, and Brigitte Gabriel, *They Must Be Stopped: Why We Must Defeat Radical Islam and How We Can Do It* (New York, 2008), p. 4.

[12] Reinhold Loeffler, *Islam in Practice: Religious Beliefs in a Persian Village* (Albany, 1988).

possible under existing circumstances.[13] For example, Lurey Khan, the daughter of a Punjabi Muslim man and an African American woman, reported that her father could not find other Muslims in Boston around 1912 when he immigrated to the United States, so in place of the noon congregational prayer, he "prayed alone on his rug every Friday at sunset. Then he would give alms in the form of fruit and candy to the neighbor's children."[14] In Cedar Rapids, Iowa, most Muslim-owned grocery stores in the 1930s and 1940s could not afford to close down around noon on Fridays. Not only would they have had to forgo sales if they did, but closing at noon on Fridays would have brought unwanted attention to them. So in place of conducting the obligatory noon congregational prayers on Friday, they performed them on Thursday nights, and followed it with some socializing and a lecture or reading of the Qur'an.[15]

Some enslaved Muslims outwardly converted to Christianity, but in practice, they worshiped in a way that highlighted the commonalities between Islam and Christianity, so as not to offend their owners nor to cut their own ties with the ummah. This is exemplified in the autobiography of 'Umar ibn Said, who treats the Qur'an and the Gospels as functional equivalents of one another. He writes, "I am 'Umar who loves to read the scripture, the Great Qur'an. General Jim Owen along with his wife read the Gospels. They read the Gospels to me a lot."[16] 'Umar was not interested in scriptural rivalry. He apparently sought common ground with Christians within his own Islamic worldview. While acknowledging in his autobiography that he and his master's family were brought up with different scriptures, he asked, "God our Lord, our Creator, and our Ruler, the Restorer of our state ... open my heart to the Gospels, to the path of guidance." He followed this with a phrase from the Qur'an, "Praise belongs to God, the Lord of the Worlds" (Qur'an 1:2, 6:45, 40:65), and then went on to quote the Gospel, "Because the Law

---

[13] It is, of course, possible for some practices that were originally intended as improvisations to become adaptive by becoming customary and being retrospectively justified in terms of Islamic law or theology. It is nonetheless important to distinguish between improvisational and adaptive practices as heuristic categories because improvisational practices have been a significant aspect of the history of Islam in America, and many of these improvisations have not endured as adaptations of Islam to an American context.

[14] Lurey Khan, "An American Pursues Her Pakistani Past," *Asia*, March–April 1980, p. 34.

[15] Hussein Ahmed Sheronick, "A History of the Cedar Rapids Muslim Community: The Search for an American Islamic Identity" (B.A. thesis, Coe College, 1988), p. 37.

[16] 'Umar ibn Said, "The Life of 'Umar ibn Said (1831)," reprinted in Marc Shell and Werner Sollors, eds., *The Multilingual Anthology of American Literature: A Reader of Original Texts with English Translations* (New York, 2000), pp. 88–89. My translation.

[*shar'*] was made for Moses and grace [*al-ni'ma*] and truth [*al-haqq*] were for Jesus the Messiah"[17] (John 1:17). 'Umar simultaneously stepped in and out of both Islamic and Christian scriptures, improvising a prayer, under slavery, based on a shared conception of God as the Creator, Lord, and Ruler of all of existence. Tellingly, 'Umar cited a verse from the Gospel of John that would not offend his Muslim co-religionists; he ignored both preceding and proceeding verses that describe Jesus as the Son of God or as the Word having been made flesh. This shows that he was fully aware of the differences between Islam and Christianity but improvised a religious practice that would allow him to maintain his relationship with God and the ummah while at the same time entering into a relationship with his non-Muslim masters, whom he admired for their kindness.[18]

Improvisational Islamic practices are not limited to the early history of Islam in America. A contemporary leader of the Shadhiliyyah Sufi Order in Portland, Oregon, whom the Portland Muslim History Project interviewed in 2004,[19] indicated that when, on her way to her evening shifts, she gets stuck in traffic at the time of the sunset (*maghrib*) ritual prayer, she says the prayer without the prostrations in her car rather than risk missing the prayer. Nor are these improvisations always divorced from the Islamic legal tradition (*fiqh*). Some American Muslims, for example, who are uncomfortable washing their feet in public bathrooms as part of the ablution for the daily ritual prayers, quickly take off their shoes and wipe water over their socks. This improvisation is based on a legal debate about whether or not it is permissible, under certain circumstances, for one who has put on *khuffayn* (leather outer boots or socks) while in a state of ritual purity (*tahara*) to perform ablution by simply wiping a wet hand over one's footwear rather than washing one's bare feet.

In the United States, as members of a religious minority, Muslims form social, political, and economic ties with non-Muslims and non-Muslim institutions that hinder the strict observance of Islamic precepts. Through improvised religious practices, some Muslims practically acknowledge that there are norms by which Islamic acts of worship ought to be performed. They thus maintain their personal ties with God and their communal ties with the ummah that presumably upholds these norms, while at the same time forming new communal ties with

---

[17] 'Umar ibn Said, "Life," pp. 88–91.

[18] See 'Umar ibn Said, "Life," pp. 80–81.

[19] Some of the reports produced by this project are available at http://pluralism.org/affili-ates/ghaneabassiri/index.php, accessed October 22, 2011.

non-Muslims in their American context. Through their improvisations, they seek to harmonize the relation between individual, God, and their expanded community without demanding recognition as American Muslims either from members of their expanded community or from members of the ummah. Improvised religious practices thus make do with what is possible at a given point in time; they do not construct enduring religious identities.

TRADITIONAL PRACTICES

Traditional practices refer to the reproduction of normative practices from Muslim-majority contexts in the United States. Though mostly done by immigrants, some American-born Muslims also learn these practices from Muslim immigrants or by traveling to or living in Muslim-majority societies. Because practices from many different Muslim-majority societies and Muslim groups have been transplanted in the United States, examples of traditional practices are too varied and numerous to enumerate. Some of these traditional practices, such as adherence to the Five Pillars, are generally recognized as Islamic, even though the way in which they are performed may differ according to cultural and sectarian differences. For example, during Ramadan, following what they believe to be a tradition established by Prophet Muhammad, many Sunnis attend mosques to perform supererogatory prayers known as *tarawih*. The Shi'a reject tarawih prayers as an innovation introduced by the second caliph, 'Umar ibn al-Khattab. Muslim sartorial practices are also influenced by traditions reproduced in the United States. The *niqab*, which covers the face of a woman, only allowing the eyes to show, is one such example. It is more frequently found among Muslims from the Arabian Peninsula, where the practice is more common, than among Muslims from Eastern Europe or other parts of Asia.

Many more examples of this sort could be cited, but mentioning them is unnecessary. Out of all the types of Islamic praxis I discuss, the notion of reproducing traditional practices from Muslim-majority contexts in the United States is most straightforward and intuitive. What is significant about traditional practices is that they reproduce different sectarian and cultural communal identities found in Muslim-majority contexts in the United States. Consequently, they engender diversity in Islamic praxis in the United States, and as Muslims from varying cultural and sectarian backgrounds encounter one another's variations on Islamic praxis, they find traditions that were normative in their Muslim-majority communities relativized in the U.S. context.

Rather than rethinking the normativity of their traditional practices in light of such relativizing experiences with diversity, many Muslims in the United States opt to practice Islam solely within the context of their own tradition. These American Muslims gather in mosques with people from their own ethnic, racial, or sectarian background, where they can hear sermons in their own language and continue their particular traditions. They relate the individual and God through specific traditional practices that define their community more narrowly. Consequently, traditional Muslim practices result in a form of "denominationalism" within American Islam. Varying traditional practices "denominate" Islam for specific communities according to the way in which Islam was interpreted and practiced within the Muslim-majority context with which they are familiar. Thus, in major metropolises, we find Muslims categorizing mosques not just in terms of their sectarian affiliation (e.g., Twelver Shi'i, Ahmadi) but also in terms of their ethnic makeup (e.g., Bosnian, Somali, Turkish, South Asian, Arab, etc.).

ESSENTIALIZING PRACTICES

Another way American Muslims have sought to make sense of the diversity of Islamic practices in the United States is by essentializing Islam, that is, by identifying essential characteristics and practices in Islam that they construct as universal. Essentialist understandings of Islam idealize the practice of Islam by divorcing praxis from context. This is done in at least two different ways, which could be defined as scripturalist and perennialist. Scripturalist understandings of Islam rely on contemporary, literal readings of the Qur'an as divine revelation and hadith as directly inspired by God, thus containing the purest expression of Islam, to define practices and beliefs that are essentially Islamic. Those who adhere to scripturalist, essentialist understandings of Islam, for example, oppose the use of gravestones because they see it as a form of innovation that has no precedent in the texts of the Qur'an and hadith. Similarly, they oppose the widespread veneration of holy figures among Muslims because they believe there is no precedent for such practices in the Qur'an or the hadith.

This essentializing of Islam through literal readings of the Qur'an and hadith seeks to differentiate the religion of Islam from Muslims' varying cultures. This differentiating of religion from culture introduces a spectrum on which Muslim practices could be placed. Those practices explicitly mentioned in the Qur'an and the hadith become essential to Islam and are thus defined as "religious," while practices that Muslims developed over time within varying Muslim societies are viewed as "cultural" and thus dispensable to the practice of Islam in the United States.

No religion, however, exists outside of culture. Religious practices always occur in a historical context, and contemporary essentialist, scripturalist understandings of Islam have their roots in the late nineteenth- and early twentieth-century reform movements in Islam that sought to define an Islam for the modern era. Muslim reformers at this time often distinguished between the teachings of Islam encapsulated in its scriptures and the practices of Muslims. The latter they found backward and in need of reformation in order for Muslim-majority societies to progress and shed the yoke of European colonialism.

By the mid-twentieth century, as Muslim-majority countries were gradually gaining independence, some Muslims influenced by such essentialist understandings of Islam traveled to Europe and North America with the aim of gaining technical expertise with which they could return to develop their own countries. They found in Europe and North America an ideal context where they could put their essentialized understandings of Islam into practice. The cultural, ethnic, racial, and class diversity found among Muslims in the United States provided an opportune testing ground for their universalizing theories of Islam and Islamic practice. Moreover, unlike Muslim-majority societies, there were no established Islamic traditions in the United States with which their essentialized understandings of Islam had to vie. Of course, tens of thousands of Muslims lived in the United States before the 1950s and 1960s, but these new Muslim immigrants quickly dismissed the practices of earlier Muslim communities as un-Islamic adaptation to American society. Indeed, when the Muslim Students Association was founded in 1963, one of the tasks its leadership (which shared in essentialist, scripturalist views of Islam) set before itself was to educate earlier American Muslims about "true Islam."[20]

This essentializing of Islam through a contemporary literal reading of the Qur'an and the hadith, irrespective of context, relates individual, God, and community through the utopian notion that God's commands, individuals' understandings of those commands, and the communal enactments of God's commands are all one and the same. Universalist practices are thus intended to eradicate any tensions between God, individual, and community and establish the Muslim community as a "single unit" brought together through "Islamic ideology." Because

---

[20] Kambiz GhaneaBassiri, *A History of Islam in America* (Cambridge, 2010), p. 269.

such a utopian, universalist Muslim community is not found in history, the practice of essentialist, scripturalist understandings of Islam in the United States has generally required community activism and the building of new institutions that reflect the view that Islam is a singular way of life. Indeed, adherents of this understanding of Islam have been at the forefront of building mosques and national Muslim organizations in the United States.

The process of building mosques and organizations in the United States requires interfacing with various branches of government and American society. It also requires support, not only financially but also morally, from the larger Muslim community with all of its diversity. Consequently, putting essentialist, scripturalist understandings of Islam into practice has often required adaptation, improvisation, and recognition of cultural differences within the Muslim population of the United States. As mosques and other institutions have been formed around essentialist, scripturalist understandings of Islam, they have also transformed Islamic practice in the United States. They have homogenized the practices that define one as a Muslim by reducing an Islamic identity to a minimal set of beliefs (namely the recognition of the Qur'an and hadith as the only sources of Islam) and practices (namely the Five Pillars, modest dress, and abstinence from pork and alcohol).

This essentializing of Islamic identity has not only made Islamic communities mobile, because one could uphold these minimal beliefs and perform these minimal practices irrespective of one's cultural, social, or political context, but it has also made Islamic activism transferable from one group or cause to the next, sometimes in surprising ways. As Leila Ahmed has shown, women activists have come to lead the struggle for gender equality in Islam in the United States. Ahmed notes that for these women activists "their identity as Muslim Americans clearly trumps and supersedes their sense of identity and community as grounded in either ethnicity or national origins. In the foreground of their work is their identity as Muslim Americans: a trait which sharply distinguishes them from many other Americans of Muslim heritage" who are secular or come from backgrounds that were not formed by mosques and institutions that essentialized Islamic practices and identity.[21]

Perennialist, universalist understandings of Islam, unlike scripturalist understandings, do not seek a minimal common denominator among Muslims; rather, they see Islam as the ultimate expression of a timeless

---

[21] Leila Ahmed, *A Quiet Revolution: The Veil's Resurgence, from the Middle East to America* (New Haven, 2011), pp. 285–286.

religiosity shared by humanity in general. Muslim intellectuals who adhere to such an understanding of Islam have had the broadest appeal of all American Muslim intellectuals among non-Muslim Americans. The most prominent of these individuals is the leading figure of the Maryamiyyah Sufi order, Seyyed Hossein Nasr (b. 1933), a native of Iran and a prolific scholar who has a volume dedicated to him in the prestigious Library of Living Philosophers series.[22]

For adherents to such understandings of Islam, practice is not simply an act of worship that God commands but rather an expression of an innate disposition (*fitra*) that was instilled in humanity by God to call humankind to the recognition of God's unicity (*tawhid*).[23] Consequently, Islamic practices need not be prioritized in terms of what is obligatory and supererogatory but rather in terms of their reflection of humanity's fitra. Whatever practice is seen as most reflective of this innate nature is valued. This has led some perennialist Muslims to be more conscientious about performing *dhikr* (ritual remembrance of God) in Sufi circles than salat in neighborhood mosques. In fact, salat (and other acts of worship) in this view are seen as existential acts of divine remembrance. As Nasr explains,

> The life of the practicing Muslim is punctuated ever anew by the daily prayers, which break the hold of profane time upon the soul and bring men and women back to a sacred time marked by the meeting with God and to a sacred space pointing to the supreme center of the Islamic universe, Mecca, where the celestial axis penetrates the plane of earthly existence.[24]

By relating the individual to God through fitra rather than scripture or a set of divine commands, perennialist understandings of Islam conceive of community more in terms of like-minded universalists than in terms of the ummah.

ADAPTIVE PRACTICES

Adaptive practices refer to the adaptations of traditional practices to changing times. These practices differ from improvised practices in that their practitioners do not regard them as temporary attempts to make do under existing conditions. Rather, they are seen as enduring

---

[22] Lewis Edwin Hahn et al., eds., *The Philosophy of Seyyed Hossein Nasr* (Chicago, 2001).

[23] Seyyed Hossein Nasr, *The Heart of Islam: Enduring Values for Humanity* (New York, 2002), pp. 6–7.

[24] Nasr, *Heart of Islam*, pp. 131–132.

adaptations to changing circumstance from within Islam's legal, intellectual traditions or religiocultural traditions.

One of the most common forms of adaptive practices is adaptation to technology. Today, for example, Muslims can download searchable copies of the Qur'an, along with its recitation and translation, on smart phones. They can buy watches and clocks that play recordings of the call to prayer. They can download programs that calculate the direction of prayer (*qiblah*). Among Muslims in the United States, as among Muslims in the modern world in general, technological adaptations tend to have a homogenizing effect. For example, while there are disagreements among Muslim schools of law about how to calculate the time or direction of prayer, only a few of the programs developed allow their users to choose the school of law by which they wish to have the program calculate the time or direction of prayer. They thus make the time and direction of the prayer the same for every Muslim – Sunni or Shi'i, Hanafi or Shafi'i – who wishes to take advantage of the conveniences of technology. This homogenizing effect also furthers the notion that isolated Muslims could remain intimately and spiritually connected with the ummah through their practices. The aforementioned Job Ben Solomon had to guess at the direction of prayer by observing the movement of the sun and stars, not knowing where Maryland was with respect to his homeland or Mecca; today, however, American Muslims could travel anywhere in the world on vacation or business trips and access calculations of times of prayer and the qiblah down to the minute or latitudinal degree from their hotel room. They would not need to connect with any physical community to feel as though they are religiously communing with it.

Other forms of adaptive practices include such practices as the hosting of *iftars* at mosques. Muslims usually break the fast during Ramadan at home with their families. In the United States, many do not have their family members with them, or their families and friends are not Muslim, so the mosque becomes a surrogate family during Ramadan where religious ties are reinforced. The presence of a mosque community in the absence of family also encourages individual Muslims to maintain the practice of fasting in a society in which they feel no social pressure to do so.

Adaptive practices, similar to improvised practices, not only maintain communal boundaries but also shift them. We have already seen how adaptations to technology tend toward homogenization. For adaptations to take root, traditional Muslim practices need to be modified in relation to contemporary circumstances. As such, adaptation necessarily requires a recognition of the status quo ante; adaptive practices modify traditional practices in order to make them relevant to the relations and technologies that already shape American Muslims' lives. Qiblah programs, for example, do not push Muslims to use computers but make Muslims' use of computers relevant to the practice of Islam. In turn, if the adaptation takes root, these programs make the use of computers more integral to the ritual prayer. Similarly, mosque iftars do not push Muslims to shun family but make it possible for American Muslims who cannot break the fast with their families to experience the communal dimension of Islamic practice, which inadvertently makes the family less relevant to communal acts of worship.

Within the larger context of American society and politics, wherever American Muslims have already formed an understanding of the relation between individual, God, and community in their lives as citizens, students, laborers, employers, professionals, refugees, religious leaders, etc., adaptive practices allow for the practice of Islam to remain relevant in their lives. A good example is when American Muslims participate in Islamic events hosted by non-Muslim governmental officials, such as iftar dinner or Eid celebrations. Governmental officials recognize that sharing in religious practices builds community, and they seek to reinforce nationalistic ties through their state sanction of Muslim practices. President Obama exemplified this point in his welcoming remarks at the August 13, 2010, iftar dinner at the White House:

> Here at the White House, we have a tradition of hosting iftars that goes back several years, just as we host Christmas parties and seders and Diwali celebrations. And these events celebrate the role of faith in the lives of the American people. They remind us of the basic truth that we are all children of God, and we all draw strength and a sense of purpose from our beliefs. These events are also an affirmation of who we are as Americans.[25]

Muslims participate in these state-sponsored rituals even though an iftar hosted by non-Muslims makes very little sense religiously. They do so because their participation allows them to reaffirm their preexisting citizenship ties through their religion. Through such adaptive practices, they merge individual Muslims' relationship to the state with individual Muslims' relationship with the larger Muslim community and thus help establish a distinct American Islam.

[25] "Remarks by the President at Iftar Dinner," Office of the Press Secretary, August 13, 2010, http://www.whitehouse.gov/the-press-office/2010/08/13/remarks-president-iftar-dinner, accessed October 22, 2011.

CONCLUSION

I began with the assertion that Sadiq's detention upon arrival in the United States resulted from a misconceived notion that religious laws and beliefs are productive of behavior. I have argued that an examination of Islamic practice shows us that religious beliefs and behavior are shaped not only in relation with one another but also in relation to varying contexts. This does not mean that they are relativistic and thus not constitutive of religious norms. Rather, their relationality is maintained by the structure of Islamic practices, which bring the individual, God, and community into an interdependent triangular relation through which normativity is varyingly negotiated by harmonizing different individual desires and understandings with divine commands and communal needs and traditions.

Religious normativity as such is best conceived as a product of a particular process rather than legal or scriptural dictums. The latter obscures the polyvalence of religious beliefs and practices that allows for religions to relate to different sociohistorical circumstances. The practice of Islam in the United States draws attention to the polyvalences and relationality of religious beliefs and practices – not only because of the enormous diversity of Muslims in the United States but also because Islamic traditions and authorities do not necessarily play a formative role in shaping American Muslims' lives. The structure of Islamic practices that allow for varying understandings of God and community to come into relation through individual acts of worship has pluralistically shaped Islamic normativity and conceptions of community among American Muslims.

Further Reading

Abdullah, Zain, *Black Mecca: The African Muslims of Harlem* (New York, 2010).
Asad, Talal, *The Idea of an Anthropology of Islam* (Washington, D.C., 1986).
Barzegar, Abbas, "Discourse, Identity, and Community: Problems and Prospects in the Study of Islam in America," *Muslim World* 101:3 (2011): 511–538.
Bell, Catherine, *Ritual Theory, Ritual Practice* (New York, 1992).
Ghamari-Tabrizi, Behrooz, "Loving America and Longing for Home: Isma'il al-Faruqi and the Emergence of the Muslim Diaspora in North America," *International Migration* 42:2 (2004): 61–86.
Hammer, Juliane, *American Muslim Women, Religious Authority, and Activism: More than a Prayer* (Austin, 2012).

Lewis, Thomas A., "On the Role of Normativity in Religious Studies," in Robert Orsi, ed., *The Cambridge Companion to Religious Studies* (New York, 2012), pp. 168–185.

Loeffler, Reinhold, *Islam in Practice: Religious Beliefs in a Persian Village* (Albany, 1988).

Rouse, Carolyn M., *Engaged Surrender: African American Women and Islam* (Berkeley, 2004).

13 Muslim Spaces and Mosque Architecture

AKEL ISMAIL KAHERA

The subject of this chapter is threefold. First, in a brief historical summary, we examine the origins of the American mosque in the postbellum era up to the present day. Then we discuss the theoretical assumptions on the aesthetic language and function of the American mosque, highlighting the spatial and cultural elements, public space, and gender by way of three examples. Finally, we critique the political tensions and the contentious political discourse in the post-9/11 era, especially the widespread misunderstanding of the so-called Ground Zero Mosque.

The design conceptualization of an American mosque and its aesthetics support two primary themes: to preserve the identity of the various forms that constitute the elements of a religious edifice for men and women and the relationship between spiritual repose and aesthetics; and to organize the communal worship and public space of the mosque according to religious practice and the *shari'ah* (sacred law). Furthermore, there is a common consensus that Muslim religious aesthetics is a theo-centered dogma. This conceptual framework must also consider the unique aesthetic language, which explains the elements employed in spatial treatment within a mosque. In the Muslim world, shari'ah has substantive meaning for the study of urbanism in the *madinah* or the premodern Islamic city.[1] In the West, this formula holds true with the added proviso that the North American urban context has no parallel to the Muslim world.

That Islam had not survived in the antebellum era in an organized practice among Muslim captives does not mean that it did not flourish in some rebellious form during slavery.[2] Indeed, some African Muslims succeeded in following the precepts of their faith through religious practice, mostly in the form of individual practice but, on occasion, also in small communities. Several of these captives stood out as men of education

[1] Akel Ismail Kahera, *Reading the Islamic City: Discursive Practices and Legal Judgment* (Lanham, 2011).
[2] *Prince among Slaves*, dir. Andrea Kalin, 2006.

and knowledge, for example, Omar ibn Said (1770–1864), after whom a mosque at Fayetteville, North Carolina, is now named. No one knows how many Muslims were among the contingent of slaves brought to America between 1619 and 1808, when the slave trade officially ended.[3] Likewise, no one knows how these early Muslims worshiped, if they were allowed to worship at all; even more problematic is the dating of the first mosques on American soil. In the 1940s, Malcolm Bell Jr. (1913–2001) photographed and interviewed many coastal Georgia Blacks as part of the Works Progress Administration program. The results of this project were published in a monograph, *Drums and Shadows: Survival Studies among the Coastal Georgia Negroes*. Bell interviewed descendants of former slaves who were Muslims, and a few of them described the daily ritual prayer that was still being performed at the time of the interview.[4] One interview mentions a building that a slave master ordered to be torn down, the description of which suggests that it could have been intended to be a gathering place for Muslims (*musalla*) rather than a domicile.[5]

In 1984 Allan Austin brought the importance of this research to our attention with the publication of *African Muslims in Antebellum America*.[6] Austin's research uncovered the fact that the Hausa, the Mandingo or "bookmen," and the educated Fulani from West Africa were part of the slave population in the antebellum South.

The Albanian Muslim community of Biddeford, Maine, one of the first associations established by immigrant Muslims in the United States, built a mosque (*masjid*) shortly after the community was formed in 1915; by 1919, another mosque was built. With the passage of the U.S. immigration quota laws in 1921 and 1924, Muslim immigrants from Syria, Lebanon, Jordan, and the Arab provinces of the Ottoman Empire, began to arrive in North America.[7] Immigrant communities were established at Ross, North Dakota, in the 1920s, and in Cedar Rapids, Iowa, in the 1930s. Contrary to popular belief, the mosque at Ross is not the oldest mosque in America because African Muslims were already present in

---

3   See Richard Brent Turner, Chapter 2 in this volume. According to Phillip Curtain, in *Africa Remembered*, from 1711 to 1810 British and French slave traders brought 1.6 million African slaves from *bilad al-Takrur* (West Africa).

4   Muriel Bell and Malcolm Bell Jr., *Drums and Shadows: Survival Studies among the Georgia Coastal Negroes*; Savannah Unit Georgia Writers' Project, Works Progress Administration (Athens, 1940).

5   The interview indicated that Ben Sullivan, the grandson of Salih Bilali, was eighty-eight and living on St. Simons when interviewed by WPA in the 1930s.

6   Allan Austin, *African Muslims in Ante-Bellum America* (New York, 1997).

7   Barbara Daly Metcalf, *Making Muslim Space in North America and Europe* (Berkeley, 1996).

North America in the antebellum period. In 1934 Lebanese immigrants built a mosque at Cedar Rapids.[8] In 1930 African American Muslims established the First Muslim Mosque in Pittsburgh; Jameela A. Hakim documented the history of this community in a monograph, *History of the First Muslim Mosque in Pittsburgh, Pennsylvania.*[9]

The First Cleveland Mosque, founded by al-Hajj Wali Akram in 1932, is now the oldest continuously running Muslim institution in America. Jabal Arabiyya, a Muslim village in Buffalo, New York, was founded by a small group of African American Muslims during the Great Depression (1929–1945).[10] It was also during this time that the Ad-Deen Allah Universal Arabic Association was established under Professor Muhammad Ezaldeen, an African American who had studied in Cairo from 1931 to 1935.[11] In 1955 Sheikh Daoud Ahmed Faisal established the State Street Masjid in Brooklyn, New York. The mosque is still in use today and represents a noteworthy point in the historic development of the American Muslim community. In 1962 the Brooklyn-based Darul Islam movement, an African American Muslim community, evolved from the State Street Masjid. The Darul Islam established a mosque at 1964 Atlantic Avenue in Brooklyn but would eventually settle at 52 Herkimer Place in 1972 after gathering to pray at a number of temporary locations; the organization eventually spread to Philadelphia and Cleveland. Many other mosque communities came into existence in the 1960s to the 1970s, including the Mosque of Islamic Brotherhood (New York), the Islamic Party (Washington, D.C., and the Caribbean), and the Hanafi Community (Washington, D.C.). Almost every major American city on the East Coast had a mosque affiliated with one of these communities.[12]

THE URBAN MOSQUE

In inner city neighborhoods all across America – in cities such as Boston, Atlanta, Detroit, New York, Houston, and Chicago – the urban mosque

[8] Omar Khalidi, "American Mosques," in Yvonne Haddad and John L. Esposito, eds., *Muslims on the Americanization Path?* (Oxford, 2000), pp. 317–334.
[9] Jameela A. Hakim, *History of the First Muslim Mosque of Pittsburgh, Pennsylvania* (n.p., n.d.).
[10] Robert Dannin, *Black Pilgrimage to Islam* (New York, 2002).
[11] Michael Nash, *Islam among Urban Blacks, Muslims in Newark, New Jersey: A Social History* (Lanham, 2008).
[12] Yusuf Nuruddin, "African-American Muslims and the Question of Identity: Between Traditional Islam, African Heritage and the American Way," in Haddad and Esposito, *Muslims on the Americanization Path?*, pp. 215–262.

Figure 13.1. The Al Farouq Mosque, Atlanta, Georgia (Photo courtesy of Anis Basheer)

represents perhaps the largest edifice dedicated to communal worship, education, and social activities. Three prominent examples are the Islamic Cultural Center in Washington, D.C. (1957), The Islamic Center of New York in Manhattan (1991), and a rural edifice, the Dar al-Islam in Abiquiu, New Mexico (1980). Urban and rural mosques may differ in size and ancillary function, often determined by construction cost or the availability of land. While no prescriptive form for the mosque occurs in the Qur'an, the need for communal worship among American Muslims has led to the development of a particular American blueprint for mosque buildings but one that generates a diversity of structures and designs. Differing in more than just outward appearance, the North American mosque gives priority to a balanced mix of functions and innovative aesthetic features. Mosques serving primarily immigrant communities have a two-tiered identity, in which many differ according to the cultural interaction of the émigré. "Diaspora aesthetics," cultural sentiments informed by nostalgia, customs, traditions, and present-day beliefs, associate the mosque with memory and, as such, adopt styles from the country or region of origin. Stylistically, the design of a mosque falls within three common genres: first, a strict adherence to an aesthetic tradition influenced by sign, symbol, and building convention; second, an attempt at design interpretation employing experimental and popular ideas, resulting in a hybrid image; and, finally, a faithful attempt to understand modernity, tradition, and urbanism.

CULTURAL VALUES AND RELIGIOUS AESTHETICS

Five aesthetic principles have shaped the formative aesthetics of mosques since the seventh century: namely, the structure of *belief, order, space, materials, and symbols.* These formative principles can be found in mosques built in the United States since the 1950s; in this context they have largely been responsive to the religious, cultural, and practical needs of Muslim immigrants. The design process, choice of building materials, and the resulting aesthetic image are three aspects that are part of a web of relationships centered on forces of sustainability. Every edifice continues to be endowed directly or indirectly with a set of cultural values by the architect, but here again we may question the extent to which the architect has control over the final product or expression and the extent to which that expression has engaged with viable processes of production.

The necessity of keeping the Prophet's example, the *sunnah,* alive in public memory may explain how later mosques have emerged. In general, art historians have focused on individual patrons and stylistic details, treating the mosque solely as a work of art, but they have essentially ignored the religious component of mosque design and construction. The interpretation offered here seeks to explain the long-standing influence of the architectural language and its relationship to the sunnah. However, mosques are not built according to divine specifications as neither the Qur'an nor hadith provide clear indications for how a mosque should be constructed and how it should look. The Qur'an stresses only the value of the edifice as a place for the remembrance of God, and prophetic tradition prescribes a list of profane actions that are not allowed to take place in a mosque. For example, the absence of human or animal imagery (iconography) in a mosque means that the essence of sacred art remains reflective, contemplative, and theo-centric. Three American mosques present an interesting overview of architecture and religious values.

THE ISLAMIC CULTURAL CENTER, WASHINGTON, D.C.

The cornerstone of the Islamic Center in Washington, D.C., established primarily for the diplomatic community, was laid in 1949, and President Dwight Eisenhower formally inaugurated the mosque in

Figure 13.2. Islamic Cultural Center, Washington, D.C. (Photo courtesy of the Library of Congress)

1957. The mosque's motifs can best be understood by studying the inscriptions, which reflect both meaning and style. Almost without exception, the inscriptions draw the attention of the viewer. Several verses of the Qur'an have been arranged in a symmetrical configuration and in various patterns on the interior walls and ceilings of the primary prayer hall. The Divine Names of Allah (*al-asma Allah al-husna*) and several familiar and often-quoted verses from the Qur'an such as Al-Alaq, 96:1–5, are inscribed in large framed borders of Arabic (*thuluth* style) script with smaller framed panels of ornamental Kufic script.

Two inscription bands run horizontally across the face of the prayer niche (*mihrab*), the upper band of which reads, "Verily we have seen the turning of your face to the heaven," and the lower band, "surely we shall turn you to a *qiblah* [prayer direction] that shall please you" (Al-Baqara, 2:144). The mihrab's decorative treatment follows the Iznik and Bursa tradition of using glazed tiles, blue, red, and green, which are commonly found in Ottoman Turkish buildings.

The plan of the building contains three halls (*iwan*) framed by an exterior double arcade (*riwaq*), which serves as an *extra muros* space or *ziyada*. The orthogonal arcade remains perpendicular to the street, but the *masjid* is set out at a tangent to conform to the qiblah axis, which has been calculated on the basis of using the great circle or the shortest distance when facing Mecca. In the building there is a small court (*sahn*) open to the sky, but the whole central space of the mosque is covered with a modest clerestory dome. An arcade consisting of five contiguous arches serves as an entry portal and a key part of the facade.

The entry portal runs parallel to the street, and for added emphasis it is recognized by an inscription band of Kufic script at the upper part of the facade, which reads, "In houses of worship which Allah has permitted to be raised so that His name be remembered, in them, there [are such as] extol His limitless glory at morning and evening" (Al-Nur, 24:36). The mosque's composition epitomizes an array of Muslim aesthetic themes; the overall *image* the inscriptions evoke is significant in regard to the use of epigraphy from two aspects: as a devotional theme, and as an emotional device with symbolic meaning that satisfies a quiet devotional disposition. Historically, three kinds of visual patterns can be found in myriad examples: designs derived from plant life, often called "arabesque" in the West; Arabic calligraphy, the most revered art form in Islam because it conveys the word of God; and tessellation, or the repetitive "ordering" of a geometric pattern. Like similar religious buildings elsewhere, difficulties remain with regard to interpreting the stylistic qualities of the North American mosque, which are mainly derived from a "mixed bag" of conventions, whether from Muslim art forms or from the diverse circumstances of diasporas in North America.[13]

An aesthetic profile consisting of émigré's place or history makes up most of the stylistic variations that exist today. Many immigrant communities invoke a cultural style and imagery drawn from their country of origin and based on nostalgia. The most important element in the mosque is the fellowship hall, where men and women gather to pray on a daily basis. Some buildings have schools attached; at Masjid at-Taqwa in Houston, Texas, for example, both a school and a clinic are part of the mosque complex. A Muslim or non-Muslim architect who is commissioned to design a mosque must therefore decide on such guidelines independently.[14] And if we also consider the sensibilities attached to

[13] Akel Ismail Kahera, *Deconstructing the American Mosque: Space, Gender, and Aesthetics* (Austin, 2002).

[14] Gulzar Haider, "Brother in Islam, Please Draw Us a Mosque: Muslims in the West; A Personal Account," in Hyat Salam, ed., *Expressions of Islam in Buildings* (Singapore, 1990), pp. 155–166.

Figure 13.3. Interior of the *musalla* (sanctuary) of the Islamic Cultural Center, Washington, D.C. (Photo courtesy of Mark Susman)

the culture of each diaspora community, such as dress, language, diet, religious practice, and the use of public and domestic space, memory appears to be crucial as a mechanism for maintaining various habits and customs, thus keeping them alive and making them mutually meaningful to the immigrant community.

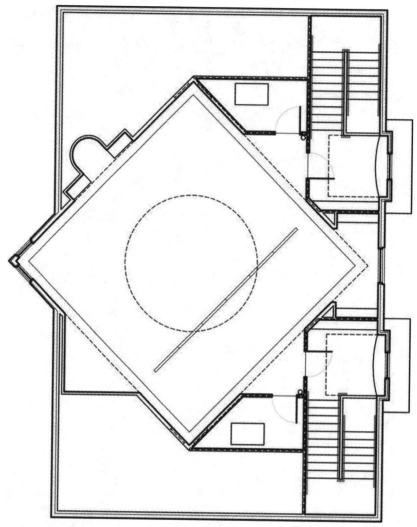

Figure 13.4. Plan of the Islamic Center of Huntington, West Virginia (Courtesy of McCoy Architects LLC)

DAR AL-ISLAM, ABIQUIU, NEW MEXICO

In 1980 the late Hassan Fathy (d. 1989) was commissioned to design the master plan for a Muslim village, the Dar al-Islam (Abode of Islam) at Abiquiu, New Mexico. The master plan for the mesa site is framed by surrounding arid hills and several snow-capped mountains that are visible in the distance. In Abiquiu, the Charma Valley and its immediate surrounding have a long history, having been populated before the

Figure 13.5. Mosque in Abiquiu, New Mexico (Photo courtesy of Ronald Baker)

1598 arrival of the Spanish by several native Indian peoples. The harsh environmental conditions at Abiquiu provided an ideal setting for using adobe construction. Hassan Fathy remained faithful to a long-established building tradition that endorsed the notion, "Small is beautiful." As Fathy puts it, "Tradition is a key element of culture; when the craftsman was responsible for much of the work of building, traditional art came out of the subconscious of the community.... it is held together by an accumulated culture, rather than by one individual's idea of harmony."[15]

Fathy's mosque and its ancillary buildings undoubtedly belong to the site, while the mosque also offers a clean demarcated space for worship facing Mecca. The traditional building technique works well for the choice of site and the project itself; the design principles of Dar al-Islam can be applied elsewhere in North America. Hassan Fathy's religious building complex keeps questions of body, mind, spirit and soul in the foreground, signaling a major paradigm shift that demonstrates correspondences between knowledge, intuition, faith, philosophy, and science. The traditional adobe technique worked well for the choice of

[15] Kahera, *Deconstructing the American Mosque*, 81–90; Akel Ismail Kahera, "Hassan Fathy: On Architecture and Human Existence" *Muslim Quarterly Magazine* 1:1 (Spring 2010): 14–23.

site and the project itself. By using adobe construction, Fathy remained faithful to his "sustainable" tradition.

THE ISLAMIC CULTURAL CENTER OF MANHATTAN, NEW YORK CITY

The Islamic Cultural Center of Manhattan (completed in 1990) explores the use of modern technology as a compositional device.[16] The mosque confronts both tradition and modernity by seeking to reinterpret various aesthetic themes associated with extant models found in the Muslim world. First, the surface motifs reflect geometric themes, which are employed as a unifying element throughout the mosque's interior and exterior. These motifs can be seen primarily on the carpet where worshipers assemble for prayer in horizontal and parallel rows facing the qiblah. They also appear in the surface treatment of the *minbar* (pulpit) and the exterior facade, and in several other interior elements as well. Geometry is a fundamental theme in Islamic cosmology and Muslim art, but in this instance it comes closer to a modernist, secular interpretation rather than a traditional, cosmological interpretation. The inscriptions, which are included in the decorative features of the mosque's interior, are rendered in a geometric Kufic style. They are set in a straight horizontal and vertical arrangement, which accommodates a modernist concept of order. For instance, around the mihrab the geometric Kufic script reads, "Allah is the Light of the Heavens and the Earth."

Admittedly, the use of traditional inscriptions as a decorative element is in some respects incongruent with the idea of a secular, modernist interpretation of surface treatment. Using geometry as a spatial theme, with the aid of a corresponding angular Kufic inscription, provides a visual affinity; the aesthetic treatment of the interior of the dome over the central prayer hall further illustrates this last point. The dome's structural ribs have been left bare and rudimentary, which provides a bold geometric texture to the dome's inner face when seen from below. The inner drum of the dome is covered with a band of angular Kufic inscription, but the pattern of concentric ribs clearly dominates the composition, especially since the text of the band is largely unreadable from the main prayer hall below. Both compositional elements, epigraphy and geometry, were clearly intended by the architect to be an operative aesthetic device. Many of these aesthetic themes are tied to the affinity of four key themes: the value of time; the value of context; the

---

[16] Kahera, *Deconstructing the American Mosque*, pp. 72–76.

Figure 13.6. Islamic Cultural Center of New York (Photo courtesy of Zain Abdullah)

value of space; and the value of memory. By looking at these four themes in the aesthetic treatment of the American mosque, we detect a concomitant relationship between diaspora, cultural and religious beliefs, and aesthetics.[17]

SPACE AND GENDER

Because the visual and architectural expression of the American mosque is rather unique in many ways, each architectural expression reflects possible background conditions including, diaspora, culture, ethnicity, nostalgia, and above all ways of interpretation. These features provide the basic function of a mosque, the system of aesthetics, and the making of architectural space and the modalities of architectural expression. In simple terms, when we take into account the specific nature of the seventh-century Prophet's mosque built at Medina – an archetypal building, a "spatial sunnah" – it was an architectural precedent that continued to affect the physical planning of later mosques. The designation, "spatial sunnah" gives clarity to the distinction and the

[17] Akel Ismail Kahera, with Craig Anz and Latif Abdulmalik, *Design Criteria for Mosques and Islamic Centers: Art, Architecture & Worship* (Oxford, 2009).

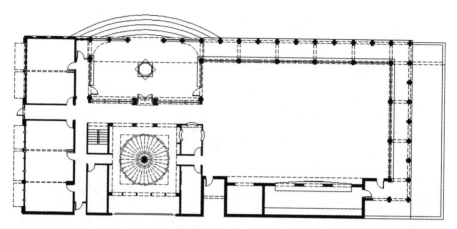

Figure 13.7. Plan of Islamic Cultural Center of Austin, Texas (Drawing courtesy of Integrated Metropolis, Austin, Texas – Craig Anz, Akel Ismail Kahera, and Ian Kerr)

connection between the archetypal model and the American interpretation. Another aspect of the sunnah is an overall agreement or consensus (*ijma'*); it must not be overlooked. Explicit examples of the hadith record the behavioral mannerisms of the faithful in the assembly of a mosque; therefore, the term "spatial sunnah" may be substituted for the term "sanctioned enclosure" without doing damage to the essence or meaning of the sunnah.[18] "Spatial sunnah" is a formula that explores three primary design features: first, it examines problems of visual propriety apropos to efficacy and expression; second, it examines problems of appearance and spatial obligation, especially the obligation to women that allows them free and unfettered access to the mosque; finally, it is an important obligation for a community of adherents to set aside a space for communal gathering. Communal worship is a devotional act, and space and place can be expressed in terms of a referential cognition or the "spatial sunnah," which regulates the plan of a mosque. Because of the authority of the "spatial sunnah" in the Medina plan, women were not physically segregated, as we know from the hadith and historical sources. The practice of "female segregation" today originates in immigrant communities that subscribe to familiar cultural and social customs (without question) from their country of origin. Another explanation may be the influence of patriarchy. While the principle of gender equity is implicit in the text of the Qur'an, male commentators

---

[18] Kahera, *Deconstructing the American Mosque*, pp. 41–46.

Figure 13.8. Women performing the prayer, Fayetteville, Georgia (Photo courtesy of Amirah A. Kahera)

have long been accustomed to state that private worship for women at home is preferable.

Three descriptive markers – cultural and social norms, religious belief, and religious practice – further characterize the institution of congregational worship and, in many crucial respects, give reason to dispute various statements about the physical component of women's prayer space.[19] First, religious practice defines the etiquette of women and men, who share the same right of entry to the mosque, for the performance of the five daily prayers, the Friday prayer, and the Eid or feast prayers. Second, while both premodern and present-day commentators point to the merits of public worship without gender distinction, scholarly discourses and legal consensus differ owing to the interpretation of hadith. The view that supports the merits of public worship for women is derived in part from the prophetic statement that rewards for congregational prayers are twenty-seven times greater

[19] S. M. Darsh, *Islamic Essays* (London 1979); Asma Sayeed, "Early Sunni Discourses on Women's Mosque Attendance," *International Institute for the Study of Islam in the Modern World Newsletter* 7 (March 2001): 10.

than those for prayers offered alone.[20] American Muslims, men and women, have debated and negotiated spaces in mosques as well as access to them and segregation within them for several decades and continue to strive for practices and interpretations that build communities and include all of their members. Most useful for comparison is the mention of the word *masjid* (mosque) in the Qur'an, which does not attribute a hermeneutical status to male or female worshipers. In fact, the Qur'an makes no distinction between the sexes: "I will not suffer the work of any worker among you to be lost whether male or female" (Q. 3:194). The etymology of the word *masjid* can be traced to the Arabic verb *sajada*, to prostrate or bow down to God in worship (Q.72:18; 24:36; 9:18).

Finally some urban mosques support an emancipatory vision of female congregants, in support of the collective act of communal worship. Most important is the fellowship hall where men and women gather to pray on a daily basis, to read the Qur'an, and to engage in a host of pious activities.

THE CONSTRUCTION OF MOSQUES AFTER SEPTEMBER 2001

Undoubtedly the freedom of religion is guaranteed under the First Amendment to the constitution: "Congress shall make no law respecting the establishment of religion, or prohibiting the free exercise thereof; or abridging the freedom of speech, or of the press; or the right of the people peaceably to assemble, and to petition the Government for a redress of grievances." Mosques, such as Park51 in 2010, however, have become the subjects of contentious debate. Park51 was not the first instance that the construction of a mosque was challenged; in 2006 a court case erupted over the construction of the Islamic Cultural Center in Roxbury, Massachusetts. The case was dismissed by the court in 2007.[21] The so-called Ground Zero Mosque was considered by some critics to be an illegitimate religious edifice. Many have asked if the Patriot Act (Public Law 107–56) has been instrumental in composing and decomposing expressions of uncertain religious beliefs that put all Muslims in the West off balance? If the First Amendment implicitly supports religious space for all Americans and all religious faiths, then the

---

[20] This hadith appears in *Sahih Bukhari*, one of the canonical hadith collections.
[21] *Islamic Society of Boston & others v. Boston Herald, Inc. & others*, 2006-P-1358.

Figure 13.9. Sanctuary of the Islamic Center of Huntington, West Virginia (Photo courtesy of McCoy Architects LLC)

rhetorical stance of contentious politics posits the following question: How should the First Amendment guarantees apply to current controversies and contentions in the political discourse about religion, public space, and public life?

It is telling that construction of new mosques built after September 11, 2001, has often stalled for various reasons, with some projects such as Park51 receiving national attention. The resistance to the building of mosques is therefore bound to the political climate and the infrastructure of our cities. No one will deny that there is a connection between particular expressions of Islamophobia and anti-Muslim bias and exclusion on the one hand and the aftermath of 9/11 on the other. In other words, while mosques continue to serve as institutional spaces for worship, charitable activities, education, and safe spaces for community members, the connection between resistance and opposition to mosque construction is not always made explicit in public discourse. The symbolism projected onto Park51 and other sites continues to impact mosque developments across America.

Figure 13.10. Mihrab and sanctuary of the Al Farouq Mosque, Atlanta, Georgia (Photo courtesy of Akel Ismail Kahera)

Further Reading

Bayoumi, Mustafa, "Shadows and Light: Colonial Modernity and the Grand Mosque of Paris," *Yale Journal of Criticism* 13:2 (2000): 267–292.

Ebaugh, Helen Rose, and Janet Saltzman Chafetz, *Religion and the New Immigrants: Continuities and Adaptations in Immigrant Congregations* (New York, 2000).

Gale, Richard, "Representing the City: Mosques and the Planning Process in Birmingham," *Journal of Ethnic & Migration Studies* 31:6 (2005): 1161–1179.

Haider, G., "Brother in Islam Please Draw us a Mosque: Muslims in the West a Personal Account," in Hyat Salam, ed., *Expressions of Islam in the Buildings of Islam* (Singapore, 1990), pp. 155–166.

Kahera, Akel Ismail, *Deconstructing the American Mosque: Space, Gender, and Aesthchis* (Austin, 2002).

"Two Muslim Communities: Two Disparate Ways of Islamizing Public Spaces," *Space and Culture* 10:4 (2007): 384–396.

Metcalf, Barbara, ed., *Making Muslim Space in North America and Europe* (Berkeley, 1996).

Sardar, Ziauddin, "Towards an Islamic Theory of the Environment," *Arts & the Islamic World* 3:1 (1985): 12–24.

Sayeed, Asma, "Early Sunni Discourses on Women's Mosque Attendance," *ISIMNewsletter* 7:1 (2001): 10.

Serageldin, Ismail, and James Steel, *Architecture of the Contemporary Mosque* (London, 1996).

14 Islamic Education in the United States: Debates, Practices, and Institutions

ZAREENA A. GREWAL AND R. DAVID COOLIDGE

A DIVERSE PEDAGOGICAL LANDSCAPE

Historically, Muslim American pedagogical discourses were characterized by an antiestablishment streak; however, Islamic educational practices in the United States are increasingly conforming to the institutional status quo of American primary, secondary, and higher education. While the scrutiny of Muslim institutions in the wake of September 11, 2001, has driven some of these mainstreaming trends, the political climate alone cannot account for this sea change in Islamic education. Despite the derivative nature of most Islamic pedagogy, Muslim educators hold firmly to their conviction that Islamic education remains a unique and important alternative in the pedagogical landscape of the United States.

The demand for Islamic primary and secondary schools is evident in their rapid growth and expansion and, in some cases, waiting lists of more than one hundred students. Parents cite a wide range of motivations for sending their children to Islamic K–12 schools. Some hope to instill Islamic knowledge and values and foster a strong religious identity in their children, while others are attracted only by second-language instruction. Some parents hope to shelter their children from racial and religious discrimination and other social ills in public schools (including bullying and dating), while others see Islamic schools as sources of behavioral reform in cases of sexual activity, drug and alcohol use, and gang involvement. Most American Muslim families do not send their children to full-time Islamic schools. One estimate is that just under 4 percent of Muslim American youth attend full-time Islamic schools, a small minority even in the subset of "mosqued" Americans.[1] Far more American Muslims participate in supplemental, part-time religious

[1] Karen Keyworth, "Islamic Schools of America: Data-Based Profiles," in Yvonne Y. Haddad et al., eds., *Educating the Muslims of America* (Oxford, 2009), pp. 21–38. "Mosqued" here means Muslims who regularly participate in activities in mosques and community centers.

programming, such as Islamic Sunday schools at local mosques, summer camps led by national organizations, and paid and unpaid tutors who teach children how to read the Qur'an at home.

Although the largest investments of Muslim American capital and labor are in pedagogical institutions for children, most innovation in Islamic pedagogy happens at the level of higher education. There are few formal institutions of Islamic higher education in the United States; however, informal religious education for adults thrives in study circles, a pedagogical form that has enjoyed a renewed popularity as a result of the late twentieth-century global Islamic revival. All over the world, small groups of like-minded Muslim adults study in these unofficial classes presided over by those deemed most knowledgeable among them. Some Muslim Americans have merged the study circle with its contemporary corollary in American culture, the adult book club. Such gatherings are as likely to happen on the floor of a mosque as around a table in a bookstore café. Alongside these unofficial, organic pedagogical and social activities, mosques and Islamic centers serve adult congregations across the United States through the sermons, lectures, and classes offered by Muslim preachers and teachers, both local speakers and those on international tours. The most popular preachers develop large followings among Muslim Americans, attracting thousands of adult learners at local and national Islamic conferences and retreats throughout North America. Islamic learning, however, does not only happen in the direct, face-to-face contexts of homes, classrooms, cafés, mosques, and auditoriums. One of the defining features of the global Islamic revival is that it coincided with a media revolution. Islamic teachings are transmitted through books, pulp religious literature, pamphlets, cassette tapes, CDs, video tapes, DVDs, YouTube videos, iPod downloads, webinars, online classes, and Internet streams of sermons and public debates. Islamic media are the primary site of religious instruction for large segments of the Muslim American population, and recorded Islamic teachings are freely distributed or marketed throughout Muslim American communities.

This chapter aims to provide an illustrative sketch of pedagogical practices and formal institutions in Muslim communities in the United States over the course of the twentieth century and the first decade of the twenty-first.[2] Throughout this period, Muslim American pedagogical

---

2   Islamic pedagogy in unique settings, such as U.S. prisons, and Islamic forms of learning, such as the spiritual training of Sufi communities, are not discussed in this chapter because they are characterized by particularities that deserve separate treatment. On Islamic learning in U.S. prisons, see Anne Bowers, "The Search for Justice:

practices and institutions have been diverse and diffuse, ranging widely in their purpose, scope, content, and structures. Many Islamic pedagogical institutions have demonstrated remarkable agility, successfully attracting students, youth and adults alike, over generations, but others became vestiges of American Muslim history. We restrict our focus to formal, full-time pedagogical institutions, even though they make up only a small part of a much more complex Islamic pedagogical landscape that is primarily informal and unsystematic. Although not always representative of Muslims' pedagogical practices as a whole, this narrow focus on formal institutions brings key shifts in the antiestablishment ethos of Muslim American pedagogy into sharp relief. While Muslim populations in the United States date back to the colonial period, the history of formal Islamic pedagogical institutions begins in the 1930s.[3]

PRIMARY AND SECONDARY ISLAMIC EDUCATION

The Nation of Islam and the University of Islam

The Nation of Islam established the first formal Islamic pedagogical institutions in the United States for adults and children in the 1930s, although their schools for children quickly surpassed their adult programming. In 1930 W. D. Fard, an enigmatic immigrant silk peddler, founded the Nation of Islam (NOI) in Detroit. He also established a school in Detroit named the University of Islam in the home of one of his first converts, Elijah Muhammad, who assumed leadership of the NOI after Fard's disappearance. In 1934, as part and parcel of the government's systematic harassment and surveillance of the NOI, the Detroit Board of Education tried unsuccessfully to close the school.[4] Despite these political pressures, NOI communities grew and thrived throughout the urban centers of the Northeast and Midwest in the 1930s, and University of Islam satellites were established in these communities. Although called universities, the schools offered kindergarten through twelfth grade; naming them "universities" was a way to indicate that the curriculum

---

Islamic Pedagogy and Inmate Rehabilitation," in Haddad et al., *Educating the Muslims of America*, pp. 179–208; on the diverse forms of Sufism in America, see Marcia Hermansen, "Hybrid Identity Formations in Muslim America: The Case of American Sufi Movements," *Muslim World* 90:1–2 (2000): 158–197.

3   Although much of the religious activities of African Muslim slaves and the first Muslim immigrants arriving in the eighteenth century has yet to be documented by historians, it can be assumed that wherever and whenever Muslims congregated for ritual prayer, they also congregated to teach and learn religious knowledge.

4   For a detailed account of this history and the surveillance of the NOI, see Edward Curtis IV, Chapter 1 in this volume.

was universal and advanced, and an alternative to the deplorable condition of public schools in urban America, characterized by poor quality of education and structural racism. While esoteric knowledge, secretly concealed or willfully withheld, looms large in NOI cosmology, the NOI curriculum included standard disciplines such as math, science, history, and reading, as well as life-skills training. NOI mosques (initially called temples) consistently offered adult congregants opportunities to learn practical skills and bodies of knowledge that could improve their day-to-day lives, from how to cook and eat a healthy diet to steps to start and grow a small business.

The pedagogical vision of the NOI paved the way for both the Black nationalist independent education movement and the Afrocentric education movement that came out of the civil rights movement, offering an alternative to the public school system.[5] In what is now a classic in American literature, *The Autobiography of Malcolm X*, the NOI's most famous convert recounts his own painful experience as a talented and popular student in his nearly all-white school. Despite achieving excellent grades and even the class presidency in seventh grade, Malcolm's ambitions were undermined by a racist teacher in eighth grade. Upon hearing Malcolm muse about becoming a lawyer, the teacher dissuaded him, urging him to become a carpenter instead, a station the teacher believed was more suited to his skin color.[6] This moment of disillusionment was the beginning of a downward spiral that led him to drop out of school and pursue a life of crime until he was sent to prison, where he encountered the transformative message of Black empowerment in the Nation of Islam. His religious conversion marked an intellectual transformation as well, as Malcolm began to expand his vocabulary by painstakingly copying a dictionary in the prison library, page by page.[7] Malcolm's story is a testament to the NOI's cultivation of a strong ethos of self-improvement, with education for children and adults at its core.

By the mid-seventies there were forty-one University of Islam schools throughout the United States, but the seventies was also a period of massive transformation for the NOI and, therefore, for the schools. After Elijah Muhammad passed away in 1975, his son Wallace D. Muhammad took over the leadership of the NOI, even though his own conversion

5 Zakiyyah Muhammad and Hakim M. Rashid, "The Sister Clara Muhammad Schools: Pioneers in the Development of Islamic Education in America," *Journal of Negro Education* 61:2 (1992): 178–185.

6 Alex Haley, *The Autobiography of Malcolm X* (New York, 1987), pp. 32–38.

7 Haley, *Autobiography*, p. 175.

to Sunni Islam had been an on-and-off point of contention between father and son. Renamed Imam W. D. (Warith Deen) Mohammed, he inspired the majority of NOI members to move toward Sunni Islam during this period. Louis Farrakhan became the rival leader of a smaller community of Black Muslims who remained committed to the original teachings of Elijah Muhammad. Under Imam W. D. Mohammed's leadership, the forty-one Universities of Islam were renamed the Sister Clara Muhammad schools, honoring W. D. Mohammed's mother, the pioneer teacher. Although the Sister Clara Muhammad schools retained their emphasis on high academic standards and cultivating Black pride in their students, Sunni thought and theology replaced the NOI theology classes. In reaction to W. D. Mohammed's curricular reforms, Louis Farrakhan reestablished the University of Islam K–12 schools in inner cities across the country in 1989, with religious instruction in the original theology of the NOI.

Sunni Primary and Secondary Schools

This history accounts for only a small part of the national picture of Islamic schools today, most of which (85 percent) were established in the nineties by recent immigrants, primarily from the Middle East and South Asia. The eighties marked the beginning of a period of expansive growth of Islamic K–12 schools in predominantly Sunni immigrant mosque communities, which continues to the present day. Of the approximately 250 full-time Islamic schools in the United States, only a few are identified as Shi'a, although many Islamic schools founded by Sunnis attract Shi'a students as well.[8] With their overlapping, explicitly Sunni religious instruction, the Sister Clara Muhammad schools have joined schools founded by predominantly immigrant Muslim communities in umbrella organizations, such as the Council of Islamic Schools of North America. Sister Clara Muhammad schools also attract Muslim students from other ethnic and racial backgrounds. In 1991 the original University of Islam in Detroit became an independent Sunni school, renamed Al-Ikhlas Training Academy. Serving Yemenis and Bangladeshis as well as African American students, it is both the first and longest continuously running Islamic school in the United States.[9] Conversely, Islamic schools founded by immigrants attract many African American Muslim students.

---

[8] Shi'a schools in the U.S. include Al-Iman in New York and Al-Hadi in Houston.
[9] Sally Howell, "Competing for Muslims: New Strategies for Urban Renewal in Detroit," in Andrew Shryock, ed., *Islamophobia/Islamophilia* (Bloomington, 2010), p. 216.

In fact, Islamic schools often reflect far more racial, ethnic, class, and even sectarian diversity than the congregations of the mosque communities that found them. For example, in 1999 the mosque congregation in Ann Arbor, Michigan, was predominantly Arab American; however, the enrollment of the first-grade classroom of the Michigan Islamic Academy, housed in the mosque, included white, African American, Jordanian, Libyan, Malaysian, Saudi, Somali, Palestinian, Pakistani, and Venezuelan students. In addition to their ethnic, racial, linguistic, and national diversity, the demographics of the school population reflected a wide spectrum of religious devotion, socioeconomic class, and citizenship status. The school attracted the children of "devout" white, African American, and Latino converts as well as "non-practicing" immigrants from the Middle East; wealthy third- and fourth-generation immigrants and poverty-stricken, newly arrived refugees; international university students, and semiliterate day laborers.[10]

In the case of primary and secondary education, Islamic schools in the United States are increasingly modeled closely on American public schools and faith-based private schools. Before September 11, there were numerous innovative curricular reform programs aimed at integrating Islamic studies across disciplines, often termed the "Islamization of Knowledge" after the programmatic vision of leading reform-minded Muslim intellectuals. With the politicization of Islamic education after September 11, holistic Islamic instruction increasingly became synonymous with integrating a character curriculum based on Islamic values, a considerable departure from the pedagogical ambitions of many Muslim educators in the eighties and nineties, who labored to develop uniquely Islamic approaches to the teaching of all disciplines. Today, most full-time Islamic schools' methods and curriculum match those of American public schools down to the textbooks. Thus, what makes many Islamic schools "Islamic" is simply that Islamic studies and sometimes Arabic are additional courses and that the Muslim-majority school environment creates an Islamic ethos that normalizes Islamic practices and cultivates pride and a strong "Muslim-first" identity in students.

The metrics of success adopted by Muslim educators increasingly conform to those of the American education system at large. If teacher certification is taken as a quality measure, only 10 percent are fully staffed by certified teachers, and many of these teachers are not Muslim. If religious studies are excluded, the percentage of certified teachers jumps to 46 percent. If standardized testing is taken as a measure, some Islamic

---

[10] Author Zareena A. Grewal was employed at the school during this time.

schools meet or exceed state standards, while others fall far short.[11] Few
Islamic schools refuse to measure their worth by such official, external,
and mainstream standards, at least academically. In other words, there is
no Islamic school in the United States that would identify itself with a
pedagogically "progressive" philosophy, although a few incorporate pedagogical practices drawn from experimental pedagogical methods, such as
Montessori. A handful of Islamic schools have built solid, national repu-
tations in Muslim American communities. For example, the Al-Ghazaly
School in Jersey City boasts alumni who have graduated from Ivy League
universities, such as Harvard, Yale, Cornell, and Columbia.[12] While the
most academically reputable Islamic schools (and the ones with the
most impressive facilities) tend to be ones financed by wealthier immigrants in the suburbs, the Sister Clara Muhammad schools have also
improved and expanded over the years, including in their extracurricular
offerings, such as their celebrated athletic, step dance, and debate teams.
W. D. Mohammad High in Atlanta distinguished itself in 2006 when its
women's varsity basketball team, the Lady Caliphs, competed for the
Georgia state championship. Both academic and athletic achievements
are increasingly defined by Muslim Americans in terms of reference
points common to the broader society.

After September 11, 2001, mainstream media coverage of American
Islamic schools with inflammatory headlines such as "What Are Islamic
Schools Teaching?" or "U.S. Islamic Schools Teaching Homegrown
Hate?" stoked fears about a Muslim fifth column.[13] Contrary to the stereotype, researchers consistently demonstrate that American Islamic
schools place great emphasis on civic-mindedness.[14] In reaction to this
increasingly hostile and suspicious political climate, more Islamic
schools are restricting Islamic studies curriculum to material written
by American Muslim authors, such as the "I Love Islam" series. Not
all mainstream media representations of Islamic schools are negative.
In 2004 an Islamic school was featured on PBS's *Postcards from Buster*,
a nonanimated spinoff of its popular cartoon *Arthur*, in which Buster
narrates mini-documentaries filmed from a knee-cap vantage point. In
the episode "Sense of Direction," Buster meets a Pakistani American

[11] Keyworth, "Islamic Schools of America: Data-Based Profiles."
[12] Tariq Mahmoud, personal communication with Zareena Grewal, October 28, 2010.
[13] Daniel Pipes, "What Are Islamic Schools Teaching?" *New York Sun*, March 29, 2005;
Kenneth Adelman, "U.S. Islamic Schools Teaching Homegrown Hate," FOX News,
March 15, 2007.
[14] Louis Cristillo, "The Case for the Muslim School as a Civil Society Actor," and
Jasmine Zine, "Safe Havens or 'Religious Ghettos'? Narratives of Islamic Schooling in
Canada," in Haddad et al., *Educating the Muslims of America*, pp. 39–84.

girl named Farah who gives him a tour of her Islamic school in Chicago, explaining how Muslims face Mecca in prayer and why she chooses to wear a headscarf only at school.[15]

Although the post-9/11 political environment profoundly constrained debates among Muslim educators over the nature and scale of Islamic pedagogy, it also redirected Muslim charitable giving and nurtured institutional growth. One of the unintended effects of the state's stricter policing of Muslim Americans' charitable giving in the wake of 9/11 was the growth of domestic Islamic charities, including schools. Many internationally focused Islamic charities were closed, frozen, or simply choked out of existence by the government's post-9/11 crackdown, even when the pending investigations and lawsuits were dropped. Although Islamic schools also face increased state scrutiny, Muslim Americans wary about charitable giving in this hostile political climate often opt to support Islamic schools because they are perceived to be relatively "safe" and "apolitical" institutions. Since the 2010 campaign against the so-called Ground Zero Mosque, Islamic schools across the country, like mosques, have faced a national grass-roots movement organizing to keep them out of particular municipalities or at least to prevent building expansion. The dramatic growth in Islamic schools after September 11 may thus be short-lived.[16]

Madrasas

There are a few Islamic schools in the United States that self-identify as madrasas, despite the stigma of militancy associated with these traditional Islamic seminaries in the minds of many Americans. The longest-running institutions are the Institute of Islamic Education (IIE), founded in 1989 in Chicago, and Darul-Uloom Al-Madania (DUM) in Buffalo, founded in 1992. The teachers are products of the Deobandi movement, which emerged in India in the latter half of the nineteenth century in reaction to British colonial policies.[17] Deobandi madrasas worldwide are organized into two tracks, a memorization track, which focuses exclusively on the memorization and melodic recitation of the entire Qur'an, and a scholarly track, focusing on classical Islamic disciplines as laid out in the relatively uniform Dars-e-Nizami curriculum.

---

[15] "Postcards from Buster: A Sense of Direction" season 1, episode 3.

[16] Kathleen Foley, "'Not in Our Neighborhood': Managing Opposition to Mosque Construction," Institute for Social Policy and Understanding (Washington, D.C., 2010).

[17] Barbara Daly Metcalf, *Islamic Revival in British India: Deoband, 1860–1900* (Delhi, 2002).

Most American madrasa students are South Asian but the schools also attract other students. Like the enrollment trends in regular Islamic primary and secondary schools, parents' motivations to send their children to madrasas range widely, including as a form of punishment and rehabilitation.[18] Older students in the academic track (*"alim* programs") are usually there by choice, and they tend to be much more devoted to the ideological orientations of the Deobandi school of thought. Strict gender segregation is a norm at these schools, as is a general pattern of social isolation from the broader American society, unlike most Islamic K–12 schools.

These American madrasas replicate the intellectually insular orientation shared by many Deobandi-affiliated madrasas throughout the global South Asian diaspora.[19] The DUM is made up of two separate schools, one for grades K–2 which establishes basic reading, writing, and math skills and a second for grades 2–10 that is focused primarily on religious studies taught in Urdu and Arabic. Graduates often do a correspondence course in order to get a General Education Diploma. Unlike DUM, IIE's instruction is primarily in English; however, its secular curriculum is still minimal. In the fall of 2005, four twelfth-grade students at IIE reached their last year of high school without ever being assigned a novel to study, until a substitute teacher assigned the American classic *The Catcher in the Rye*.[20] This disinterest and disengagement from the broader society stands in sharp contrast to the growing mainstreaming trends in most Islamic schools.

Homeschooling

While most Islamic K–12 schools are derivative either of American public and private schools or of South Asian Deobandi madrasas, Muslim Americans are being far more inventive and innovative in homeschooling, perhaps the fastest growing demographic of homeschooling families in the United States.[21] In the nineties, Hamza Yusuf, a renowned Muslim preacher based in northern California, popularized the growing

---

[18] For one female student's account, see Sunaina Maira, *Missing: Youth, Citizenship, and Empire after 9/11* (Durham, 2009), pp. 190–193.

[19] For a comparison with similar schools in the United Kingdom, see Peter Mandaville, "Islamic Education in Britain: Approaches to Religious Knowledge in a Pluralistic Society," in Robert Hefner and Muhammad Qasim Zaman, eds., *Schooling Islam: The Culture and Politics of Modern Muslim Education* (Princeton, 2007), pp. 237–239.

[20] Author R. David Coolidge was the substitute twelfth-grade English teacher while a student in the Qur'anic memorization track.

[21] Priscilla Martinez, "Muslim Homeschooling," in Haddad et al., *Educating the Muslims of America*, pp. 109–122.

homeschooling movement in Muslim American communities on a much wider scale. Before his public advocacy of programs such as the Kinza Academy, it was not uncommon to find Muslim families, especially working-class African American Muslims and immigrant Muslims, homeschooling their children, daughters more often than sons. This choice was usually framed as a suboptimal solution in the face of the poor social and educational conditions in their neighborhood public schools. Yusuf introduced a harsh critique of American education, positing homeschooling not as a reluctant compromise but as a pedagogical ideal that surpasses the best American education had to offer. Yusuf has insisted in his speeches and his writings that modern schools deaden inquiry and expose impressionable children to social ills. In one speech, Yusuf invoked the Prophet Muhammad's instruction of his daughter Fatima as an example of homeschooling, and he named Ali ibn Abu Talib, the fourth caliph in Islamic history, as an example of a homeschooled genius. Yusuf connects his religious critiques of American education with the work of secular radical educational reformers, such as John Taylor Gatto and Dorothy Sayers.[22] Although homeschooling is one area in which Muslim Americans are making pedagogical innovations in curricular content and pedagogical form rather than simply adding an Islamic veneer to mainstream pedagogical practices and curricula, Muslims have been far more innovative (albeit far less invested) in Islamic higher learning.

Innovating and Institutionalizing Islamic Higher Learning

The wide range of institutions of higher learning established by Muslim Americans has had diverse outcomes: some pedagogical experiments have failed and disappeared, others have been reinvented and resuscitated, and several are clearly growing and successful. It is relatively common to hear Muslim educators claim that in order to secure the future of Islam in the United States, American Islamic higher learning must "move from personalities to institutions." Personality-based institutions, such as the Nawawi Foundation in Chicago, support the work of a single scholar-in-residence, with occasional guest teachers. Nawawi's Umar Faruq Abd-Allah, a white American convert to Islam, former Islamic studies professor, and internationally renowned Sufi master

---

[22] Hamza Yusuf Hanson, "Lambs to the Slaughter," in John Taylor Gatto, Hamza Yusuf Hanson, and Dorothy Sayers, eds., *Beyond Schooling* (Toronto, 2001); Hamza Yusuf Hanson, "New Lamps for Old," in John Taylor Gatto, Hamza Yusuf Hanson, and Dorothy Sayers, eds., *Educating Your Child in Modern Times: Raising an Intelligent, Sovereign, and Ethical Human Being* (Hayward, 2003).

and preacher, conducts independent research on topics of importance to American Muslims and offers courses for adult students. Criticisms against such personality-based institutions include their instability and short life-span; these institutions die when the teacher moves or passes away, or if he or she no longer attracts students. In fact, most institutions of Islamic higher learning failed not because of their structure but owing to lack of resources. Examples include a short-lived Shi'a institution of higher learning established in New York in the nineties[23] and the defunct Muslim Teachers College in Virginia, which trained primary and secondary teachers to work in the Sister Clara Muhammad schools and its own boarding school.

The platitude that American Muslims must "move from personalities to institutions" is often overstated. In this formulation, the core problem is the lag in evolution from pedagogical practices centered on an individual religious leader's charisma to the development of pedagogical institutions that allow for greater longevity and breadth. In fact, personality-based institutions are not the norm and are short-lived; most Muslim religious authorities in the United States teach without establishing a formal institution; rather, they attract students by establishing a scholarly reputation and disseminating their teachings. Increasingly, the directive to move from "personalities to institutions" is not lodged against the personality-based schools, which are clearly in decline in the United States; even the successful Nawawi Foundation froze programming in 2012. The criticism is directed at those institutions that are overwhelmed by their charismatic religious leaders. In other words, it would be more precise to express the criticism this way: Islamic educational institutions must move beyond their personalities. Founders of these institutions often express concern over whether their pedagogical vision and programming will survive them, a fear that materialized in the case of the first major Islamic institution of higher education in the United States.

International Institute of Islamic Thought and the American Islamic College

The International Institute of Islamic Thought (IIIT) in Herndon, Virginia, and the American Islamic College (AIC) in downtown Chicago were both founded in 1981 by reform-minded Muslim American intellectuals, led

---

[23] Abdulaziz A. Sachedina, "A Minority within a Minority: The Case of the Shi'a in North America," in Yvonne Y. Haddad and Jane I. Smith, eds., *Muslim Communities in North America* (Albany, 1994), p. 12.

by the modernist reformer and seminal Muslim American figure Isma'il al-Faruqi (d. 1986). Al-Faruqi, a Palestinian American professor of Islamic Studies at Temple University, and his Saudi colleague, AbdulHamid AbuSulayman, linked what they saw as the civilizational decline of Muslim societies to an epistemological crisis that was the result of an ethical and conceptual gap between Western social and natural sciences and Islamic values and intellectual traditions. Their "Islamization of Knowledge" paradigm holds that a prerequisite of the revival of Muslim societies is the harmonization of Islamic scholarly traditions and values with the secular academic social and physical sciences. In other words, the process of bringing Islamic scholarly traditions to bear on disciplines such as anthropology, sociology, and political science ought to yield an "Islamized" sociology or political science, recognizable as conceptually linked to a reformed Islamic scholarly tradition but also recognizable as intellectually sound in theory and method by secular academics. Their pedagogical vision was simultaneously an antiestablishment critique of secular academia as well as a conciliatory intellectual project. Their vision was enormously influential in mosque communities and trickled down to Sunni primary and secondary schools founded by revivalist immigrants in the eighties and nineties.

Their pedagogical vision manifested itself in the establishment of Islamic pedagogical institutions in the United States and abroad, such as the American Islamic College in Chicago.[24] The AIC was acquired with financial support from international Islamic organizations such as the Organization of the Islamic Conference and the Muslim World League, and initially the college promised to offer a program granting a bachelor's degree in Islamic Studies and Arabic with a rigorous curriculum that brought the best of the liberal tradition of Western higher education to a reform-minded, modernist study of Islamic disciplines. Classes began in 1983 with al-Faruqi at the helm as chairman. Reformist Muslim thinkers, such as Asad Husain, a political scientist, and Ghulam Aasi, a professor of Islamic studies, were recruited from Pakistan to teach both secular disciplines and Islamic studies. By 1986, however, the college was near financial ruin, and the brutal murder of al-Faruqi left a vacuum in leadership from which it never fully recovered. AIC was never accredited, nor did it offer more than a handful of classes in computer science, sociology, history, and political science. By the late 1990s, the AIC was struggling to survive, attracting very few students. Ultimately, AIC lost

---

[24] See Karen Leonard, Chapter 10 in this volume, for a discussion of its Graduate School of Islamic Social Sciences.

its basic academic license but continued to offer not-for-credit classes. Its operational budget could barely maintain the extensive building, let alone provide reasonable salaries to members of the faculty, who supplemented their incomes by taking adjunct positions at local colleges. The dorms were used to house male Muslim international students attending other universities throughout Chicago, and the facilities were often rented to other faith communities for social and educational events of their own. Unfortunately, the multiple uses of the facility led to a lengthy lawsuit over the control of the property.

IIIT supported the careers of several generations of reform-minded Muslim American academics through endowed scholarships and continues to publish their books as well as a peer-reviewed, academic journal, the *American Journal of Islamic Social Sciences*, with the Association of Muslim Social Scientists. Although the Muslim educators associated with IIIT were pioneers in the field of Islamic higher education in the United States, their programmatic vision of the "Islamization of Knowledge" never reached fruition as a coherent pedagogical approach in U.S. institutions.[25] It began to fall out of step with the national Muslim conversation about Islamic education in the nineties, particularly with the rising popularity of Hamza Yusuf, a fierce critic of the approach. In addition, IIIT and its related institutes were subject to intense political scrutiny after September 11. Both the offices and homes of those affiliated with IIIT were raided by federal agents; the taint of federal investigation further dried up donor and student interest.[26] Although formal charges were never made, the organization is still recovering.

In 2010 the intellectual direction of the AIC was assumed by Turkish American educators who are part of the Gülen movement, an Islamic pedagogical movement that embraces secular education and has a markedly less ambitious pedagogical vision than the AIC's founders. Turkish Gülen communities throughout the United States are characterized by a highly centralized, corporate structure, with each satellite following a strict chain of command back to its leader, Fethullah Gülen, who resides in rural Pennsylvania. In the fall of 2010, they organized a conference on the future of Islam in America, featuring many of the most popular Muslim preachers and scholar-activists in the United States, rather

[25] IIIT had relatively greater success in Muslim-majority countries. See Mona Abaza, *Debates on Islam and Knowledge in Malaysia and Egypt: Shifting Worlds* (New York, 2002).

[26] Indeed, another Islamic college also in the D.C. area, a satellite branch of Imam Muhammad ibn Saud Islamic University in Saudi Arabia, was completely shut down due to the hostile political environment following September 11.

than Gülen preachers who have had little appeal beyond the Turkish community. Civic-minded, apolitical, assimilationist, and professional in all of its religious outreach activities, the Turkish Gülen group in Chicago successfully generated new excitement for the AIC but with little trace of the original, holistic, antiestablishment pedagogical vision of its founders.

Zaytuna College

Zaytuna Institute was founded in Hayward, California, in 1996 by the aforementioned Hamza Yusuf and a local businessman. They aimed to revive "traditional Islamic education," both in terms of curricular content (classical texts in Islamic law, theology, rhetoric, etc.) and in terms of pedagogical method.[27] Yusuf's vision is to revive Islam's mystical tradition of Sufism and its pedagogical model of initiatic transmission, specifically the *ijaza* system that formed the basis for the transmission of the religious disciplines within Sunni Islam, among American Muslims.[28] In what they called the "traditional" system, the teacher and the student read texts in each core discipline together, and the teacher expounded upon the usually terse text that was written with the purpose of being memorized. Once the student completed (and occasionally memorized) the text and displayed sufficient understanding of its contents, the student would be granted an ijaza, a license authorizing the student to teach the text and move to studying an intermediate text in the same discipline. The direct relationship between the teacher and the student, through the medium of the text, was seen as the proper methodology for transmitting sacred knowledge and teaching piety. Yusuf argues that the creation of modern universities in the Arab world was not a step forward but a dilution of Islam's rich scholarly tradition. Yusuf's vision embodies the antiestablishment tenor of discourses on Islamic pedagogy in the United States, in which unofficial, "traditional" training often has far more cache than a formal academic degree in Islamic studies. Importantly, Zaytuna explicitly distinguishes its alternative, holistic pedagogical vision from the "Islamization of Knowledge" approach, noting: "Muslim thinkers of the past never felt the need to 'Islamize' [knowledge] as many modern Muslim thinkers have, a development

---

[27] Zareena Grewal, *Islam Is a Foreign Country: American Muslim Youth and the Global Crisis of Authority* (New York, 2013).

[28] For more on the particular intellectual and political genealogies of Hamza Yusuf, see Scott Kugle's book *Rebel between Spirit and Law: Ahmad Zarruq, Sainthood, and Authority in Islam* (Bloomington, 2006).

that has led to an unnecessary Western/secular vs. Islamic/revelatory dichotomy."[29]

In 2004 Zaytuna launched a pilot seminary program as a conscious attempt to create a systematic curriculum that could be used to train future generations of Muslim scholars in the United States. Zaid Shakir, a nationally recognized African American preacher, joined Yusuf to form the nucleus of the growing Zaytuna faculty. Through a national fundraising campaign, they promoted Zaytuna as an inclusive institution of higher learning that would revive the Islamic scholarly heritage. Although originally billed as a seminary, the founders made Zaytuna College a B.A.-granting institution after much internal debate. The reasons given for this change to dismayed donors were threefold. First, Zaytuna was modeled on historic Islamic institutions of higher learning, memorialized for *not* separating but integrating religious subjects and "worldly" disciplines; therefore, the creation of a full-fledged university would better approximate this Islamic ideal than the creation of a specialized seminary. Second, it was in the students' interests to have coursework that could be recognizable and transferable to other institutions of higher learning throughout the United States. Third, Zaytuna aimed to have an impact on the wider society and therefore ought to prepare students for a range of different careers.[30] In August 2010 Zaytuna College welcomed its first freshman class of fifteen students and received considerable positive coverage in the mainstream media.[31] Also in 2012, they purchased a campus in Berkeley near the Graduate Theological Union and established a formal relationship with the GTU and its affiliate colleges, which includes the use of their library.

American Learning Institute for Muslims

The American Learning Institute for Muslims (ALIM), established in Detroit, Michigan, in 1999, aims to empower American Muslims through a basic but conceptually rich Islamic education. Despite its acronym, which means "scholar" in Arabic, ALIM is much more pragmatic and humble in its ambitions: to give American Muslims a stronger religious "literacy." Literacy here is not literal but rather refers to nurturing a comfort level with scripture, Islamic disciplines of scholarship, and contemporary debates in American mosques. To this end, ALIM offers a

---

[29] http://www.zaytunacollege.org/academics/related_topic/general_Education_approach, accessed April 3, 2012.

[30] Imam Zaid Shakir, personal communication with R. David Coolidge, June 2010.

[31] Scott Orb "American Islam," *Chronicle Review*, March 18, 2012, http://chronicle.com/article/American-Islam/131154, accessed April 3, 2012.

one-month summer course in Detroit at a college campus and weekend courses that move across the country. ALIM is far less wedded to the model of "traditional" Islamic pedagogy espoused at Zaytuna, although members of the core faculty have this "traditional" training as well as academic degrees in Islamic studies from prominent, secular American universities. Their best-known teacher is Sherman "Abdul Hakim" Jackson, an Islamic studies professor at the University of Southern California and a popular Muslim preacher among Muslim youth in the United States, Canada, and Europe. In addition to the core faculty, guest scholars, including teachers associated with Zaytuna and other institutions, teach at ALIM. ALIM distinguishes itself in two important ways: the diversity of its faculty and its incorporation of the liberal arts college seminar as a pedagogical model. ALIM's faculty members reflect not only the rich demographic diversity of American Muslims but a wide spectrum of religious perspectives; even its core faculty members have very different, though not necessarily opposing, religious orientations. Each perspective is presented respectfully but from a critical point of view, yielding an eclectic curriculum made cohesive by its academic quality. ALIM aims to cultivate critical thinking skills and commitments to particular, American expressions of Islam in its students. Despite its English-only format, inclusive spirit, and American thematic focus, ALIM has struggled with its student enrollment more than its peer institutions. One critique often lodged against ALIM is that it is "too academic" and, therefore, inaccessible even to many college-educated Muslim Americans. Some consider ALIM's fusion of critical and confessional approaches to the study of Islam irreverent and object to the format or the teaching styles of the instructors, which put a primacy on open questions and debates.[32] The faculty holds that a critical engagement with the tradition ultimately empowers students and solidifies their faith and confidence as Muslims.

AlMaghrib Institute

Despite intense political scrutiny because of its link to Saudi Arabia and the global Salafi movement, AlMaghrib Institute is one of the most demonstrably successful institutions of higher learning in the United States, particularly in terms of measures such as numbers of students enrolled, successful marketing, and curricular and structural innovation.[33]

---

[32] Nadia Inji Khan, "'Guide Us to the Straight Way': A Look at the Makers of 'Religiously Literate' Young Muslim Americans," in Haddad et al., *Educating the Muslims of America*, pp. 123–154.

[33] Boasting an annual revenue in 2010 of $1.2 million, thirty-six thousand current and former students, tens of thousands of Facebook fans and Twitter followers devoted

Founded in 2002 by Muhammad Alshareef, an Egyptian Canadian graduate of the Islamic University of Madinah, AlMaghrib is headquartered in Houston, though the instructors are spread throughout North America. Most of AlMaghrib instructors are graduates of the Islamic University of Madinah, which is why AlMaghrib is characterized as Salafi in ideological orientation, despite founder Muhammad Alshareef's commitment to not using labels other than "Islam" and "Muslim" to describe its approach. Some of AlMaghrib's faculty are popular preachers in their own right, such as Yasir Qadhi, securing a loyal student base. Like ALIM's weekend courses, AlMaghrib adopts a mobile classroom model that moves from city to city across the country. The sites for the classes range from a rented university lecture hall to a local mosque. AlMaghrib boasts a sleek and user-friendly Web site with an incredibly active forum that connects the instructors with their students across long distances. The logistical details for the classes are the responsibility of local student volunteers, giving them a sense of ownership, and these local volunteers play a critical role in developing an esprit de corps among the students. They are often organized into *qabeelas* (Arabic for "tribe") with male and female leaders, a self-conscious attempt to echo the social reality of the founding period of Islam. The qabeelas are encouraged to outdo one another in advertising, Web site construction, exam results, and other areas of healthy competition. AlMaghrib also had a brief partnership with an on-site Arabic-immersion course named the Al-Bayyinah Program, based in Dallas. AlMaghrib founders are working toward establishing an M.A.- and Ph.D.-granting Islamic seminary with a permanent campus in the United States, featuring teachers as full-time faculty.[34]

In terms of pedagogical form and content, AlMaghrib differs from ALIM and Zaytuna in important ways. The AlMaghrib experience is more akin to a didactic, corporate retreat than the American college classroom, with little room for the critical approach to the kind of religious study ALIM instructors encourage. Zaytuna's veneration of historical pedagogical forms and its spiritual retreat ambience are also absent. AlMaghrib weekend retreats offer individual classes over the course of back-to-back weekends, just as weekend continuation courses serve busy professionals in the corporate world. Each of AlMaghrib's classes is a coherent whole rather than cumulative, although students have an option to follow the curriculum

---

to its faculty, and hundreds of sermons on YouTube, AlMaghrib has eclipsed many of its competitors. Andrea Elliott, "Why Yasir Qadhi Wants to Talk about Jihad," *New York Times*, March 17, 2011, http://www.nytimes.com/2011/03/20/magazine/mag-20Salafis-t.html?pagewanted=all, accessed April 3, 2012.

[34] Yasir Qadhi, personal communication with Zareena Grewal, July 2010.

as laid out on its Web site. Its Islamic studies curriculum is simple and accessible, authored by the faculty, and its lowest-common-denominator approach to the curriculum enhances its comparative success in drawing students with a wide range of religious observance. Despite its successful mobile-classroom model and weekend conference approach, AlMaghrib has a glaring gap in its student population: African American Muslim students.[35] Far more than Zaytuna and ALIM, AlMaghrib's students are primarily of Arab and South Asian descent. The absence of Black students is particularly surprising at AlMaghrib because the Salafi strain of Islam identified with AlMaghrib is popular in some African American Muslim communities. AlMaghrib, ALIM, and Zaytuna compete for students, which has resulted in a rivalry that has surged and waned over the years. Generally speaking, the institutes have settled into a live-and-let-live attitude toward each other, encapsulated in the oft-repeated slogan coined by Hamza Yusuf: "Let the best da'wah (mission) win."

Virtual Institutes

As evinced by AlMaghrib, the use of technology has played a major role in reshaping the landscape of formal institutions of Islamic higher learning in the United States. Qibla.com (formerly Sunnipath.com) is arguably in the vanguard of virtual Islamic education. It is an online school originally based in New Jersey, but its offices and American staff have moved to Amman, Jordan. Qibla's accessibility and the high quality of its curriculum appeal to many English-speaking Muslims worldwide. Seekers Guidance, run by former Qibla teacher Faraz Rabbani, offers a similar level of quality and depth in a new format but is tailored specifically to the needs of North American and Australian Muslim audiences. Many Muslim educators, even those invested in physical institutions and direct teacher-student interaction, recognize they must have a virtual presence in order to stay relevant.[36] Brick-and-mortar institutions of Islamic higher learning now compete with emerging and often relatively more successful virtual institutes.

CONCLUSION: PROFESSIONAL FUTURES

Muslim preachers and religious leaders are increasingly expected to demonstrate "professional" mastery of bodies of knowledge both within

---

[35] Yasir Qadhi, personal communication with Zareena Grewal, July 2010.
[36] Despite its commitment to initiatic learning, even Zaytuna has adopted this distance-learning approach.

the Islamic tradition and beyond it. Interestingly, professional graduate degrees from universities in the United States are increasingly folded into contemporary constructions of religious authority. In contrast to most Muslim American intellectuals in the academy, who remain largely unknown and unread by lay Muslim Americans, Muslim academics such as Nawawi's Abd-Allah and ALIM's Jackson are regularly invited to large, mainstream Muslim American conferences and preach to tens of thousands of Muslim Americans each year. Their Ph.D. degrees from prestigious American universities augment the stamp of religious authority that comes from their unofficial religious instruction overseas. For some American Muslims, the imprimatur of "traditional" religious study overseas is sought because of a lack of appealing institutions of Islamic higher learning in the United States. For others, the preference for study abroad is linked to the ascription of a cultural and religious authenticity, which either has not or cannot be replicated in the United States.[37]

Islamic chaplaincy programs, such as the one based at Hartford Seminary, offer a uniquely American model of religious authority and a professional Islamic education. The program trains Muslim chaplains to serve in hospitals, universities, the military, and prisons. While the curriculum is relatively light on normative Islamic knowledge, such as theology and law, these programs focus instead on developing applied skills such as counseling, interfaith relations, and leading a congregation. Male and female alumni have many employment opportunities, particularly in hospitals, prisons, and elite universities. As resources within mosque communities, chaplains do not command much religious authority by means of their degree, but their skill sets as counselors, conflict-mediators, and public spokespeople are in high demand. Muslim chaplains play an important role in educating the wider public about Islam and Muslims. For example, in 2012 New York University's chaplain Khalid Latif was a guest on Comedy Central's popular show *The Colbert Report*, and he regularly blogs on CNN.com.

Muslim American educators are embracing more and more of the pedagogical norms of American educational institutions, a significant change from the antiestablishment streak of Islamic pedagogical discourses in the twentieth century. Islamic pedagogical institutions in the United States will have to negotiate skepticism toward their mainstreaming trends in their efforts to attract Muslim students and donors to invest in distinctly "Islamic" and "American" education, however these terms are defined. Whatever the outcome of that negotiation, one

---

[37] Grewal, *Islam Is a Foreign Country.*

can expect that Muslim American students will still quote verses of the Qur'an, study the hadith, and debate the meanings and forms of the Islamic tradition as students have done since the earliest study circles in the central mosques of Mecca and Medina.

Further Reading

AbuSulayman, AbdulHamid A., *Crisis in the Muslim Mind* (Herndon, 1993).

Doumato, Eleanor, and Gregory Starrett, eds., *Teaching Islam: Textbooks and Religion in the Middle East* (Boulder, 2007).

Grewal, Zareena A., *Islam Is a Foreign Country: American Muslim Youth and the Global Crisis of Authority* (New York, 2013).

Haddad, Yvonne Y., Farid Senzai, and Jane I. Smith, eds., *Educating the Muslims of America* (New York, 2009).

Hefner, Robert, and Muhammad Qasim Zaman, eds., *Schooling Islam: The Culture and Politics of Modern Muslim Education* (Princeton, 2007).

Kadi, Wadad, and Victor Billeh, eds., *Islam and Education: Myths and Truths* (Chicago, 2007).

Korb, Scott, *Light without Fire: The Making of America's First Muslim College* (Boston, 2013).

Sarroub, Loukia, *All American Yemeni Girls: Being Muslim in a Public School* (Philadelphia, 2005).

15 Muslim Public Intellectuals and Global Muslim Thought

TIMUR R. YUSKAEV

Edward Said once noted that an "intellectual is an individual endowed with a faculty of representing, embodying, articulating a message, a view, an attitude, philosophy or opinion to, as well as for, a public." Specific audiences speak in specific ways. To influence change, an intellectual must know how to speak their language and "when to intervene" in it.[1] American Muslim intellectuals have served as guiding voices in local Muslim discourses, which have always been intertwined with global currents of Muslim thought. How have they spoken the language of American Muslim audiences? How and when have they intervened in it? What has been local and global in such interventions? Finally, what has been "public" about them?

Two sermons by (Shaykh) Hamza Yusuf (1960–), delivered shortly before and after September 11, 2001, can help us answer these questions. Yusuf, who is white, converted to Islam in 1977 and studied for a decade under the tutelage of Muslim clerics in the Middle East and North Africa. Drawing on his education in Muslim seminaries, he presented himself as a "traditional scholar," stressing that his intellectual lineage and methodology represented a continuation of premodern Islamic traditions of theological, legal, and mystical thought.[2] In the late 1990s, and especially after 2001, he became the most recognizable English-speaking Muslim preacher on the Internet, reaching a worldwide audience.[3] At this stage in his career, his primary audience consisted of second-generation immigrant and African American Muslims, as well as converts.

The language of his audience, which in a broader sense includes collective memory, reflected developments in American Muslim

---

[1] Edward Said, *Representations of the Intellectual* (New York, 1996), p. 11.
[2] See Zareena A. Grewal and R. David Coolidge, Chapter 14 in this volume.
[3] On Yusuf's international appeal, see Garbi Schmidt, "The Transnational Ummah – Myth or Reality? Examples from the Western Diasporas," *Muslim World* 95:4 (2005): 575–586.

discourses following 1965, the year of the assassination of Malcolm X and the Immigration Act. Yusuf incorporated in his speeches the influence of Malcolm X, who by the late 1990s had become an iconic figure in American Muslim memory, with many converts of all racial and ethnic backgrounds still referring to him as the reason for their embrace of Islam.[4] Yusuf's rhetoric was also a product of the demographic change that occurred after the Immigration Act, which dramatically increased the numbers and diversity of Muslim immigrants. With increased numbers came greater capacity to establish mosques, schools, and regional, national, and international organizations, such as the Muslim Students Association (MSA), Islamic Society of North America (ISNA), and Islamic Circle of North America (ICNA),[5] and publishing houses, such as Kazi Publications. Larger audiences and more capable institutions fostered demand for local Muslim articulations provided by preachers, like Yusuf, and other intellectuals whose influence is notable in his sermons.

Yusuf's sermons then serve as windows to American Muslim discourses. I focus on contributions by the post-1965 generation of American Muslim intellectuals.[6] Whether in agreement or disputation, Yusuf alluded to their ideas on both occasions. Of course, the story of American Islam is similar to many other American religions in one crucial aspect: it originated elsewhere and was reshaped by its American adherents. With this in mind, I observe three ways in which intellectuals served as cultural translators of Islam: they translated Muslim discourses from abroad into general notions of "normative Islam"; they employed such "normative" ideas to develop American interpretations; and they ventured to speak as American-based authorities for the benefit of global audiences.

Uttered shortly before and after 9/11, these sermons also bring to light what makes the work of American Musilm intellectuals public. In Yusuf's case, it was a testimony to his sense of timing. The events of 9/11 challenged American Muslims to formulate their participation in public life during the "War on Terror." After 9/11 Yusuf became a public intellectual in the sense of speaking to broad and public, as opposed to limited and parochial, concerns. As he spoke, he built upon other authorities.

---

4 See Steven Barboza, *American Jihad: Islam after Malcolm X* (New York, 1994).
5 See Karen Leonard, Chapter 10 in this volume.
6 On the importance of 1965 as a watershed year in American Muslim history, see Kambiz GhaneaBassiri, *A History of Islam in America* (Cambridge, 2010), pp. 272–282.

TWO SERMONS

Sometime at the end of the 1990s, Yusuf spoke to an audience of
hundreds of college-age Muslims in Toronto, Ontario. His listeners were
locals and travelers from other parts of Canada and the United States.
Later, the speech became one of the most watched Muslim sermons
on the Internet. This sermon, "Making Sense of Our Past," was introspective and transformative.[7] It reviewed the "current condition" and
the past that led Muslims into the present predicament, which Yusuf
summarized by the word "modernity." He defined modernity as a per-
mutation of the eternal sin of *kufr*, rejection of God. The modern kufr,
he said, began with the corruption of the mind, brought about by those
Western philosophers who projected the supremacy of human reason over divinely inspired knowledge. Modernity's spread around the
world made it akin to a disease: "[It is] like syphilis, and this is a syphilitic culture, right?" Yusuf's example of this "syphilitic culture" was
Americans' obsession with materialism. He demonstrated it through the
Qur'anic story about Qarun, the biblical Korah, a spectacularly wealthy
contemporary of Moses. Qarun became so arrogant in his wealth that
he rejected his dependence on God. To add an American twist, Yusuf
explained that Bill Gates, the paradigmatic billionaire of the 1990s, "is a
modern Qarun." Gates, of course, was not Muslim. Yet this example of
a flaw in a non-Muslim "other" led to the articulation of the sermon's
central point: modernity, with its cult of material success, had become
a Muslim disease as well. Muslims became infected by it over the past
two centuries, when they borrowed Western ideologies, like nationalism
and secularism. Yusuf laid the blame for this at the feet of some Muslim
reformers: they reformulated Islam, "and people don't realize this, that
the whole new version of Islam is written. And it begins emphasizing
things like 'love of the nation is from *iman* [faith].'" And so, "we no
longer see ourselves as within the fold of Islam, the brotherhood that
Allah has given us.... We see ourselves – I am an American Muslim,
he's a Pakistani Muslim, ... and on and on, false designations that Islam
rejects completely." This critique was the sermon's transformative
moment, which confronted the audience with a dilemma: How could
they be saved in this modern "cornucopia of materialism" when even
their religion was affected by it? Yusuf's answer was to concentrate on
private religiosity, specifying that, "at an individual level, all of us have

---

[7] Hamza Yusuf, "Making Sense of Our Past," online video, http://www.aswatalislam.
net/DisplayFilesP.aspx?TitleID=50096&TitleName=Hamza_Yusuf, accessed April
25, 2008. Until recently the video was available on YouTube but was flagged as
inappropriate.

to make an absolute commitment to studying our *deen* [religion], in its most comprehensive and broad-based orthopraxic tradition."

Now compare this to "Give and Take for God's Sake," a sermon Yusuf gave at ISNA's 2003 national convention in Chicago.[8] On this occasion, he no longer spoke about retreating into private spaces to study and preserve tradition. Rather, as a "traditional scholar," he authorized Muslims' involvement in American politics and public life. He began by citing Qur'an 17:20–21 and 6:12, and reminding that God "is self-committed to grace," that he "bestows freely" on "all human beings, the righteous and the transgressors," and that Muslims must "give out" from what God has given them. This reminder shaped the central theme of the speech, a theme of God-conscious citizenship in which humans must reciprocate God's grace by treating each other with mercy and respect. As in his pre-9/11 speech, Yusuf employed here the approach of highlighting a flaw in the Western "other." And, as in that speech, the transformative moment came when he noted that "we" are just like the Western "them." But it was a different kind of transformation. Now he urged his listeners to recognize that "we can no longer speak of us vs. them because we are us and we are them." "Muslims are part and parcel of the tapestry of this country. We have been here from the beginning and we are here to stay." "We are not anti-American. We are adhering to the finest principles of this country. And if we don't recognize those principles and recognize that they are Islamic principles and stand by them, then we have failed to live up to the historical task of this community." Yusuf encapsulated this historical task by presenting Muslims as "inheritors of the struggle" of such people as Martin Luther King Jr. "to keep this country in course with its founding principles." To do so, he preached, Muslims must act as responsible citizens and speak truth to power. "Our Prophet said, 'speak the truth even if it's bitter.' We must speak the truth. This is our right and obligation [because] we are Americans and we are Muslims."

PUBLIC INTELLECTUALS AND AMERICAN MUSLIM DISCOURSES

I introduced Yusuf's sermons as windows into the language of the post-1965 generations of American Muslims. So whom among American and global Muslim intellectuals did Yusuf echo?

---

[8] Hamza Yusuf, "Give and Take for God's Sake," online video, http://www.youtube. com/watch?v=1hACtSI56DQ and http://www.aswatalislam.net/DisplayFilesP.aspx?T itleID=50096&TitleName=Hamza_Yusuf, accessed April 25, 2008.

There is an almost militant tenor to Yusuf's sermons. In Toronto, he mocked the dominant culture's stress on material success as evidence of its "syphilitic" nature. In Chicago, he called on his audience "to speak the truth" to power. He told that he followed the model of the Prophet Muhammad and Martin Luther King Jr. And yet what some surely heard were the echoes of Malcolm X, who famously declared that he did not "see any American dream" but only "an American nightmare." This oppositional quality of both speeches reflected the language of Yusuf's audiences who grew up in the shadow of Malcolm X's legacy and incorporated the influence of African American critiques of American realities.

In terms of content, Yusuf's Toronto speech was closest to the works of Seyyed Hossein Nasr (b. 1933), an Iranian American philosopher. Born in Tehran and educated in the United States, Nasr is the most recognized Muslim representative of Perennial Philosophy, which has its roots in antimodernist Catholic discourse. After his graduate studies in the United States, he spent some thirty years in Iran, where he served as an intellectual bridge between the secular-educated and the religious elites. He returned to the United States after the 1979 revolution. Throughout his life, Nasr wrote for "those Muslims with a modern education who have been torn away from the integral Islamic tradition."[9] This term, "integral Muslim tradition," was his contribution to the widespread twentieth-century Muslim and Iranian call for the return to tradition as the answer to current crises. Nasr insisted that proper Islamic tradition integrates all facets of premodern Muslim heritage, philosophy, theology, law, art, and mysticism. In numerous books, he advanced a vision of modern history that is strikingly similar to Yusuf's: modernity is a disease that is marked by hypermaterialism and secularism; it originated in the West but spread into the Muslim world; a return to tradition is the answer; and proper tradition must privilege religious knowledge over secular.

Like Yusuf's pre-9/11 speech, Nasr's works characterized "current political life" as consumed by nationalism and materialism. For example, in a book directed at "young Muslims" residing in the West, he advised that "in order to understand the political aspect of the modern world, one has to go beyond the very complicated patterns, actions and reactions and events which dominate the political scene today." Instead of jumping into political activism, he urged his readers to examine "the roots and causes" of the modern "rebellion" against spiritual

---

[9]   Seyyed Hossein Nasr, *Ideals and Realities of Islam* (Chicago, 2000), p. xxvii.

and temporal authorities.[10] Such skepticism toward "current political life" is a mark of the rhetoric of traditionalism shared by Yusuf and Nasr. Nasr presented himself in his works as a global intellectual and philosopher who provided overarching critiques and appeared distant from local squabbles. This emphasis on "essential" and universal aspects of Islam was representative of those immigrant intellectuals of the first post-1965 generation who chose to stress Muslim identity over ethnic identity. This, in turn, had a salient impact on the shaping of American Muslim, as opposed to ethnic, discourses.

A telling example here is Fazlur Rahman (1919–1988), a Pakistani American interpreter of the Qur'an. Rahman, an advocate of reform in Islamic law and many other areas, has been characterized as a modernist opposite of Nasr. The two, however, share many similarities: both studied in the West and returned to native countries, and both had to emigrate to the United States because of political turmoil, in Rahman's case in 1968. While in Pakistan and Iran, neither Rahman nor Nasr was explicitly political. Their works, however, had profound political connotations. Nasr's writings, for example, emphasized that Marxism was a symptom of the modern "rebellion" against traditional authorities. This message corresponded with the official line of Iran's Shah Mohammad Reza Pahlavi. At the same time, Rahman interpreted Islamic texts while serving as an adviser to the reforms instituted by Pakistan's ruler, General Ayyub Khan. During their sojourn in Iran and Pakistan, their vagueness on politics was quite political. During their decades in the United States, that same vagueness played a different role; it became important in the process of cultural translation. Their presentation of "essential" Islamic ideas made such ideas global. Instead of local particulars, both authors stressed "normative Islam," a phrase they frequently used. Their American Muslim readers then translated such "normative" ideas in locally resonant ways.

The tendency to formulate essential and universal ideas resonated with the institutional needs of the first post-1965 generation. Isma'il Raji al-Faruqi (1921–1986), a Palestinian American academic, can also be seen as an antipole to Nasr. While Nasr stressed the importance of Sufism, al-Faruqi opposed it because he saw in it a reason for the perceived stagnation of the Islamic civilization. Like Nasr, he was critical of secularism. However, al-Faruqi saw no contradiction between religion

[10] Seyyed Hossein Nasr, *A Young Muslim's Guide to the Modern World* (Chicago, 1993), pp. 193–194.

and modern modes of knowledge. Indeed, religious reason to him was always rational. An incessant activist, he spoke and wrote about America as the place where the new Muslim community could fulfill the vision of Islam as a progressive and rational religion, away from what he saw as the shackles of medieval and colonial baggage in Muslim-majority countries. While teaching at Temple University in Philadelphia, al-Faruqi was instrumental in establishing Muslim institutions, like the International Institute of Islamic Thought (IIIT) in Herndon, Virginia, which had an international orientation, and the MSA, which served the needs of Muslim students in the United States and Canada. It is in the field of building institutions that Nasr and al-Faruqi met. The language of Pan-Islamic values resonated with the inclusive character of such organizations as the MSA, where Nasr was also a leading voice. In the early stages, the MSA was a broad effort by Muslims of all possible orientations. In addition to Pan-Islamic tropes, what united them was a rhetorical opposition to Western secularism. This was a marker of distinction from the larger society, which inspired religiously motivated activism and responded to the fear of assimilation.

While agreeing or disagreeing on specific points, Yusuf's pre-9/11 sermon echoed the works of Nasr and Rahman. Like Nasr, Rahman, and al-Faruqi, he engaged with the issues of modernity and Islamic reform, which was indicative of the transnational character of Muslim discourses in the United States. Yusuf, however, spoke as a representative of a more recent development. Unlike the other three intellectuals, he stressed not "tradition" in general terms but "tradition" as it has been embodied for centuries by Muslim scholars and institutions of learning. In addition to Sufism, his form of traditionalism emphasized the continuity of Sunni and Shi'i methodologies of jurisprudence. In the United States and Europe, this "traditionalist" trend began in the 1990s and has had several prolific advocates. People representing this approach, like Yusuf's Mauritanian teacher Shaykh Abdallah bin Mahfudh ibn Bayyah, have presented themselves as *'ulama* (scholars) who confront a global "protestantization of Islam," characterized by them as a break with historically continuous Islamic traditions. They lay the blame for this at the feet of Muslim reformers who reformulated Islam and turned it into "an ideology" and, in the process, usurped the authority of the 'ulama.

This was the line of argument Yusuf advanced in Toronto. And, although he did not mention names, the intellectuals whose heritage he portrayed as dangerous most likely included such individuals as Muhammad 'Abduh (1849–1905), the famous Egyptian reformer of Al-Azhar University, and Sir Sayyid Ahmad Khan (1817–1898), the father of Indian Muslim modernist tradition who included Western post-Enlightenment rationalism in his religious interpretations. Yusuf's stress on the study of Islam in its "orthopraxic tradition" was a call toward a reconceptualization of Muslim revival.

Of course, the ideology of revival connected many reformist movements and thinkers in the nineteenth and twentieth centuries. As historian Chase E. Robinson noted, the return to Islam of the legendary Prophetic era was a shibboleth of the Muslim language of revival in the past two hundred years.[11] This was the approach of 'Abduh, who called for a return to the practices of the companions of the Prophet Muhammad, *al-Salaf al-Salih*. The movement he commenced came to be known as Salafiyya. Its most noted representatives in the Middle East were Hasan al-Banna (1906–1949) and Sayyid Qutb (1906–1966). The former was the founder of the Muslim Brotherhood; the latter, its most influential ideologue. In the Indian subcontinent, a parallel development was associated with Abu al-'Ala al-Mawdudi (1903–1979) and the movement he created, the Jam'at i-Islami. Thinkers such as 'Abduh, al-Banna, Qutb, and Mawdudi shared an orientation that Yusuf criticized and attempted to reverse. They all circumvented the discursive tradition of the jurisprudence and other Islamic disciplines, including mysticism, produced by the 'ulama in the centuries that separate modern Muslims from the generations closest to the Prophet. Yusuf's call to follow the "orthopraxic tradition" was a subtle declaration of difference: he stressed the importance of continuation of the four Sunni schools of jurisprudence, as well as an acknowledgment of the parallel importance of the Shi'i clerical tradition.

In this way, Yusuf's Toronto sermon was also a critique of al-Faruqi and Rahman. After all, while critical of nationalism, which he called "a despicable Western virus," al-Faruqi's articulation of Islam borrowed heavily from the vocabulary of twentieth century's Pan-Arabist and Pan-Islamic ideologies.[12] In addition, his vision, summarized by one of his students, was "to raise this new [American Muslim] community in accordance with the teachings of the Qur'an, the Sunnah, and no particular legal school of thought."[13] Rahman's agenda was comparable, but more subtle. Instead of repudiating "schools of thought," he formulated

[11] Chase E. Robinson, "Reconstructing Early Islam: Truth and Consequences," in Herbert Berg, ed., *Method and Theory in the Study of Islamic Origins* (Leiden, 2003), p. 105.

[12] Ismail R. al-Faruqi, *Tawhid: Its Implications for Thought and Life* (Kuala Lumpur, 1987), p. 9.

[13] Muhammad Shafiq, *The Growth of Islamic Thought in North America: Focus on Isma'il Raji Al Faruqi* (Brentwood, 1994), pp. 114–115.

a new methodology of Qur'anic interpretation, which he applied to the sunnah as well. Like 'Abduh, Qutb, Mawdudi, and many other modern Muslim exegetes, Rahman carried out a thematic interpretation of the Qur'an. He explicitly stressed the dramatic epistemological gulf between seventh-century Arabia, the Qur'an's historical and cultural setting, and contemporary Muslim contexts. Influenced by the Indian poet Muhammad Iqbal (1877–1938), he fashioned the recognition of constant movement in human history into a tool of interpretation. He presented Qur'anic themes as essential and yet flexible guidance that has to be continuously reinterpreted for new times and places. For example, he argued that, although the Qur'an expressed itself in ways that resonated with the patriarchal language and culture of its initial audiences, an uncritical following of such expressions in contemporary contexts would violate its essential ideas of divine justice and human equality.[14]

This insight, as well as Rahman's methodology of thematic interpretation, had a profound impact among American Muslim advocates for gender justice, such as Amina Wadud (b. 1952), an African American exegete, and Azizah al-Hibri (b. 1943), a Lebanese American scholar of constitutional and Islamic Law.[15] Wadud became internationally known for serving as the prayer leader at a mixed-gender Friday service in New York City in 2005.[16] In the 1990s, her *Qur'an and Woman* was among the most widely read books on gender and the Qur'an in such places as Malaysia, South Africa, and the United States. She is an example of an intellectual who simultaneously translated the universal articulations of Rahman, as well as Mawdudi and Qutb, into American and transnational contexts. First published in Malaysia, *Qur'an and Woman* addressed Malaysian, American, and global Muslim audiences. Wadud illustrated the Qur'an's connection to its historical context by bringing up "the tropics of Malaysia," where the Qur'anic description of the paradise as a bountifully irrigated garden would not have been as dramatic as it was in the arid Arabia. At the same time, in this book, most of her examples from contemporary experience came from "post-slavery America."[17] Interestingly,

---

[14] See Fazlur Rahman, *Major Themes in the Qur'an* (Minneapolis, 1994) and *Islam and Modernity: Transformation of an Intellectual Tradition* (Chicago, 1982).

[15] Rahman's influence on Muslim feminist authors is immense. See, for example, Asma Barlas, *"Believing Women" in Islam: Unreading Patriarchal Interpretations of the Qur'an* (Austin, 2002), and Nimat Hafez Barazangi, *Woman's Identity and the Qur'an: A New Reading* (Gainesville, 2004).

[16] See Juliane Hammer, *American Muslim Women, Religious Authority, and Activism: More Than a Prayer* (Austin, 2012).

[17] Amina Wadud, *Qur'an and Woman: Rereading the Sacred Text from a Woman's Perspective* (New York, 1999).

Wadud's book followed the outline of an agenda for Qur'anic exegesis formulated by al-Hibri in a 1982 article.[18] In addition to her scholarship, al-Hibri became known for establishing Karamah, an educational institution focused on training women in American and Islamic law.

Al-Hibri's scholarship and activism demonstrate a complicating feature of the ongoing process of cultural translation of global Muslim thought into American discourses. I introduced such immigrant intellectuals as Nasr, Rahman, and al-Faruqi by saying that they carried out the first step in the cultural translation of Muslim discourses in the United States. That first step was an articulation of universal and essential ideas. Converts such as Yusuf and Wadud are examples of intellectuals who took the second step and gave such concepts their American character. Yet key in this process was not whether a person was a convert, or a first- or second-generation Muslim, immigrant, African American, or any other. Rather, what mattered was their ability to respond to the needs of their constituents. If these needs were specifically local, then the responses were also local and specific, such as in al-Hibri's bridging of American and Islamic jurisprudence. In addition, al-Hibri, like Wadud and Yusuf, became an important voice in international Muslim discussions. Speaking and writing as an American Muslim, she contributed to the third step in the development of American Muslim discourse, translating it into a local articulation that speaks to global concerns.

So far, I have examined the echoes of other intellectuals in Yusuf's pre-9/11 sermon. What about his 2003 speech? It is important to note that his post-9/11 transformation into an advocate for Muslim participation in American public life followed in the footsteps of other intellectuals, like al-Faruqi, who issued similar pronouncements in the 1970s and 1980s. What is unique about Yusuf's transition is that before him, the virtual monopoly in this line of argument belonged to people like al-Faruqi, who envisioned the United States as a land of opportunity for practical Islamic reforms, which some of Yusuf's followers would characterize as "modernist." After 9/11, public speakers of all stripes had to respond to their audiences' increased concern with public life. Yet how could Yusuf carry out this transition given the legacy of his own language?

Yusuf's speech followed an important precedent that occurred in the mid-1970s. His 2003 formulations resembled those of Imam Warith Deen Mohammed (1933–2008). A son of Elijah Muhammad, the Nation of

---

[18] Azizah al-Hibri, "A Study of Islamic Herstory: Or How Did We Ever Get into This Mess?" *Women's Studies International Forum* 5:2 (1982): 207–219.

Islam's longtime leader, W. D. Mohammed inherited his father's position in 1975 and transformed the group into a Sunni Muslim community. Given the Nation of Islam's legacy of staunch separatism, his transformation toward inclusivity came as a shock to many observers. In 1976 he symbolically lifted the American flag during the movement's annual convention. In 1977 he followed by giving a series of sermons on "The Birth of the American Spirit." Central in these sermons was the theme of an inherent correspondence between American and Qur'anic ideals. He elaborated on this theme on thousands of occasions over the next three decades. For example, in a 1987 sermon, he offered an interpretation of the Qur'anic phrase "one community" as a divine sign that corresponds to the ideals of America as "one nation under God." In the same speech, he noted how difficult it was to urge African Americans, Muslims and non-Muslims, to become full participants in public life: because of the history of slavery and discrimination, they had an understandable skepticism toward mainstream politics. And yet, he said, if they did not claim their share and did not "inherit this home," they would continue to be exploited as "servants and slaves."[19]

In 2003 Yusuf echoed Mohammed's theme of ownership when he declared that American Muslims were "inheritors" of American struggles; that they "have been here from the beginning and are here to stay." Key in Mohammed's strategy was a rhetorical decoupling of American ideals, such as "one nation under God," from its history. For Elijah Muhammad, this country was inherently evil, and its racist practices reflected its essence. For W. D. Mohammed, the essence was positive and resonant with Islamic ideals. Similarly, after 9/11, Yusuf disassociated America, in its essence, from the sins of modernity. This enabled him to authorize Muslim engagement in politics without compromising his "traditionalist" critique of modernity. In this speech, discursive threads – his own and those of broader American Muslim discussions – were not broken but realigned.

CONCLUSION: WHAT IS "PUBLIC" ABOUT AMERICAN MUSLIM INTELLECTUALS?

My analysis highlights some of the ways in which the two sermons echo some American Muslim intellectuals and reflect broader local and global discussions. I emphasize the role intellectuals play as cultural

---

[19] Warith Deen Mohammed, "National Imams Meeting: Yusuf Analogy," CD (Chicago, 2008).

translators. The ways in which they communicate demonstrate their global-local connections, as well as the changing expectations of their audiences. Politics and gender are examples of areas where intellectuals respond to and intervene in the language of their listeners and readers. My last note is on what is "public" about them.

Telling here is a correspondence between Yusuf's and W. D. Mohammed's formulations and the rhetorical move made by American Catholic intellectuals after World War II. Muslims after 9/11, like Catholics half a century before, were engaged in reshaping their language. Yusuf's antimodernism finds direct parallels in American and international Catholic thought of the late nineteenth and early twentieth centuries. As Catholics' place in American society became more secure, Catholic intellectuals absolved America from the sins of modernity.[20] Likewise, Mohammed's decoupling of America from the sins of slavery and Jim Crow marked his constituents' increased confidence about their place at the table of the American republic after the victories of the civil rights era. In his post-9/11 sermon, Yusuf referenced African American experience and echoed formulations of such Catholic intellectuals as John Courtney Murray (1904–1967).

This new stance of Yusuf, and before him Mohammed, should lead students of American Islam to think deeper about the public aspects in the work of American Muslim intellectuals. When people like Yusuf addressed Muslims as actors in American public life, they intervened in the already existing language and were responding to the reality their audiences already lived. By the end of the first decade of this century, American Muslims and their institutions had a long history of participation in this country's public life. With their income and education levels largely mirroring or exceeding those of other groups, they attempted to actively overcome marginalization imposed on them in the wake of 9/11.[21] Of course, like Catholics and African Americans, Muslims' standing as an established minority has not been unproblematic, which makes intellectual formulations of Muslim public discourses even more vital. In further historical parallel, American Catholics became an important global voice precisely at the moment when they began to speak as Catholics and Americans, when they transformed their American

---

[20] R. Scott Appleby, "The Triumph of Americanism: Common Ground for U.S. Catholics in the Twentieth Century," in Mary Jo Weaver and R. Scott Appleby, eds., *Being Right: Conservative Catholics in America* (Bloomington, 1995), pp. 37–62.

[21] Pew Research Center, "Muslim Americans: Middle Class and Mostly Mainstream," 2007, http://www.pewresearch.org/2007/05/22/muslim-americans-middle-class-and-mostly-mainstream/.

identity from a dilemma into an advantage. Similarly, when Muslim intellectuals began to speak as "Americans and Muslims," we witnessed the emergence of a new, more confident voice of a Muslim culture with global importance.

Further Reading

Esposito, John L., and John Voll, eds., *Makers of Contemporary Islam* (New York, 2001).

Haddad, Yvonne Y., Jane I. Smith, and Kathleen Moore, *Muslim Women in America: The Challenge of Islamic Identity Today* (New York, 2006).

Hammer, Juliane, *American Muslim Women, Religious Authority, and Activism: More Than a Prayer* (Austin, 2012).

Leonard, Karen, "American Muslim Politics: Discourses and Practices," *Ethnicities* 3:2 (2003): 147–181.

Strum, Philippa, ed., *Muslims in the United States: Identity, Influence, Innovation* (Washington, D.C., 2006).

Waugh, Earle H., and Frederick M. Denny, eds., *The Shaping of an American Islamic Discourse: A Memorial to Fazlur Rahman* (Atlanta, 1998).

Yuskaev, Timur R., *Speaking Qur'an: The Emergence of an American Sacred Text* (forthcoming).

16 Cultural and Literary Production of Muslim America

SYLVIA CHAN-MALIK

In December 2010, the *New York Times* ran an article on Muslim American artists in the San Francisco Bay Area entitled "Muslim American Artists Strive to Bridge a Chasm."[1] The piece featured a diverse range of writers, musicians, and visual artists, such as playwright Wajahat Ali, décor and event designer Khadija O'Connell, and members of the hip hop collective Remarkable Current, all of whom, reporter Thalia Gigerenzer wrote, were engaged in work of "reimagining one of the country's most complicated compound identities: Muslim American."[2] Their efforts, Gigerenzer continued, were motivated by a desire to counter the racist and Orientalist stereotypes that had come to characterize Islam and Muslims in the years since 9/11, the ways in which, as Ali was quoted, "our narrative has been stolen from us."[3] The creation of distinctly Muslim American cultural forms, the article noted, would "expand understanding of their faith among non-Muslims as well as bridge American and Islamic traditions," thus addressing "the chasm" between Islam and America, between Muslim Americans and practices of their faith.[4] Said Javed Ali, founder of *Illume*, a Muslim online news, arts, and culture magazine, "We're at a point where Islam is really being defined in this country, and it's going to be through the arts."[5] While Gigerenzer's piece was a welcome alternative to narratives of anti-Muslim bias so pervasive in the media at the time, it also reinforced long-standing Orientalist notions of a vast gulf – the "chasm" – between "Islam" and the "United States," between "Muslims" and "America," as well as portraying the emergence of Muslim American artistic and cultural production as a wholly post-9/11 phenomenon. Yet,

---

[1] Thalia Gigerenzer, "Muslim American Artists Strive to Bridge a Chasm," *New York Times*, December 16, 2010.
[2] Gigerenzer, "Muslim American Artists."
[3] Gigerenzer, "Muslim American Artists."
[4] Gigerenzer, "Muslim American Artists."
[5] Gigerenzer, "Muslim American Artists."

as various writers and scholars have noted, "Islam" has long influenced American culture, both in how Islamic and Arab cultures have shaped cultural production in the United States and in the ways Muslims in the United States have significantly contributed to the creation of art, music, literature, and other cultural forms. In other words, "Islam" and "Muslims" have in fact long been part of the cultural fabric of the United States, shaping various forms of cultural and literary production. What changed in the post-9/11 era was the unprecedented level of media, political, and cultural scrutiny upon Islamic practices and Muslim communities in the United States, a shift that ultimately led to the increasing categorization of cultural and literary production emerging from various Muslim communities in the United States as "Muslim American."[6]

Yet the post-9/11 "reimagining" of Muslim American cultural identities is not the result of a "chasm" between Islam and American but of a shift in what sociologist Pierre Bourdieu called "the space of possibles": those systems of logic that define the "universe of problems, references, intellectual benchmarks" within a cultural field.[7] Bourdieu says, "When a new literary or artistic group makes its presence felt in the field of literary or artistic production." as with the new generation of Muslim American artists, "the whole problem is transformed."[8] Within the post-9/11 United States, Muslim Americans have necessarily and actively engaged, as other minoritized groups have done in the past, in cultural strategies of "claiming America," of asserting a Muslim presence in the United States and highlighting the contributions of Muslims in the creation of American literary and cultural forms, in order to counter and resist racial-religious violence in political and public life. As a result, the "problem" of Muslim American culture and literature, if we follow Bourdieu, has become not *whether* Muslims in the United States

---

[6]   For the purposes of my chapter, I employ the term "Muslim American" (as opposed to "American Muslim") to signify the cultural and literary works in question and thus extend this usage to identify the cultural practitioners and the communities they serve. Within the U.S. Muslim community itself, the question of how to self-identify has been debated, with many arguing that whereas racial and ethnic identifiers (e.g. "Asian American," "African American," etc.) are aptly used as qualifiers for "American-ness," a *religious* identity, such as "Muslim" should function as the primary term, with "American" being used as the qualifying adjective. While I understand the importance of such distinctions, and might go so far as arguing that "American Muslim" more aptly captures the transnational nature of Muslim identity formation in the United States, I believe at this time that "Muslim American" is a more inclusive term that allows for the flexibility and fluidity of Muslim identities in the United States, as a number of artists and writers I discuss here might not strongly self-identify as Muslim.

[7]   Pierre Bourdieu, *The Field of Cultural Production* (New York, 1993), p. 176.

[8]   Bourdieu, *The Field*, p. 32.

are engaged in literary and cultural production (which, of course, they always have), but *what* the precise nature of "Muslim American" culture and literature might be. More questions then follow: What renders a song, a painting, a poem "Muslim American"? What are the category's defining characteristics and features, and how do we determine its parameters of inclusion? What is the "universe of problems, references, and intellectual benchmarks" of this emergent field of cultural and artistic expression? In what follows, I explore these questions by offering a generalized overview of Muslim American cultural and literary production, first considering the racialized contexts out of which the artistic expressions of Muslims in the United States have emerged and evolved, then turning to a selective history of Muslim American culture and literature. In closing, I consider how these various forms of artistic expression have converged in the contemporary moment, and how the hypervisiblity of Islam and Muslims in the United States has resulted in an unprecedented diversity and range within Muslim artistic expression in the United States.

As with Islam itself in America, the cultural expressions of Muslims in the United States are rooted in the African American experience. From the Islamic influences on blues and jazz, to its constitutive presence in movements of Black nationalism and civil rights, to its current impact on contemporary hip hop culture, Muslim American cultural and literary production is inexorably entwined with the cultural politics of Blackness and the ways in which African Americans, both Muslim and non-Muslim, have incorporated elements of Islam into expressions of Black culture. As such, to declare that Muslim American artists and culture have only emerged in the years since 9/11 leaves out how African American Muslims have long engaged in artistic expressions that have sought to imagine and reimagine their complex compound identities as African Americans, Muslims, and Americans. At the same time, it is crucial to understand the space of African American Muslim cultural politics I refer to here as an infinitely heterogeneous one, forged through a process of racial and religious exchange between African American and immigrant Muslims, mainly from South and West Asia, and through Black engagement with the transnational flows of knowledge and capital through which Islamic ideologies and Muslim cultural practices have always reached the United States. As a result of Islam's rootedness in Black America, even the artistic expressions of post-1965 waves of South Asian and Arab Muslim immigrants, which might initially seem far-removed or as existing discretely from the African American history of Islam, must subsequently reckon with this racialized past through their inclusion in the field of Muslim American culture.

Thus, to acknowledge the racial and religious confluence at the heart of Muslim American culture constitutes a critical first step in understanding the space of possibles of Muslim American literature and culture. Akin to historian Robin D. G. Kelley's notion of polyculturalism, which he uses to discuss how "most black people in the Americas are products of a variety of different 'cultures' ... which live in and through us every day," this syncretism provides insight into how Muslims in the United States have consistently negotiated their self-imaginings as simultaneously local, national, and transnational citizens.[9] This is due to how, as miriam cooke has written, Islam's "very material connection to Arabia, where it found its beginnings, provides unusual possibilities for constructing a territorialized transcultural identity."[10] Muslims, cooke continues, "can think transnationally while continuing to live locally, recognizing themselves as citizens of the world while retaining deep connections with a specific place, whether it be of birth, of choice, or of compulsion."[11] As we will see in what follows, it is in this confluence that the "universe of problems, references, and intellectual benchmarks" of Muslim American artistic expressions is found.

ISLAM AND THE BLUES

In *Blues People: Negro Music in White America*, LeRoi Jones (Amiri Baraka) writes that

> it is impossible to say exactly how old blues is – certainly no older than the presence of Negroes in the United States. It is a native American music, the product of the black man in this country; or to put it more exactly the way I have come to think about it, blues could not exist if African captives had not become American captives.[12]

As Jones infers, the blues were the cultural by-product of the transatlantic slave trade in the United States. Though the genre did not rise to popular prominence until the early twentieth century (through artists such as W. C. Handy, Leadbelly, and Robert Johnson), the blues were undeniably rooted in the southern plantation, its direct predecessors the

---

[9] Robin D. G. Kelley, "People in Me," *Colorlines Magazine*, Winter 1999.
[10] miriam cooke, "Multiple Critique: Islamic Feminist Rhetorical Strategies," *Nepantla: Views from South* 1:1 (2000): 91–110.
[11] cooke, "Multiple Critique."
[12] Amiri Baraka, *Blues People* (New York, 1999), p. 17.

work songs and field hollers sung by slaves to endure backbreaking labor and relentless dehumanization.

However, while the blues were born on the plantation, the music's origins lay in West Africa, where upwards of 30 percent of slaves were born. Historian Sylviane Diouf estimates that of the roughly 400,000 African captives who were first transported to the United States, 15 to 20 percent were Muslims who came from an area known as the Sahel, a vast area in Africa "stretching from Senegal in the West to Sudan in the east."[13] This region, known as Senegambia, was fundamentally shaped by the contact between its natives and the Arab-Berber Islamic world since the eighth century. Islamic influences infused the local culture, in particular, the region's music. Subsequently, West Africans deported through the trans-Saharan trade brought their music and rhythms (including those that had already been changed by the Arab-Islamic contact) north to the Maghreb. As Diouf writes, "There was much cross-fertilization on both sides of the desert and it is this complex heritage that West African Muslim captives brought to the United States where it found a fertile ground."[14] Unlike non-Muslim slave groups from coastal West Africa and Central Africa, who relied heavily on drumming and chants for their musical expression, slaves from Senegambia stood a much better chance of preserving their musical culture because of the region's traditional emphasis on string and wind instruments. Because southern plantation owners feared slave revolts and uprisings, drumming and group chants were outlawed, while Sahelian slaves were able to adapt their skills to local instruments such as the fiddle or guitar, later even producing the banjo as an American incarnation of their traditional lute. As a result of the seemingly less threatening nature of their style, they were allowed to perform their music, sometimes even at slaveholders' balls, which allowed for the music's migration across the Deep South, including Mississippi, the birthplace of the blues.

JAZZ AND THE REEMERGENCE OF ISLAM IN THE TWENTIETH CENTURY

The blues traveled north at the start of the twentieth century, as Black migrants from the South flooded to northern industrial centers such as Chicago, Detroit, New York, Philadelphia during the post-Reconstruction

---

[13] Sylviane A. Diouf, "African Muslim and American Blues," *Muslim Voices: Arts and Ideas*, http://muslimvoicesfestival.org/resources/african-muslims-and-american-blues, accessed April 25, 2013.

[14] Diouf, "African Muslims and American Blues."

era. Seeking work and new opportunities, many came in contact with burgeoning discourses of Pan-Africanism, guided by the philosophies of early Black nationalist thinkers such as Edward Wilmot Blyden and Marcus Garvey, who expressed a deep respect and admiration for the teachings of Islam. Pan-Africanist thought fueled interest in Islam, spurring the widespread appeal of early twentieth-century Islamic organizations such as the Moorish Science Temple (MSTA), the Ahmadiyya Movement in Islam, and the Nation of Islam (NOI). Both Pan-Africanism and Islamic organizations such as these called for the redefinition of Black cultural and political identities in ways that rejected the racist and oppressive ideologies of the plantation and the Christian church. Characterized by a spirit of internationalism, a refusal of white European supremacy, and the acknowledgment of the creativity of Black urban cultures, such Pan-Africanist and Islamically oriented ideologies were instrumental to the development of a Black cultural renaissance across the North, exemplified by the Harlem Renaissance in the 1920s and 1930s. Described by Jamaican American journalist J. A. Rogers in 1925 as "one part American and three parts American Negro ... the nobody's child of the levee and the city slum," jazz was the soundtrack of the times.[15] Reaching the height of its popularity at the close of the First World War, the improvisational art form exuded, to cite Rogers once more, "a fresh joyousness" through which audiences found "a temporary forgetfulness ... a tonic for the strong and a poison for the weak."[16] From the 1930s to the 1950s, when the genre reigned as the nation's most popular musical form, numerous prominent Black jazz musicians converted to Islam, including pianist Ahmad Jamal, saxophonist Yusef Lateef, drummer Art Blakey (Abdullah Ibn Buhaina), pianist McCoy Tyner (Sulieman Saud), vocalist Dakota Staton (Aliyah Rabia), and bassist Ahmed Abdul-Malik (best known for his work with Thelonious Monk).

Almost all entered the religion through the Ahmadiyya movement, a group Richard Brent Turner has called "unquestionably one of the most significant movements in the history of Islam in the United States in the twentieth century, providing ... the *first multi-racial model* for American Islam" (emphasis in original).[17] Founded by Hazrat Mirza Ghulam Ahmad, the Ahmadiyya was a South Asia–based missionary movement that appealed to Black Americans because of its racially

[15] J. A. Rogers, "Jazz at Home," *Survey Graphic Harlem* 6:6 (1925): 665–667.
[16] Rogers, "African Muslims and American Blues."
[17] Richard Brent Turner, *Islam in the African American Experience* (Bloomington, 1997), p. 110.

inclusive doctrines, ambitious internationalist scope, and notion of continuous prophecy. To these musicians, Ahmadiyya Islam was "a force which directly opposed the deterioration of the mind and body through either spiritual or physical deterrents,"[18] a respite from racism, nights in smoke-filled clubs, and the perils of drugs and alcohol. At the same time, as trumpeter Dizzy Gillespie noted in his autobiography, many musicians converted to Islam merely to escape Blackness; as one musician says: "Man, if you join the Muslim faith, you ain't colored no more, you'll be white. You get a new name and you won't be a nigger no more."[19] Thus, conversion to Islam was a "tonic" as well, providing jazz musicians spiritual protection from the harmful trappings of their profession, alongside a political safeguard from white supremacy, an identity that at times allowed them to transcend their parochial identities as "Blacks" and embrace a global community of Muslims. Giving their songs titles like "Prayer to the East," "Eastern Sounds," and "Abdullah's Delight," African American Muslim musicians combined Islamic themes and messages of Black protest in their recordings, while donning Islamic *kufis* and *thobes*, and incorporating Asian and Middle Eastern musical sounds and elements into their work.[20]

However, various Black Ahmadi Muslim musicians also soon learned that their membership in the ummah did not shield them from censure within their communities, in particular, their South Asian co-religionists. Aminah McCloud has written that "the subject of music was often a source of debate with the subcontinent Ahmadis," as many of the Indian missionaries of the movement "insisted on Indian customs and interpretations" of Islam and did not view African Americans as "having something to offer American Islam."[21] However, with relatively few immigrant Muslims (of both South Asian and Middle Eastern origin) in the United States, such religious opinions had little to no effect on the cultural work of African American Muslim jazz musicians at the

---

[18] C. O. Simpkins, cited in Turner, *Islam in the African American Experience*, p. 139.

[19] Dizzy Gillespie, *To Be, or Not...to Bop* (Minneapolis, 2009[1979]), p. 291.

[20] This encounter between jazz and Islam reverberated beyond the lives of converts themselves. For example, saxophonist John Coltrane's *A Love Supreme*, recorded in 1964 and often called the greatest jazz album of all time was deeply shaped by Coltrane's exposure to Ahmadiyya Islam through pianist Tyner, his wife Naima, and a drummer named Nasseridine, who played within Coltrane in Philadelphia in the 1950s and 1960s. In the album's liner notes, Coltrane writes, "Now and again through the unerring and merciful hand of God, I do perceive his ... OMNIPOTENCE ... HE IS GRACIOUS ... AND MERCIFUL." These words directly echo the opening lines of almost every chapter in the Qur'an: *Bismillah al-Rahman al-Rahim*: "In the name of Allah, the gracious, the merciful."

[21] Aminah McCloud, *African American Islam* (New York, 1995), p. 21.

time, who mostly worked with and played for Black and white peers and audiences. This dynamic would fundamentally change in the decades following the passage of the 1965 Hart-Celler Immigration and Nationality Act, as a dramatic increase in the number of South Asians and Arabs living and working in the United States irrevocably changed the composition of Muslim America and thus, dramatically altered the trajectory of Muslim American identity, community, and cultural formation.

BLACK NATIONALISM AND THE BIRTH OF MUSLIM AMERICAN LITERATURE

Islam was foundational to the development of American popular music, from the roots of the blues to the creative heights of jazz, and emanated almost entirely from the Black cultural imaginary. While adopted by musicians as either a spiritual or political refusal of white supremacy, "Islam" had heretofore yet to be advanced within U.S. cultural production as an *explicit* symbol of racial resistance, a positioning that would fundamentally change during the course of the politically turbulent 1960s. As film historian Donald Bogle writes, "In 1960, Negroes were quietly asking for their rights. By 1969, blacks were demanding them. The decade moved from the traditional goal of cultural and academic assimilation to one of almost absolute separatism and the evolution of a black cultural aesthetic."[22] Islam functioned as a major factor in this cultural and political shift, as the Black separatism of the Nation of Islam captivated Black America, while inspiring fear and loathing in white Americans as, in the infamous words of a 1959 CBS News special hosted by Mike Wallace, "The Hate That Hate Produced." During this time, a distinctly Muslim American *literary* presence emerged, first through the publication of Alex Haley's *The Autobiography of Malcolm X* in 1965 and, later, through the poets, writers, and playwrights of the Black Arts Movement. These texts represented, in the words of writer and scholar Mohja Kahf, "the first set of writings in American literature to voice a cultural position identifiable as Muslim."[23] In other words, whereas the Islamic influences on the works of Muslim American blues and jazz artists were subtle, indicating their Muslim identities without actively promoting any sort of Islamic ideology or practice, the Islam of

[22] Donald Bogle, *Toms, Coons, Mulattoes, Mammies, and Bucks: An Interpretive History of Blacks in American Films*, 4th ed. (New York, 2001 [1973]), p. 195.
[23] Mohja Kahf, "Islam: Portability and Exportability," paper presented at the UCLA Center for Near Eastern Studies, 2007.

these literary expressions was bold and uncompromising, asserting the religion as integral to a Black American cultural identity, which lay at the heart of the era's revolutionary zeitgeist.

The Autobiography of Malcolm X, written with the assistance of Alex Haley, was originally published in November 1965 and, in the years since, has become "the most popular autobiography of an African American in print," selling millions of copies in paperback in the United States alone.[24] At once "a political tract, a religious conversion narrative, and an underground commentary on twentieth-century American culture,"[25] the text not only is part of the American literary canon but has become an iconographic fixture in American popular culture, in particular following director Spike Lee's film adaptation of the text in 1992. While speculation around its authorship and accuracy continues, the text is still widely viewed in the popular and political U.S. imaginaries simultaneously as a Black nationalist screed, decrying the evils of white supremacy and giving voice to the racial ideologies of the Nation of Islam (of which Malcolm was member from 1952 to 1963), and as a tale of religious and racial universalist triumph, due to Malcolm's renunciation of the NOI's racial ideologies following his pilgrimage to Mecca in 1964. Neither of these readings captures the full complexity of Malcolm X's narrative, a consequence mainly due to a lack of attention to how his story reflects an African American Muslim – and thus a distinctly Muslim American – history and legacy. As Samory Rashid noted in 1993, "an analysis of the Islamic aspects of his life is essential to understanding Malcolm X ... attempts to understand him through the lens of America's perennial racial debate trivialize his message and the universality of his significance."[26] Beginning with Malcolm's father's participation in Marcus Garvey's Pan-Africanist Universal Negro Improvement Association (UNIA) during his childhood in Nebraska, to his move to the northern urban industrial centers of Detroit, Philadelphia, and New York, to his membership in the Nation of Islam, and subsequent move toward the teachings of Sunni Islam, the *Autobiography* is, beyond a personal narrative, a concise mapping of Islam's historical lineage in the twentieth-century United States. The early politics of Black nationalism, the racial mythology of the NOI, the move towards Sunnism, and finally to Malcolm's distinctly Muslim American ideological positioning

---

[24] Thomas Doherty, "Malcolm X: In Print, on Screen," *Biography* 23:1 (2000): 29–48.

[25] Thomas Doherty, "Malcolm X: On Print, on Screen," *Biography* 23:1 (Winter 2000): 29–48; 30.

[26] Samory Rashid, "The Islamic x Aspects of the Legacy of Malcolm X," *American Journal of Islamic Social Sciences* 10:1 (1993): 60–71; 64.

through his simultaneous and passionate commitments to a Black nationalist politics and an ideology of Islamic universalism at the end of his
life – these components reflect the trajectory of Islam's cultural presence
in America and reveal the distinctive interplay between race and religion
in this formation. As we see through the story of El-Hajj Malik El-Shabazz,
to be *both* a fiery advocate of racial and class liberation and a committed
Muslim can be part and parcel of the cultural politics of American Islam.

This discursive intertwining of Islam's cultural significance
with the struggles for racial justice of the 1960s and 1970s was further solidified through an engagement with the poets and writers of
the Black Arts Movement, founded directly after Malcolm's X's assassination on February 21, 1965. During that time, poet and writer
LeRoi Jones (author of *Blues People*, cited earlier) established Harlem's
Black Arts Repertory Theatre/School, amid heated debates of African
American intellectuals and activists concerning the split between
Malcolm and the Nation of Islam and the most viable way forward
for the Black revolutionary struggle. According to Melani McAlister,
the *Autobiography*'s publication that same year created "a sensation
within the circles of young, increasingly radicalized men and women
who had listened to Malcolm X's speeches, and were now riveted by
the story of his life."[27] In this context, McAlister continues, Jones/
Baraka set out to create

> a community based black popular theatre and to invent a form and
> language that would reach African American audiences with a mes-
> sage of black (post)nationalism … its founding was an inspiration
> to a new generation of poets and playwrights, (creating) a flowering
> of African American cultural production unlike anything since the
> Harlem Renaissance.[28]

Within the Black Arts "renaissance," Islam was portrayed as a staunchly
Black religion, its adaption and inclusion in the realm of Black cultural
struggle viewed as a means of rejecting the white man's god. Merging
with popular discourses of Afrocentrism, the religion became part of a
critical vocabulary of Black resistance, in which cultural and political
struggles were considered one and the same.

Baraka himself converted to Sunni Islam in 1968 (though he
renounced the faith in 1974, citing an ideological shift to Marxism/

[27] Melani McAlister, *Epic Encounters: Culture, Media, and U.S. Interests in the Middle East since 1945* (Berkeley, 2005), p. 101.
[28] McAlister, *Epic Encounters*, p. 105.

Leninism). Initially inspired by the political organization and strength of the Nation of Islam, Baraka composed a short play before his conversion in 1965 entitled *A Black Mass*, which adapted Elijah Muhammad's story, "Yakub's History," in which the NOI leader explained how white people had been created as a "race of devils" from the world's original Black inhabitants six thousand years ago by a "big-headed" Black scientist named Yakub. The play "turns the Nation's myth into a reinterpretation of the Faust story and a simultaneous meditation on the role and function of art,"[29] in particular, challenging the notions of art for art's sake, and instead emphasizing that all artistic expression should and must work toward political ends. Islam, Baraka would say later, was a holistic spiritual framework through which Black people could reclaim their true connections to the Divine and that art was a vehicle to achieve this contact. "As you begin to beat your way back through the symbols, getting close to what the source of Black art was, " Baraka stated in a 1968 interview, "you begin to see that it comes out of Islam. The closeness of man with natural evidence of Divinity is what art was about in the beginning ... that's what art is supposed to be about: to collect that Divinity, to show its existence, to praise it."[30]

One of Baraka's closest colleagues in the Black Arts Renaissance was poet, playwright, and essayist Marvin X, best known for his one-act plays *Flowers for the Trashman* (1965), and *The Black Bird* (1969), the latter advancing explicitly Islamic themes. In 1968 he published a book of poems entitled *Fly to Allah*, which melded themes of Black anger, militancy, and masculinity with Islamic themes and imagery in lines such as "who killed uncle tom / who killed uncle sam / Allah! / Fly to him / if you are from him."[31] In the years since, Marvin X – who has remained a Muslim – has continued to produce writings reflecting the interplay between Black nationalism and Islamic conceptions of justice, struggle, and equality. Calling him the "Father of Muslim American Literature," scholar and writer Mohja Kahf says of Marvin X, "While *The Autobiography of Malcolm X* is a touchstone of Muslim American culture, Marvin X and other Muslims in BAM were the emergence of a cultural expression of Black Power and Muslim American identity ... what I see as the starting point of Muslim American literature."[32]

---

[29] McAlister, *Epic Encounters*, p. 105.
[30] Imamu Amiri Baraka, *Conversations with Amiri Baraka* (Jackson, 1994), p. 54.
[31] Marvin X, *Fly to Allah: Poems* (Fresno, 1969).
[32] Kahf, "Islam: Portability and Exportability."

Kahf also characterizes Marvin X and his peers as "sexist as all get out, in the way that is common for men of his generation and his radicalism."[33] Indeed, the history of Muslim American culture and literature as reflected is undeniably dominated by men, as well as, in many cases, rooted in patriarchal conceptions of gender and sexuality. It is important to note, however, that this is not due to the inactivity of Muslim women in the United States in the realms of cultural and literary production but most likely the result of what Ula Taylor has called the "crisis of archival recognition" for African American women, in which Black women's stories and voices are historically devalued and thus "subject to be overlooked, misheard, misinterpreted, misrepresented, and ultimately misappropriated."[34] Indeed, the deeply masculinist character of the Nation of Islam and the politics of Black nationalism functioned to sequester and silence the voices of Black women, whom Elijah Muhammad saw as "the field to produce (the Black) nation" and thus instructed Black men to "control and protect... his crop."[35] In regards to the recounting of Muslim American women's cultural and literary histories, it is arguable that such a devaluation of women has been further compounded by debates among scholars of Islam concerning women's performance and artistic expression. According to Sarah Weiss, writing in regard to Muslim women and musical performance, the cultural expressions of Muslim women tend to be associated with a "relaxing of morals.... When women are involved in performance, it is common to assume that they themselves are not pious."[36] Thus, in conjunction with the ideologies of both Black nationalism, such an association between art and immorality served to put Muslim American women "in their place" in the home, as mothers, and as supporters of men. They were to remain cloistered, closeted, and out of the public eye.

Despite this, within the context of the Black Arts Movement, Black feminist poet and writer Sonia Sanchez, who joined the Nation of Islam in 1972, created work that illuminated the intersections between Black nationalism, Islam, and Black, Third World, and Islamic feminist ideologies. In her poetry, Sanchez stressed the importance for Black women to be committed to the advancement of a strong and unified Black

---

[33] Kahf, "Islam: Portability and Exportability."

[34] Ula Taylor, "Women in the Documents: Thoughts on Uncovering the Personal, Political, and Professional," *Journal of Women's History* 20:1 (2008): 187–196; 188.

[35] Elijah Muhammad, *Messages to the Blackman* (Philadelphia, 1965), p. 58.

[36] Sarah Weiss, "Arts. World Music," in Suad Joseph, ed., *Encyclopedia of Women and Islamic Cultures* (Leiden, 1997), pp. 188–195; 188.

revolutionary struggle, and like Baraka and Marvin X, she viewed Islam as a spiritual and political framework through which to engage the struggle; in other words, Sanchez's desire for Black mobilization and empowerment led her to adopt Islam's religious teachings. While she ultimately left the NOI in 1975 to embrace a Pan-Africanist feminist philosophy, she wrote prolifically during her years in the organization, creating prose and poetry that placed Muslim women at the center of Black revolutionary struggles, as well as in the presence of the Divine, a juxtaposition clearly revealed in a poem from the 1974 volume, *A Blues Book for Black Magical Women*:

> WE ARE MU.S.LIM WOMEN!
> dwellers in light
> New women created from the limbs
> Of Allah
> We are the shining ones
> Coming from dark ruins
> Created from the eye of Allah.
> And we speak only what we know
> And do not curse God
> And we keep our minds open to light
> And we do not curse God
> And we chant Alhumdullilah
> And do not curse God.[37]

FROM HIP HOP TO NEW MUSLIM COOL

As with the nation itself, the 1970s were a transformative decade for Islam and Muslims in the United States, in regard to both the racial, ethnic, and ideological composition of Muslim American communities and national attitudes concerning Islam and Muslims in the U.S. political and cultural imaginaries. These shifts were a result of a number of factors, including (but not limited to) political turbulence in West Asia and North Africa, specifically the ongoing oil crisis and the Iranian hostage crisis of 1979; the steady waning of Black nationalist and revolutionary political movements; the death of Elijah Muhammad in 1975 and the transition of the NOI's leadership to his son, Warith Deen Mohammed; and the ever-growing numbers of Muslim immigrants from South Asia and the Middle East entering and subsequently living and working in

---

[37] Sonia Sanchez, *A Blues Book for Black Magical Women* (Detroit, 1973).

the United States. Taken together, these political and social developments facilitated a fundamental shift in both Islam's cultural meanings and community presence in the United States, in particular the manner in which conceptions of Islam and Muslims became conflated with the notion of an orientalized foreign threat, a development that ultimately served to distance the religion from its long-standing presence and culture associations within Black communities in the United States.

Of course, Muslims from South and West Asia had long been present in the United States.[38] However, in the realm of cultural and literary production, it was not until the 1980s and 1990s that writers emerging out of South Asian, West Asian, and North African Muslim diasporic traditions began to make their presence more strongly known in American literary and cultural fields. In the 1980s and 1990s, writers such as Kashmiri American Agha Shahid Ali and Palestinian American Naomi Shihab Nye produced work infused with Islamic sensibilities that resonated forcefully within the multicultural rhetoric of those decades, while former Beat poet and white American convert to Islam Daniel Abd al-Hayy Moore drew upon his engagement with Islam's mystical Sufi tradition and his extensive travels through North Africa to produce works such as *The Ramadan Sonnets* and *Mecca-Medina Timewarp*, both published in the 1990s. It was also during this time that thirteenth-century Muslim poet and Sufi mystic Rumi became the most widely read poet in the United States, as a result of the release of the adaptation of his poetry by American poet and writer Coleman Barks.

At the same time, the steady rollback of civil rights gains enacted during Ronald Reagan's presidency in the 1980s ushered in a resurgence of Black nationalist ideologies via the realm of hip hop. Rappers such as Chuck D of Public Enemy, Paris, Nas, and others touted their affiliations with Black Muslim leaders such as Louis Farrakhan and expressed their respect for the teachings of Islam, while the release of Spike Lee's 1992 film biography of Malcolm X rendered the Muslim American leader a central icon of the hip hop generation. As with Islam's earlier incarnations in Black American communities, the religion's manifestations in the 1980s and 1990s hip hop culture were rooted in antiracist ideologies, both political and spiritual, as its main presence arrived through the Five Percenters, a movement that preached the divinity of the

---

[38] Some of these histories have been well documented, such as those of Bengali Muslim seamen in Harlem in the 1930s, Indian Muslim farm laborers on the West Coast, and Arab immigrants mainly from Syria and Lebanon in the Northwest and Midwest. See the historical chapters in this volume and their further reading sections.

Black Man, whom the group's members called "Allah."[39] Even more so than the NOI, Five Percent views have been deemed heretical by other Muslims, though the group has had the largest impact among hip hop artists themselves and the genre's terminology, symbols, and ideology. At the same time, while Five Percenters do not generally consider themselves Muslims, preferring instead to be called Five Percenters or simply, "Gods," the influence of Islam's symbols and terminology on the group is undeniable. From the late 1980s on, rappers affiliated with the Five Percenters were extremely influential in the evolutions of rap music and hip hop culture, in terms of both commercial success and critical acclaim. Among these artists were Rakim Allah, Big Daddy Kane, Poor Righteous Teachers, Busta Rhymes, Leaders of the New School, Guru, Pete Rock, Mobb Deep, Queen Latifah, Erykah Badu, and members of the groups Wu Tang Clan and Digable Planets. Despite such pockets of influence within popular and literary culture, however, Islam and Muslims for the most part remained largely "underground" throughout the 1980s and 1990s, as Soviet-style communism remained the nation's preeminent foe until the fall of the Berlin Wall in 1990, and the nation engaged in heated debates over multiculturalism and national identity during the culture wars of the 1990s. Muslim American communities, both African American and immigrant, mostly remained out of the public eye, as the former strived to recalibrate and restructure their communities in the wake of the 1970s political struggles, and the latter developed and strengthened their own communities, as well as attempting to assimilate and weave themselves into the fabric of American society.[40]

This relative lack of visibility was forever altered on September 11, 2001, as "Muslim Americans" were abruptly thrust into the national spotlight, broadly characterized through associations with terrorism and Islamic fundamentalism. Images of the male Muslim terrorist and the oppressed and submissive Muslim woman flooded the U.S. media and popular culture, reinvigorating age-old Orientalist stereotypes for

---

[39] The basic premise of the organization is that 85 percent of people are without knowledge, 10 percent are bloodsuckers of the poor who have knowledge and power but use it to abuse the 85 percent, and the 5 percent are the poor righteous teachers who preach the divinity of the Black man who is God manifest and will save the 85 percent from destruction.

[40] As stated earlier, following the death of the Honorable Elijah Muhammad in 1975, the Nation of Islam came under the leadership of Muhammad's son, Warith Deen Mohammed, who transitioned the organization toward the teachings of Sunni Islam and eventually renamed the group the American Society of Muslims. Another group, led by Muhammad's disciple Louis Farrakhan, maintained the group's racial separatist beliefs.

the contemporary era. Under such difficult circumstances, Muslim Americans of all races, ethnicities, and national origins were forced to articulate and define their identities as Americans, as well as seeking out points of commonality within their communities. As a result, the post-9/11 cultural and literary expressions of Muslim Americans not only articulated myriad racial, ethnic, and cultural identities and histories encompassed by their communities but also recounted their shared experiences as a community under suspicion. The decade since 9/11 has witnessed a proliferation of voices "identifiable as Muslim," due to both a heightened public interest in Islam and Muslims and the desire of Muslims in the United States to share their stories. Many of the expressions have taken up the traditions of political activism and social justice struggles represented by Islam's long-standing role in Black American cultural politics. For example, on November 7, 2001, Palestinian American poet and New York native Suheir Hammad published "First Writing Since (Poem on Crisis of Terror)" in the online poetry journal *In Motion*, in which she emphasized the presence of Arabs and Muslims in the United States and expressed her pain over the attacks:

> one more person ask me if i knew the hijackers.
> one more motherfucker ask me what navy my brother is in.
> one more person assume no arabs or muslims were killed. one more
>   person
> assume they know me, or that i represent a people.
> or that a people represent an evil. or that evil is as simple as a
> flag and words on a page ...
> if there are any people on earth who understand how new york is
> feeling right now, they are in the west bank and the gaza strip ...[41]

Linking the pain of New Yorkers following the attacks to that of Palestinians struggling under Israeli occupation in the West Bank, Hammad conveys the rage, grief, and ambivalence of Muslims and Arabs, particularly women, in post-9/11 America. Hammad has only reluctantly identified with the label Muslim though. The poem was later discovered by hip hop mogul Russell Simmons, who asked her to perform her work on his *Def Poetry Jam* series on HBO in 2002 and join the series tour, with which Hammad performed for the next two years.

As Hammad's example demonstrates, the urban cultural milieus of hip hop and the spoken word scene have been natural outlets for the post-9/11 voices of Muslim American artists. Aligning themselves with

[41] Suheir Hammad, "First Writing Since," *In Motion Magazine*, November 7, 2001.

working-class, people-of-color, and grass-roots activist communities, spoken word artists such as Hammad, Bay Area female spoken word artists Calligraphy of Thought, Puerto Rican American Muslim convert Liza Garza, Milwaukee-based slam poet Muhibb Dyer, Bay Area poets and rappers Amir Sulaiman and Baraka Blue, and many others utilized their work to critique the War on Terror, the conditions of urban America, and racial, gender, and class inequality, all the while speaking to the evolving realities of being Muslim in the post-9/11 United States. Like Amiri Baraka, Marvin X, and Sonia Sanchez before them, these poets and artists attempted to merge their artistic and political visions, emphasizing Islam's focus on justice, racial egalitarianism, and the importance of charity and good works. In the realm of hip hop, artists also advanced such principles, for example, Washington, D.C.–based rappers Native Deen, and a number of artists who have emerged from or been associated with Bay Area hip hop collective Remarkable Current, including its founder, DJ, and producer Anas Canon, rappers and vocalists Tyson Amir and Kumasi, and Puerto Rican Muslim American duo Mujahideen Team, or M-Team, featuring brothers Hamza and Suliman Perez (aka Doc Zhivago). In addition, well-known hip hop artists such as Yasiin Bey (formerly Mos Def), Ali Shaheed Muhammad, Q-Tip, Lupe Fiasco, and Busta Rhymes began more publicly proclaiming their identities as Muslims. The links between Islam and Black culture and identity have also been explored in Muslim American novelist Murad Kalam's *Night Journey* (2004), as well as the writings of white American convert Michael Muhammad Knight, whose nonfiction works *Blue-Eyed Devil* and *The Five Percenters: Islam, Hip Hop, and the Gods of New York*, offer – as the subtitle to the former reads – an "odyssey through Islamic America."

The realities of Islam in urban post-9/11 America have also begun to be more fully explored in American film and cinema. Rapper Hamza Perez's life was the focus of 2009's *New Muslim Cool*,[42] a documentary directed by Bay Area–based filmmaker Jennifer Maytorena Taylor, which aired as part of PBS's acclaimed *POV* documentary series. Perez and his brother Suliman are also featured in the 2010 documentary *Deen Tight*, directed by Mustafa Davis, which explores the phenomenon of hip hop in Muslim cultures, focusing on the struggles of Muslim hip hop artists trying to, in the film's words "find a balance between their culture and their religion." In 2011 two feature-length films exploring the lives of

---

[42] See Su'ad Abdul Khabeer and Maytha Alhassen, Chapter 17 in this volume, for further discussion.

African American Muslim men, *Bilal's Stand* (dir. Sultan Sharieff) and *Mooz-lum* (dir. Qasim Bashir) also premiered in U.S. theaters. Michael Muhammad Knight's first novel, *The Taqwacores*, a fictional account of an Islamic punk rock scene in the United States published in 2004, spawned a real Islamic punk movement, which was the subject of an award-winning 2009 documentary titled *Taqwacore: The Birth of Punk Islam* and was dramatized as *The Taqwacores* (dir. Eyad Zahra) in 2010. As these examples demonstrate, the aforementioned literary, musical, and cinematic expressions unearth an always-evolving, yet deeply rooted ethos of social, political, and cultural protest that has been at the heart of Muslim American identity and culture. As Hishaam Aidi (citing postcolonial critic Robert Young) has written, "Islam is at the heart of an emerging global, anti-hegemonic culture ... that combines diasporic and local cultural elements, and blends Arab, Islamic, Black and Hispanic factors to generate 'a revolutionary Black, Asian and Hispanic globalization, with its own dynamic counter-modernity ... constructed in order to fight global imperialism.'"[43] While such a categorization poses the danger of inaccurately constructing Islam as a romanticized mode of cultural resistance – when it should in fact be viewed as a complex, contradictory, and at times deeply conservative intermixture of cultural, political, and religious ideologies – Islam appears to continue to constitute a "galvanizing force" among working-class and people-of-color communities in the post-9/11 United States.

Since the 1970s, however, distinctive Muslim American identities have also developed and evolved out of "immigrant" Muslim communities across the country. Numerous first- and second-generation Muslims of South Asian, West Asian, and North African origin have come forward to tell their stories in the post-9/11 era, mainly in the literary realm. Many of the novels, short stories, poetry, and plays bear much in common with Asian and Arab American immigrant literatures, exploring themes of generational conflict, cultural divisions, and the difficulties of assimilation. Novels such as Afghani American Khaled Hosseini's *The Kite Runner* (2004), Samina Ali's *Madras on Rainy Days* (2004), Mohja Kahf's *The Girl in the Tangerine Scarf*, and Shaila Abdullah's *Saffron Dreams* (2010) offer Muslim American perspectives beyond the urban contexts detailed here, providing a glimpse into the ways Muslim immigrants to the United States have created communities in places like Bloomington, Fremont, and immigrant ethnic enclaves in the metropolitan centers

---

[43] Hisham D. Aidi, "Let Us Be Moors: Islam, Race, and 'Connected Histories,'" *Souls* 7:1 (2005): 36–57; 46.

of New York and Philadelphia. Other texts, such as Mohsin Hamid's *The Reluctant Fundamentalist* and H. M. Naqvi's *Homeboy* explore the effects of state profiling and surveillance practices, detailing the lives of young "immigrant" Muslim men, in this case both Pakistani, who must endure their labeling and interpellation as "terrorists" in various ways. On the stage, Pakistani American playwright Wajahat Ali's *The Domestic Crusaders* (mentioned in the introduction) and the *Hijabi Monologues* project – a series of monologues exploring the realities of Muslim women who wear the *hijab*, or headscarf – have garnered large audiences and critical acclaim, and continue to be staged in theaters across the United States. Beyond stereotypical media images as terrorists and fanatics, Muslims have also begun to appear on mainstream American television: NBC's situation comedy *Outsourced*, set in a call center in India, debuted in 2010 and features a number of Muslim characters and actors, while comedian and media pundit Jon Stewart's popular satirical program *The Daily Show* has regularly featured commentary from actor and comedian Aasif Mandvi, a Muslim American of Indian descent. Beyond the arenas of literature, music, and film, a Muslim American cultural ethos has also been developing in the fields of fashion and art, as clothing retailers such as Shukr ("thankfulness" in Arabic) and Artizara (and many others) offer modest, urban-inspired, and decidedly fashion-forward Islamic garments, while artists such as Australian-based Peter Gould merges vibrant and sleek graphics with Islamic visuals. Muslim American comedy is also on the rise; prominent comedian Dave Chappelle, who converted to Islam in 1998, began publicly discussing his faith in 2005, while a 2008 documentary *Allah Made Me Funny* follows Muslim American comedians Azhar Usman, Preacher Moss, and Mo Amer, who are, respectively, Indian American, African American, and Palestinian American.

In other words, in the post-9/11 era, racial and religious confluence continues to be the hallmark of Muslim American cultural and literary production, as absolutely no hard and fast lines divide "immigrant," from "African American," Islam from America. While Islam's cultural history in the United States is grounded in Black communities and culture, to look toward Muslim America's future is to understand the new set of social, political, and cultural conditions shaping its contemporary formations, which are always, irrevocably, and simultaneously tied to domestic and transnational affiliations of race, ethnicity, class, nation, and religious identity. While Black Americans in the early to mid-twentieth century found the teachings of Noble Drew Ali, Elijah Muhammad, and Ahmadiyya missionaries in their transition to the

North following the Great Migration as a means to reverse decades of dehumanization engendered through the institution of slavery, young Muslim American artists and writers in the post-9/11 United States reveal how a new set of narratives – of 9/11, globalization, neoliberalism, feminism, gender and sexuality, transnational religious discourse, immigration, and multiracialism – are now an integral part of the past, present, and future of Islam in America.

Further Reading

Bayoumi, Moustafa, "East of the Sun (West of the Moon): Islam, the Ahmadis, and African America," *Journal of Asian American Studies* 4, no. 3 (2001): 251–263.

"Moorish Science," *Transition*, no. 80 (1999): 100–119.

cooke, miriam, and Bruce B. Lawrence, eds., *Muslim Networks from Hajj to Hip Hop, Islamic Civilization and Muslim Networks* (Chapel Hill, 2005).

Curtis, Edward E., IV, *Muslims in America: A Short History* (New York, 2009).

Marr, Timothy, *The Cultural Roots of American Islamicism* (New York, 2006).

McAlister, Melani, "One Black Allah: The Middle East in the Cultural Politics of African American Liberation, 1955–1970," *American Quarterly* 51:3 (1999): 622–656.

McCloud, Aminah Beverly, *African American Islam* (New York, 1995).

Turner, Richard Brent, *Islam in the African American Experience* (Bloomington, 1997).

17 Muslim Youth Cultures

SU'AD ABDUL KHABEER AND MAYTHA ALHASSEN

Young people are central actors in the formation of American Muslim cultures, and their cultural production engages questions of identity. This self-making through culture does not occur in a vacuum but has been shaped by specific contextual realities. For one, American Muslim youth cultures are shaped by the contemporary moment in which the convergence of a bad economy, racism, and the "War on Terror" has made their very existence a cause for national concern. As a result, Muslim youth in the United States are typically represented and analyzed through two narrow prisms: as potential jihadis or as upwardly mobile model minorities. The cultures of young American Muslims respond to this binary, both explicitly and implicitly.

Young U.S. Muslims are in dialogue with the expectations of "parent culture," the perspectives of often dominant older American Muslims, both immigrants and converts. Parent culture holds a series of ideals about who young people should be and their proper role in community life. A primary consequence of these beliefs is that many Muslim youth feel marginalized in traditional spaces of American Muslim sociality, such as the mosque. For some youth, part of their identity work resists parent culture by creating alternative spaces and frameworks for American Islam. Yet resistance is not the only response to the parent culture. Some young Muslims aspire to these "parental" ideals and find room to live out their sense of religious identity within them.

Finally, although young Muslim cultures in the United States are grounded in local contexts, this identity work is also transnational. This is partly due to the ways that Muslim identity remains informed by intra-Muslim debates that cross national boundaries.[1] Technology also plays a role in making Muslim youth cultures transnational. Young U.S. Muslims, like youth across the globe, embrace technology as a tool to

---

[1] miriam cooke and Bruce Lawrence, eds., *Muslim Networks from Hajj to Hip Hop* (Chapel Hill, 2005).

make and share culture. Blogs and social media have become critical sites of communication and debate in which actors have a stake in shaping U.S. Muslim youth cultures.

We identify Muslim youth as females and males of diverse racial, ethnic, and socioeconomic backgrounds. Some were raised in Muslim families, and others are converts to Islam and in fact, many converts are leading cultural producers. Thus there is an important caveat to be made in any discussion of American Muslim youth cultures. Since its emergence in the United States in the 1950s, the category "youth" is typically associated with adolescence. Accordingly, "youth culture" is defined as an age-based set of styles, practices, and interests. However, consideration of American Muslim youth cultures demands a more expansive notion of the category "youth." American Muslims who are now well into their thirties remain critical actors in the production of American Muslim youth cultures in the United States. Although no longer adolescents, they came of age as Muslims in the United States and have now become the artists, activists, and academics that are paving the way for subsequent generations of American Muslim youth.

Young American Muslim cultures have taken shape and taken up space in a variety of locations, yet three key areas stand out: music, fashion, and new media. These sites of inquiry, often studied within broader academic youth studies scholarship, are key arenas in which cultural production is youth generated.[2] While U.S. Muslim youth are in dialogue with parent culture and broader discourses on youth and society at large, these sites are more autonomous and thus more centrally guided by youth interests, perspectives, and anxieties than other spaces youth occupy such as schools, universities, and workplaces.

MUSIC

From the late 1990s, music, from *nasheeds* to punk, began to emerge as a significant site of Muslim youth cultures. The form and content of music composed by American Muslims has ranged widely. Some music focuses on religious themes and adheres to religious opinions that only use of the male voice and the drum is Islamically permissible in creating music. These performers have typically been endorsed by parent

---

[2] Dick Hebdige, *Subculture: The Meaning of Style* (London, 1979); Julian Sefton-Green, *Digital Diversions: Youth Culture in the Age of Multimedia* (London, 1998); Norma Mendoza-Benton, *Homegirls: Language and Cultural Practice among Latina Youth Gangs* (Malden, 2005); Sunaina Maira and Elisabeth Soep, *Youthscapes* (Philadelphia, 2004).

culture. Other music pushes boundaries by relying on different readings of religious texts and histories of music in Muslim communities, such as Qawwali and Gnawa, to argue for not only the permissibility but the centrality of music to Islam.[3] This music is also broader thematically. Some young American Muslim musicians even push back against the necessity of being identified as a "Muslim" artist. Troubling the boundary between "religious" and "secular," these artists argue for what they see as a more holistic understanding of religion's relationship to art. Three genres dominate the soundscape of Muslim youth cultures: hip hop, punk, and nasheed.

There is a synergistic relationship between American Islam and hip hop that is rooted in values of self-determination and community empowerment spread within urban Black and Latino communities by the Nation of Islam (NOI), the Five Percenters, and Sunni Islam. As a result, themes and motifs related to Islam are standard elements of hip hop music and culture. This synergy is also what made hip hop the first musical genre to be seriously engaged by young U.S. Muslims. Some of the earliest hip hop productions by young Muslims were novice rhymes, such as the 1990s MYNA raps. These early songs were typically composed by teenagers, performed at youth camps, and sold on cassette tapes. This music related to the everyday experiences of young American Muslims, reinforcing particular notions of Islamic piety while appealing to the aesthetic tastes of teenagers. These objectives have become cornerstones of hip hop music produced within the American Muslim community such that we argue that the perceived needs of young American Muslims have been the central motivational force behind the creation of all "American Muslim music."

Though skeptics question the genre's religious permissibility, hip hop's significance to young Muslims is unequivocal. As a result, Muslim hip hop has become standard at Muslim events. Yet, for the artists who perform at these venues, the climate toward hip hop is complicated by race. Invitations to perform are typically accompanied by stipulations about what artists can do on stage, illustrating that in many communities hip hop is still held at arm's length. Some artists have argued that this is the product of anti-Black racism. In the documentary *Deen Tight*, poet Amir Sulaiman describes his experiences performing for Muslim audiences as: "[It seems as if] what makes you black and American is *haram*."[4]

3 Suad Abdul Khabeer, "Rep that Islam: The Rhyme and Reason of American Islamic Hip Hop," *Muslim World* 97:1 (2007): 125–141.
4 Mustafa Davis, *Deen Tight* (Abu Dhabi, 2010).

Sulaiman is one of many U.S. Muslim hip hop "heads" (artists, promoters, activists, or fans) who have encountered a mix of hostility and ambivalence toward music in general, and hip hop in particular, from other Muslims. This mix stems from anti-Black racism as well as interpretive religious stances that prohibit music. For many Muslim hip hop heads, this has meant isolation from community life. One response to this isolation was the creation of an email listserv called *Muslims in Hip Hop*. Launched in 2002, by event promoter Christie Z-Pabon and her husband, Pop Master Jorge "Fabel" Pabon, *Muslims in Hip Hop* provides Muslim hip hop heads with a virtual community space. Over the listserv and Facebook page, relationships of mutual support developed among members who were negotiating the demands and needs of contemporary Muslim artists. Coming from distinct local contexts both within *and* outside of the United States, Muslim hip hop heads share commitments to hip hop and to Islam. We argue that these transnational networks have produced dialogic relationships between Muslims that have the potential to challenge the religious hegemony of the "Muslim world" as well as the cultural imperialism of the United States. Likewise, they will have significant localized effects on Muslim youth cultures in the United States.

Young Muslims frequently cite the 2004 novel *The Taqwacores*,[5] about a group of young Muslims who negotiate American Muslim identity through punk music and culture, as playing a seminal role in their engagement with punk music as *Muslims*. For example, Kouroush Poursalehi started his own band, Vote Hezbollah, after reading *The Taqwacores*. Others, such as the band Al-Thawra, were already consuming punk and creating music. Yet reading *The Taqwacores* seemed to give young punk Muslims more confidence. The stories told in *The Taqwacores* reflected their own frustrations with mainstream American culture and the ideological and social norms of their local Muslim communities.

"Taqwacore" is a term that brings together *taqwa*, the Islamic precept of God-consciousness, with core, a reference to hardcore or specifically hardcore punk. Blending punk and Islam comes as a surprise to many. Punk is typically characterized as deeply irreverent, and Islam is seen as demanding conformity in belief and ritual practice. For Muslim punk bands and fans, taqwacore was not a paradoxical term. Rather, young Muslims "have embraced punk rock as … a form of open

5   Michael Muhammad Knight, *The Taqwacores* (New York, 2004; 2nd ed., New York, 2009).

resistance to both mainstream American society and traditional Islam, as a means of community development, and identity building in the context of U.S. government policies and prominent media stereotypes of Muslim Americans."[6] The music they create retains connections to the cultural traditions and histories of the Muslim cultures in which they were reared.

Not all audiences see value in taqwacore. In 2007 taqwacore bands including the Kominas, Al-Thawra, Vote Hezbollah, and Secret Trial Five, an all-female band, formed to do a "Taqwa-tour." This tour, featured in the 2009 documentary *Taqwacore*, made a stop at the 2007 convention of the Islamic Society of North America (ISNA) and signed up for the evening's youth entertainment night. However, their lyrics and incorporation of female vocalists came in direct conflict with ISNA's vision of Muslim entertainment. There were reports that the young Muslim audience enjoyed taqwacore, yet ultimately the bands were not able to negotiate with the ISNA officials onsite. Rather, their sets ended early as the local police arrived to remove the Taqwa-tour bands from the premises. Regardless, the event was interpreted as a success by Muslim punk artists, who saw these types of encounters as useful in pushing boundaries for social change.

A similar confrontation took place at the same conference during a hip hop performance, and it is worth noting that those objecting were not "parents" but other young Muslims. This speaks to the diversity among American Muslim youth and underscores the fact that youth cultures, Muslim or otherwise, are not necessarily subversive but can be aligned with what is considered normative. Accordingly, whereas hip hop and punk are typically framed as socially transgressive by parent cultures, the contemporary English-language nasheed genre, made famous in the United States by artists such as Native Deen, Maher Zain, and Dawud Wharnsby, is more broadly embraced across generations. The nasheed is a devotional song that has its roots in majority-Muslim countries. Nasheeds typically privilege voice and percussion, in adherence to aforementioned religious rulings, yet popular nasheed artists in the United States, Canada, and Europe have increasingly incorporated a broader range of instrumentation, and their music has reflected the influence of the "secular" musical genres of pop, R&B, and hip hop.

---

[6] Sarah Siltanen Hosman, "Muslim Punk Rock in the United States: A Social History of the Taqwacores" (Master's thesis, University of North Carolina at Greensboro, 2009), p. 14.

Native Deen, who started out with MYNA raps, has emerged as a premier group of the genre. Exemplifying the value of identity, piety, and aesthetics in American Muslim music, Native Deen songs emphasize faithfulness, moral fortitude, and Muslim pride. Native Deen's audience, like many nasheed groups, includes Muslim adolescents *and* their parents. Furthermore, in addition to stateside concerts, Native Deen has visited fans outside the United States through events such as *Evening of Inspiration*, a concert series held in the United Kingdom by the international charity, Islamic Relief. The worldwide appeal of nasheed artists underscores the transnational circulation of a set of ideals regarding Muslim identity and Islamic piety, ideals that are tied to American Muslim youth yet more often than not align with parent cultures.

Nasheed artists also reached global audiences by way of concert tours in Muslim-majority nations sponsored by the U.S. Department of State. These performances, in which some Muslim hip hop artists have also participated, can be seen as complicity or an alignment with another kind of mainstream, the U.S. empire. Hishaam Aidi notes that "the U.S. government's growing use of hip hop in public diplomacy, counter-terrorism and democracy promotion [is] an attempt to harness the genre towards various political objectives," such as improving the image of the United States abroad.[7] These artists are not unaware of the controversy surrounding these trips. For Native Deen, the response has been to evaluate collaborations with the state in light of the principles that guide its artistic production. Band member, Abdul Malik Ahmad has stated that "if it's our mission to spread tolerance and faith, it can be O.K. to take this [particular] offer."[8]

In all these genres, save to some extent punk, women performers have been marginal. This marginalization stems from certain religious taboos regarding women's bodies and patriarchal notions of male and female desire. Restrictions around women's bodies find their roots in "certain elements of the classical Muslim tradition [that] treat female sexuality as dangerous, with potentially disruptive and chaotic effects on society."[9] Accordingly, female sexuality, if left unchecked, will unleash heterosexual male desire and social discord or *fitna*. The association of women with fitna has precipitated practices and discourses that restrict

[7] Hishaam Aidi, "Leveraging Hip Hop in U.S. Foreign Policy," *AlJazeera*, November 7, 2011.

[8] Mark Oppenheimer, "A Diplomatic Mission Bearing Islamic Hip Hop," *New York Times*, July 22, 2011.

[9] Kecia Ali, *Sexual Ethics and Islam: Feminist Reflections on Qur'an, Hadith and Jurisprudence* (Oxford, 2006).

women's bodies and activities. Accordingly, for some scholars and communities, Muslim women's *awrah* (private parts), unlike a man's, includes her voice. This had particular implications for female Muslim vocalists. As one U.S. Muslim hip hop artist, Miss Undastood, explained: "It's harder because people don't think that I should be so vocal ... I had one brother tell me it is not becoming of a Muslimah [Muslim woman] to do this."[10]

These norms are in alignment with the patriarchy endemic in the wider hip hop scene and broader U.S. culture. Women in hip hop struggle against being cast primarily as objects of male desire and anxiety rather than artists in their own right. American women find themselves facing gender-based discrimination, which is often also attenuated by race and class. The marginal position of young female Muslim artists underscores the limits of "resistance" in Muslim youth cultures. In terms of race, Muslim youth cultures are often at odds with parent cultures, yet seem to more commonly reproduce traditional gender norms.

FASHION

Like music, fashion is also a central location of Muslim youth culture in the United States. The styles of U.S. Muslim youth culture have been developed by individual designers, many of whom are formally trained in fashion design, as well as everyday "fashionistas" who mark their bodies in daily negotiations of American Muslim identity. Critically, these designers and consumers co-constructed an "Islamic Fashion Scape," a broad field of "sartorial possibilities open to" Muslims, by "developing distinctive Islamic styles inspired by different types of regional dress" and by "selecting, altering and re-combining elements of mainstream fashion to create new Islamically sensitive outfits."[11] "Islamic" is not defined here as one form of dress over another but rather indexes the stylistic choice to dress modestly according to particular understandings of religious requirements. These choices are meaningful because the visual is deployed not only as individual self-expression but also as an "intervention and medium of debate" in public spheres of Muslim life.[12]

---

[10] Khabeer, "Rep that Islam," p. 132.

[11] Emma Tarlo, *Visibly Muslim: Fashion, Politics and Faith* (Oxford, 2010), p. 225. Writing from the British Muslim context, Tarlo dates the beginnings of this Islamic Fashion Scape in the late 1990s. However, we argue that in the U.S. context the Islamic Fashion Scape has its origins in the sartorial practices of African American Muslim communities from the 1960s, if not earlier. This included a consumer market and events such as fashion shows.

[12] Annelies Moors and Emma Tarlo, "Introduction," *Fashion Theory* 11:2–3 (2007): 138.

They may infer competing and complementary notions of religiosity, race, and nation between youth culture and parent culture.

Modest dress is a broadly accepted virtue among Muslims. However, what precisely defines a practice as modest or "Islamic" is contested. For young American Muslims, the desire to dress modestly can be a youthful complement to parent culture's notions of pious dress or be in competition by pushing boundaries through choices such as color, shape, and scarf style. Further, young Muslim sartorial choice sometimes functions as a critique of parent culture, whose own styles are seen as "more 'cultural' and 'traditional' than 'religious' and therefore less 'Islamic.'"[13] Moreover, the same debates over women's bodies and male desires implicated in the contestations over music are also at play in Muslim youth fashion. As a result, the Islamic fashion scape has been dominated by designs that respond to growing demands by young American Muslim women for modest wear. Sites such as Shukr Islamic Clothing, Primo Moda, and Artizara as well as individual designers such as Nzinga Knight and Nailah Lymus, seek to cater to this growing market, offering fashion choices that reflect Islamic principles with flair. In addition to these sites, blogs and Web sites advise young Muslim women on how to transform the latest fashion trends into hijabi-friendly styles.

Young Muslims also seek attire that reflects their concerns with their own marginalization in a U.S. political and cultural climate. T-shirts, the "iconic item of global youth culture,"[14] became particularly popular. Online and at events, young Muslims choose T-shirts with satirical messages such as: "Whoops! There goes my Wudu," "Go Ahead, Profile me," and "This is what a radical Muslim Feminist Looks Like."[15] These T-shirts are assertions of Muslim identity. By centering on shared religious practices, like ablution, with humor, these T-shirts reproduce bonds of communal affiliation and can even encourage piety. Further, in a context where being identifiably "Muslim" is likely to mark one as an enemy of the state, these T-shirts also directly confront state-sponsored civic ostracism.

While the Islamic fashion scape, like the broader fashion industry, is dominated by women's styles, some of the more dynamic fashion trends that young Muslims are creating on the ground are for and by young men. These are male styles of dressing that incorporate urban and hip hop inspired fashions such as large white T-shirts and sneakers

---

[13] Moors and Tarlo, "Introduction," p. 139.
[14] Emma Tarlo, *Visibly Muslim*, p. 217.
[15] www.hijabman.com.

with clothing items from Muslim-majority regions, such as the *izar*, or male wrap skirt. As seen in major urban centers like Philadelphia in the first decades of the twenty-first century, a young Muslim man might be found wearing a denim izar over capri-length pants, matching Air Jordans, and a beard under a short-brim hat or a more simple ensemble of a *thobe* (long-sleeved long garment) paired with Timberland boots and a puffy vest. These choices epitomized the hybridity at the heart of young Muslim fashion, which links identifications of race, age, class, gender, region, and religion. These styles underscore religious commitments as each is tied to prophetic tradition. Yet they are also specific iterations of the prophetic tradition for male dress as articulated through Salafist or other literalist approaches commonly found in urban centers in the United States. This highlights the important role of the local in shaping Muslim youth culture. Yet these styles are also seen in other cities around the nation and around the ummah, underscoring U.S. Muslim youth culture's ties to transnational Muslim discourse. The use of denim, Timberlands, short brims, and white T-shirts further demonstrates that Islamic fashion, like Muslim youth culture more generally, is not only tied to particular notions of religiosity but also "related to national, regional and ethnic belonging."[16]

NEW AND SOCIAL MEDIA

Another location wherein Muslim youth culture has made critical interventions is new media. This new media ecology includes social networking sites such as Facebook, Twitter, and YouTube and activities like blogging and social activism. Scholarship of "Islam online" has traced the sociocultural impact of new technology on individual and communal Muslim identities, notions of religious authority and authenticity, and transformations in the Muslim public square(s).[17] For Muslim youth, new media platforms function as promising spaces for religious self-making and cultural (re)definition. At times, social media allow for an expansive conception of "community" that engages a "virtual ummah" of "collective Muslim identities."[18] Yet, as Muslim youth connect to their counterparts across difference in the "virtual ummah,"

---

[16] Moors and Tarlo, "Introduction," p. 136.

[17] Dale Eickelman and Jon Anderson, eds., *New Media in the Muslim World: The Emerging Public Sphere*, 2nd ed. (Bloomington, 2003); Gary Bunt, *iMuslims: Rewiring the House of Islam* (Chapel Hill, 2009).

[18] Mohammad el-Nawawy and Sahar Khamis, *Islam Dot Com: Contemporary Islamic Discourses in Cyberspace* (New York, 2009).

they also police boundaries of "Muslimness" that remain grounded in local Muslim contexts in which race and gender are central.

Young Muslims use social media sites as their non-Muslim peers do: status updates, retweets, "liking," posting comments and photos, and generating their own content. In late 2011 a popular YouTube video "Shit Girls Say," a montage of sayings stereotypically associated with young white women, inspired spin-off videos using the meme "Shit X says" or "Stuff X says" to parody a wider range of groups like "parents," "New Yorkers," and hijabis. Young Muslim women produced videos such as "Stuff Hijabis Say" and "Stuff People Say to Hijabis" and "Stuff MGT Say" that use satire to critique stereotypes signified by the hijab, such as Muslim women are uniquely pious or repressed.[19] These young Muslim women use social media to intervene in a religious and cultural milieu where Muslim women are marginalized. Indeed, while all Muslim youth may feel marginal in many mainstream Muslim community spaces, gender creates an added level of exclusion. Yet new media has the potential to engender more equitable community space. Through humor as well as more serious webzines and dailies, like *AltMuslimah* and *Muslimah Media Watch*, young Muslim women have used new technologies to challenge gender-based exclusion.

Activism through social media extends beyond questions of gender. By 2010, advocacy messaging, like the Twitter hashtags #Jan25, #Syria, #Yemen, and #AllAmericanMuslim as well as Facebook campaigns had become an increasingly popular medium for creating awareness and, to a certain extent, mobilization around specific causes.[20] At the intersection of gender, race, religion, and social media was the 2012 campaign "We Are All Abeed." According to the Chicago-based blogger Hind Makki, this campaign was prompted by an incident where the n-word was used against a student of African descent at an all-girls Muslim high school whose population is predominately Arab. Tying this incident to a pattern of anti-Black racism in the Middle East, the United States, and the American Muslim community, a former student began the "We Are All Abeed" awareness campaign. This is an effort to recuperate the term "abeed" which literally translates as slave and, in the Qur'anic sense, references servitude to God but has historically been used as a

---

[19] MGT is short for Muslim Girls Training and General Civilization Class (MGT-GCC), an auxiliary unit of the NOI that is dedicated to the religious education and socialization of female members.

[20] #Jan25, #Yemen, and #Syria were forms of virtual support for antiregime efforts in Egypt, Yemen, and Syria, respectively. #AllAmericanMuslim trended in support of the 2011 TLC docu-series, *All American Muslim*.

derogatory term for Black people. Like other youth-generated social media campaigns, there was a Facebook page, which had links to purchase campaign-related merchandise including T-shirts and wristbands, which have become icons of an uneasy contemporary marriage between consumerism, fashion, and activism. This campaign, spearheaded by a young woman, engaged intra-Muslim discourses around race and gender but also participated in the broader culture of youth-generated social media activism.

Social media was also the site of youth-generated responses to revelations of a New York City Police Department (NYPD) secret surveillance program targeting American Muslims by ethnicity and religious practice. In response, the Yale Muslim Students Association created the Facebook page "Call the NYPD," which mocked the alleged threat posed by Muslim college students through photos of individuals holding signs with phrases such as "I am a … Blonde, Call the NYPD." The hashtag #mynypdfile derided NYPD surveillance of Muslims, with quips such as the tweet by @msentropy: "Sir, she's been known to talk publicly about ijtihad. Sounds close enough to jihad to me. #mynypdfile." This online social activism by young Muslims contradicts the academic scholarship and broader popular discourse that tends to view the online activities of young U.S. Muslims only in terms of potential terrorist recruitment.[21]

While "U.S. Muslim youth online" remains an understudied topic, our preliminary research suggests that one major consequence of new media is that it has helped to decenter the mosque, typically dominated by parent culture, as the primary setting for the authentication of Muslim identity and religious authority. Although new technologies were initially contested by parents and other agents of "tradition," it was not long before even the most "traditional" leaders were blogging, tweeting, and updating their Facebook pages. Thus there are complex and, at times, tense negotiations between youth culture and parent culture online.

These negotiations were at the fore of online debates on the multimedia blog, "30 Mosques." Each day during the month of Ramadan, a duo of twenty-something South Asian American Muslims, Aman Ali and Bassam Tariq, would visit a different mosque to break their fasts and later post a blog entry that documented their observations of the local mosque culture. The project, which began in 2010 and was continued

²¹ David Drissel, "Online Jihadism for the Hip-Hop Generation: Mobilizing Diasporic Muslim Youth in Cyberspace," *International Journal of Interdisciplinary Social Sciences*, 2:4 (2007): 7–20.

in 2011, received international media attention and was praised by Muslims and non-Muslims alike for showcasing the U.S. Muslim community as diverse rather than monolithic. Yet this showcase did not go unchallenged by other young Muslims. Some commentators read the visits with an openly gay Imam in 2010 and in 2011 to an Ahmadi mosque as progressive and others as an attempt to legitimate transgressions. Likewise, some hailed their effort to document women's spaces in mosques. Others, such as blogger Peter Gray, argued the visit was a violation of women's privacy and that their commentary on what they saw as inequities in the women's space was a smug performance of patriarchy.

This online back and forth reflects a transposition of the offline tug of war over the boundaries of "Muslimness." The public sphere of cyberspace is a locale of contestation. Parent culture and its youthful advocates seek to recenter the locus of power and authority back in the hands of traditional leaders, as agents of boundary-pushing Muslim youth cultures seek unconventional sources. New and social media have created alternative spaces for religious dialogue and cultural production, yet young Muslims have not completely shifted the centers of power and authority, and not all desire to do so. Whatever the perspective, young Muslim engagement with new media stands as evidence of the ability of Muslim youth cultures to shift the terms of engagement.

CONCLUSION

This chapter is in no way meant to be exhaustive, as the cultural production of young American Muslims is dynamic and changing rapidly. However, the specific examples provided here do illustrate a common thread found in all forms of Muslim youth culture: identity. Race or ethnicity, gender, and class as well as the expectations of parent culture, long-standing religious debates, and contemporary geopolitics frame the negotiation of identity by young U.S. Muslims. At the convergence of all these factors is contemporary Muslim youth culture, which, by way of resistance, alignment, and ambivalence, young Muslims have and will continue to shape their social worlds.

Further Reading

Aidi, Hishaam, "Verily, There Is One Hip-Hop Ummah: Islam, Cultural Protest and Urban Marginality," *Socialism and Democracy* 18:2 (2004): 107–126.
Alim, H. Samy, *Roc the Mic Right: The Language of Hip Hop Culture* (New York, 2006).

Bunt, Gary, *iMuslims: Rewiring the House of Islam* (Chapel Hill, 2009).

cooke, miriam, and Bruce Lawrence, eds., *Muslim Networks from Hajj to Hip Hop* (Chapel Hill, 2005).

Hosman, Sarah Siltanen, *"Muslim Punk Rock in the United States: A Social History of the Taqwacores"* (Master's thesis, University of North Carolina at Greensboro, 2009).

Khabeer, Suad Abdul, "Rep That Islam: The Rhyme and Reason of American Islamic Hip Hop," *Muslim World* 97:1 (2007): 125–141.

el-Nawawy, Mohammad, and Sahar Khamis, *Islam Dot Com: Contemporary Islamic Discourses in Cyberspace* (New York, 2009).

Rashid, Hussein, "Taqwacore Roundtable: On Punks, the Media, and the Meaning of 'Muslim,'" *Religion Dispatches*, February 10, 2010.

Student Press Initiative, *This Is Where I Need to Be: Oral Histories of Muslim Youth in New York City* (New York, 2008).

Tarlo, Emma, *Visibly Muslim: Fashion, Politics and Faith* (Oxford, 2010).

18 Sexual Identity, Marriage, and Family

DEBRA MAJEED

Since the days of the Prophet Muhammad, when Muslims of seventh century Arabia first regulated the number of wives a husband could marry and legislated behavior between men and women, sexual identity, marriage, and family life have represented three intersecting markers of submission to G-d at both the individual and communal levels.[1] They are spaces in which the ethical codes that govern the public and private spheres of everyday Muslim life collide and connect. The amount of attention afforded these markers in authoritative sources of Islam confirms their dominance as the material ground upon which a Muslim's surrender to G-d's will is most evident or absent to other followers of the religion, and the intrinsic connection between spirituality, sexuality, and the family.

Regardless of the diverse geographic, social, or historical contexts in which adherents practice Islam or the religious ideology they uphold, sexual identity, marriage, and family life in Islam continue to be sites of contestation. Through them, Muslims are routinely imagined as oppressed or oppressors, pious individuals shackled by modernity, or liberated people of faith who consciously choose to dress, worship, or self-identify in ways that may be contrary to the dominant society in which they live. Of course, the issue of female choice or agency is often questionable in a patriarchal tradition such as Islam.[2] Generally, the relational and familial power of males is presumed.

The author wishes to thank Laury Silvers, Juliane Hammer, Beatrice McKenzie, and Linda Sturtz for their comments and suggestions.

[1] Muslims adhere to a system of governance that is similarly reflected in ritual matters and ethical thought of many Jewish communities. See, for example, Umar F. Abd-Allah, "Theological Dimensions of Islamic Law," in Tim Winter, ed., *The Cambridge Companion to Classical Islamic Theology* (Cambridge, 2008), pp. 239–240.

[2] I ground discussions of patriarchy in the work of both Asma Barlas and Zillah Eisenstein. Engaging the work of Eisenstein, Barlas defines patriarchy as "a continuum at one end of which are representations of God as Father and of fathers as rulers over wives/children, and at the other end, a politics of sexual differentiation that privilege

Even as female Muslims are "imaginatively constituted" in both scholarly and popular discourses by Muslims and non-Muslims, they also are rendered as the "face" of Islam by default. Alongside male Muslims, they are minorities in a nation that does not always understand their rituals, practices, or beliefs. The tension inherent within the social marginalization of Muslims can compound identity concerns that are particular to women. Indeed, in a world presumed to be largely shaped by and for its male members, Muslim women invariably encounter doubts about their roles and place, as if neither is shaped by multiple factors. They also face questions about the extent to which they are complicit in their own exploitation, are proactive in exercising their rights, or assume second-class status as divine will. Perhaps most importantly, female Muslims must contend with their personal exegetical frameworks, as well as self- and other-imposed expectations or obligations. Many choose to do this "work," according to Asma Barlas, because the alternative of silence would leave unexamined common portrayals of Muslim life.[3] Such silence also would continue a practice of legitimating male domination on the basis of religion, from the perspective of Muslims who strive for gender justice. Evidence of patriarchy in Islam has evolved from the absence of egalitarian readings and widespread acceptance of gender inequality in treatments of marriage within classical *fiqh* (human and thus fallible jurisprudence). By the eighth century, classical jurists were writing these texts within and based upon human experience in the patriarchal context of Arabia. Gender equality rarely visited the lived reality of Muslim women's lives because equality was not a concern of these premodern writers. Thus, most contemporary Muslim women and men have personally encountered or accepted via tradition a normative concept of gender in classical fiqh that contains the "core of the patriarchal logic" for the subjugation of women in the private sphere, particularly in regards to issues of intimacy and family life.[4] In addition to the religious beliefs and practices (e.g., belief in G-d, daily performance of prayers) that are expected of all Muslims, male followers have benefited from the institutionalization of male domination and female subjugation and the invocation of fiqh as divinely ordained. Today, the lived

males while Otherizing women." Asma Barlas, "Does the Qur'an Support Gender Equality? Or do I Have the Autonomy to Answer This Question?" an address to the University of Groningen, November 24, 2006; Zillah Eisenstein, *The Female Body and the Law* (Berkeley, 1988), p. 90.

3 Asma Barlas, "Does the Quran Support Gender Equality?"
4 Ziba Mir-Hosseini, "Islam and Gender Justice," in Vincent J. Cornell and Omid Safi, eds., *Voices of Islam*, vol. 5: *Voices of Change* (Westport, 2007), p. 88.

realities of Muslim women and men continue to complicate and fuel debates over sexuality, marriage, and family in Islam.

This chapter explores self-identity, marriage, and family life as three intersecting markers of divine submission. It first considers the experiences of American Muslims and the identity challenges they face in their attempts to be Muslim in a non-Muslim environment. Consideration of sexual identity draws attention to the significance of culture and community in the ways Muslim women and men perceive and represent themselves in private and public spheres. It makes note of the complicated relationship that continues to exist between some men and women, and communal ideas that constitute what it means to be a "good" Muslim. Second, an exploration of marriage as a significant institution to American Muslims points out the marriage forms Muslims consider, particularly the illegal practice of a husband with multiple wives. Finally, family life offers a glimpse of the nucleus of Muslim society. While I point to the tensions of upholding Muslim family values, I also recognize that Muslim communities are not immune from the trauma of abuse and divorce, as divorce, too, demonstrates the force of religious ideas to women and men. All three markers take account of the widespread diversity that exists among the six million to seven million Muslims in the United States. Theirs is a context defined both by its strength and by its challenges.

SEXUAL IDENTITY

For contemporary Muslims, sexual identity can be understood as a sense of one's self as a sexual being and how one is represented to and in society as well as before G-d. For American Muslims, that sense of self is often tied to their physical beings and the adoption of religious systems, how they negotiate societal norms associated with gender, and how they respond to cultural expectations of women as the symbol of family honor and men as the maintainer of and provider for women. Sexual identity signifies interior self-descriptions as well as exterior categories that are assigned to individuals.[5] It involves balancing self-understandings of one's faith and communal exegeses with cultural representations of sexuality that constitute popular images of American Muslims. In the United States, as in other Western settings where the lack of cohesion about Muslim ideals and practices leads to monolithic images of gender,

---

[5] Momin Rahman, "In Search of My Mother's Garden: Reflection on Migration, Sexuality, and Muslim Identity," *Nebula* 5 (December 4, 2008): 1–25.

sexual identity is often constructed in terms of fascination with the role and status of women. More often than not, this fascination zeroes in on dress and representations of the female body. As Zillah Eisenstein has persuasively argued, "the body is most often the starting point for a discussion of sex 'difference,'" albeit not the most logical point of departure.[6] Just as culture and experience are social constructs, what we think we know about the body, particularly the gendered body, cannot be separated from our own backgrounds, experiences, and what we have been taught. This reliance on culture and context renders the female body a "symbolic construct" that obscures thoughtful consideration of the sexual or biological differences of woman and man.[7] Nicole-Claude Mathieu has observed:

> As a result of unconscious presuppositions about the sexes, there is almost never a symmetrical analysis of the status of man and woman and of father and mother, since they are in fact considered relevant to different levels of reality.[8]

Issues surrounding the concepts of "male" and "female" open the door to consideration of masculinity and femininity, of what it means to be a good father or mother, a good Muslim.

At first glance, the dress of Muslims, particularly how women cover themselves and how much of them remains hidden, may seem to represent exclusively a visible sign of Muslim culture or piety (or both). In addition to Friday *khutbahs*, a wide variety of materials, including DVDs, YouTube videos, audiobooks, journal essays, pamphlets, blogs, novels, books, and other media, are devoted to debating, questioning, or instructing Muslim women about how best to use their bodies to fulfill Islamic requirements or retain local customs. Precise data do not exist on the number of American Muslim men and women who wear religious symbols as the embodiment of modesty. Still, the presence nationwide of men who wear long, untrimmed beards and the men and women who cover their heads (men with a turban or *kufi*, a small cap) or adopt modest styles of dress, indicates that many American Muslims are comfortable being associated with a particular religious marker that accentuates their visibility. Although the term *hijab* is the common reference for the manner in which Muslim women cover their ears, neck,

---

6 Eisenstein, *The Female Body and the Law*, pp. 90–91.
7 Eisenstein, *The Female Body and the Law.*
8 Nicole-Claude Mathieu, "Biological Paternity, Social Maternity," *Feminist Issues* 4 (Spring 1984): 70, as cited in Eisenstein, *The Female Body and the Law*, p. 91.

and head and body (from the neck to the ankle), some Muslims insist that hijab "applies to Muslim men as much as women" and is a way to "fortify modesty" between and among the sexes. For them, the "basic hijab" for Muslim men involves a dress code (covering the body from the belly button to below the knee) and the requirement of employment to financially support their families.[9] As in other regions where Muslims are not in the majority, sexual identity can mark perceived differences between Muslims and non-Muslims, pious and non-pious Muslims, and thus intersecting narratives of culture, privilege, oppression, self-defined agency, and ontology.[10]

The Qur'an speaks directly to the physical appearance of Muslims, enjoining both men and women to dress modestly. However, historical "particularities" coupled with gender relations within a patriarchal context have kept the mantle of moral responsibility on women in the form of their sexual identity.[11] For most women, hair covering and modest dress are the dominant image; wearing *niqab*, or a face veil, is the choice of a minority. Perhaps the common sight of American Muslim women with covered heads walking side-by-side with clean-shaven Muslim men wearing T-shirts or shorts is evidence that women are more likely to assume this moral mantle. Indeed, dress and demeanor reflect sexual identity, or how American Muslim women see and retain some control over the representations of their sexual selves. When considering how to best project their self-image in a sexualized culture like the United States, many Muslim women who adopt hijab in whatever version strive to direct attention to their personality, character, and personhood, rather than to their physical shapes. Given its widespread attention, it is not surprising that in the United States, the hijab is the single most recognized "symbol of belonging to a Muslim community" for men and women.[12]

For Muslims affiliated with lesbian, gay, bisexual, transgendered, and queer communities, negotiating sexual identity is a more difficult and challenging task. In Islam, spirituality and sexuality are interrelated. In the atmosphere of heterosexual privilege, nonheterosexual representations of males and females are taboo for most Muslims. Even discourses

[9] Maria Zain, "Definition of Hijab for Muslim Men: How Modesty Is Incorporated into the Islamic Dress Code for Men," Men's Fashion@suite 101, http://maria-zain. suite101.com/definition-of-hijab-for-muslim-men-a444107.

[10] Rahman, "In Search of My Mother's Garden."

[11] Ziba Mir-Hosseini, *Islam and Gender: The Religious Debate in Contemporary Iran* (Princeton, 1999), p. 3.

[12] Geneive Abdo, *Mecca and Main Street: Muslim Life in America after 9/11* (Oxford, 2006), p. 22.

around sexuality can become violent ones in American mosques (as in Muslim-majority regions). Considerations of "intimate citizenship" serve as a reminder that the personal, emotional, and sexual dimensions of a Muslim's life have public and often political consequences.[13] Indeed, the struggles of LGBTQ Muslims are often silent or ostracizing experiences. Similarly, national studies about Muslim Americans, such as the 2009 Gallup study, "Muslim Americans: A National Portrait," avoid discussion of homosexuality, choosing instead to focus on more acceptable topics like race and gender as traditionally understood.[14] Perhaps more progress is visible among Muslim activists who promote the Qur'an as an authoritative text that supports human diversity but does not condemn homosexuality or transgender behavior, or take a clear stance on either issue. Indeed, historian Scott Kugle and members of Al-Fatiha, the first international organization for gay Muslims, are among a growing contingent of Muslim activists who refuse the presupposition of heterosexual authority. While these Muslims acknowledge that conversations about sexualities in Islam can be complicated, they argue that such conversations are necessary to challenge patriarchy and ensure justice. Ultimately, for many American Muslims, even those who do not view homosexuality as a sexual offense, multiple sexual identities are a Western construction. Even with such insistences, promotion of gender equity may be one visible means by which American culture can contribute to the quality of life for all Muslims. As Talal Eid has observed, "As American society at large moves towards greater gender equity, opening more opportunities for women in education and employment, gender roles are shifting."[15]

American college and university campuses represent one site of shifting gender roles, if not gender equity. Here, Muslim women are as likely as American Muslim men (42 percent to 39 percent) to complete a college degree or courses beyond high school, according to the Gallup poll. Interestingly, the study also found that Muslim women are among the two most "highly educated female religious groups."[16] The road to equity is often mired in tension between traditional demands

---

[13] Scott Siraj al-Haqq Kugle, "Sexuality, Diversity, and Ethics in the Agenda of Progressive Muslims," in Omid Safi, ed., *Progressive Muslims: On Justice, Gender, and Pluralism* (Oxford, 2003), p. 181.

[14] Gallup Inc., "Muslim Americans: A National Portrait; An In-Depth Analysis of America's Most Diverse Religious Community" (Washington, D.C., 2009).

[15] Talal Youssef Eid, "Marriage, Divorce, and Child Custody as Experienced by American Muslims: Religious, Social, and Legal Considerations" (D.Th. diss., Harvard University, 2005), p. 105.

[16] "Executive Summary," in "Muslim Americans: A National Portrait," p. 11.

and cultural norms, however, especially in regards to female autonomy and mix-gendered mingling. For instance, most Muslims would insist that female college students should not live away from home in a non-Muslim environment until they are married. Even those parents who perceive college to be a fitting environment for young adults to wrestle with or engage in individual identity construction, are fearful that their daughters might be tempted to bow to physical desires or peer pressure and engage in *zina*, or premarital sex. (As with many other religious and secular communities, less attention is devoted to the sexual proclivities of sons.)

Among the ubiquitous concerns of some Muslim parents is whether the "Islam" they practice is the "Islam" to which their children will ascribe even in a context void of a visible Muslim presence – as are many academic institutions. These concerns often translate into two different but related questions: "What will happen when religious beliefs meet the campus culture where casual sex and underage drinking may be the norm?" and "What is my child experiencing that I may not know about or approve of?" Like other parents who prefer (or mandate) their children's adherence to the Islamic rule against sex before marriage, some Muslim parents discover that their children become or continue to be sexually active while in college. In search of a middle ground, these Muslims strive to send their daughters to institutions, like Brigham Young University in Provo, Utah (if anywhere), that are known for promoting strict moral values, modest dress, and abstinence before marriage. Still, on college campuses nationwide, Muslim women and men, like other religious students, face struggles to reconcile their faith and their sexual longings. Once the battle of admission has been waged and won, many Muslim students join their peers in contemplating a range of questions: "Who am I?" "What do I really believe?" "What matters to me and why?" "What if I am gay?" "How far should I go with a secret love?"

Though the "face" of Islam presented to the West is usually a female whose head is covered and is assumed to follow the dictates of her husband or male guardian, American Muslim women and men grapple with complex choices about modesty, identity, and family. Today, examining the contours of sexual identity and formation serves as a reminder that sexual identity is a social construction that constitutes one's version of reality. How American Muslims negotiate their own sexual identity can reveal the extent to which they view themselves as American *and* Muslim and how they will face the joys and responsibilities of companionship and family life associated with marriage.

MARRIAGE

The institution of marriage has assumed a number of configurations throughout American history, whereby property marriage, love marriage, arranged marriage, and other forms of commitment and intimacy were esteemed and celebrated. As in most human societies, marriage for American Muslims is a significant event of adulthood – an institution with both religious and social significance that fulfills basic individual and social needs.[17] As a public practice, marriage provides the contact through which family, the nucleus of Muslim society, comes into existence and reproduces itself. Most Muslims believe that Allah created men and women as company for one another, and so that humanity may procreate itself and live in peace and tranquillity.

Although a tradition of gender segregation is maintained on some level in mosques around the world, several of the "getting to know" practices of single Muslims in the United States mirror the dating patterns of their neighbors, including the use of intermediaries and social media; excursions to shopping malls, karaoke bars, and clubs; and (though sometimes reluctantly) the family setup. Clearly, new information and communication technology has changed the landscape of Muslim meeting and dating and social interaction. "Speed-dating" and "Muslims for Marriage" matrimonial events at national conferences, along with Internet chat rooms, Facebook, and other Web sites devoted to dating and marriage have increased since the 1990s, expanding opportunities for unmarried and never married Muslim women and men to meet and contemplate marriage. Moreover, the expanding presence of *shisha* cafés, named for the Arab water pipe, offers an alcohol-free alternative for mixed conversations. Found in thirty-eight states, shisha cafés (also referred to as *hookah* bars) are attracting attention from anti-tobacco activists who caution against characterizations of the shisha as an "Islamically viable alternative."[18]

On college campuses in the United States, Muslims also meet prospective partners as dorm neighbors or classmates; at athletic, political, or social events; and by acquiring cell phone numbers or instant message identifications from mutual friends. Understandably, debates

[17] "Vital and Health Statistics Series 23, Number 28, Marriage and Cohabitation in the United States: A Statistical Portrait Based on Cycle 6 (2002) of the National Survey of Family Growth," U.S. Department of Health and Human Services (Washington, D.C., 2010), p. 4.

[18] Hamza A. Bajwa, "Last Gurgle for the Binge-Shisha-Smokers," Islamic Awakening. Com, http://www.islamicawakening.com/viewarticle.php?articleID=1299.

about whether the "Islamic" way of courtship is truly compatible with "Western" practices, and the extent to which young (and older) Muslim adults should adhere to the traditional ways or expectations of their families are ongoing conversations for Muslims regardless of gender, culture, or economic status. Ultimately, the majority of Muslims get to know members of the opposite sex for the purpose of marriage. Many also limit mate selection to their own ethnic, cultural, or language group. While Muslim men frequently date or marry non-Muslim women, Muslim women continue to be less likely to date or marry non-Muslim men. The Islamic regulation that children follow the religion of the father and cultural prohibitions are major roadblocks that heavily restrict whom Muslim women can seek out for marriage.

As with most couples in the United States, the road to marriage for American Muslims features a proposal, a public ceremony, and a witnessed document-legitimating proceeding, though the establishment of Muslim marriage does differ from its non-Muslim counterparts as do marriage practices between and within various American Muslim communities. Moreover, in Islam, marriage is a binding, social contract, complete with obligations and observances that have spiritual and legal consequences. Most Muslims begin the process with an offer of marriage (typically extended by the male) and an agreed upon *mahr*, also referred to as a dower, or gift the prospective groom promises to his soon-to-be bride. The *mahr* can be divided into two parts: what is paid or given at the time of marriage, and what is deferred until a predetermined time or at the dissolution of the marriage by death or divorce.[19] The definition of mahr in Morocco is typical of its global understanding. There, the dower is defined as "the property given by the husband to indicate his willingness to contract marriage, to establish a family, and to lay the foundation for affection and companionship."[20] Regardless of definition, the mahr is not a bride-price to be paid to the father or guardian but rather is designed for receipt by the bride herself.[21] It is, in the most rudimentary manner, the husband's payment for sexual access to his wife. Understandably then, the exchange or promise of the marriage dower is an essential part of the legitimacy of the marriage. Nevertheless, while the mahr is considered to be one of the financial obligations related to

[19] Pascale Fournier, "Comparative Law at the Intersection of Religion and Gender," EUI Working Paper RSCAS 2009/50, European University Institute, Florence, 2009, p. 2.
[20] Jamal J. Nasir, *The Islamic Law of Personal Status*, 2nd ed. (London, 1990), p. 86.
[21] Lindsey E. Blenkhorn, "Islamic Marriage Contracts in American Courts: Interpreting *Mahr* Agreements as Prenuptials and Their Effect on Muslim Women," *Southern California Law Review* 76:1 (November 2002): 199.

marriage, whether it is paid in full or at all is often dependent upon the resources and determination of the bride and her representatives.

Typically, both mutual consent and evidence of the mahr are expressed in the marriage contract, also known as *nikah*, the Arabic term for marriage and the word generally used to refer to the marriage ceremony. To varying degrees, the contract documents the obligations and rights a prospective husband and wife possess in regard to each other in their chosen form of marriage. As Kecia Ali has observed, "Aside from the basic requirement of 'mutual good treatment,' which is not legally defined, these rights and duties are differentiated by gender. They are also interdependent: a failure by one spouse to perform a specific duty may jeopardize his or her claim to a particular right."[22]

Marriage contracts are particularly critical for women, for, with them, American Muslim women can stipulate their expectations of financial, spiritual, and physical support during the marriage, and what grounds determine its end. They can also specify the type of marriage they are willing to accept (e.g., monogamy or polygyny) and under what terms. In fact, some American imams refuse to certify marriages that involve polygyny – union between a husband and a second, third, or fourth wife – or require couples to commit to monogamy only.[23] Like other legal documents, the Muslim marriage agreement requires the making and acceptance of an offer in the presence of witnesses. Although the marriage contract is designed to help women assert their rights under religious law, its enforcement in American courts has been inconsistent – perhaps, due, in part, to Christian underpinnings of American law that lead some judges to mistake the Islamic contract for a prenuptial agreement because of the promises the spouses make. The length of a nikah varies from a single paragraph to multiple pages. Most Muslim couples design their own, preferring to articulate and sometimes publicize their personal expectations, responsibilities, and dreams. A relatively few American Muslims, including some who legalize their unions by obtaining a marriage license, choose either to adopt a "fill-in the-blank" standard contract or to forego this aspect of the road to marriage. To the

[22] Kecia Ali, "Special Focus: Islam, Marriage Contracts in Islamic Jurisprudence," The Feminist Sexual Ethics Project, http://www.brandeis.edu/projects/fse/Pages/marriage-contracts.html.
[23] The term *imam* refers to the one who leads the congregation in prayer. Consistent with many other religious leaders in the United States, imams provide other services to their congregations, such as premarital counseling, family mediation, grief support, and burial services. I distinguish between Muslim polygyny and other forms of multiple marriage for men, whereby they are able to marry any woman and as many women as they desire.

latter group, the contract symbolizes the "religious" nature of the process that they prefer not to acknowledge. Still, most imams strongly encourage couples to register their marriages with civic authorities. Some American imams require premarital counseling and refuse to perform marriages without a license or in cases of polygyny.

The nikah as wedding ceremony can and often does occur in homes, mosques, and other locations and can be witnessed by Muslims and non-Muslims. The ceremony is often followed by a reception, whose location is dictated by cultural preferences and financial resources. (Regardless, the reception can last well into the night and cost tens of thousands of dollars.) The ceremony usually includes a sermon in the language of the couple (but with an introduction in Arabic), reading and reflection upon passages from the Qur'an, and the exchange of vows. The number and gender of required witnesses depends upon the school of law to which the couple ascribes, as do the context, possible gender segregation, and the extent to which Western marriage practices (e.g., bride's maids, wedding bouquets, traditional wedding gowns) are interspersed with Islamic practices. While they are still a rarity, a few Muslim American women have, in the words of Kecia Ali, "acted on a frontier" by officiating at Muslim weddings. Perhaps the first American Muslim to publicly administer vows when she officiated at a nikah in 2004, Ali is quick to point out that the imam's role in a Muslim wedding is similar to the official's role in the Jewish ritual – ceremonial. Indeed, unless the officiant is licensed to conduct a wedding, the couple may also have a civil servant or an authorized individual present at their nikah to sign their license, certifying that the marriage is in accordance with U.S. civil law. Some Muslims do, however, forgo governmental interference into their private affairs and do not register their unions. In such cases, these couples may face a legal quagmire if their marriage ends or they separate.[24]

Like many other Americans, the sexual lives of Muslim couples are considered private affairs. Culture, age, and education often influence the extent to which husbands and wives share any aspect of their physical, spiritual, or emotional concerns. Additionally, the prohibition of dating that continues with some American Muslims, whereby a prospective couple spends little if any time alone, occasionally places couples in the position to share intimate details in the presence of trusted

---

[24] Julie Macfarlane, "Understanding Trends in American Muslim Divorce and Marriage: A Discussion Guide for Families and Communities," Institute for Social Policy and Understanding (Washington, D.C., 2012), p. 12.

relatives or friends. When considering when or how to start a family, for example, some American Muslim wives refuse to use contraceptives, believing instead that every birth is a "contribution" to the *ummah*, or body of believers. Sometimes they are encouraged or forced to bear children by husbands or families that view children as evidence of prosperity or as future labor in family businesses. Muslim women and men with reproductive or sexual dysfunctions are expected to be upfront with that information before marriage, particularly if they are in conversation with prospective husbands or wives who are not yet parents and want to be. The emphasis on marriage and family in Islam makes discussions about children a routine topic for most Muslim couples. Even those who are "childless by choice" routinely confront internal and or external expectations to build the ummah and raise future Muslims.[25] Equally significant for some American Muslims is the expectation that they remain open to ways of organizing households that go beyond heterosexual monogamy.

When American Muslims contemplate establishing a household, most choose the one-man, one-woman tradition in overwhelming numbers.[26] Yet some Muslims initiate, welcome, or acquiesce to other family forms, such as unions with a fixed time limit or those with multiple wives. *Mut'ah*, or temporary marriage, is socially accepted among some Muslims but far less practiced than polygyny. Sunni scholars equate mut'ah with "pleasure marriages" or prostitution; Shi'a leaders consider the bond "religiously legal." While the agreed upon timeframe for mut'ah is fixed, it can be set for as brief as one hour to as long as ten years. Couples in these unions typically agree not to have children, and if a wife becomes pregnant, abortion may be an option. As is common with monogamy and polygyny, the bride's dower is stipulated for a mut'ah. Still, in all three forms of marriage, abuses occur, often victimizing women and children the most.

The American polygynist population is estimated to be between 30,000 and 100,000, but how and whom experts count is unclear.[27] Still,

---

[25] Laura S. Scott turned the "Childless by Choice Project" into *Two Is Enough: A Couple's Guide to Living Childless by Choice*, http://www.childlessbychoiceproject. com/Childless_by_choice_book.html.

[26] Ihsan Bagby, Paul M. Perl, and Bryan T. Froehle, "The Mosque in America: A National Portrait; A Report from the Mosque Study Project," Council on American-Islamic Relations (Washington, D.C., 2001).

[27] In contrast to self-identified "fundamentalist Mormons," many Muslim women whose husbands are married to multiple wives do not characterize themselves as polygynists. Rather, they say they are monogamously married and that only their husbands practice polygyny. A Georgetown Law professor and NPR limit the size of the American

visible promoters of polygyny tend to be "religious and conservative."[28] In addition to self-identified former Mormons, they include evangelical Christians and Muslims. While U.S. prosecution of polygyny is rare, formal allegations of criminal activity, such as child abuse in multiparty families, has led to increased attention by law enforcement officials.[29] While Muslims have appeared in U.S. courts since the 1970s, few court cases have involved polygyny, which has been illegal since the late 1800s, when Utah joined the Union. For the small minority of Muslims in America who choose polygyny, the religious law supersedes the civil.

In seventh-century Arabia's patriarchal, misogynistic society, the physical survival of women often necessitated depending upon provision from the men in their lives, through whom women also negotiated their legitimacy and social honor. Women displaced by war without a husband or male relative, for instance, were suddenly on their own in a society that confused value with material wealth. Widows also were undervalued in a male-privileging society that not long before murdered female infants at birth. Within this environment, the Prophet received the revelation of the Qur'anic verse Al-Nisa 4:3. A popular English translation of this verse directs its male listeners as follows: "If you fear that you shall not be able to deal justly with the orphans, Marry women of your choice, Two or three or four; but if you fear that you shall not be able to deal justly (with them), then only one, or (a captive) that your right hands possess, that will be more suitable, to prevent you from doing injustice."

This verse and its companion, 4:129, which stipulates that even men with the best of intentions remain unable to treat multiple wives fairly, attempt to address an inequity concerning the rights and maintenance of women and children, and the existing customary practice that both became the property of men when they married in pre-Islamic Arabia.[30]

polygynist population to 50,000. See Jonathan Turley, "Polygamy Laws Expose Our Own Hypocrisy," *USA Today*, October 4, 2004, and "Polygamy in America," NPR, February 10, 2010. More than a decade earlier, historian Mildren M. El-Amin estimated the population to be as high as 100,000. See *Family Roots: The Qur'anic View of Family Life* (Chicago, 1991), p. xiii.

[28] Michael G. Myers, "Polygamist Eye for the Monogamist Guy: Homosexual Sodomy ... Gay Marriage ... Is Polygamy Next?" *Houston Law Review* 42:5 (Spring 2006): 1451–1487; Elise Soukup, "Polygamists, Unite! They Used to Live Quietly, but Now They're Making Noise," *Newsweek*, March 29, 2006.

[29] For example, Tom Green was convicted in Utah in 2001 on four counts of bigamy, and in 2002 of child rape. In 2007 Warren Jeffs was convicted of two counts of first-degree felony rape. The Utah Supreme Court overturned his conviction three years later.

[30] See, for example, John L. Esposito, *Women in Muslim Family Law*, 2nd ed. (Syracuse, 2001), p. 12. Roger Mitton, "The Polygamy Debate: Many Women Are Saying That One Is Enough," *Asiaweek*, December 20, 1996, p. 24.

Thus, the revelation of the Qur'an did not accompany the introduction of polygyny, but with it, one form of plural marriage was regulated and restricted.[31] While examinations of Islamic legal materials routinely promote these verses as a divinely inspired reform in Arab history that served to repudiate one expression of patriarchy and protect women and children from abuse and destitution, no consensus exists about how, where, or when Al-Nisa's instructions should be invoked today. Indeed, opponents of polygyny routinely protest against attempts to subvert civil laws, while declaring that "the love between a husband and wife should not be divided."[32] They make the additional argument that polygyny is inherently unjust to secondary wives because their unions cannot be recognized in a society that does not adhere to Islamic law. In contrast, proponents of polygyny hold that the U.S. prohibition against plural marriage violates their religious freedom and should be set aside in favor of what they believe to be divine law. Indeed, both supporters and opponents of the practice within American Muslim communities defend their positions with divergent interpretations of these verses. Even so, both sides agree that the Qur'an addresses a personal or family matter that should be adjudicated in a way that privileges the Islamic legal position on marriage, a union in which members are garments of one another and possess ontological equality.

Most American Muslim women living in polygynous households have accepted communal interpretations that, at best, give men *permission* to take up to four wives and, at worst, confirm the *right* of men to do so. Others intentionally choose polygyny because they prefer to maintain independent lifestyles while also reaping the benefits of the status afforded to married women. Nevertheless, the extent to which American Muslim women consciously agree to polygyny is a complex issue. To concede or to consent to sharing one's husband suggests that a Muslim woman exerts agency freely, that, at least in her mind, she knowingly has a choice. The question is whether a Muslim woman married to a polygynous man possesses what Saba Mahmood calls "positive freedom," or the ability to form her actions by her own will."[33] Most often the answer depends upon the woman and whether she has been socialized to encounter the Qur'an as a living document that speaks

---

[31] As Jamal Badawi and others persuasively argue, associating polygyny with Islam continues to be a feature of the Western mythology of the Islamic religion and practice. See J. Badawi, *Gender Equity in Islam: Basic Principles* (Indianapolis, 1995).

[32] Mitton, "The Polygamy Debate," p. 24.

[33] Saba Mahmood, *Politics of Piety: The Islamic Revival and the Feminist Subject* (Princeton, 2005), p. 11.

to the individual, and in the context of justice. Equally significant are Muslim women's perceptions of polygyny as a response to "domestic terrorism" that links them to their first-generation Muslim ancestors.

FAMILY LIFE

The family unit is the single most recognized entity in Islam, based on blood relationships or affinity.[34] After the nikah ceremony, the American Muslim husband and wife establish a home and life together and, in most cases, agree to raise children. Thus, the family continues to serve as "an organizing system for both social and legal regimes."[35] Through the years and across the nation, Muslims in America have worked diligently to foster family values rooted in Islamic law and applicable within a secular context. According to a religious leader in Iowa, "Family is one of the biggest challenges. We are in a melting pot, but we don't want our identity to melt."[36] Fostering a Muslim identity has not been easy, especially within a culture that tends to privilege individuality, rather than communal responsibility. As one reporter noted,

> Both liberal and conservative Muslims offer a family vision that sometimes seems like an Islamic Norman Rockwell painting. Muslims see family in ways similar to orthodox Jews or evangelical Christians. They set themselves against the sirens of popular culture.[37]

Nevertheless, like just about any aspect of life for the estimated six to seven million American Muslims, from identity construction to marriage processes, family life is not monolithic. Influences, such as culture, education, age, gender, country of origin and its relationship with the West, economic class, and life in America help determine the family dynamics of American Muslims. Many view their households and mosques as safe spaces for developing and protecting the well-being of children. However, unhealthy relationships between children and parents do occur, often as a result of differing cultural expectations, mental health issues, or the

---

[34] Hunt Janin and Andre Kahlmeyer, *Islamic Law: The Shari'ah from Muhammad's Time to the Present* (Jefferson, N.C., 2007), p. 37.

[35] Asifa Quraishi and Najeeba Syeed-Miller, "No Altars: A Survey of Islamic Family Law in the United States: Introduction," in Lynn Welchman, ed., *Women's Rights and Islamic Family Law: Reflections on Reform* (London, 2004), p. 179.

[36] Jamal Tibi as quoted in Robert Marquand and Lamis Andoni, "Islamic Family Values Simmer in a U.S. Melting Pot," *Christian Science Monitor* 88:43 (1996).

[37] Marquand and Andoni, "Islamic Family Values Simmer in a U.S. Melting Pot."

parents' experience as child abuse victims or with the "trauma of intimate partner violence."[38]

The rate of divorce among American Muslims has risen sharply
since 1987, and women often find themselves entering a new marriage
with children from former unions and then adopting or caring for the
children of their new husband or agreeing to have children with him.[39]
These combined families contribute to findings by the Pew Research
Center that Muslims and Mormons have the largest households. In fact,
15 percent of Muslims are raising three or more children in their households, and 5 percent have five or more children living at home, according
to the Pew survey.[40] In contrast, divorce or the need for family mediation
follows incidents of intimate partner violence in some Muslim households or disagreements about children and finances. Another major conflict issue involves the role of women within public and private spheres.
Typically, according to the MacFarlane report on divorce from 2012,
couples struggle more often when the wife desires a college education
and a career and the husband prefers her to focus exclusively on creating a happy home life.[41] In a related study, Dena Hassouneh-Phillips
has demonstrated the influence of spirituality on the abuse experiences
of American Muslim women, drawing particular attention to manipula-
tions of religious texts as a source of vulnerability and the rejection of
patriarchal ideology as a tool of empowerment.[42]

Clearly, not all Muslims believe wives should remain within the
home and under the authority of their husbands, or that husbands are
the primary decision makers and sole providers. Similarly, religiously
observant family life may or may not involve raising children, particularly in the case of same-sex couples for whom parenting options may be
limited. Organizations like Karamah, the Washington, D.C., legal outreach and resource center, and Women's Islamic Initiative in Spirituality
and Equality (WISE), a New York–based global social network, strive to
educate Muslim communities through the empowerment of women
and girls and work diligently to support Muslims to live healthy and
secure lives in America. Marriage and family education and support

[38] Dena Hassouneh-Phillips, "Strength and Vulnerability: Spirituality in Abused American
Muslim Women's Lives," *Issues in Mental Health Nursing* 24 (2003): 681–694.
[39] Macfarlane, "Understanding Trends in American Muslim Divorce and Marriage," p. 5.
[40] *U.S. Religious Landscape Survey*, Pew Research Center's Forum on Religion and
Public Life, January 29, 2009, http://pewforum.org/Income-Distribution-Within-U.S.
-Religious-Groups.aspx.
[41] Macfarlane, "Understanding Trends in American Muslim Divorce and Marriage."
[42] Hassouneh-Phillips, "Strength and Vulnerability," pp. 688, 692.

also are evident in the activities of numerous mosques and through the teaching and scholarship of male and female Muslim scholars. For example, Atlanta Mosque of Al Islam in Georgia, Masjidul Waritheen in Oakland, California, the Islamic Circle of North America (ICNA), and The Muslim Alliance in North America (MANA) are among the varied mosques and organizations that support healthy American Muslim families. Similarly, when Zaid Shakir and Hamzu Yusuf cofounded Zaytuna College in 2009, they designed the curriculum for the first Islamic institution of higher education to include courses on marriage, divorce, and family life.

CONCLUSION

By 2007, two of three Muslims in the United States were immigrants, coming from more than eighty nations.[43] They joined American-born Muslims, largely African Americans, to form one of the most diverse religious communities. Because of the efforts of members of this ummah and their ancestors, Islam is an American religion today. While male and female Muslims share values, beliefs, and practices in common, they also differ on how these considerations reflect what it means to be a "good Muslim," and how best to represent their individual and collectives selves within a secular environment and among neighbors who still fear them. The increasing number of failed marriages, the struggles that young adults face as they strive, sometimes unsuccessfully, to maintain their morality on college campuses dominated by the culture of casual sex, restrictions governing sexuality and gender that oppress rather than empower, and the sexist paradigms that confine and marginalize women are challenges that twenty-first-century American Muslims continue to confront. Debate continues regarding who and what hold the power to define Islam, and in regard to secular and religious ideas about liberation and identity. Acknowledging such challenges is not a call for despair. It does afford an opportunity to examine the assumptions and interpretations upon which Muslims attempt to regulate and celebrate their lived realities. "We see messaging around us about being Muslim that is not open to fact, but opinion," remarked Rubina Ismail, from Southern California. "We have that double-edged kind of challenge."[44] How they

---

[43] Yvonne Y. Haddad and Jane I. Smith, "Introduction: The Challenge of Islamic Education in North America," in Yvonne Y. Haddad, Farid Senzai, and Jane I. Smith, eds., *Educating the Muslims of America* (Oxford, 2009), p. 5.

[44] Rubina Ismail and her daughter participated in the "Free to Be Me: Empowering Women and Girls," a WISE seminar for female Muslims that confronted key issues:

reconcile the three intersecting markers of divine submission – sexual identity, marriage, and family life – will help determine the future they bequeath to subsequent generations.

Further Reading

Ali, Kecia, *Sexual Ethics and Islam: Feminist Reflections on Qur'an, Hadith and Jurisprudence* (Oxford, 2006).

Hoodfar, Huma, Sajjad Alvi, and Sheila McDonough, eds., *The Muslim Veil in North America: Issues and Debates* (Toronto, 2003).

Karim, Jamillah, *American Muslim Women: Negotiating Race, Class and Gender within the Ummah* (New York, 2008).

Mattu, Ayesha, and Nura Maznavi, eds., *Love, InshAllah: The Secret Love Lives of American Muslim Women* (Berkeley, 2012).

Rouse, Carolyn Moxley, *Engaged Surrender: African American Women and Islam* (Berkeley, 2004).

Safi, Omid, ed., *Progressive Muslims: On Justice, Gender, and Pluralism* (Oxford, 2003).

Tipton, Steven M., and John Witte Jr., *Family Transformed: Religion, Values and Society in American Life* (Washington, D.C., 2005).

self-esteem, media literacy, and health and wellness. "Making a Difference: Muslim Women Dispel Stereotypes," MSNBC, May 19, 2011.

19 Studying American Muslim Women: Gender, Feminism, and Islam

JULIANE HAMMER

Eminent feminist theorist and historian Joan Scott raised a series of questions in the introduction to a 2007 volume called *Women's Studies on the Edge*, in which she and other contributors to the volume were debating the past, present, and future of women's studies as part of institutions comprising the American academy:

> What does it mean to make "women" the object of our studies? What are the exclusions performed by insisting on a homogeneous category of "women?" When inclusion is the aim, are there alternatives to the endless proliferation of specific (racial, ethnic, religious, geographic, national, sexual, class) identities? Is there such a thing as feminist theory or feminist methodology? What counts as emancipation and for whom?[1]

The concerns expressed evolved around the inscription of "women" and "gender" as exclusive and dominant categories, the emergence of "feminist fundamentalism," and the shifts of power dynamics involved in defining the "orthodoxy" of feminist thought and politics.

This debate about women and gender as categories of inquiry is significant to this volume because of the complex ways in which Muslim women (mostly as objects of study and reflection) have been part of the conversation for several decades. While many of the chapters in this volume address women as well as questions of gender dynamics as integral to the description and analysis of their given topic, for much of its short history, the still-emerging field of American Muslim studies (spread between a range of academic disciplines and not always recognized as a field at all) has separated the study of women from other topics, primarily by maintaining a focus on Muslim men as normative, thus treating Muslim women as an exception to that norm. Once Muslim

---

[1] Joan Scott, "Introduction: Feminism's Critical Edge," in Joan Scott, ed., *Women's Studies on the Edge* (Durham, 2008), pp. 1–13; pp. 7–8 for quotation.

women became a topic of academic (and political) interest, there was no shortage of scholars and journalists willing to produce study after study of Muslim women's lives, discourses about Muslim women, and other related questions.

There are indeed a significant number of academic studies of American Muslim women. After all, the focus on (if not obsession with) Muslim women, is only second to the enduring fascination of American academics and journalists with Islam's assumed propensity to violence, religious extremism, and their uses for political purposes. It could even be argued that the construction of the inherently violent nature of Muslim men in the past and present is perfectly paired with their oppression of Muslim women. Not surprisingly then, the academic study of Muslim women in various parts of the world has gone through several stages that chronologically line up with parallel political developments and, equally important, with stages in feminist theory and practice. One could even start a historical timeline of such works with descriptions of Muslim women's lives penned by European women travelers dating back to early European colonialism, or with the reflections of male travelers and European musings on and fascination with harem life and secluded Muslim women. Such works set the stage for many later representations of Muslim women and, more importantly, provided ideological support for an unholy marriage of colonialism and European feminism by coding the oppression of Muslim women as an important reason for the civilizing mission brought to Muslim societies by European colonial powers.[2] Studies from the mid-twentieth century onward often focused on concerns with Muslim women's poor social status and its religious sources, that is, Islam. The 1980s, in part through the emergence of Muslim women scholars as voices in the academic study of Islam, saw not only the development of works that located within Islam an egalitarian impulse thwarted by the pressures of its patriarchal contexts but also arguments for the positive value of gender-separated spaces in Muslim societies, which created specifically feminine spheres and life experiences. The 1990s witnessed studies of the Qur'an by women scholars claiming an unimpeachable basis for women's rights, holding up the Qur'anic ideal of equality as a standard by which to judge social realities.[3] More recently, scholars have sought to complicate the view

[2] See Leila Ahmed, *Women and Gender in Islam* (New Haven, 1992), pp. 127–168; and Charlotte Weber, "Unveiling Scheherazade: Feminist Orientalism in the International Alliance of Women, 1911–1950," *Feminist Studies* 27:1 (Spring 2001): 125–157.

[3] For the most prominent example, see Amina Wadud, *Qur'an and Woman: Rereading the Sacred Text from a Woman's Perspective* (New York, 1999).

of Muslim women's unrelenting oppression and have worked instead to recover evidence of past and present female resistance and agency, including studies of how Muslim women are carving out spheres of interpretive autonomy and are successfully negotiating their public and private lives within the constraints of broader social structures.

In a less chronological fashion, works on Muslim women and gender in Islam can also be divided, with somewhat blurry lines, into three categories: studies of Muslim women's lives and experiences, studies of discourses on women and gender in Muslim societies, and exegetical works engaging with Qur'an, sunnah, and Islamic law. The last category is most obviously the domain of Muslim scholars (female and male), while the first two have been carried out by scholars with various secular and religious identities.

The study of American Muslim women in many ways follows these patterns and aligns well with the politics and dynamics described in the quotation from Joan Scott. In this chapter, I want to offer some reflections on these dynamics and the state of the study of American Muslim women in the first part, and a featured focus on American Muslim women as scholars in the American academy as a case study for thinking further about the dynamics of activism, feminism, and the secular academy in the second. In the first part I advance the argument that the study of gender dynamics, after having focused mostly on women as a category of inquiry and as an object of study needs to move beyond such binary gendered focus to the integration of gender as a category of inquiry in all areas of the study of American Muslims. The second part of the chapter aims to link Muslim women's scholarly contribution to the American academy with constantly negotiated questions of secularism, feminism, and the possibility of interweaving scholarship and activism.

TAKING STOCK: STUDYING AMERICAN MUSLIM WOMEN

Are women equally represented in studies of American Muslims? The short answer is no; however, two conceptual problems appear in this attempt to review the existing field of American Muslim studies in search of Muslim women. The first is somewhat of a conundrum: when looking at how American Muslim women have been studied, we are much more likely to come across works that have focused on women and their experiences, histories, and lives than we are to find other approaches to incorporating gender into the analysis of the past and present of American Muslims. In other words, the women we are concerned with may be much less visible in works that do not loudly proclaim to be studies of Muslim women. The second is a now standard acknowledgment that women as part of what has been termed the "subaltern" have been marginalized if not entirely ignored in historiographic research as well as in historical sources and documents because of a direct link between power and the ability to "write" history. This dynamic is certainly at work in the scarcity of information about female Muslim slaves during the era of the American slave trade and into the twentieth century, most prominently in studies of African American Muslim groups and organization. However, it must also be acknowledged that most of the early Muslim immigrants to the United States (in the late nineteenth and early twentieth centuries) were men; thus women's history would have played a smaller part in this period.

Curiously, some of the earliest available studies focusing on women did so through discussions of family. While it could certainly be argued that a focus on marriage practice, family models, and traditions suggests a rather standard reduction of women to particular societal spheres and a deterministic approach to women's roles in society, it may also be argued that a gendered approach to issues of marriage and family represents an early attempt to integrate reflections on gender with the study of women and men in their societal interactions. Examples such as *Muslim Families in North America*[4] and *Family and Gender among American Muslims: Issues Facing Middle Eastern Immigrants and Their Descendants*[5] provided important insights into gendered interactions and the negotiation of practices and traditions that are formative for gender relations in American Muslim communities. It is noteworthy, that the first volume contained one essay on African American families,[6] while the second, in its title and scope, focused on immigrant Muslims of Middle Eastern origin. Both volumes contain essays that delineate community structures along ethnic lines and reflect an insistence on differences between those communities rather than their interconnectedness. One can only speculate as to why this line of inquiry, focusing on gendered interaction but not exclusively women, all but disappeared from research on American Muslims. One possible explanation is the aforementioned insistence on studying women qua women – in order

---

[4] Earle H. Waugh, Sharon McIrvin Abu-Laban, and Regula Burckhardt Qureshi, eds. (Edmonton, 1991).

[5] Barbara Aswad and Barbara Bilge, eds. (Philadelphia, 1996).

[6] Na'im Akbar, "Family Stability among African-American Muslims," in Earle H. Waugh, Sharon McIrvin Abu-Laban, and Regula Burckhardt Qureshi, eds., *Muslim Families in North America* (Edmonton, 1991), pp. 213–231.

to develop and apply certain lines of feminist inquiry, and to carve out spaces for the study of a historically understudied and underrepresented group in society.

As a result, works appeared in the later 1990s, increasing in number after 2001, which focused on American Muslim women. They include Carolyn Rouse's *Engaged Surrender*, a study of African American Muslim women in a community in Los Angeles; *Aversion and Desire: Negotiating Muslim Female Identity in the Diaspora*, a study of Muslim women immigrants in Canada by Shahnaz Khan; and *Muslim Women in America: The Challenge of Islamic Identity Today*, a volume coauthored by three of the preeminent scholars in the study of American Muslims, Yvonne Haddad, Jane Smith, and Kathleen Moore.[7] Notably, chapters or entire sections on women can be found in several earlier volumes edited by Haddad and/or Smith.[8] Jane Smith's introduction to *Islam in America* (1999 and 2010) in both editions also contains a chapter on Muslim women.[9] Volumes such as *The Muslim Veil in North America*,[10] by virtue of their topic, also focused on Muslim women. The only study to concentrate on the aforementioned division between "immigrant" and African American Muslim women by making their interactions the focal point of the research is Jamillah Karim's *American Muslim Women: Negotiating Race, Class, and Gender within the Ummah*.[11]

Karen Leonard has argued that negotiations of Muslim identity in America, as well as discussions of the distinction between religion and culture, have often taken place through negotiation of gender norms and women's roles in society.[12] This assessment echoes the link between colonialism and feminism in that the "moderness" of colonized and postcolonial Muslims was often assessed through their discourses and practices regarding women in their societies. However, it ascribes a much larger degree of agency to Muslims, in this case American Muslims, in determining how women's roles and rights can and should figure into

---

[7] Carolyn Rouse (Berkeley, 2004); Shahnaz Khan (Toronto, 2002); Yvonne Haddad, Jane Smith, and Kathleen Moore (New York, 2006).

[8] For example, Y. Haddad, ed., *The Muslims of America* (New York, 1991); Y. Haddad and J. Smith, eds., *Muslim Communities in North America* (Albany, 1994); Y. Haddad and J. Esposito, eds., *Muslims on the Americanization Path?* (Oxford, 2000).

[9] Jane Smith (New York, 1999 and 2010).

[10] Sajida Sultana Alvi, Homa Hoodfar, and Sheila McDonough, *The Muslim Veil in North America: Issues and Debates* (Toronto, 2003).

[11] Jamillah Karim, *American Muslim Women: Negotiating Race, Class, and Gender within the Ummah* (New York, 2009).

[12] Karen Leonard, *Muslims in the United States: The State of Research* (New York, 2003), pp. 92–99.

debates about American Muslim identities and community practices. It is in this context of negotiating gender norms that we have to look harder for "women" and "men" in order to adequately assess the status of Muslim women's studies.

However, the area of discursive gender debates is also the arena in which Muslim women scholars made their entrance from the 1980s onward. Described as Muslim feminists, Muslim feminist theologians, and Islamic feminists, by others and in their own works, they have negotiated their gender reform agendas, their presence in the secular American academy, and their identification with American feminist projects and discourses.

SETTING THE STAGE: WOMEN APPROACH SACRED TEXTS

In the more than fourteen hundred years of Muslim history, there is evidence of the work and significance of women as scholars in a variety of Islamic sciences, including the production of Qur'anic commentary or *tafsir*. However, only fragments of their works survive, and it is clear from the sources that women were a minority among Qur'anic scholars and often their voices (such as the ubiquitously cited Rabi'a) are heard through male interlocutors. Women scholars engaged in reinterpretations of sacred Islamic texts, most notable the Qur'an, appear on the historical stage of modernity in the early twentieth century, often preceded by male Muslim reformist thinkers who, through colonialism, contact with modernist ideas, and profound changes in their societies since the European enlightenment included new ideas about gender roles and women's rights into their discourses and treatises. For them, methods and strategies for reinterpreting the Qur'an in a manner consistent with the demands of modernity was perhaps the most important path to keeping Islam relevant for Muslims.

The 1960s and 1970s also saw the arrival of Muslim students and later intellectuals and scholars to America, some of whom would become important trailblazers for the development of American Muslim thought. Of the three giants of that first generation, Seyyed Hossein Nasr (from Iran, b. 1933), Ismail al-Faruqi (from Palestine, d. 1986), and Fazlur Rahman (from Pakistan, d. 1988), it was Rahman who would provide Muslim women scholars with the hermeneutical tools to carry out their gendered reinterpretations of the Qur'an.

It was at the crossroads of postcolonial and nation-state developments, Muslim reformist thought, and American feminist theory and practice that the mother generation of American Muslim women scholars emerged. First to publish among them were Riffat Hassan and Azizah al-Hibri. Hassan moved from Pakistan to the United States in 1972 and started her work as a Muslim feminist theologian shortly thereafter. She has focused her approach to the Qur'an on her insistence that it provides the blueprint for human rights as women's rights and has argued that it is misguided male interpretation in Muslim history and in the present that have deprived Muslim women of their God-given rights.[13] Azizah al-Hibri, born and raised in Lebanon, has focused her work on reinterpreting Islamic Law based on the Qur'an by arguing, in a parallel manner, that patriarchal interpretations and legal rulings have prevented Muslim women from reaching their full rights and dignity as mandated by the Qur'an. In 1993 al-Hibri founded Karamah, Muslim Women Lawyers for Human Rights, a nonprofit organization concerned with worldwide and domestic activism for Muslim women's rights.[14] Both Hassan and al-Hibri were working closely with American Jewish and Christian feminists, drawing on shared experiences and similar approaches to historical and textual rethinking of their respective traditions.

The 1990s saw the emergence of a second generation of Muslim women thinkers, foremost among them Amina Wadud. A child of the civil rights movement, who converted to Islam at age seventeen, Wadud went on to earn a Ph.D. in Islamic studies and became a professor of Islamic studies at Virginia Commonwealth University in Richmond, Virginia. Her first book, based on her dissertation and completed while she was teaching in Malaysia, was titled *Qur'an and Woman: Rereading the Sacred Text from a Woman's Perspective*. It was first published in Malaysia (1992) and appeared on the U.S. market in 1999, published by Oxford University Press. Wadud had a strong connection to gender activism, most notably in her affiliation with Sisters in Islam, a Malaysian women's rights organization, and through an international network of women activists. Around the same time, two other women scholars, Asma Barlas and Nimat Barazangi, offered important contributions to American Muslim thought with a focus on gender justice and equality. Barlas, from Pakistan, was teaching political science at Ithaca College,

---

[13] See, for example, Riffat Hassan, "The Issue of Woman-Man Equality in the Islamic Tradition," in Leonard Grob, Riffat Hassan, and Haim Gordon, eds., *Women's and Men's Liberation: Testimonies of Spirit* (New York, 1991), pp. 65–82.

[14] See Azizah Al-Hibri, "Azizah Al-Hibri – Founder; Karamah (Muslim Women Lawyers for Human Rights)," in Anne Braude, ed., *Transforming the Faiths of Our Fathers: Women Who Changed American Religion* (New York, 2004), pp. 47–54; and www.karamah.org.

when she wrote an oft-quoted work that intertwined feminist theory with Qur'anic hermeneutics. Barlas, similar to Wadud, reread the Qur'an from a gendered perspective and offered revisionist commentary on passages that in her view have historically been used to oppress Muslim women.[15] Nimat Barazangi, originally from Syria, argued that Muslim women could gain their equal rights only if they became educated on the sacred grounding of such rights in the Qur'an and sunnah. Her plea for Islamic higher learning for women linked the exercising of God's will in human society to women's education and access to exegesis on their own terms.[16]

An emerging young generation of Muslim women scholars is notable both in their increasing numbers and in the fact that many if not most of the women in this generation are American born, thus reflecting shifts in demographics and patterns of American Muslim community building. The most important scholar of this generation to date is Kecia Ali, professor of Islamic studies at Boston University and the author of the ground-breaking *Sexual Ethics and Islam* (2006), which refocused hermeneutical debates on the significance of rethinking Islamic Law while directly addressing the North American context in order to think of gender justice and equality in direct connection with sexual ethics.[17]

From the 1980s to the mid-2000s American Muslim women scholars cannot be described as an American Muslim women's "movement," as most of them have worked on their own rather than in direct cooperation. However, some, including Amina Wadud and Kecia Ali, were part of a larger progressive reform movement with distinct American characteristics. Documented by the publication of *Progressive Muslims: On Justice, Gender, and Pluralism* in 2003 and edited by Omid Safi, self-described Muslim progressive thinkers and scholars offered their contributions to rethinking Islamic notions of justice, the significance of gender for any kind of justice, and the role of pluralist ideas in Muslim thought and practice. Thus, here and elsewhere, Muslim women scholars contributed their thought and simultaneously shaped broader Muslim reform projects in tandem with their male counterparts, rather than in a gendered and thus feminine vacuum. Or, to put it differently, American Muslim women scholars have both influenced the thought of

15 Asma Barlas, *"Believing Women" in Islam: Unreading Patriarchal Interpretations of the Qur'an* (Austin, 2002).
16 Nimat Barazangi, *Women's Identity and the Qur'an: A New Reading* (Gainesville, 2004).
17 Kecia Ali, *Sexual Ethics and Islam: Feminist Reflections on Qur'an, Hadith, and Jurisprudence* (Oxford, 2006).

male Muslim intellectuals and been influenced by their ideas and her-meneutical methods.

In terms of content and despite many differences in nuance, emphasis, and priorities, Muslim women scholars' exegetical projects have in common a focus on gender and notions of gender justice and equality within a framework of human equality. This can take the form of arguing for women's rights as human rights, claiming that human equality is the only way to acknowledge and honor God's omnipotence (Wadud's tawhidic paradigm),[18] criticizing patriarchy as *shirk* (to asso-ciate anything with the level of God, which violates absolute mono-theism),[19] and distinguishing between Islam as gender-just and Muslim societies in the past and present as misinterpretations of that ideal. All the Muslim women scholars discussed in this chapter have focused their reform projects on the reinterpretation of sacred texts, most importantly the Qur'an.

They employ and share hermeneutical methods, which they bring together with their own values of gender justice and equality, namely:

1. A thematic approach to the Qur'an
2. Arguments for a historical-critical approach to the text
3. The idea of the necessity of a "conscientious pause"

All three of these exegetical moves can be found in other modern (or modernist) interpretations of the Qur'an, and even attention to gender issues is not limited to the scholars discussed here. In their thematic approach to the Qur'an as well as in their argument for the historical contextualization of the Qur'an as text, the women scholars follow in the footsteps of Fazlur Rahman, who developed what he called the "double movement" in approaching the Qur'anic text,[20] which involved first recognizing the historical context of the revelation of the Qur'an (seventh-century Arabian society) and then deducing how that histori-cally contextualized revelation could and should be applied to contem-porary circumstances.

A thematic approach to the Qur'an abandons the more traditional verse by verse interpretation of the text in favor of thematic readings of collected passages that evidently address the same topics. It also often

[18] See Amina Wadud, *Inside the Gender Jihad* (Oxford, 2006).
[19] See Barlas, *"Believing Women" in Islam.*
[20] Fazlur Rahman, *Islam and Modernity: Transformation of an Intellectual Tradition* (Chicago, 1982), p. 7.

involves a search for the spirit of the text over the letter and thus a renewed search for God's will as expressed in the text.

The third exegetical move of many of the women scholars, especially prominent in the work of Amina Wadud, draws on Khaled Abou El Fadl's use of the term "conscientious pause." Abou El Fadl defines the necessity of this "pause" as caused by a conflict between principles of one's faith and textual evidence.[21]

Here, Abou El Fadl not only offers an approach to the Qur'anic text that allows any Muslim to object to Qur'anic injunctions under certain circumstances but, through the idea of a conscientious pause, also implies that the Qur'an does not carry absolute authority and is not the only source of religious and moral conviction, because the text needs to be interpreted in order to be understood and applied to Muslim lives and practices. Muslim women scholars have also pointed out that by definition all tafsir is a product of the backgrounds, values, and circumstances of the respective exegetes and their times.[22] Thus, the exegetical projects of American Muslim women scholars may employ new methods for their approaches to the Qur'anic text and bring different sensibilities, values, and even analytical categories to the text, but they are as much products of their own times and circumstances as earlier texts were. They are shaped by a century of feminist discourses (whether they agree with them or not), by experiences of racial and ethnic discrimination through racism in North America or colonial and neocolonial projects of domination and Muslim women's liberation, and by the particular dynamics of American Muslim communal histories and experiences. Wadud acknowledges as much when she states, "I have moved to a new, albeit uncomfortable reflection: neither their 'Islam' nor my 'Islam' has ultimate privilege. We are all part of a complex whole, in constant motion and manifestation throughout the history of multifaceted but totally human constructions of 'Islam.'"[23]

FEMINISTS AND FEMINISMS

While some Muslim women scholars very comfortably use the term feminist to describe themselves and their intellectual projects, others have struggled with the designation and its implications. In discussing

---

[21] Khaled Abou El Fadl, *Speaking in God's Name: Islamic Law, Authority and Women* (Oxford, 2001), p. 94.

[22] See, for example, Ali, *Sexual Ethics and Islam*, p. xxi.

[23] Wadud, *Inside the Gender Jihad*, p. 6.

Muslim women's studies earlier in this chapter, I point out the alliance between colonialism and nineteenth-century feminism. Arguably, this association is one of the reasons for the rejection of the feminist label. The accusation of being a feminist, for Muslim women in America and elsewhere, has sometimes been used as a means to undermine their projects and claims, namely by accusing them of being agents of an imagined "West" that wants to destroy Islam and Muslim communities. If reform projects are represented in this way, it becomes much easier to reject them as inauthentic and thus not worthy of further consideration. The legacy of colonial feminism is revived every time the plight and oppression of Muslim women are used as an ideological tool to justify war and military intervention, such as before and during the 2001 invasion of Afghanistan. More broadly, Muslim women's oppression by Islam has also been a useful backdrop for the projects of American and European feminists, in the same breath critiquing their own lack of equality, and patronizing those who in this view are in an even worse situation.

Muslim women scholars have also joined other marginalized women, especially women of color, in critiquing earlier waves of feminism as representative of white middle-class women's interests, and in gross neglect of other perspectives and agendas. Muslim women have also negotiated a complex divide between secular and religious forms of feminist thought and activism. It is safe to say that the majority of American feminists were secularists, if not outright antireligious in their sentiments, seeing religions as one of the main tools for patriarchal domination of women. Not unlike their Jewish and Christian counterparts somewhat earlier, American Muslim women who insisted on religious frameworks for feminist or gender equality projects had to defend their approaches and argue against the general rejection of their religious tradition, which would have situated them outside their communities of faith.

And last but not least, Muslim women reformers and intellectuals have had to struggle against a sense of historical disadvantage that, combined with the previously described use of Muslim women as a foil for other feminists' projects, has led to a complicated and continuously disadvantaged position in feminist interfaith projects.

EXEGESIS, ACTIVISM, AND THE SECULAR ACADEMY

This dynamic in combination with having to carve out spaces for religiously normative and exegetical work in the context of the secular academy has put Muslim women scholars in a complicated position. Their male predecessors, certainly in their first generation represented by Nasr, al-Faruqi, and Rahman, seem to have not encountered any difficulties in being hired into university positions while actively pursuing prescriptive intellectual projects and agendas. Likewise, the work of scholars such as Khaled Abou El Fadl, Abdullahi an-Na'im, Ebrahim Moosa, Farid Esack, and Omid Safi, while all on a progressive or reformist spectrum, seems to indicate that the secular American academy in fact does have spaces for such scholars.

Asma Barlas has argued that it is their very presence in the American context (and freedom) that allows them to carry out their projects when she points out that the distinctive feature of modern reinterpretations of the Qur'an is direct involvement of the state "in defining the framework for the production of religious knowledge.... In such a milieu, rereading the Qur'an in egalitarian modes is an exercise that has the potential to impinge on the hegemony of the state itself."[24] Thus, Muslim women scholars in North America are afforded the freedom to develop their readings of the Qur'an in an environment that is not free of coercion or pressures but is also not a threat to their well-being or personal safety.

It can thus be argued that certain spaces within the American academy in fact provide room for reformist reinterpretation projects, thereby enabling work that could otherwise not be done. However, it is also worth noting that the precondition for acceptance in the academy then may be the very progressive nature of such projects. This in turn privileges projects that legitimize the perceived need of Muslim women's liberation from an oppression that is the cornerstone of the entire argument. Muslim women scholars have discussed the merits and dangers as well as their experiences of exclusion and tokenism in different venues. One early product of such discussions is the valuable volume *Windows of Faith*, edited by Gisela Webb,[25] which is the product of two academic panels in the years preceding its publication. The volume demonstrates not only intra-Muslim intellectual cooperation and dialogue but also the diversity of approaches and projects of the women involved. It also reformulates a question that has dominated much of feminist discourse in the twentieth century, namely how the feminist project can and should be both theoretical and applied.[26] Here, the question as to how a scholar's agenda is shaped and determined by activist commitments and vice

---

[24] Barlas, *"Believing Women" in Islam*, p. 89.
[25] Gisela Webb, ed. (Syracuse, 2000).
[26] Saba Mahmood has argued that there is "a deeper tension within feminism attributable to its dual character as an *analytical* and a *politically prescriptive project*," which has been noted by feminist theorists for some time. Saba Mahmood, *Politics of Piety* (Princeton, 2005), p. 10 (emphasis in the original).

versa is at the center of reflection and debate. While the ideal of scholarly objectivity, which has rightly been identified as an objectification of (usually male) positions as normative by feminist thinkers, has been left behind in much of the humanities and some of the social sciences, an explicit activist commitment, as well as an insider position in studies of one's own community or faith tradition, is still often perceived as limiting rather than enriching. Thus, the intersection of insider-outside, analytical-exegetical, and scholar-activist has shaped and often limited the work of American Muslim women scholars in distinct ways.

AUTHORITY, COMMUNITY, AND BEYOND

Exegetical projects are directly linked to questions of authority and tradition. This link is not particular to women or to Muslims. Whether someone's interpretation matters in a more than theoretical way is connected to two main areas, one's authority in the faith community, and one's authority outside of it. In the case of Muslim women scholars, their faith commitments may be perceived as diminishing their scholarly authority, while their "feminist" and academic commitments may simultaneously be perceived as diminishing or even negating their religious authority in the eyes of their communities.

Barlas, for example, reflects openly on her rejection by non-Muslims based on expectations of the Muslim woman "other" as silent or conforming to preconceived notions of "proper" feminist expression.[27] However, she also recognizes the potential limits of her religious authority when she writes at the end of her book:

> That is the end toward which I undertook this work: in the hope that it will be among those egalitarian and antipatriarchal readings of Islam that will, in time, come to replace misogynist and patriarchal understandings of it. Yet, I remain aware that such a possibility is remote, at least in my lifetime.... As for me, I belong to no sanctioned interpretive community, nor am I a male, or even a recognized scholar of Islam (the chances of being accepted as a scholar by most Muslims if one is not a man are slim to begin with). However, as a Muslim woman, I have a great deal at stake in combating repressive readings of the Qur'an and also in affirming that Islam is not based in the idea of male epistemic privilege, or in a formally ordained interpretive community.[28]

[27] Barlas, *"Believing Women" in Islam*, p. xii.
[28] Barlas, *"Believing Women" in Islam*, pp. 209–210.

More generally, American Muslim women scholars have struggled with maintaining or building interpretive communities that center around their exegetical project, with the transformations of Muslim communities that would entail, and with their full inclusion and acceptance in the American academy.

CONCLUSION

What does the study of American Muslim women have to do with American Muslim women scholars in the American academy? The joint study of and reflection on both in their dynamics, setbacks, and contributions point to theoretical and methodological issues that may transcend even questions of gender, femininity, and masculinity. The insights gained from thinking about our field, the study of American Muslims, in its multiple dimensions, disciplines, and its history, can help us rethink and refine our methodological tools and theoretical assumptions. The future of the study of American Muslim women, in my view, lies in the mainstreaming of gender as a category to think *with*, rather than to think *about*. Muslim women, as Amina Wadud notes, are "half of humanity," and thus half of American Muslim communities as well. It is in transcending assumptions about religious authority and practice, political participation, institution building, and the many other facets of American Muslim lives as normatively male that the field will make its mark as much more than the study of a religious minority community in American society.

Further Reading

Ali, Kecia, *Sexual Ethics and Islam: Feminist Reflections on Qur'an, Hadith, and Jurisprudence* (Oxford, 2006).

Ali, Kecia, Juliane Hammer, and Laury Silvers, eds., *A Jihad for Justice: Honoring the Work and Life of Amina Wadud* (e-book, 2012), http://www.bu.edu/religion/files/2010/03/A-Jihad-for-Justice-for-Amina-Wadud-2012-1.pdf.

Barlas, Asma, *"Believing Women" in Islam: Unreading Patriarchal Interpretations of the Qur'an* (Austin, 2002).

Haddad, Yvonne, Jane I. Smith, and Kathleen Moore, *Muslim Women in America: The Challenge of Islamic Identity Today* (New York, 2006).

Hammer, Juliane, *American Muslim Women, Religious Authority, and Activism: More than a Prayer* (Austin, 2012).

"Identity, Authority and Activism: American Muslim Women's Approaches to the Qur'an," *Muslim World* 98:4 (October 2008): 442–463.

Hoodfar, Huma, Sajjad Alvi, and Sheila McDonough, eds., *The Muslim Veil in North America: Issues and Debates* (Toronto, 2003).

Rouse, Carolyn Moxley, *Engaged Surrender: African American Women and Islam* (Berkeley, 2004).

Wadud, Amina, *Inside the Gender Jihad: Women's Reform in Islam* (Oxford, 2006).

Webb, Gisela, ed., *Windows of Faith: Muslim Women Scholar-Activists in North America* (Syracuse, 2000).

Index

Aasi, Ghulam, 257–258
Abd al-Ati, Hammudah, 93
Abd-Allah, Umar Faruq, 255–256, 263–265
Abdel Nasser, Gamal, 59–60, 62–63
Abduh, Muhammad, 272–274
Abdullah, Shaila, 296–297
Abdullah, Zain, 65–82, 179
Abdul-Malik, Ahmed, 284
Abdul Rauf, Feisal, 156–157, 161, 165–167
Abdul Rauf, Muhammad, 165–166
Abdur-Rashid, Talib, 72
"Abode of the Message," 195
Abou El Fadl, Khaled, 24–25, 176–177, 339, 340–341
Abu Muslima, Sayd, 93
Abu Namous (Imam), 166
AbuSulayman, AbdulHamid, 256–259
academic research on American Islam
    Cold War–era synthesis and expansion in, 58–63
    identity politics and scholarship on African slaves and, 43–44
    Muslim American women's studies, 332–335, 340–342
    post-9/11 proliferation of, 23–26
    women's studies and, 330–332
activism of Muslim women, 340–342
adaptive practices in American Islam, 223–225
Ad-Deen Allah Universal Arabic Association, 230
Adenu Islamic United Arabic Association, 57
adhan (call to prayer), 45

Adib, Dawud, 93
advocacy groups, Muslim American creation of, 102–103
aesthetic principles of mosque construction, 232
Afghanistan, U.S. involvement in, 93
Africa
    enslaved Muslims from, 29–30
    religious-political wars in, 33
    repatriation efforts of American Muslims back to, 30
African American Institute for Islamic Research, 179
African American Jewish groups, 88–89, 194
African American Muslims
    academic research on, 22
    Ahmadiyya movement and, 87–88
    community organization by, 170–174
    conversion by, 83
    cultural production and experience of, 281–282
    demographics of, 98–100, 172–173
    early research on, 15–26
    gender issues for, 24–25
    Great Migration and, 88–92
    historical emergence of, 46
    indigenous/immigrant boundaries and, 95–96
    institutions and organizations for, 174–180
    literary influence of, 286–291
    mid-twentieth-century increase in, 51–57
    mosque construction by, 228–230